What they're saying about

The Learning Revolution
by Gordon Dryden and Jeannette Vos

"*The Learning Revolution* has given my wife and me more ideas to help our children than I have gathered together in 15 years of workshops on teaching. And its unique format enables you to speed-read the entire book in about 15 minutes."

> Graham Hookey, head of Meadowridge School, Maple Ridge, Canada

"This book is truly causing a new revolution in China. It sold a phenomenal 2,007,691 copies in only three weeks —and 7.5 million copies in 25 weeks. All 1,000 members of our own company have bought copies: and this year we donated 10 more to each member of our staff as Chinese New Year gifts for families and friends. *The Learning Revolution* is changing the future of the world's oldest civilization and its 1.3 million people."

> Song Chaodi, President, Clever Software Group Company, China

" Wow! The most inspiring and informative book on the brain and accelerated learning that I have ever read. Bound to become a classic."

> Diane Loomans, President of Global Leading, San Diego, California,
> and author of *Full Esteem Ahead*

"If today every parent and every teacher alive read this book, the world would change for the better by tomorrow. I know only one other thing which has that power."

> Glenn Doman, Philadelphia, USA, author of *Teach Your Baby To Read*

"Congratulations on your superb effort . . . a very positive message of our potential, toward learning specifically and toward life in general."

> Professor Marian Diamond, University of California at Berkeley,
> California, the scientist who dissected part of Albert Einstein's brain

"This is the book that I wish I had written. It is accessible, important and transformational. It will change lives. And it should change education."

Sir Christopher Ball, Chairman of Britain's Campaign for Learning

"When a book sells 30,000 copies in a nation of 3.8 million people, and goes through three editions in five months, you know it's spot on target. Outstanding for business, schools, families—and everyone rethinking the future for a new century."

Reg Birchfield, publisher, *Management* magazine, New Zealand

"Now more than ever, the whole concept of education and learning needs to be reinvented. This book brilliantly shows us how."

Charles Handy, United Kingdom, author of *The Age Of Unreason*

About 35,000 copies of *The Learning Revolution* have so far been sold in Sweden. Over 25,000 business innovators and educators have attended Learning Revolution seminars and workshops. A truly brilliant interactive passport to the 21st century."

Ingemar Svantesson, publisher and author, Sweden

"One of the most important books of the decade. With Stephen Covey's *The 7 Habits of Highly Effective People, The Learning Revolution* has become one of our two main guidebooks in helping to transform 44,000 staff into an active learning organization."

John Hoerner, Chief Executive, The Burton Group Plc., United Kingdom

"Absolutely outstanding. The entire book is the most inspiring and comprehensive pulling together of all the various strands of learning research that I have ever seen."

Colin Rose, co-author of *Accelerated Learning For The 21st Century*

"With the publication of *Common Sense,* Thomas Paine launched a revolution in the 13 American colonies. May this wonderful book launch The Learning Revolution throughout the world. It is a master-piece of research . . . not about what might be done someday, but what is being done and can be done now. A blueprint for the 21st century—now."

Steven Snyder, President, Steven Snyder Seminars, California, USA

"As soon as I took it out of the mail, *The Learning Revolution* became a desktop resource in our office. It provides information and perspective that have been tremendously beneficial to me personally and to hundreds of others receiving parts of it shared in presentations."

Jeanne Forrester, Ed.D., Governor's Education Adviser,
State of Mississippi, USA

"With this book, *The Learning Revolution,* Gordon Dryden and Jeannette Vos establish themselves as world leaders in that same revolution. *The Learning Revolution* is what books on education should be: a masterful blend of knowledge, care, optimism and very practical advice. It provides a superb tour of the main advances and main concepts that will affect education and learning in the 21st century. It is also a *tour de force!"*

Tony Buzan, England, author of *The Mind Map Book*

"Simply the best book I have seen about modern teaching methods, and presented in the same exciting way that it promotes for effective learning. When it was first published, we air-freighted supplies into Singapore for each of our teachers. Teacher applicants also receive a copy as an indication of our teaching method goals. This is an outstanding overview and a practical guide."

David A. Perry, Chairman, Overseas Family School, Singapore

"This book is absolutely superb and will stimulate, challenge and inspire many educators in the future. Inspirational and exciting in that it presents very practical suggestions about doing something now!"

Raymond A. Daley, Principal, St. Ives Primary School, Sydney, Australia

"The best in learning from around the world . . . catapults the reader into the possibilities of education's future. An important book . . . invaluable for anyone interested in learning."

Bobbi DePorter, Oceanside, California, USA, Past President,
International Alliance for Learning, and author of *Quantum Learning*

"An exciting and very positive blueprint for the future, for both parents and educators."

Ronald Hockwalt, Superintendent, Walnut Valley Unified School District,
Walnut Creek, Los Angeles, California, USA

"A ripper!"

Glenn Capelli, Perth, Western Australia, co-author of *Maximizing Your Learning Potential: a handbook for lifelong learning*

How to skim-read this book in 15 to 30 minutes

 1 Every second page in this book is a 'poster page'. Each one highlights key points: an overview of the book.

2 'Poster pages' at the start of each chapter summarize its theme.

3 So turn to page 18, and start to skim-read each left-hand 'poster page' very quickly. If the poster page is detailed, skim only the headings.

4 That skim-read will tell you which chapters you must read thoroughly and which you can 'skim'.

5 Read the 'must-read' chapters first, 'highlighting' key points with a colored marker pen or pencil.

6 Skim the other chapters to refresh yourself on important points, again highlighting key information.

7 If you're not trained in rapid reading, turn to page 157 for some simple tips.

If the total subject-matter is new to you, you're welcome to read every chapter thoroughly and at your own pace. But we still recommend steps 1 to 3 above—before you read the whole book or the parts that affect you immediately. They will give you an advance overview. That makes it much easier to remember the main points, and much easier to see how each chapter fits into the big picture.

How to remember all the main points

If you're a teacher or trainer

Duplicate any 'poster page' in this book on a photocopier. Then enlarge that page and print on bright colored poster paper. Display the posters on walls as permanent reminders of main points. To make your posters more attractive, print each one in a different solid background color with the type and illustrations "reversed" so the black printing and pictures appear as white against the solid backgrounds of different colors. See next page for an even better idea.

If you're a student of any subject

Make a Mind Map® of any chapter you're studying. A good Mind Map* starts like the illustration above, computer-generated by Dilip Mukerjea, of Singapore, and reprinted from his book *Superbrain.* Mind Maps record information as the brain does, like branches on a tree, and make it very easy to recall key points. See pages 164-167 for simple tips.

* Mind Map is a registered trade mark of Tony Buzan.

Run 16 slide-shows with our CD-ROM

The English language

 Has a total of 550,000 words

 abc Has 26 letters, only 44 sounds

 2,000 make up 90% of speech

ea igh ough Has 70 spelling combinations

 400 words form 65% of writing

bat once 50% of words are phonetic, 50% not

This is a black-and-white sample of the color slides that form the basis for 16 separate presentations on The Learning Revolution CD-ROM. They also include Mind Maps on the main points of each chapter.

 1 This book has also been made into 16 color slide-shows on a CD-ROM.

 2 It includes one color-slide presentation for the Introduction and one for each chapter.

 3 Each set comes with a recorded commentary so you can run a series of professional slide-shows for yourself or students: on Mac or Windows.

 4 You can also select slides for your own presentations, and print on an ink-jet or laser color printer.

 5 You can then enlarge them on a color photocopier as posters to use around your room to remind you and students of key points.

 6 Students and teachers can also use the CD-ROM as a template to produce their own slide-shows or study projects—mixing with material from the Internet.

 7 See page 498 for more details and the last page of this book to order more CD-ROM/book packages.

But does it work?

We've been careful to include in this book only results that have been proven. Here are some:

In Flaxmere, New Zealand, 11-year-olds up to five years behind at school are catching up in under ten weeks, using a tape-assisted reading program. The average gain is 3.3 years in eight to ten weeks. Details, page 384

In a United States Army trial, soldiers using the techniques recommended in this book have achieved 661 per cent better results when learning German: more than twice the results in one-third the time. Details, page 333

Before changing to new teaching methods, 52 percent of chemistry students at Tempe High School in Arizona, USA, achieved A, B or C grades in examinations. Now it's 93 percent. Details, page 335

On one course at the giant American Intel group, staff achieved a 507 percent knowledge gain, compared with 23 per cent by 'normal' teaching methods. Details, page 505

Students at a high school in Sydney, Australia, have learned a three-year French course in eight weeks. Details, page 331

At Montessori International in Montana, USA, every child can read fluently, write clearly and do basic arithmetic by age five. Details, page 263

In Christchurch, New Zealand, a seven-year-old has passed the senior high school mathematics exam. Details, pages 511

Also by Gordon Dryden and Jeannette Vos

Videotape and audiotape series:

The Learning Revolution

Also by Gordon Dryden

Books:

Out Of The Red
The Reading Revolution (with Denise Ford)

Parenting program:

FUNdamentals (with Colin Rose)

Television series:

New Zealand: Where To Now?

The Vicious Cycle
Right From The Start
The Vital Years
Back To Real 'Basics'
The Chance To Be Equal
The Future: Does It Work?

16-part United States series:
The Learning Revolution

Also by Jeannette Vos

Doctoral dissertation:

An Accelerated/Integrative Learning Model Program
The Music Revolution (teacher-trainer program)

The Learning Revolution

To change
the way
the world
learns

**Gordon Dryden and
Dr. Jeannette Vos**

the
learning
web

The Learning Revolution

To change the way the world learns

Published by:

The Learning Web
Torrance, CA, USA, and Auckland, New Zealand
www.thelearningweb.net
email: orders@thelearningweb.net
In U.S. and Canada: toll-free 1-800 637-6893
Address details on page 544.

ISBN: 1-929284-00-4

Contents

Contents   13

Notes: 1. Figures throughout are in U.S. dollars unless stated. 2. Billions are also in American terminology; thus one billion is 1,000 million, and a trillion is a million million. 3. Spelling is American-English.

A challenge from seven million readers to the rest of the world

When Chinese parents line up to buy 251,000 copies of a book in one day—and 7.5 million copies in 25 weeks—you know publishing history is being made.

But *The Learning Revolution* is much more than the world's best-selling book. It is a catalyst to change the way you think, live, learn, work, teach and act.

It is certainly doing that in the world's oldest civilization, where it has become the centerpiece for a national debate on how 1.3 billion people can best prepare for the 21st century.

The co-authors' message is simple, graphic—and of overwhelming importance:

❑ *We live at the start of history's most profound revolution.*

❑ *We now know how to store all humanity's combined knowledge and wisdom, and make it instantly available to almost anyone on earth.*

❑ *We need a learning revolution to match the revolution in instant communication—and that revolution is well under way.*

❑ *Every family, school or business can take advantage of this new age of networked intelligence.*

This book shows how.

Already its impact has also been as striking as its presentation.

The Mandarin edition is on track to sell 10 million copies in well under a year— since the co-authors first appeared on Chinese television screens in December 1998 in a half-hour national program.

Around 35,000 copies of an earlier edition have been sold in Sweden. More than 25,000 Swedes have flocked to co-author Jeannette Vos's seminars and workshops. Other international innovators in education have followed.

In New Zealand, the original book went through three editions in the first five months. In a nation of 3.8 million people, 30,000 copies have been sold: equal to more than 2 million copies in the United States.

Many companies around the world have responded to the book's message by ordering copies for their staff.

One Chinese company has gone even further. Clever Software Company is China's biggest educational software company. It was so impressed with *The Learning Revolution that* Clever arranged to become sole mainland distributor for the first Chinese-language edition.

Since that decision was made the book's impact has been phenomenal.

The reason is not hard to discern. *The Learning Revolution* summarizes research from a wide range of disciplines. It synthesizes that into a new theory of learning and a learning society. It reports succinctly how that knowledge is already bringing about revolutionary breakthroughs in learning, education, business and families.

It also presents its findings crisply and clearly so that anyone can read it easily and understand. Its unique layout helps that process.

Since those earlier editions appeared in 1993 and 1994, the world has changed dramatically. And this completely updated edition explores how breakthroughs in electronic, multimedia technology can produce learning miracles, particularly when linked to the latest brain research.

Some may argue that this makes the book more suited only to advanced economies: those which can afford the latest home computers and Internet connections.

The co-authors think the opposite. They believe *The Learning Revolution* shows how even poor countries can marry the world's most effective technologies to the world's most effective learning and teaching methods—then use that marriage to bypass the industrial revolution and leap directly into new era of networked intelligence.

Certainly millions of Chinese are embracing this message. And in doing so they're sending out a challenge to citizens, parents, teachers and students around the world: to grasp the core of *The Learning Revolution* to produce a truly learning society.

If you can dream it, you can do it.

WALT DISNEY

History's newest revolution: the power to change your life

The Learning Revolution is based on eight main beliefs:

1. The world is hurtling through a fundamental turning point in history.

2. We are living through a revolution that is changing the way we live, communicate, think and prosper.

3. This revolution will determine how, and if, we and our children work, earn a living and enjoy life to the fullest.

4. For the first time in history, almost anything is now possible.

5. Probably not more than one person in five knows how to benefit fully from the hurricane of change—even in developed countries.

6. Unless we find answers, an elite 20 percent could end up with 60 percent of each nation's income, the poorest fifth with only 2 percent.[1] That is a formula for guaranteed poverty, school failure, crime, drugs, despair, violence and social eruption.

7. We need a parallel revolution in lifelong learning to match the information revolution, and for all to share the fruits of an age of potential plenty.

8. Fortunately, that revolution—a revolution that can help each of us learn anything much faster and better—is also gathering speed.

This book tells its story. It also acts as a practical guide to help you take control of your own future.

The main elements of the revolution are twofold. They link the modern marvels of brain research with the power of instantly available information and knowledge.

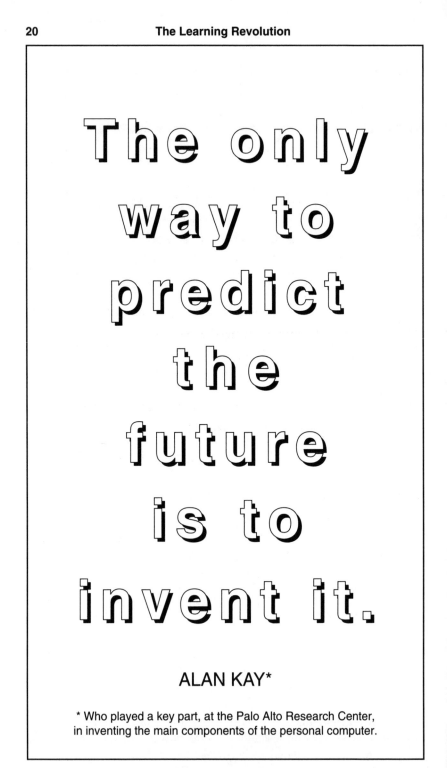

The only way to predict the future is to invent it.

ALAN KAY*

* Who played a key part, at the Palo Alto Research Center, in inventing the main components of the personal computer.

For the first time, we now know how to store almost all the world's most important information and make it available instantly, in almost any form, to almost anyone on earth—and to link everyone together in a global networked learning web.

This power enables even developing countries to bypass the industrial revolution and leap straight into the age of information and innovation.

The obvious face of the communications revolution is the world total of 250 million personal computers—growing to 500 million by 2002—and the worldwide Internet that links them together. But "pulsating below the surface are the invisible catalysts for change: the 6 billion noncomputer silicon chips embedded in your car, stereo, ricecooker and thousands of other items."[2] The computer in your cellular phone has more power than all the computers used during World War II combined.[3]

More important is the network revolution. Says Canadian researcher and author Don Tapscott in *The Digital Economy*: "We are at the dawn of an Age of Networked Intelligence—an age that is giving birth to a new economy, a new politics, and a new society."

The seismic scope of this change forces us to completely rethink everything we've ever understood about learning, education, schooling, business, economics and government.

In fact, schools can successfully introduce information technology only if they rethink the role of teaching and learning. If every student can retrieve information when required, then the teacher's main role is no longer that of an information-provider.

At last we are also learning to make use of the most brilliant human resource of all: the almost limitless power of the billions of cells and trillions of connections that make up the average human brain.

The possibilities are breathtaking:

To prosper in the new one-world economy, **would you like to learn to speak a foreign language fairly competently in only four to eight weeks?***

In a world where school dropouts have no future, **would you like to be guaranteed that your children will catch up at school in under ten weeks—even if they are now three years behind?**

In a world where knowledge is exploding, **would you like to be able**

---

* *Breakthroughs summarized early in this book are explained fully later, and some chapter notes are sourced to those fuller explanations.*

Learning is most effective when it's fun.

PETER KLINE
The Everyday Genius*

* Published by Great Ocean Publishers Inc, 1823 North Lincoln Street, Arlington, VA 22207.

to skim through four books in a day—and remember what you read?

*In a world of instant communications, **would you like to be able to tap into the combined knowledge and talents of humanity—on your own personal computer or TV screen?***

*In a world where perhaps only a quarter of all people will have fulltime jobs as we now know them, **would you like to earn an excellent living doing the things you love to do?***

*In a world where education systems are under severe criticism, **would you like some guaranteed methods to reduce the current failure rate?***

*In a world where everyone will have to plan for several different careers in a lifetime, **would you like to learn the key principles about any new job simply, easily and quickly?***

*In a world where 20 percent of the population will soon be over 60, **would you like to know how you can go on enjoying life well into your 80s or 90s?***

*In a world where soaring taxation and deficits threaten to strangle democracy, **how can we achieve these results without spending an extra cent?***

If these questions sound like the start of a glowing advertisement, relax. Every one of these results is possible right now. All are being achieved somewhere in the world:

❏ In Finland, the Government has engaged 5,000 students to teach their teachers how to use computers and information technology.[4]

The Learning Revolution model: Everyone is now a teacher as well as a learner. And "for the first time ever children are taking over critical elements of a communications revolution".[5]

❏ In China, eight-and-nine-year-olds at the Beijing 21st Century Experimental School are learning to speak fluent English by playing with giant crossword puzzles, quiz shows and other fun-filled games.

The Learning Revolution model: For most people, learning is most effective when its fun.

❏ In New Zealand's Tahatai Coast Primary School, six-year-olds use computers to make CD-ROMs and plan their own "school of the future". Other six-year-olds build Technic Lego working models of their "21st century home". And they use computers to activate the solar- and wind-powered units designed to make each house self-sufficient in energy.

The Learning Revolution model: Create the right environment and

All children are born geniuses, and we spend the first six years of their lives degeniusing them.

BUCKMINSTER FULLER

even children from poorer families explode into self-directed learning.

❏ In isolated Montana, America's least-populated state, all four-year-olds at the Montessori International nursery school can now read, write, spell and do basic mathematics even before starting school.

The Learning Revolution model: The best time to develop your learning ability is before you start school—because most of your brain's major pathways are laid down in those vital early years. [6]

❏ In California, former schoolteacher Jan Davidson and her husband Bob, who borrowed $6,000 from their son's college savings to start an educational multimedia company, have since sold it for almost $1 billion.[7]

The Learning Revolution model: Great teachers can now teach millions of people, through the marvels of interactive electronic communications: and make a fortune doing the things they love to do.

❏ In Christchurch, New Zealand, Michael Tan has passed his seventh-form (13th grade) high school mathematics examination—at age seven. And 12-year-old Stephen Witte—regarded by teachers as a disciplinary problem—passed six university bursary examinations and won the Papanui High School's Physics Prize, but only after being given the opportunity to bypass four grades.

The Learning Revolution model: People learn best when they want to learn, not at some predetermined age.

❏ In China, a 24-volume set of color encyclopedias, that once sold for $1,000, can now be pressed as a compact disc for less than 50 cents. Bill Gates has become America's richest person partly by giving away such CD-ROM encyclopedias to sell other computer software.

The Learning Revolution model: Even the "have-nots" can benefit from technology—but farsighted visionaries can do even better.

❏ In America, staff on one "accelerated learning" course at the giant Intel group increased their subject-knowledge 507 percent compared with a 23 percent gain by students learning by "normal" methods.[8]

The Learning Revolution model: The new methods are paying off big in staff training.

❏ In Arizona, high-school teacher Leo Wood—using similar methods—has lifted his students' achievements in chemistry from 52 percent getting A, B and C grades to 93 percent.[9]

The Learning Revolution model: Even complex information can be

To learn it, do it!

ROBERT C. SCHANK
*Engines For Learning**

* Published by Laurence Erlbaum Associates, 365 Hillsdale, New Jersey 07642.

absorbed easily, and remembered, when learners are fully involved.

❑ In Hastings, New Zealand, 11-year-olds up to five years behind in their reading are catching up in eight to ten weeks through a "tape-assisted reading program". A typical gain in that time is 3.3 years.[10]

The Learning Revolution model: Even if you're well behind at school, it's not too late to catch up, using integrated learning methods.

❑ In California, the scientist who dissected Albert Einstein's brain, Professor Marian Diamond, is rearing the world's most intelligent rats—and providing big breakthroughs to speed up learning in humans.

The Learning Revolution model: The brain research shows intelligence can soar in the right environment—and for humans too.

❑ In Beijing, China, the Clever Software Group Company employs 1,000 specialists to produce *Computer Tutor* and other CD-ROM programs that guarantee student examination passes. And CSC links all its staff members around China in an internal Intranet, which is now also being used as a model for schools.[11]

The Learning Revolution model: Interactive learning technology provides some of the world's best business opportunities.

❑ In St. Louis, Missouri, the teachers at New City School[12] have collectively written an entire book, on how they're teaching every subject, at every grade, by catering to many different types of intelligence.

The Learning Revolution model: There is more than one type of smartness—and we each have a learning style as individual as our fingerprints. Effective schools should recognize that and cater to it.

❑ In Alaska, students at Mt. Edgecumbe High School run four pilot companies. One order: $600,000 for smoked salmon to Japan—as they study marketing, business, economics and Japanese.[13]

The Learning Revolution model: Use the real world as your classroom, and to learn it, do it.

❑ Millions of youngsters have now learned the basics of geography from a CD-ROM game devised by two young Iowa trivia-quiz fans: *Where In The World is Carmen Sandiego?*

The Learning Revolution model: Computer games can transform many aspects of learning.

❑ In Singapore, the Government is spending $US1.5 billion[14] to bring the world's best information technology to its schools and homes.

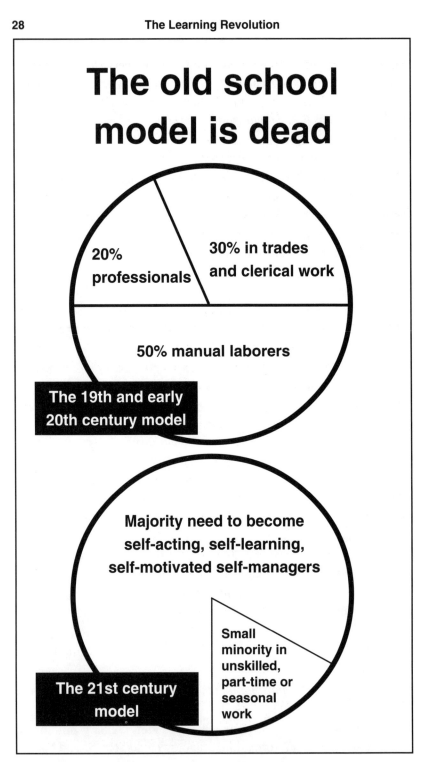

The old school model is dead

20% professionals

30% in trades and clerical work

50% manual laborers

The 19th and early 20th century model

Majority need to become self-acting, self-learning, self-motivated self-managers

Small minority in unskilled, part-time or seasonal work

The 21st century model

All schools are getting at least one computer for every two students; all students their own free Internet connection—to link with the 150 million others already "Net surfing" in 1999. Prime Minister Goh Chok Tong has laid out a vision of *Thinking Schools, Learning Nation*[15] as the 21st century goal. The five-year IT budget totals $2.5 million per school.

The Learning Revolution model: You don't have to be a giant country or state to lead the world. Visionary government helps.

❏ In Sydney, Australia, students at Beverley Hills High School have learned to speak fluent French by compressing a three-year course into eight weeks—using revolutionary do-it-yourself learning methods.[16]

The Learning Revolution model: Accelerated learning has been proven for years in foreign-language schools; now it's everybody's turn.

Those examples may look like isolated facts. Yet they typify the most important revolution in human history. They hold the secrets to take us all confidently into the 21st century, no matter how small, big, rich or seemingly poor the country. But the flip side of the future is bleak:

❏ In affluent western Europe, 19 million people cannot find jobs.[17]

❏ In even richer America, almost 27 million people are now living in poverty. More than 40 percent of that nation's poor are children. Forty percent of teenagers in New York City are unemployed; 20 percent in the rest of the country[18]—while high-tech companies cry out for staff.

❏ At Britain's worst-performing schools, the average 11-year-old is reading at a five-year-old level, while top-achieving schools are three years ahead of average.[19] Some political leaders are talking about a ten-*year* program to lift all 11-year-olds to an 11-year-old achievement-level[20]— while just one of the successful programs covered in this book shows how that can be achieved in ten *weeks!*[21]

❏ More than half of America's young people leave school without the knowledge or foundation required to find and hold a good job.[22]

❏ In America more than 270,000 students carry guns to school, and the New York City school system now operates the eleventh largest security force in the United States, with more than 2,400 officers.[23]

This book recognizes that downside, but does not dwell on it. *The Learning Revolution* is about practical, proven alternatives: actions and programs that work, effectively and simply, to build a better future for ourselves, our families, schools, businesses, communities and countries.

Above all, it is a book about your personal learning revolution: how

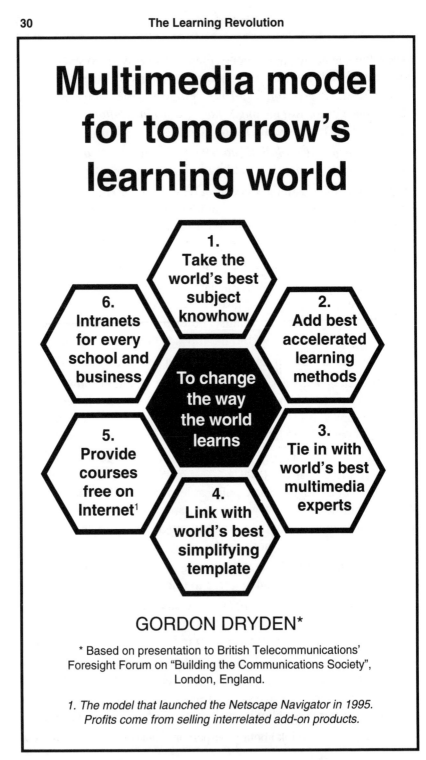

Multimedia model for tomorrow's learning world

1. Take the world's best subject knowhow

6. Intranets for every school and business

2. Add best accelerated learning methods

To change the way the world learns

5. Provide courses free on Internet[1]

3. Tie in with world's best multimedia experts

4. Link with world's best simplifying template

GORDON DRYDEN*

* Based on presentation to British Telecommunications' Foresight Forum on "Building the Communications Society", London, England.

1. The model that launched the Netscape Navigator in 1995. Profits come from selling interrelated add-on products.

to develop your own unique talents: to learn by using all your senses and your natural abilities.

These guidelines have come not a moment too soon. The old school model is as dead as the industrial revolution that spawned it. It may well have been fine 50 years ago to "educate" 20 percent of the population to be professional workers, 30 percent for trades and clerical jobs, and to leave the remaining 50 percent to be largely-uneducated farm and manual laborers. But to continue that policy creates a national and international disaster. Nearly all students now need to become self-acting, self-confident, creative "managers of their own future". The tragic alternative is to continue to create a dispossessed, unemployed underclass, as most of the old manual jobs disappear.

And even for graduates, knowledge gained in a degree course is often outdated even before graduation. Overall, the instant-communications revolution enables us to regularly update that information, and make it available, on demand, when it is needed by anyone who possesses the tools to access it.

We can thus now define many new models for the new digital age. In the multimedia model, it means we can:

❑ Harness the ability of the world's best "subject experts";

❑ Link their talents with the world's best specialists in simple, new, interactive, fun-filled learning techniques;

❑ Marry them to the world's most brilliant methods of interactive multimedia communications;

❑ Crystallize that work into simplified templates that make it easy to teach anyone anything in a way that suits each person's own style;

❑ Make such courses available instantly, free, to virtually everyone in the world through inexpensive network computer/TV sets—and almost as easy to operate as your TV.

❑ Set up intranet networks that can link each school with the Internet in a way that makes individual learning much more effective and much more fun—with teachers as professional managers and mentors, and schools as new interactive lifelong learning centers.

Some of the answers are so simple and self-evident it's amazing that no country has yet adopted them as national policy:

❑ *Fifty percent of a child's ability to learn is developed in the first four years of life.* [24] *This makes parents the world's most important*

Your own model for a new learning world

YOU LEARN BY

What you SEE

What you HEAR

What you TASTE

What you SMELL

What you TOUCH

What you DO

What you IMAGINE

What you INTUIT

What you FEEL

JEANNETTE VOS

From her Learning Revolution International workshops.

educators. Yet not one government spends even one percent of its educational budget on training its most vital educators.

❏ *Self-directed learning is a major key. And if you provide the right environment and tools for self-learning even tiny children become enthusiastic and lifelong self-educators.* Maria Montessori, Italy's first woman doctor, was providing such environments almost 100 years ago,[25] and showing how three- and four-year-old "retarded" children could "explode" into writing, reading and basic mathematics. Yet most countries are still not achieving that result even for "normal" children.

❏ *We now know that every one of us has a unique learning, working and thinking style.* Yet many high schools and universities still "teach" as if every student learns in the same way—the academic, abstract, theoretical way. "Research clearly illustrates that only about 30 percent of people learn best that way."[26] The other 70 percent learn in a wide variety of styles—best of all by actually *doing.*

❏ *We are also living in an era where most people have the chance to extend their active life to well beyond 75 or 80 years.* Yet political leaders are locked in debate about how to secure "retirement" benefits for this aging population, when one of the real challenges is to create a new third age of active participation in a lifelong learning community.

Fortunately we now know how to reverse those policies. All the main answers are being practiced somewhere in the world.

This book obviously represents, of course, strong personal views. Everyone's ideas are mixed in a different cauldron. Ours have bubbled through a score of different brews. From one author's career that spans 50 years of business, marketing, advertising, public relations, journalism, radio and television. From the other's life teaching at every level, from preschool to university. From our joint efforts this decade in putting the new methods into practice around the world.

From that combined background comes a simple set of beliefs:

1. Virtually anything is now possible. We can achieve almost all the things that Utopians could once only dream about.

2. Nearly every problem has been solved, in part, somewhere in the world. Choose the best solutions and you'll lead the world.

3. Where problems have not been solved, we now have simple techniques to produce great new solutions.

4. You don't have to be a giant country, a giant state, a big company

Prove it to yourself in two minutes

How to learn to count in Japanese by seeing, speaking and doing

English	Japanese	Say	Do
one	ichi	Itchy	Scratch your
two	ni	knee.[1]	knee.
three	san	Sun,	Point to sky.
four	shi	she	Point to girl.
five	go	go	Walk.
six	roku	rock.	Rock 'n' roll.
seven	shichi	shi-chi	Double sneeze.
eight	hachi	hat-chi	Put on hat.[2]
nine	kyu	coo	Coo like a dove.
ten	ju	ju	Don Jewish cap.[2]

*Adapted from an accelerated-learning Japanese language-training course, demonstrated by Creative Learning Company, Auckland, New Zealand.

1. Say, "Itchy knee" and "Sun, she go rock," as sentences while you mime the actions.
2. If you haven't a hat or cap, mime the action with your hands.

or a large school to lead the world. In fact some of the most spectacular breakthroughs are coming from small schools and companies.

5. We are now at a key historical turning point. For hundreds of thousands of years our ancestors roamed earth as ill-clad hunters. Then, around 12,000 years ago they first learned to grow crops and put animals to work. This ushered in the world's first great social breakthrough. Between 200 and 500 years ago they unleashed the power of the printing press, science and steam to pioneer the next burst forward. Now we've entered the age of instant communication with almost anyone on earth, and the world will never again be the same.

This book is based in part on these beliefs. It's also based on a remarkable coincidence. In the early 1990s, the co-authors were working on different projects, in different parts of the world. Jeannette Vos was completing a seven-year research project for her doctorate in education. Her specific subject: methods that saw high-school underachievers making dramatic turn-rounds in only ten days at *SuperCamp.* [27] But it entailed much wider research: to check the world's best learning methods. Around the same time Gordon Dryden was touring with a television crew videotaping the world's best learning breakthroughs.

We first met by chance at a 1991 international learning convention in Seattle, Washington, U.S.A. When the TV series and doctoral dissertations were finished, we swapped copies and background research. The similarities were amazing. The television and academic research dovetailed. The findings were dramatic, the truth simple:

It is possible for anyone to learn almost anything much faster— often anywhere from five to 20 times faster—and often ten times to 100 times more effectively, at any age. Those learning methods are simple, easy to learn, fun-filled, common sense—and they work.

Better still, in the years since we first met, both authors have had the opportunity to tour the planet and to seek out new breakthroughs in schools, corporations and communities. In varying ways, we've acted as observers and participants in the excitement of the information revolution. We've also been honored to act with many other catalysts to successfully change the way the world learns.

The Learning Revolution tells you how that can be done—and is being done. And how the future is yours to shape.

Gordon Dryden, Auckland, New Zealand
Jeannette Vos, Ed. D., San Diego, California, U.S.A.

The 16 key trends to shape your future

1 The age of instant communications.

2 A world without economic borders.

3 Four steps to a one-world economy.

4 Internet commerce and learning.

5 The new service society.

6 The marriage of big and small.

7 The new age of leisure.

8 The changing shape of work.

9 Women in leadership.

10 Your amazing brain rediscovered.

11 Cultural nationalism.

12 The growing underclass.

13 The active aging of the population.

14 The new do-it-yourself boom.

15 Cooperative enterprise.

16 The triumph of the individual.

The 16 major trends that will shape tomorrow's world

A revolution is changing your life—and your world.

You are part of the first generation to live in a new age: an age that offers an unlimited choice of futures in an era where virtually all things are possible.

Your children's world will be like none other before. Their future, too, depends on the ability to grasp new concepts, make new choices, and go on learning and adapting throughout life.

Rich countries have already made the leap from an industrial society to an age of information: an age where human brainpower, knowledge and creativity will continue to replace machinery and buildings as the main capital in society.

Poor countries now have the enormous opportunity to telescope history: to leap over the industrial era and straight into the new *age of networked intelligence*.

But that new age also poses stark alternatives. For those with the new knowledge: a world of opportunity. For those without: the prospect of unemployment, poverty and despair as the old jobs disappear, the old systems crumble.

The main thrust of this book is that new methods of learning are urgently needed if most people are to benefit. And not just for a new generation, but for those who are already adults.

But learning can be fully effective only if it enables each of us to link directly to the needs of the new age. Of all the trends, we believe at least 16 main ones will dictate what and how we now need to learn:

History's landmarks

The world	4.5 billion years old
Life	3.5 billion years ago
Humans	2 million years ago[1]
'Modern' humans	35,000 to 50,000 years ago?[a]
Farming	12,000 years ago
The plow	5,000 years ago
The wheel	5,000 years ago
Steam-power	250 years ago
Computers	40-50 years ago
And now	The age of instant communications

Communications

First brains	500 million years ago[b]
Speech	35,000 to 50,000 years ago[c]
Writing	6,000 years ago
Alphabet	4,000 years ago[d]
Printing	1040 AD in China, 1451 AD in Europe
Telephone	1876
Moving pictures	1894
Television	1926
Transistor	1948
Fiber optics	1988: 3,000 messages at once
	1996: 1.5 million
	2000: 10 million (prediction)

Main sources: *Reader's Digest Book of Facts*, *The Inventions That Changed The World* and *The World Book Encyclopedia*.

a. Most anthropologists differentiate between *homo habilis (handy man)*, dating back 1.5 to 2 million years, *homo sapiens (wise human beings)* and *homo sapiens sapiens,* our own species, whose earliest discovered remains have been dated to 35,000 years ago.

b. Early "brains," of course, were very simple nervous systems.

c. No one knows for certain when understandable speech developed. But the latest brain research has identified the parts of our brain that deal with speech, thought and reasoning: all are in our forebrains which are most fully developed in *homo sapiens sapiens.*

d. The earliest alphabet emerged about 1700 B.C., but the more modern Greek version was not introduced into Europe until around 1000 B.C.

1. The age of instant communication

The world has developed an amazing ability to store information and make it available instantly in different forms to almost anyone. That ability is revolutionizing business, education, home life, employment, management and virtually everything else we take for granted.

Our homes will reemerge as vital centers of learning, work and entertainment. The impact of that sentence alone will transform our schools, our businesses, our shopping centers, our offices, our cities— in many ways our entire concept of work.

Our ability to communicate is one of our key human traits. Most scientists say the world has existed for 4,500 million years,[1] that humans in somewhere near their present form have been here for maybe two million years, and as "modern humans" for 35,000 to 50,000 years. Yet our ancestors—whatever arguments exist over their origins—did not invent any form of writing until 6,000 years ago.

It took another 2,000 years before they created the first alphabet—the unique concept that eventually enabled all knowledge to be recorded by rearranging only 26 symbols. But not until the 11th century AD did the Chinese start printing books. And it was not until 1451 that German inventor Johannes Gutenburg printed the first European book: transforming our ability to store and communicate knowledge by making the printed word available to millions. "Before Gutenberg, there were only about 30,000 books on the entire continent of Europe. By 1500, there were more than 9 million."[2]

Not until the last hundred-odd years did we start to speed up the process: the first typewriter in 1872, the first telephone message in 1876, the first typesetting machine in 1884, silent movies in 1894, the first radio signals in 1895, talking movies in 1922, infant television in 1926 and the computer microprocessor and pocket calculator in 1971. Since then the communications revolution has exploded.

The world is becoming one gigantic information exchange. By 1988 a single fiber optic "cable" could carry 3,000 electronic messages at once. By 1996: 1.5 million. By 2000: 10 million.[3]

In a typical year the world produces over 800,000 different book-titles.[4] If you read one a day, it would take you well over 2,000 years to complete them all. But what if you could automatically select only the information you want, when you want it, and have it fed to you through

If products such as cars and cereal followed the same trend as the PC, a mid-size car would cost $27 and a box of cereal a penny.

BILL GATES
Business @ The Speed Of Thought*

*Published by Warner Books, New York.

one of those 10 million messages that we will soon be able to transmit at the same time on one fiber optic "cable" at almost no cost? And what if you could reproduce that information at home in any form: on computer, videotape, compact disc or on your home printer? The technology is operating. And more and more you won't even need the fiber optics.

By early 1999 at least 250 million computers were in use. At least 150 million people had direct access to the Internet. Each one could directly contact 150 million others. Millions more had Internet access through their company or school. Between 2000 and 2005, many forecast that 500 million[5] to 1 billion individuals will be on the Net.

CD-ROMs, digital video discs and electronic games provide striking early examples of the shape of things to come.

When an earlier version of this book appeared in 1993 the electronic games business was already very big but CD-ROMs were mere infants. By 1995 more than 10,000 CD-ROM titles were on the market. Most were, in some form, educational. And since then the total has soared.

Several breakthroughs form typical success models:

❑ In 1979, Californian school teacher Jan Davidson set up a small teaching center in Rancho Palos Verdes, overlooking southern Los Angeles. She soon bought a $3,000 Apple II computer, and with a friend began writing programs to drill students in vocabulary and mathematics. Her company grew modestly until 1991, when "edutainment put it into overdrive".[6] Three years later she and her husband Bob floated Davidson & Associates as a public company, and in 1996 they sold it for almost $1 billion.

Now you'll find the Davidson label, with that of toy giant Fisher-Price, on a major range of high-quality, well-researched interactive CD-ROM programs. They're turning millions of homes into preschool, elementary and high-school learning centers: *Kid Phonics, Kid Works, Kid Keys, Kid Kad,* and the *Math Blaster* and *Reading Blaster* series among the leaders from Davidsons, for youngsters from four to 12 years; and from Fisher-Price a series starting even younger.

❑ In 1981 a 25-year-old American bought Q-DOS—the "Quick and Dirty Operating System"—for $75,000,[7] developed it, and turned it into the standard for the personal-computing world. Today Microsoft co-founder Bill Gates is the world's richest person. Gates' teenage dream was "a computer on every desk and in every home".[8] Now he plans, too,

You can expect to have on your wrist tomorrow what you have on your desk today, what filled a room yesterday.

NICHOLAS NEGROPONTE
Being Digital*

* Published by Vintage Books, New York.

for an age when people everywhere will be able to take the best courses, in any subject, taught by the world's best teachers—in their home.

His *Encarta* interactive encyclopedia shows another key aspect of the future: effectively given away free with millions of PCs to help establish Microsoft *Windows* as the world's leading computer system.

❑ In 1982, an 18-year-old Texas university student began tinkering with PC technology. With some other off-the-shelf components, he started producing made-to-order personal computers. Later he pioneered the selling of made-to-order PCs by direct advertising—servicing them, and selling upgrades for them, by one of the world's best-trained telephone teams.

By 1995 Michael Dell's computer company was turning over $5.3 billion and was one of the four largest PC companies in the world. And by the start of 1999, when Michael Dell was still only 34, annual sales had soared to $18 billion.

❑ In 1991 a company that formerly made simple playing cards outstripped the earnings of the massive Sony Corporation by $400 million. In 1992 the same company generated $5.5 billion in sales and $1.3 billion in pretax profits from just 892 employees: more than $6 million in sales per employee. Its name: Nintendo. Its product: electronic games. Its leadership dynamo: Hiroshi Yamauchi—the creator of the ultimate job description for the new century. When asked by his first designer: "What should I make?" Yamauchi replied: "Something great."[9]

Today Nintendo, Sega and Sony compete with a raft of others for the $15-billion-a-year electronic games market.

❑ In 1993 a 22-year-old American student working for $6 an hour created the first-ever Internet "browser". Two years later his company had still never turned a profit. Yet when it "went public" in August 1995 it created the biggest investment explosion in history. By the end of the first day's trading, shares bought for $28 were being traded for $71. By the end of 1995 24-year-old Mark Andreessen's personal stockholding was worth $137 million. And those of his senior venture capital partner Jim Clark were worth $1.3 billion.[10]

The company's name: Netscape Communications. Market worth by mid-1996: $3.1 billion. Its product: the Netscape *Navigator*. If the product's benefit was brilliantly simple, its marketing concept turned

Models for the new information age

Your child's video game

has 10,000 times the capacity of the world's first 1947 ENIAC computer.

Today's greeting card

that sings "Happy Birthday" contains more computer power than existed on earth before 1950.

Most home video cameras

contain a more powerful chip than the huge IBM system 360 computer: the giant that filled hundreds of sq. ft. of air-conditioned space in the 1960s.

Genesis offers a game

with a computer more powerful than a multimillion-dollar 1976 Cray supercomputer.

Sony has a videogame

with a 200 MIPs (millions of instructions per second) processor that not so long ago would have cost about $3 million in mainframe form.

Internet [2]

will soon connect more than 100 universities at 600 million bits per second—enough to transmit a 30-volume encyclopedia in less than 1 second.

DON TAPSCOTT*

* Condensed from *The Digital Economy*,
and the book edited by him, *Blueprint To The Digital Economy*,
both published by McGraw-Hill,
11 West 19th Street, New York, NY 1001, USA.

business wisdom upside down: give the product away—free—to become the worldwide industry standard, and make money by selling the add-ons.

By September 1996 40 million people around the world were using the *Navigator's* simple point-and-click tools to surf the Internet, to find graphics, text and video from vast information databases.

Chief Executive Officer Jim Barksdale was predicting 500 million users by early in the new century,[11] and Bill Gates' team, with its new Internet *Explorer,* was racing to dominate the same market. By early 1999 Netscape was being merged into an even bigger concept, as part of America Online, which was by then the world's biggest Internet provider.

Writes Ray Hammond in *Digital Business:* "What was particularly important about the feeding frenzy for Netscape stock was that the market suddenly grasped the concept of the Internet as a permanent new communications channel, one which will be bigger than all the others put together, a channel which will be, at one and the same time, *global, personal, interactive, low cost* and *forever-growing.* However, even these words undersell what the Internet and its successors will become and the impact it will have on business and social structures."

On its own, says Hammond, a personal computer is fairly dumb. But place it on a network, where it joins millions of others, and "the solitary PC becomes part of a neural network of intelligence which, collectively, has stunning power". Says Nicholas Negroponte, the Founding Director of the Media Lab at the Massachusetts Institute of Technology: "Thomas Jefferson advanced the concept of libraries and the right to check out a book free of charge. But this great forefather never considered the likelihood that 20 million people might access a digital library electronically and withdraw its contents at no cost."[12]

A CD used as read-only memory (CD-ROM) has a storage capacity of 5 billion bits. That's the equivalent of about 500 classic books "or five years' reading, even for those who read two novels a week".[13] Yet by early in the new century, says Negroponte, a typical CD-ROM will be able to hold ten times as much information: the equivalent of 5,000 books.

A CD-ROM can be mass-produced now for about $1 a disc in the United States and well under 50 cents in China. That's 50 cents for 500 interactive books, soon to be 5,000! And virtually every personal computer is now being delivered with the capacity to play CD-ROMs. Perhaps more importantly, there is now no need even to buy many CD-ROMs themselves. Their interactive contents can be downloaded in-

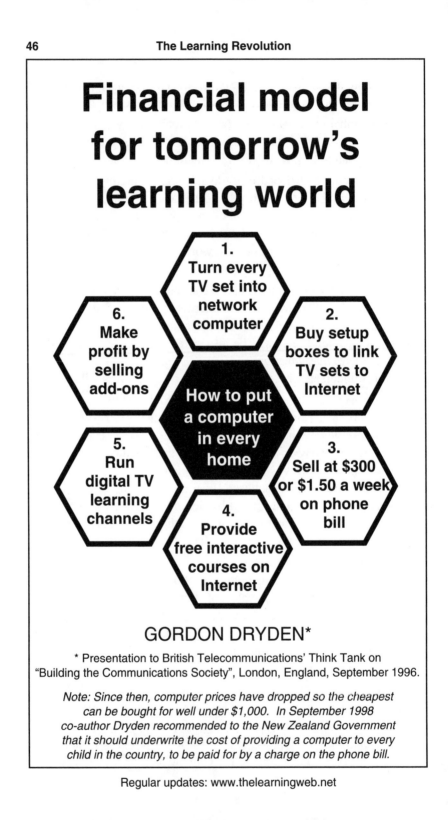

Financial model for tomorrow's learning world

1. Turn every TV set into network computer

6. Make profit by selling add-ons

2. Buy setup boxes to link TV sets to Internet

How to put a computer in every home

5. Run digital TV learning channels

3. Sell at $300 or $1.50 a week on phone bill

4. Provide free interactive courses on Internet

GORDON DRYDEN*

* Presentation to British Telecommunications' Think Tank on "Building the Communications Society", London, England, September 1996.

Note: Since then, computer prices have dropped so the cheapest can be bought for well under $1,000. In September 1998 co-author Dryden recommended to the New Zealand Government that it should underwrite the cost of providing a computer to every child in the country, to be paid for by a charge on the phone bill.

stantly from the Internet by millions of people around the world, at any time they wish. That means the more complex software programs, which tend to overload home computers, can be stored at one central point, and Internet users can plug into any program they want. The process makes a home computer almost as easy to use as a TV set. *Prime time* becomes *any time*—but you run the programs.

Tim Berners-Lee, creator of the Web, says the new "information appliance" might even come inside a cereal box. "My kids could rummage around for the free gift," he says, "take out a tube, unroll it to something flat, flexible and magnetic, stick it to the refrigerator and start navigating the Web."[14]

Says *Business Week:* "The great information-appliance race is on. The goal: to create electronic gadgets that are as simple as the TV but can instantly make the connection to the digital world."

Tie those concepts in with hire-purchase selling and you'll probably have the next big breakthrough in consumer electronics—with tremendous potential for education and learning. When a telephone, electricity or cable company can offer you instant access to the Internet and World Wide Web through a fiber-optic phone line and a combined TV-personal computer—and give you a payment choice of, say, $300 in cash or no deposit and $1.50 a week on your bill—every home will have cheap access to everyone else.

Wired magazine's executive editor Kevin Kelly calls the new economy a "tectonic upheaval". And he writes: "The irony of our times is that the era of computers is over. All the major consequences of stand-alone computers have already taken place. All the most promising technologies making their debut now are chiefly due to communication between computers—that is, connections rather than computations." [15]

Kelly says the network economy is "fed by the resonance of two stellar bangs: the collapsing microcosm of chips and the exploding telecosm of connections. These sudden shifts are tearing the old laws of wealth apart and preparing territory for the emerging economy.

"As the size of silicon chips shrinks to the microscopic, their costs shrink to the microscopic as well. They become cheap and tiny enough to slip into every—and the key word here is *every*—object we make."

While the total world population of personal computers is expected to reach 500 million by 2002, "the number of noncomputer chips now

With interactive multimedia systems, management in developing countries can bypass the industrial revolution.

STAN SHIH
Chief Executive Officer, The Acer Group*

* The Taiwan-based international computer company, number seven in the world, in author interview.

pulsating in the world is 6 billion", and Kelly forecasts there'll be 10 billion by 2005 and a trillion not long after. "As we implant a billion specks of our thought into everything we make," he says, "we are also connecting them up." And it is the explosion of low-cost—sometimes free—connections that is fuelling the new economy.

"When you go to Office Depot to buy a fax machine," says Kelly, "you are not just buying a $200 box. You are purchasing for $200 the entire network of all other fax machines and the connections between them— a value far greater than the cost of all the separate machines."[16]

Or, as Larry Downes and Chunka Mui put it in *Unleashing The Killer App:* "If you and I can call only each other . . . a phone is of little value. But if we can call nearly everyone else in the world, it becomes irresistible."

One of Asia's outstanding business leaders, the Taiwan-based Acer Group's Chief Executive Stan Shih, for instance, forecasts that low-cost, interactive, electronic multimedia systems will allow management in developing countries to bypass the industrial revolution—jumping directly into the Information Age.[17]

2. A world without economic borders

We are also moving inevitably to a world where most commerce will be virtually as unrestricted as the Internet. Ignore the short-term moves to protect some countries' farming incomes. The genie is out of the bottle: the instant transfer of money around the globe—at least $1.3-trillion dollars a day[18]—has altered the very nature of trade and world commerce.

Megatrends 2000 co-author John Naisbitt lists a global economy as one of his main predictions. "That's the undoubted direction the world is going—towards a single-market world economy. Sure, we have the counter-trends of protectionism along the way, but the main over-arching trend is to move to a world where there's free trade among all countries."[19]

And President Clinton's first Secretary of Labor, Robert B. Reich, writes at the start of *The Work Of Nations—preparing ourselves for the twenty first century:* "We are living through a transformation that will rearrange the politics and economies of the coming century. There will be no *national* products or technologies, no national corporations, no national industries. There will no longer be national economies, at least as we have come to understand that concept. All that will remain rooted within national borders are the people who comprise a nation. Each

We are clothing the globe with a network society.

KEVIN KELLY
*New Rules For The New Economy**

* Published by Viking-Penguin, New York.

nation's primary assets will be its citizens' skills."

And those will depend above all else on the ability of a nation's population to learn those new skills, particularly in defining problems, creating new solutions and adding new values.

Certainly a nation's education system can no longer be based simply on remembering a limited core of information.

3. Four leaps to a one-world economy

While international finance has spurred the growth of the one-world economy, there are four main stepping stones to that prosperous future:

1. The continued leadership of America in the vital field of electronic innovation, and now in the new world of "convergence".

2. The rebirth of Europe as a single economic entity, as a model for integrated communities.

3. The rise of dynamic "Tiger economies" as models for small countries.

4. The resurgence of China, the world's most populous country, as a model for the large population-blocs in the underdeveloped world.

The first stepping stone: the American flair for quickly turning high-tech research into breakthrough products. As the world moves into the new century, the amazing resilience of the American economy remains the base for continued world growth, particularly in the new digital age.

And nowhere does the future beckon more than in the Californian area known as Silicon Valley. Even 50 years ago the area south of San Francisco Bay was a county of orange groves and vineyards. Now it has given birth to 240 publicly-listed technology companies with a market worth of $500 billion, annual sales of $170 billion and 377,000 employees—plus at least 4,000 small non-public companies.[20]

But its lesson for the future is probably even more important: a unique series of university-business partnerships. Today's half of Silicon Valley's revenues come from companies seeded by Stanford University.

But America's emerging new catalyst is the way several of its ground-breaking industries are now converging: computers, television, entertainment and instant communications.

That convergence, too, has tremendous implications for education: and the potential to bypass the school system if that system stays locked into an outdated model.

What's needed to match Silicon Valley?

1. Major research institution
Like Stanford, Cambridge, M.I.T.

2. One megasuccess story
Like Microsoft, Nokia, Lotus, Acer

3. High-tech talent
And the ability to attract it

4. Venture capital
Israel, Taiwan now showing the way

5. Infrastructure
Singapore the Government model

6. The right attitude
Risk-taking confidence

STEVEN LEVY*

Newsweek cover story, *The Hot New Tech Cities*
(November 9, 1998).

The second stepping stone into a one-world economy is modeled by the European Union. It links 15 countries and 370 million people. Long in the shadow of the United States, Europe is once again re-emerging as the second global anchor for prosperity and stability. Europe's new single currency, the Euro, consolidates 11 different markets. And, in spite of rising unemployment in its stagnant traditional manufacturing industries, Europe's software and telecom companies have been pumping out jobs. Germany's newly-deregulated telecom companies alone created 40,000 jobs in 1998. And even in smaller European countries, Finland's Nokia, Sweden's Ericsson, and Britain's Vodafone have shown how the new technologies can revitalize the new century's economies when backed by equally dynamic educational policies.

The ancient British university town of Cambridge typifies the turnaround. It's now headquarters for an area with 1,159 high-tech firms, spearheaded by Acorn, Cambridge Display Tech and Pipex. Sir Alex Broers, Cambridge University's vice chancellor, "dreams of transforming the entire eastern region of the United Kingdom into a digital hotbed. The masterplan, hatched by officials of town and gown, is laid out in an optimistic document labelled *Cambridge 2020.*"[21] It outlines a future where the town remains a tourist-packed beehive of chapels, halls and sprawling lawns—surrounded by rings of industrial parks and chip plants.

The third stepping stone is the new model of the internationally-targeted small country, particularly such states as Taiwan, Ireland, Finland and Singapore, with pockets elsewhere such as Bangalore in India, Tel Aviv in Israel, and Kyoto in Japan.

When co-author Dryden first visited Taipei in 1964, the capital of Taiwan had only one set of traffic lights: turned on only when a visiting dignitary entered town. Now Taiwan, with 21 million people, boasts 14,000 electronic companies with total sales of $75 billion, mostly exported, including 120 high-tech public companies, with a market worth of $100 billion, sales of $27 billion and 72,000 employees. It also graduates 10,000 engineers and scientists a year and has an active policy to attract back thousands of others who have succeeded in places such as Silicon Valley.[22]

Ireland, with under four million people, is an equally dramatic example. Twentyfive years ago it was a poor farming country. Now it is the world's second largest software exporter, after the United States. It

The single most commercially minded country in the world today is the People's Republic of China.

LAURENCE J. BRAHM
China As No. 1

*Published by Butterworth-Heinemann Asia
1 Temasek Avenue, Singapore 039192.

Regular updates: www.thelearningweb.net

has attracted 1,100 international companies to start up in the republic, and these now have 107,000 employees. The country's annual exports: $25 billion, with a trade surplus each year of $11 billion.   Like Taiwan, Ireland's tax incentives to attract high-tech companies are matched by extensive policies to develop the skilled people to staff them.[23]

Finland has even a more amazing story to tell—and in many ways it is the story of one company: Nokia. Back in the 1980s, Finland's major industry was paper and pulp. Helsinki-based Nokia, the country's largest company, was known more for its rubber boots than tiny phones.   "But when the economy took a nosedive in the early 1990s, Finland turned to high tech for salvation. The Government decided to put 2.9 percent of the gross domestic product into technology research and development. Companies turned to international partners to start electronic ventures, and Nokia discovered a seemingly endless market for cellphones."[24] Soon Nokia was pulling in $32 billion a year from this new phenomenon, and its success fuelled Finland's technology boom.   As the company grew, it also invested in science parks at universities around the country, which were funded by government-venture capital groups. Today Finland has 400 high-tech firms. It has only five million people, but nearly 2.5 million of them carry cellphones.   And the land of lakes and saunas also boasts the highest number of Internet connections in Europe.

The tiny Asian island state of Singapore provides equally important lessons. Forty years ago it was a poverty-stricken island. Twenty years ago the Government began a campaign to attract high-tech multinationals—with tax incentives, a well-educated workforce, and an amazing infrastructure program.   Fired by an enormous Government-investment policy from compulsory superannuation savings, the island state's latest infrastructure project, *Singapore One*—worth hundreds of millions of dollars—will connect every household, school and office to the Internet by the end of 1999. And Singapore is probably doing more than any other nation to spend heavily on information technology in schools.

But the biggest sleeping giant of all is China.   After the stagnating years of Mao's Cultural Revolution, since 1979 it has released more people from poverty than any other society in history. In the past 20 years it has increased its economy more than 400 percent. But in many of the coastal "special economic areas" the economy has been soaring at an even higher rate. Sure: the country still has big problems, but it is now racing to apply the lessons of Singapore, Hong Kong and Taiwan.

China-led model for new century

❑ China in 1999 had only three million homes on the Internet, but 310 million homes with TV sets.

❑ Now Hong Kong's richest family and Intel are linking for a giant new television/Internet venture.

❑ This will turn millions of TV sets into low-cost network computers.

❑ Thus hundreds of millions of Asians, even in poor homes, will have access to email, the World Wide Web and distance learning.

❑ The project will include voicemail for the majority of Asians who cannot type because they write in ideograms or phonograms.

DOUGLAS C. McGILL
*Wired magazine**

* *Empire of the Son* in May, 1999, issue, on "Richard Li's Intel deal that could crack the Great Firewall of China". McGill quotes Avram Miller, Intel's business-development chief, as saying: "The scale of this will be bigger than anything else that exists in the world."

China, too, has an extra "secret weapon": the 51 million Chinese who live outside its borders. Collectively they own liquid assets worth two trillion dollars.[25] Their over-riding ethic is educational achievement. Most of their historic family links are with major areas of growth along China's eastern seafront. With their investment in those areas, and the country's own internal growth policies, the Chinese economy is set to become the world's largest no later than the 2030s, maybe earlier.[26]

Take just one project: the brainchild of Richard Li, Californian-educated second son of Hong Kong's richest man, Li Ka-shing, and one of the two main heirs to the Li family's $10 billion fortune. In the mid-1990s Richard Li sold his Star TV satellite television network to Rupert Murdoch for $950 million. Now he's prepared to invest that, and more, to provide a unique television-Internet service to hundreds of millions of Chinese and other Asian families. Fewer than 3 percent of Asian homes currently have a telephone, but 65 percent have TV. And Richard Li, in a joint venture with Intel, is to provide these families with a cheap set-top box that will turn their television sets into emailing, Web-surfing computers. Each will even be voice-activated for hundreds of millions of Asians who cannot type. Li knows full well that, with 1.3 billion people, China has an official policy to encourage one-child families. Those children could become the world's most educated. And Li's new Pacific Convergence Corporation intends to provide them with a full range of interactive services, including distance learning and Internet shopping.

4: Internet commerce and learning

Link all these first four trends to all aspects of commerce and education and you get an even more astonishing view of tomorrow's world. As Li's project shows, not only can people communicate instantly around the globe, but they can *trade* instantly and *learn* instantly.

By mid-1997, Dell was selling computers through the Internet at a rate of $1 million a day. By early 1999: $18 million a day. By then its customers were paying $18 billion a year for Dell computers which the users themselves were largely configuring on the Internet, selecting from individual components. The completed orders were then transferred electronically to Federal Express depots, and delivered overnight.

The same pattern is revolutionizing commerce in other fields.

❏ Open up *www.amazon.com* on the World Wide Web and you'll join at least 540,000 customers who each day gain instant access to 2.5

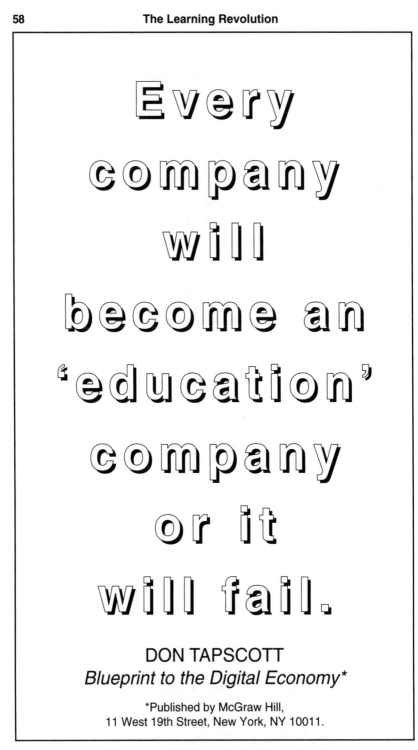

Every company will become an 'education' company or it will fail.

DON TAPSCOTT
Blueprint to the Digital Economy*

*Published by McGraw Hill,
11 West 19th Street, New York, NY 10011.

million books. Amazon does not own a shop, but its 1998 Internet sales reached $610 million. Still to turn a profit by the start of 1999, it had already assembled the world's biggest personal database of readers' book preferences.

❏ Contact *www.ImagineRadio.com* on the Web, select your favorite music styles and artists, and Imagine Radio will create your own private on-line radio station, with programs personalized for your taste. It will keep updating your own personalized radio station from the newest hits selected to suit your profile.

❏ Select *www.CDnow.com* and, from your listed preferences, it will provide you with a personalized selection from around 375,000 different music tracks and songs: a separate music service for each of its 600,000 customers.

❏ Select *www.garden.com* and Garden Escape provides an on-line nursery just for you. File your zip code and flower preferences, and it will tell you exactly when to plant what. You can even use its on-line software to landscape your home.

❏ *www.autoweb.com* arranges sales of 30,000 cars a month, totalling $660 million a year, by matching sellers with specific buyers.

Some estimates are forecasting that revenue from Internet sales will reach $327 billion by 2002. And the trend will affect education as much as business. It is creating new forms of organization that will transform both: information and service on demand.

5. The new service society

Peter Drucker, John Naisbitt, Kenichi Ohmae, Robert Reich, and many other forecasters all agree the next trend: the move from an industrial to a service society.[27] Naisbitt again: "When I got out of college in the fifties, 65 percent of the workforce in America was blue-collar. Now it's down to about 13 percent, and its falling. That doesn't mean we're producing less. In fact, around 24 percent of America's gross national product is in manufacturing, about the same as it has been every year for 40 years. The difference is that 40 years ago 65 percent of the workforce was manufacturing these products, and today only 13 percent. Now obviously that 24 percent represents many more products as our economy has grown tremendously. The big change is: we're now manufacturing with information, rather than people—with computers,

Be good, get rich but stay small.

CHARLES HANDY
Beyond Certainty*

* Published by Hutchinson (Random House UK),
20 Vauxhall Bridge Road, London SW1 2SA, England.

automation and robots instead of workers. And that industrial workforce will continue to shrink, just as the agricultural base has shrunk. A couple of hundred years ago 90 percent of the people in North America were farmers. As recently as a dozen years ago it was about three and a half percent. Now it's way below that."

Both Naisbitt and Drucker predict that by early in the new century only ten percent of the workforce in affluent developed countries like America will be working in direct manufacturing. And the figures back them up. Almost half of all routine American jobs in steelmaking disappeared between 1974 and 1988—from 480,000 to 260,000. General Motors alone wiped out 150,000 U.S. production jobs in the 1980s.

So if all a developed country's manufacturing can be done with ten percent of its workers, and all its farm products produced by another two percent, what will the other 88 percent of us do?

Some are calling our future "the new service economy". But the very terms "manufacturing" and "service" are becoming obsolete. More and more, manufacturing will be combined with service: customized for individuals—in the same way that computer hardware now represents a very small part of the total service supplied by a computer company. By far the biggest part is in specialist consulting: customized software systems and training.

Everyone now has to become a self-acting manager of one's own future. But much education still resembles the declining industrial method of production: a standard assembly-line curriculum divided into subjects, taught in units, arranged by grade, and controlled by standardized tests. This no longer reflects the world we live in. And traditional educational systems can no longer cope with the new realities.

6. The marriage of big and small

In the traditional industrial economy, bigness ruled. GM, Ford and Chrysler dominated world car production for almost half a century; IBM towered over computers; and so on in dozens of different industries.

Even 25 years ago only big companies could afford the giant computers that were then the peak of electronic achievement. That technology helped spur the ride to centralized bureaucracy, takeovers, acquisitions and mergers. Today many of those giant computers are obsolete. The world of the mini has arrived. Sure, many big companies are still there. Many of them, such as GE, are booming. Giant mergers are reported

When Amway begins selling on the Web on Sept. 1, 1999, two great 20th-century marketing forces will collide: multilevel marketing and e-commerce.

WIRED MAGAZINE*

* May, 1999.

almost every day as different industries converge. And new giants such as Microsoft, Accr, Sun and Oracle have emerged. But the earlier vast air-conditioned computer rooms lie empty or transformed.

And organizational structures are changing fast. Where the giant companies are still prospering, they have generally been split into dozens of small project teams, each self-acting and self-managing, cutting through the old specialization, the old business pyramid-style hierarchies, the old army-style management.

Tom Peters gives dozens of examples in his 834-page book *Liberation Management.* To cite just one: Zurich-based ABB Asea Brown Boveri is now one of Europe's giant companies, with revenues of $33 billion in 1995.[28] It now operates as 36 independent businesses with hundreds of autonomous profit centers. Most of these are split into ten-person, multifunction teams. And it has slashed its "head office" staff by 95 percent.

Japan's Toyota has pioneered "just-in-time" production systems, buying thousands of products from small production units—often family firms—delivered exactly when they are needed.

And in other fields—notably retailing—franchising and computerization make it possible for small distribution outlets to link with major international systems-suppliers, from McDonald's to computer and software manufacturers.

Some analysts[29] say that by early in the new century 50 percent of all retailing will be through franchises (mostly self-operating small units linked to giant systems) and direct-marketing networks (mainly individuals linked to world suppliers).

Again the examples are startling:

❏ Franchising in America involves $250 billion in annual sales.

❏ The fastest-growing franchise is Subway Sandwiches, with 7,000 outlets worldwide.

❏ Many of McDonald's 23,000 franchises around the world are run by husband-and-wife teams, but all are linked to the one central system.

❏ More than 20 million Americans are now making money from home-based industries. Over 60 percent of them are women.

❏ By far the biggest is Amway, started by Richard DeVos and Jay Van Andel, in the basement of a Michigan home in 1959. By 1996 the

90 percent of new jobs are in companies with under 50 people.

JOHN NAISBITT
co-author of *Megatrends 2000**

* In author interview.

company had 2.5 million people selling 5,000 Amway products in 76 countries, with global sales of $6.3 billion.

❑ Japan is the world's biggest direct-selling market, involving 1.2 million women distributors and a turnover exceeding $20 billion a year.[30]

❑ In 1963 Mary Kay Ash founded Mary Kay Cosmetics with a mission of promoting business opportunities for women and teaching women how to care for their skin. Today its 275,000 beauty consultants turn over $1 billion.

But the biggest growing network by far is the Internet, with its thousands of individual networks, and the opportunity for anyone to sell his or her niche products to customers around the planet.

For employment, in particular, the small companies are vital. Says John Naisbitt: "It's the young entrepreneurial companies that are creating nearly all the new jobs in the United States. In the 1980s America created 22 million brand-new jobs; there were that many more people in paid employment at the end of the eighties. And 90 percent of those 22 million jobs were in companies of 50 or fewer employees. That is the new economy. That is what's creating the new wealth-creating capacity. So if you want to see what the new company looks like, you look at the young companies, not the old household-word companies that are shrinking and are very slow to change."[31]

In many of these companies, the educational need is for thinking and conceptual skills, risk-taking, experimenting, and an openness to change and opportunity. How much of that is taught at schools?

7. The new age of leisure

British educator, broadcaster and business consultant Charles Handy puts the figures neatly in *The Age of Unreason*. When he first started work in the 1940s it was standard for each person to spend 100,000 hours in his or her lifetime in paid work, although we never thought of it in those terms. But we generally worked around 47 hours a week, for 47 weeks of the year for 47 years—generally from age 16, 17 or 18. And that worked out at just over 100,000 hours. Handy predicts that very soon— at least in developed countries—we will each need to spend only around 50,000 hours of a lifetime in paid work. And he thinks we will each split that into different and convenient "chunks".

On average the average male now lives to at least 70 years—a total of

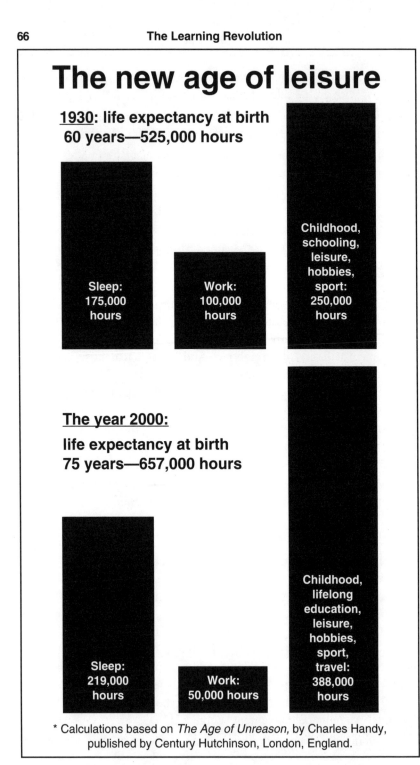

The new age of leisure

<u>1930</u>: life expectancy at birth
60 years—525,000 hours

Sleep:
175,000
hours

Work:
100,000
hours

Childhood,
schooling,
leisure,
hobbies,
sport:
250,000
hours

<u>The year 2000:</u>

life expectancy at birth
75 years—657,000 hours

Sleep:
219,000
hours

Work:
50,000 hours

Childhood,
lifelong
education,
leisure,
hobbies,
sport,
travel:
388,000
hours

* Calculations based on *The Age of Unreason,* by Charles Handy,
published by Century Hutchinson, London, England.

over 600,000 hours. And if we sleep for 200,000 hours and spend only 50,000 hours in paid employment, we will have over 350,000 hours to spend on leisure, education, travel, hobbies and everything else.

Leisure, tourism and lifelong education will be among the major growth industries. Already some of the trends are obvious. Half a billion tourists travel each year. By the year 2000, the prediction is a billion.[32]

Overcrowded Japan set goals in the mid-1980s to have 10 million of its citizens taking holidays abroad by 1991.[33] The target was achieved. Over 90 percent of Japanese newlyweds honeymoon in other countries.

In Florida, 33 million visitors a year now flock into the former swampland of Orlando — thanks to the vision of Walt Disney and the planning of his successors. More than 55 million tourists from other countries visit France each year, and the 23.6 million who visited Britain in 1995 spent $17.5 billion. London's main airport at Heathrow is now also a major shopping center, with a retail turnover of $500 million a year.

Baltimore, Maryland, once a dirty, rundown port city, now attracts eight million visitors a year to the cultural and entertainment attractions on its revamped waterfront. The giant Mall of America in Minnesota is built around a seven-acre amusement park, adapted from Knotts' Berry Farm in California. Sega has opened three virtual-reality theme parks in Japan, one in London, and it plans 50 around the world. Hyatt plans to open 25 fantasy hotels within the next few years. Legoland, at Windsor, is one of Britain's newest tourist venues. And Disneyland, in Tokyo, is Japan's biggest single tourist attraction.

Tourism is one of the few industries capable of creating vast numbers of new jobs. Achieving that will require big increases in foreign language training, culture-knowledge, hospitality service skills and the creation of exciting new leisure experiences.

And not the least of education's tasks will be to help prepare each country's citizens for a stimulating age of leisure.

8. The changing shape of work

Handy forecasts that soon a minority of working-age adults will be employed in fulltime permanent employment by traditional-style companies. Those will generally be highly-trained people, probably not starting work until their mid-twenties—with graduate and postgraduate qualifications. They are likely to provide the essential core management

By the year 2020 the largest employer in the developed world will be 'self'.

NICHOLAS NEGROPONTE
Being Digital*

* Published by Vintage Books (Random House), New York.

services. The rest, predicts Handy, will work in three separate clusters:

Cluster one will involve project groups: people coming together for specific projects, often for short periods. This will probably be the dominant high-paying work method of the coming decade. And its requirements will provide some of education's biggest challenges.

It is impossible to overstate the importance of the growing *project-group* nature of work, each person an open-minded self-acting specialist collaborating with an open-minded team to produce new solutions.

Says Handy: "The upside-down school would make study more like work, based on real problems to be solved or real tasks to be done, in groups of mixed ages and different types of ability, all of them useful. Not only would people learn more in such a school, because they would see the point and purpose of what they were doing, but it would give them a better idea of the world they would be entering."[34]

The second cluster will be part-time and seasonal workers: those who work two or three days a week in supermarkets, or weekends or summers in the tourist industry. It will be one of the few outlets for the unskilled or semiskilled. Those filling these positions are already the new-poor of the working population: the low-paid checkout cashiers, the peak-time, part-time fast-food servers.

The third cluster will be those who work individually or as a family group—often doing things they love to do. Effectively, the new world-wide information web enables competent people in any country to sell goods and services to anyone else—and to use databases to identify those customers and services. Families will be able to use such services to swap everything from holiday-houses to ideas. And we will have the choice of the world's best educators in nearly every home.

9. Women in leadership

Of the 22 million new jobs created in America in the eighties, two thirds were taken by women. Naisbitt says that the increase of women in leadership positions in America is now reaching critical mass. "Forty percent of all managers are now women. Thirty-five percent of the computer scientists are women. Half the accountants are women, as are an increasing number of lawyers and doctors. If you go to medical schools or business schools, half of the freshman class are women. And women are creating new companies at twice the rate of men."[35]

In the workplace the new technology is gender-blind.

JOHN NAISBITT
*Megatrends Asia**

* Published by Simon & Schuster, 1230 The Avenue of the Americas,
New York, NY 10020.

In *Megatrends Asia,* he underlines the explosive impact of women in the world's fastest growth area. "In Japan, nearly all currency traders are women. The number of female managers in Singapore has nearly tripled in the last decade. One in five management jobs in Hong Kong is held by a woman."

Instant access to global events through international satellite broadcasts gives Asian women a window on a world that earlier generations could not even fathom. "Education and financial independence," says Naisbitt, "will deliver what Asian women may value most — options."

The Economist says girls in many countries now seem to be outperforming boys before starting school and right through to the end of high school.[36] In many others they don't yet get the chance; there is undoubted, and often horrific, discrimination based on sex, but where the barriers are coming down, women are excelling.

There is also no doubt that in many cases women provide a different perspective. Anita Roddick is an outstanding example. In 1976 she opened her first retail venture, The Body Shop, in Brighton, England. By 1991 her worldwide chain had 709 shops, sales of $238 million and profits of $26 million. By 1993, 893 shops and a new one opening every two and a half days—nearly all of them franchises.

In her book *Body and Soul,* Roddick's perspective comes through on almost every page. "The great advantage I had when I started The Body Shop was that I had never been to business school . . . If I had to name a driving force in my life, I'd plump for passion every time . . . The twin ideas of love and care touch everything we do .

"For me there are no modern-day heroes in the business world. I have met no captains of industry who made my blood surge. I have met no corporate executive who values labour and who exhibits a sense of joy, magic or theater. In the 15 years I have been involved in the world of business it has taught me nothing. There is so much ignorance in top management and boards of directors: all the big companies seem to be led by accountants and lawyers and become moribund carbon-copy versions of each other. If there is excitement and adventure in their lives, it is contained in the figures on the profit-and-loss sheet. What an indictment!"

Just as women are changing business, so will philosophies like this change education. But how will we teach "love," "care" and "compassion?"

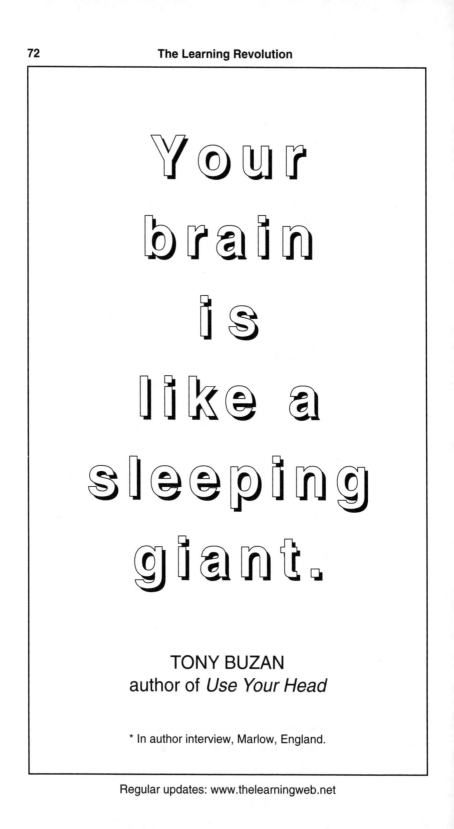

Your brain is like a sleeping giant.

TONY BUZAN
author of *Use Your Head*

* In author interview, Marlow, England.

10. Your amazing brain rediscovered

Some say the 1970s provided the decade of space exploration; the eighties, the decade of greed; and the nineties relaunched the discovery of inner-space: when we finally came to appreciate and utilize the tremendous potential of the human brain.

Tony Buzan puts it into perspective. To anyone studying education, he would seem a typically bright product of an excellent education system. He graduated in 1964 from the University of British Columbia, Canada, achieving double honors in psychology, English, mathematics and general sciences. But looking back today, he is staggered at what he *wasn't* taught.

"At school I spent thousands of hours learning about mathematics. Thousands of hours learning about language and literature. Thousands of hours about the sciences and geography and history. Then I asked myself: How many hours did I spend learning about how my memory works? How many hours did I spend learning about how my eyes function? How many hours in learning how to learn? How many hours in learning how my brain works? How many hours on the nature of my thought, and how it affects my body? And the answer was: none. In other words, I hadn't been actually taught how to use my head."[37]

Well after leaving university, he went into a library and asked for a book on how to use his brain. "The librarian said: 'The medical section's over there.' I said: 'I don't want to take my brain out; I want to use it.' And she said: 'Oh, there are no books on that.' And I thought: No books on how to use your most valuable tool. I must write one. And I did."

Since then he has written eight books. One of them, *Use Your Head,* has sold over a million copies. It is a recommended introductory text for Britain's Open University. It and the other simple Buzan techniques are essential for anyone joining The Learning Revolution.

11. Cultural nationalism

The more we become a one-world economy, the more we develop a global lifestyle, the more we will see an equal counter movement for what Naisbitt calls cultural nationalism.

"The more we globalize and become economically interdependent," he says, "the more we do the human thing; the more we assert our distinctiveness, the more we want to hang on to our language, the more

The other alternative: a rising underclass

The telephone gap

Half the world's population has never placed a phonecall.

The computer gap

Only 3 percent of the world's population uses computers, and even in the rich United States half the population cannot afford them.

The unemployment gap

Even in affluent Western Europe, 19 million people cannot find jobs.

The poverty gap

At least 27 million Americans are now living in poverty, and 40 percent of the nation's poor are children.

The education gap

More than half of America's young people leave school without the foundation needed to hold a good job.

The violence trap

270,000 American students carry guns to school.

The wealth gap

20% of Americans now earn 80 percent of the country's annual income.

The knowledge gap

The have-nots become the know-nots and do-nots.

we want to hold on to our roots and our culture. Even as Europe comes together economically, I think the Germans will become more German and the French more French."

The downside of this is obvious: the "ethnic cleansing" and horror of the civil war in the former Balkan country of Yugoslavia; the Middle East wars, often with religious overtones; rebellion in parts of the former Soviet Union; the racial bigotry in many countries.

But the positive challenges for education are equally obvious. The more technology thrives, the more the striving to capture our cultural heritage, in music, dance, language, art and history. Where individual communities are inspiring new directions in education, particularly among so-called minority groups, we're seeing a flowering of cultural initiatives—and a tremendous rise in self-esteem.

12. The growing underclass

You don't have to move too far from the center of the city in places like New York, Chicago, Philadelphia and Los Angeles to see the grim signs of a soaring underclass. It is mainly associated with color and educational failure, and overwhelmingly among unemployed youth.

Statistic after statistic shows that members of this underclass are often trapped in a self-perpetuating cycle. Back in 1970 Alvin Toffler predicted in *Future Shock* the era of the *fractured family:* more divorces, changing lifestyles, the breakdown of the nuclear family. Most of his predictions have come true. And where the fractured family has coincided with unemployment, the ingredients have formed the recipe for social disaster.

Education is a vital key to unlock an alternative future. In America's ten largest cities, the number of jobs requiring less than a high-school education has dropped by half since 1970. Two thirds of new jobs created in America since 1989 have been professional and managerial.[38] In Germany, by 2010 only 10 percent of jobs will be appropriate for unskilled workers, compared with 35 percent in 1976.[39]

But this is not only an unemployment problem. Unemployed young men tend to commit more violent crimes and not take on the responsibility of parenthood. "Adolescent boys are the most volatile and violent of all. Those under 24 are responsible for half of America's violent crime; those under 18 commit a quarter. The figures for most western countries are comparable."[40]

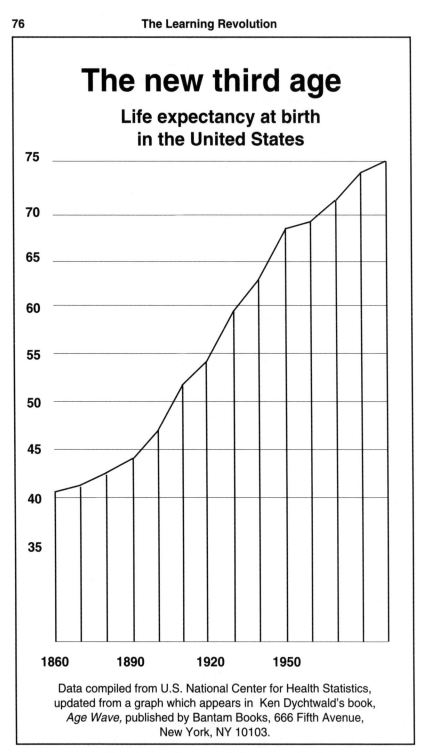

The new third age

Life expectancy at birth
in the United States

Data compiled from U.S. National Center for Health Statistics,
updated from a graph which appears in Ken Dychtwald's book,
Age Wave, published by Bantam Books, 666 Fifth Avenue,
New York, NY 10103.

Regular updates: www.thelearningweb.net

And *The Economist,* in a definitive survey, asks what restrains such behavior? "The short answer is: a two-parent home. Two-parent homes are demonstrably better at raising trouble-free children than one-parent ones."[41] All the more reason to worry that, in America in 1991, just 50.8 percent of children lived in traditional nuclear families (families where both parents were present and the children were the biological offspring of both parents). Among Hispanics, the figure was 38 percent; among Afro-Americans, 27 percent.[42]

Says *The Economist's* survey: "When men find it impossible to provide, they also seem to find it difficult to learn the nurturing bits. They may retreat into fundamentalist masculinity—the world of gangs which provides for their members a kind of rule-based behavior that boys do not get elsewhere."

Those who lack earning power, who lack self-esteem, those who get pregnant young and don't marry, those who marry young but don't have training in parenthood, and those who are poor are those most at risk of failing as parents. In turn their children have the hardest time breaking out of the poverty trap. And unfortunately that trap is not going away.

As Jeremy Rifkin puts it so well in his brilliant book *The End of Work:* "The Information age has arrived. In the years ahead, new, more sophisticated software technologies are going to bring civilization ever closer to a near-workerless world. In the agricultural, manufacturing and service sectors, machines are quickly replacing human labor, and promise an economy of near automated production by the mid-decades of the 21st century. The wholesale substitution of machines for workers is going to force every nation to rethink the role of human beings in the social process."

Even if no other factor demanded a learning revolution—and a corresponding social revolution—that paragraph screams out for one.

13. The active aging of the population

Just as economies are dramatically changing, so are demographics. And the most striking trend in developed countries is the active aging of the population.

A hundred years ago only 2.4 million Americans were over 65, under four in every 100. Today there are over 30 million—around one in eight. By 2050: over 67 million—almost 22 percent of the population.[43]

Since 1920 in America, average life expectancy has increased from

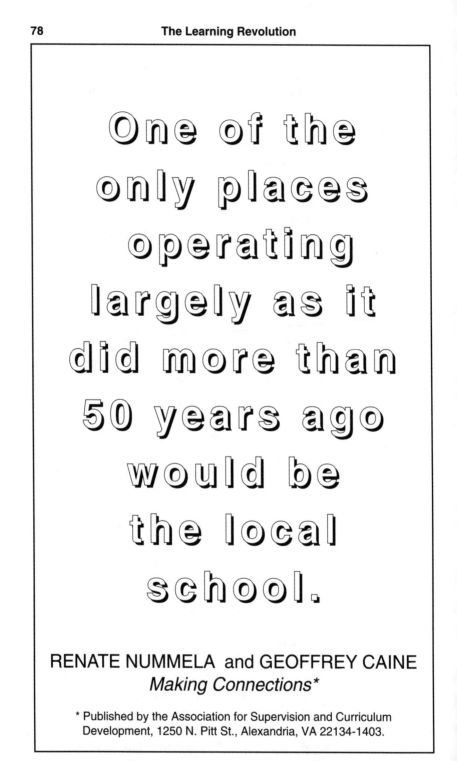

One of the
only places
operating
largely as it
did more than
50 years ago
would be
the local
school.

RENATE NUMMELA and GEOFFREY CAINE
Making Connections*

* Published by the Association for Supervision and Curriculum
Development, 1250 N. Pitt St., Alexandria, VA 22134-1403.

54 years to 75. In most developed countries, with the notable exception of Russia, the average male reaching 60 can also expect to live to at least 75, and the average woman over 80.

At current rates of growth, by the year 2025, the world's over-60 population will have increased to one billion. Little wonder that many are calling 60-plus *The Third Age*. Others are challenging us to abolish the word "retirement" from our vocabularies.

The over-60s generation also represents one of the greatest untapped resources for the future of education.

14. The new do-it-yourself boom

The industrial age also gave birth to another phenomenon: the confusion of structures with reality. Just as giant corporations arose to provide standardized mass-produced products to millions of people, so giant organizations arose to "deliver" health and education.

And so we came to confuse education with schooling; health with sickness-treatment and hospitals; law with lawyers. We came to regard education as something someone else provided for you. We believed that health was something you purchased from doctors, specialists and hospitals. Today that concept is changing rapidly. The new do-it-yourself revolution involves more than painting your home and doing your gardening. It involves taking control of your own life.

Personal computers can now provide the basis for much of what we pay experts to do: prepare wills, handle accounts, buy stocks and bonds, and figure taxes. Every sensible person now accepts that health also comes from what you do personally: what you eat and drink, and how you exercise.

But in "education" the change is slow to come. Californian educationalists Renate Nummela Caine and Geoffrey Caine explain in their book *Making Connections: teaching and the human brain:* "One function of schooling should be to prepare students for the real world. They need to have a sense of what will be expected of them, how they will be challenged, and what they are capable of doing. The assumption is that, by and large, schooling as we know it meets those goals. The reality is that it does not. On the contrary, it fosters illusions and obscures the real challenges. In particular, it fails to deal with the impact of electronic media.

"Take a close look at American teenagers. For a moment, let time run

3,000 out of Microsoft's 17,800 employees are also millionaires due to the stocks they own.

MICHAEL A. CUSUMANO and
RICHARD W. SELBY
Microsoft Secrets*

* Published by HarperCollins, 77-85 Fulham Palace Road, Hammersmith, London W6 8JB, and The Free Press, a division of Simon & Schuster, USA.

Note: by 1999 Microsoft's staff had risen to 28,000.

backwards to deprive teenagers of gadgets that are in some way dependent on electricity. One by one, we remove the television, the CD players, the computer, the videodisc, the radio, tape player, record player, electronic games, aeroplanes, air conditioning and automatic heating, shopping in large malls, and the opportunity to acquire large numbers of possessions. How well do you think our teenagers would cope? How would their lives be different? And what about our own?

"One of the only places that would reflect scarcely any difference in the scenario we've painted—and that would be operating largely as it did more than 50 years ago—would be the local school."

Obviously that criticism does not apply to those schools that are rapidly changing, and encouraging students to take control of their own world. But does it not apply to most?

Our own view is that more and more learning will become self-learning: self-directed and self-fulfilling.

15. Cooperative enterprise

The 1990s started with the collapse of Soviet-style communism, and we hope that the new decade has also heralded the decline of gambling-casino capitalism. Our own view is that both are rapidly being superseded by new concepts of *cooperative enterprise.*

In *The 100 Best Companies To Work For in America,* nearly every company listed has pioneered new forms of staff involvement: partnerships, stockholding, profit-sharing, continuing education, job-sharing, flextime, project teams and many more.

"If you want to see what the new company looks like," says John Naisbitt, "you look at the young companies, not the old household word companies that are shrinking and are often slow to change. And in the new companies you find a high degree of participative management and decision-making. You find everyone being involved in sharing the profits, including the people in the mailroom and the receptionist. You can't work for many of these new model companies unless you own stock. If you don't have the money, they lend you the money interest-free to buy stock, because you have to have literal ownership. And the company's daycare is often built-in right from the very beginning. They pay for any kind of education courses the people take in order for them to grow personally. And they create environments where people can nourish personal growth and educational growth."

There is a new generation emerging that will change the world as never before.

DON TAPSCOTT
Growing Up Digital*

*Published by McGraw Hill,
11 West 19th Street, New York, NY 10011.

16. The triumph of the individual

Around the world we're also seeing a revival of individual power and responsibility as more and more people take responsibility for creating their own future.

For around 200 years, national governments and then industrial giants have dominated almost every aspect of society.

Now the individual consumer is king—and queen—with the right and ability to choose from the best products and services around the world. This will also involve each one of us in taking the responsibility for choosing our own education—and in selecting the very best educational systems from around the world: a change with revolutionary potential.

We believe that personal revolution should take place from very early in life. As Don Tapscott summarizes it in *Growing Up Digital:* "I have become convinced that the most revolutionary force for change is the students themselves. Give children the tools they need and they will be the single most important source of guidance on how to make the schools relevant and effective."

*

Obviously, these are not the only dominant changes. We have not mentioned the spiritual revival taking place in many parts of the world, nor the regrowth of fundamentalism in many religions. The need to protect the environment is another vital trend, and has been covered in dozens of other books. So has quantum physics, and the new age of biochemistry.

But the 16 key points in this chapter represent major trends which we believe present an unchallenged case for a corresponding revolution in learning. Grasping all the opportunities will change not only the face of government and industry, but the very nature of the world we live in, and the very nature of the educational and learning systems that will groom us for the future.

A continuing theme in this book is that we cannot achieve the educational breakthroughs we need unless we make an increasing investment in new *methods* of education and learning.

No one would think of lighting a fire today by rubbing two sticks together. Yet much of what passes for education is based on equally outdated concepts.

Thirteen steps to a new learning society

1 **Rethink the role of electronic communications in education.**

2 **Learn computers and the Internet.**

3 **A dramatic improvement in parent education, especially for new parents.**

4 **A major overhaul of early childhood health services to avoid learning difficulties.**

5 **Quality early childhood development programs for all.**

6 **Catch-up programs at every school.**

7 **Define individual learning styles and intelligences, and cater to each one.**

8 **Learning how to learn, and how to think, should be on everyone's agenda.**

9 **Redefine what should be taught at school.**

10 **A four-part curriculum, with self-esteem and life-skills training as key components.**

11 **A three-fold purpose for most study.**

12 **Redefine the best teaching venues—not just at school.**

13 **Keep minds open, communicatiions clear.**

The 13 steps needed for a
21st century learning society

Imagine a 21st century community, only a few years from now.

❏ Every student has his or her own laptop computer.

❏ Every home has its own combined computer-television set at a cost of only $300, or possibly much less.

❏ Every home and every student is connected to the Internet.

❏ Every person, at almost any age, can have instant access to the world's best teachers in any subject.

❏ Each can also select at random from the world's best libraries, interactive science museums and art galleries.

❏ Each is linking up regularly with others around the world, designing their own electronic games to teach their own favorite subjects.

❏ Every new parent is trained to be able to develop each child's fantastic early potential, to be able to identify different temperaments, and different learning and thinking styles.

❏ Every four-year-old can read, write, spell, count, add, subtract, multiply, divide, compose her own stories, draw, paint—and speak three or four languages—but they've learned all this with fun and games.

❏ The health of every child from birth is regularly monitored to ensure his eyesight, hearing and other senses are in great "learning order".

❏ Every five- or six-year-old starts school with an equal opportunity to develop to its full potential.

❏ School itself is the best party in town: a base from which to explore the whole wide world of experience and knowledge.

Teachers will become managers of learning in learning centers where students will become clients, just like they are clients of lawyers or any other profession.

DAVID KERR
Chief Executive, Southland Polytechnic*

* In *Education Is Change: Twenty Viewpoints,*
edited by Harvey McQueen and published by Bridget Williams Books,
Wellington, New Zealand.

❏ Teachers are valued, highly paid professionals.

❏ Those teachers with the greatest knowledge of particular subjects have the whole world as their classroom. But the "textbooks" they create are interactive multimedia learning games, produced by the expert teams who once produced Nintendo computer games, television commercials and professional TV programs.

❏ All other teachers are skilled managers of learning centers where they act as mentors like great sporting coaches always have.

❏ Every person can plan his or her own curriculum at any age, and have access to the resources to learn the knowledge required, quickly and easily.

❏ All school-leavers have developed much higher competence than previously in such basics as reading, writing, mathematics, science, geography, history and general knowledge—what some call basic "Cultural Literacy".

❏ The three main "subjects" taught at school are learning how to learn, learning how to think and learning how to become a "self-acting manager of your own future". But they are not taught as subjects; they are integrated as working models of all study.

❏ Schools themselves have been completely redesigned. They are now round-the-clock community learning and resource centers.

❏ Introductory courses on thousands of subjects—from accounting to desktop publishing, book-writing to beekeeping—are available through the World Wide Web, and followed up with coaching at the local community resource center. One-day to six-week study courses are common.

❏ Depending on the community, each school may well have its own farm, forestry plantation, fish hatchery, newspaper or radio station—and certainly its own pilot industries, where students can test everything in practice—economics, science, accounting—and often sell the results.

❏ Everyone is a teacher as well as a student.

❏ Few active people are "retired" in the traditional sense of the word. Instead you'll find 70-year-old carpenters and engineers training yesterday's school failures to learn new skills. And together they're manufacturing the world's best manipulative learning materials for all preschool centers, not just those for affluent families.

❏ And you'll find teenage computer and Internet buffs mentoring and training parents and grandparents in their community learning center.

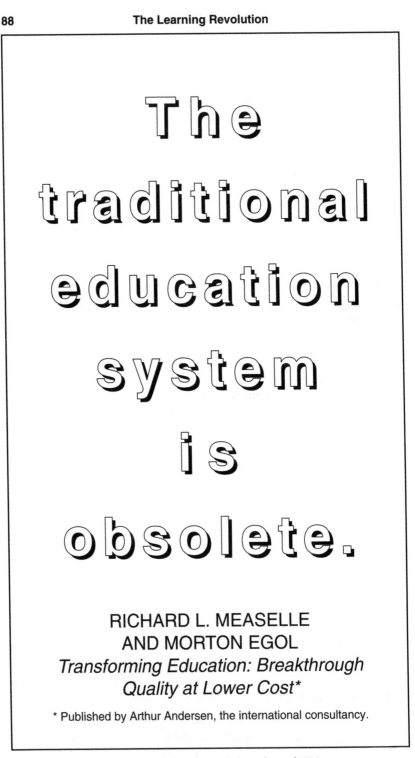

The traditional education system is obsolete.

RICHARD L. MEASELLE
AND MORTON EGOL
*Transforming Education: Breakthrough
Quality at Lower Cost**

* Published by Arthur Andersen, the international consultancy.

❏ All who want work are fully "employed". But in most "developed" countries only a minority are working "nine-to-five" for major corporations. The largest percentage are working for themselves on work they love to do, selling their goods and services on the Internet to niche markets around the world.

❏ Nearly all companies are learning organizations. Their main role is to *organize* people, not necessarily *employ* them—for most people are self-employed and contract either singly or in small groups to handle specific projects.

❏ Nearly all the new community learning centers are closely linked to business and other organizations in a full "learning community".

Does all this sound utopian? Light years into the future?

On the contrary. It is all possible now. And all aspects are being practiced in pockets around the world. We will cover examples throughout this book.

But the need is not merely to study them. It is *to actively reinvent the future of education.*

The giant Arthur Andersen consulting group puts it bluntly: "The traditional education system is obsolete."[1]

It says: "We need to replace today's assembly-line lockstep with 'self-directed' learning that is based on modern-day principles of cognitive science—including discovery, meaning-making, immersion and self-assessment—and the natural love of learning with which every person is born." It feels so strongly about it that it has designed its own model school for the 21st century.

Its thoughts are echoed by a 1995 Canadian Royal Commission: "The demands of schools have increased so greatly over the last few years," it says, "and the world has changed so drastically that nothing less than a radical reform of the school system is necessary if we are to walk boldly into the 21st century." [2] Many other countries and states are also searching for new roads to school reform.

But if your aim is only to create the world's best *schools,* then the answer is surprisingly simple: you need only to identify the best ideas already operating and link the ones that fit your needs.

But the real revolution is not only in schooling. It is in *learning how to learn, in learning how to think,* in learning new techniques that you can apply to any problem, any challenge, at any age.

This is the first generation to grow up surrounded by digital media.

DON TAPSCOTT
*Growing Up Digital**

* Published by McGraw Hill,
11 West 19th Street, New York, NY 10011.

A full learning revolution will thus involve much more than schooling. Fortunately, most of the learning breakthroughs have already been made. Many of them have come from able teachers. Many from business. Many from sports psychology and coaching techniques. Many from research into the human brain. Some from studies in nutrition. Others from health programs. And many from linking communities, schools and businesses together to replan the way ahead.

To achieve a true learning society, we believe, requires action in 13 separate but interrelated areas.

1. The new role of electronic communications

We live in the first era of human history where it is possible for everyone to communicate with everyone else.

It is also the first era in which children know more about the dominant technology than teachers or adults.

This combined Internet, computer and World-Wide-Web revolution is reshaping an entire generation: even more than the printing press, radio, the automobile and television have reshaped previous ones.

And, as Don Tapscott puts it so aptly: "What we know for certain is that children without access to the new media will be developmentally disadvantaged."

If left only to market forces, he says, the new digital economy "could foster a two-tiered society, creating a major gulf between information haves and have-nots—those who can communicate with the world and those who can't." He talks of a growing "information apartheid", where "the have-nots become the know-nots and the do-nots". And Tapscott challenges almost every form of hierarchy when he claims: "The people, companies, and nations which succeed in the new economy will be those who listen to their children."[3]

Tapscott, in one of his several excellent books on the subject, calls for all 21st century societies to "give children the tools they need, and they will be the single most important source of guidance on how to make the schools relevant and effective."[4] By using those tools, "the students teach themselves. While they're at it they can probably teach their teachers as well"—as Finland is proving in practice.

Amazingly, no country has yet completed a national program to link all its citizens into an interactive electronics instant communications

The Singapore masterplan*

❏ 'Thinking Schools' to become centers for continual learning.

❏ About $US2.5-million for each school in information technology.

❏ One computer at school for every two students within five years.

❏ Creative thinking as part of the new curriculum to match Singapore's current world leadership in mathematics and science exams.

❏ The curriculum also to build pride in Singapore's achievements, as a spur to further innovation.

❏ Previous 'top down' innovation too slow to match the 'wave upon wave' of new advances.

❏ Schools grouped in clusters to spread best new practices.

* Summarized from speech by Singapore's Minister of Education, Teo Chee Hean, April 27, 1997, subsequent author interview with the Minister, supplementary research in Singapore, and later speech reported in *The Straits Times,* July 31, 1997.

network. Singapore probably comes closest. Its 1986 National Information Technology Plan aimed to create the first fully networked society — "where all homes, schools, businesses and government agencies are connected through an electronic grid."[5]

Since then it has done much more. Early in 1997, for instance, it outlined its masterplan to spend almost $US1.5 billion over the following five years to introduce the world's best interactive information technology to its school system.

By the year 2002, Singapore's 450,000 students will share at least one computer for every two youngsters. All its schools are already linked to the Internet. Students are designing their own web sites.

And Singapore has also probably done more than any other country to link schooling, international high-tech industries and full employment. The Government has encouraged more than 3,000 international companies to locate in its tiny city state. They provide the well-paid jobs for a fully-employed workforce. And the country's education system guarantees that its school graduates have the necessary skills wanted by the new industries that will dominate the 21st century. But their example is unfortunately noticeable by its uniqueness.

Even more importantly, the digital revolution provides the catalyst for a complete rethink of learning and teaching methods. In science alone, around 10,000 new articles are published every day. No science teacher can read even a tiny fraction of that output, let alone master all the details. So where now the traditional role of the teacher as an information-purveyor? As Carol Twigg and Michael Miloff put it in a chapter in *Blueprint to the Digital Economy:* "Through the Internet, it is now possible to offer instructional materials to anyone, anytime, anywhere. Students can access courseware on information seven days a week, 24 hours a day."

Not to make full use of instant electronic communications in education would be like our ancestors failing to use the alphabet, refusing to produce typeset books or rubbing sticks together to start a fire.

According to Peter Drucker, America's most respected management thinker: in 30 years the universities of America, as we have traditionally known them, will be barren wastelands.[6]

But the first nation to fully capitalize on the explosion in digital communications, and link it with new learning techniques, could lead the world in education.

There are thousands of buildings in this country where millions of people in them have no telephones, no cable television, and no reasonable prospects of broadband services.

They're called schools.

REED HUNDT
Chairman of U.S. Federal
Communications Commission*

* Quoted by Bill Gates in *The Road Ahead,* published by Viking
(the Penguin Group), 27 Wrights Lane, London W8 5TZ, England.

2. Learn computers and the Internet

We do not place much emphasis on the need to learn too many specific trade skills too early in life. But computers and the Internet are to the 21st century what telephones have been to the 20th: and much, much more.

As Apple Fellow and visionary Alan Kay once put it: "Technology is only 'technology' for people who were born before it was invented."[7] And, according to the pioneer of learning and technology Seymour Papert, "that's why we don't argue about whether the piano is corrupting music with technology".[8] Today's technology: the personal computer, and the Internet. So, just as no one could survive in a modern economy without being able to use a telephone, so, too, should everyone become computer-smart and Internet-smart.

3. Dramatic improvement needed in parent-education

Most brain researchers are convinced that 50 percent of a person's ability to learn is developed in the first four years of life.[9] Not 50 percent of one's knowledge, nor 50 percent of one's wisdom. But in those early years the infant brain makes around 50 percent of the main *brain-cell connections*—the pathways on which all future learning will be based.

If this is true, then home, not school, is the most important educational institution in the land.   And parents, not teachers, are the main first educators. Yet even in many advanced countries, fewer than 50 percent of mothers-to-be—and a much lower percentage of fathers—attend any form of prebirth classes. And even those are often restricted to lessons about birth itself. There is an almost total lack of education for parent-hood: no training in such areas as the diet necessary for brain growth, or the best types of stimulation required by young learners.

If the present authors had to pick any priority for targeted education, and especially for educational TV, it would be parent education.

4. Early childhood health service priorities

If the first few years are vital for *learning,* the nine months before birth and the first five years of life are probably the most important for *health.* Good diet and sound nutrition are essential for learning, and so are regular health checkups.

For example, even in the wealthy United States and New Zealand, up to 20 percent of infants suffer from ear infection.[10] If undetected and

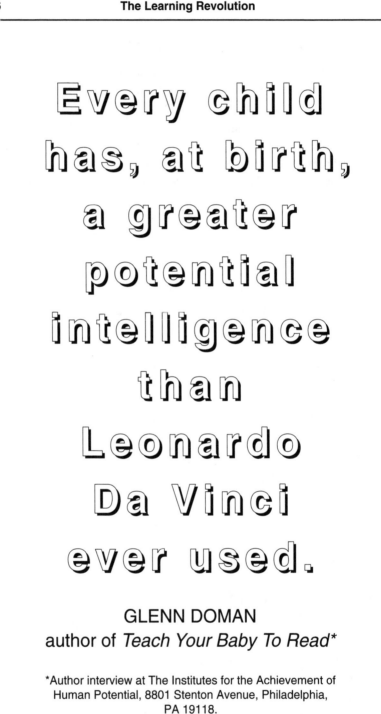

Every child has, at birth, a greater potential intelligence than Leonardo Da Vinci ever used.

GLENN DOMAN
author of *Teach Your Baby To Read**

*Author interview at The Institutes for the Achievement of Human Potential, 8801 Stenton Avenue, Philadelphia, PA 19118.

untreated, it can lead to "glue ear"—where a main hearing "tube" becomes blocked with a sticky composition that looks like glue. If that happens in both ears, a child can hardly hear. And if an infant can't hear in the years that are vital for language development—from birth to four years—he can be handicapped for life.

British research scientist Professor Michael Crawford has spent more than ten years researching the impact of diet on pregnant women and their babies. He's horrified at the overwhelming ignorance about the impact of nutrition on the developing brain, especially before an infant is born.

"Every farmer and every gardener knows perfectly well," he says, "that if he's going to have a good crop of potatoes, or if he wants to grow great roses, he's not going to run out and put some fertilizer on them the day before he wants to dig or pick them. He knows he's got to prepare the roots, almost a year before, to get beautiful roses. It's common knowledge. Everyone understands this as far as cabbages and roses are concerned. But mostly we don't even think about it when it comes to preparing to have a baby."[11]

One university study shows that 22 percent of new mothers are "at risk"—and nine percent could present a big physical danger to their babies unless they receive extra support and education.[12]

Generally they don't get it. And the self-perpetuating cycle of disadvantage continues. When they do get practical help, tied in with parent education, the change in attitudes is dramatic. A few million dollars in prevention saves billions later—in the cost of prisons and psychiatric care.

5. Early childhood development programs

Since 50 percent of the ability to learn is developed in the first four years of life and another 30 percent by age eight, then early childhood development programs should also be top priority. Most countries reverse this. Current spending per student in most universities is much, much more than elementary and high school—and all much more than preschool. Reversing the ratios should become a national priority.

6. You can catch up at any stage

Good catch-up programs abound. Many, as we will see, are at elementary or primary school. But even at the start of high school it is not too late for most.

People of all ages can learn virtually anything if allowed to do it through their own unique styles, their own personal strengths.

BARBARA PRASHNIG
The Power of Diversity*

* Published by David Bateman, 30 Taradale Grove, Albany, Auckland, New Zealand.

Regular updates: www.thelearningweb.net

And many of the new learning techniques can also be used effectively for adult learning and teaching.

7. Catering to every individual learning style

We all know that some of us learn better one way, some another. Some love to read by themselves. Others can learn best in groups. Some love to study while sitting in chairs, others lounging on a bed or a floor.

Each of us has a preferred learning style and a preferred working style. Some of us are mainly visual learners: we like to see pictures or diagrams. Others are auditory: we like to listen. Others are haptic learners: we learn best by using our sense of touch (tactile learners) or by moving our bodies (kinesthetic learners). Some are print-oriented: we learn easily by reading books. Others are "group interactive": we learn best when we're interacting with others.

Our traditional secondary school has done a great job in appealing to two of our many "intelligences": linguistic intelligence (the ability to speak, read and write) and logical-mathematical intelligence (the type we use in logic, math and science). Most of our examination systems are based on testing those limited *academic* intelligences.

But many of our current high school dropouts do not learn best by those methods. And the high school classroom techniques used to teach so-called academic learners are NOT the best methods to lift the standards of those who make up our high dropout rate. And sure, it is probably impossible to cater to every individual learning style all the time. But it is possible to design school curricula so that all learners are either tested to determine their preferred learning style or teachers are trained to observe them; and then for the styles to be catered to at school.

Equally important, it is now simple and inexpensive to provide printouts of preferred learning and work styles for everyone to plan his or her own education and future working career.

8. Learning how to learn and learning how to think

In our view, two "subjects" should form the central core of schooling, each integrated into all other studies: *learning how to learn* and *learning how to think*. This first means learning how your brain works, how your memory works, how you can store information, retrieve it, link it to other concepts and seek out new knowledge whenever you need it—instantly.

Some of these specific techniques are named "accelerated learning,"

We learn

- ❏ **10% of what we read**
- ❏ **20% of what we hear**
- ❏ **30% of what we see**
- ❏ **50% of what we see and hear**
- ❏ **70% of what we say**
- ❏ **90% of what we say and do**

VERNON A. MAGNESEN*

*Quoted in *Quantum Teaching,* by Bobbi DePorter,
Mark Reardon and Sarah Singer-Nourie, published by
Allyn and Bacon, 160 Gould Street, Needham Heights, MA 02194.

"super learning," "suggestopedia," "whole-brain learning" and "integrative learning." But it's unfortunate that such labels imply complexity. The best systems are simply "true learning". Better still, they are fun. Generally they have this in common: they encourage you to use all your "intelligences" and senses to learn much faster: through music, rhythm, rhyme, pictures, feelings, emotions and action. Overwhelmingly the best learning methods are similar to those we use as infants.

Thinking skills are also easily learned, and proven methods include Edward de Bono's *Lateral Thinking*, Alex Osborn's *Brainstorming*, Donald Treffinger's *Creative Problem Solving*, Robert Fritz's *Technology For Creating*, Stanley Pogrow's *HOTS (Higher Order Thinking Skills)*, Dilip Mukerjea's *Superbrain* and Calvin Taylor's *Talents Unlimited*. Again, the best techniques are simple, fun and effective.

9. Just what should be taught at school?

Almost everywhere in the world the debate rages about what precisely should be taught in schools.

There are at least four major curriculum "camps"—and a fifth one is growing fast.

The first is *essentialism:* the concept that teachers should pass on to students the core knowledge of an "essential" but small range of subjects.

In ancient Europe, Plato* in his *Republic* set down a curriculum for philosopher-kings or guardians. It revolved around seven "subjects". Four of them—music, astronomy, geometry and arithmetic—were designed for a "sound education". And three—grammar, rhetoric and philosophy or logic—were designed to provide methods by which essential knowledge should be studied.

This theory dominated Europe during the Middle Ages, but of course it was never intended to "educate the masses". It still dominates much of high-level British education today.

In China around 2,500 years ago, Confucius (a Latinization of Kung Fu Tzu, meaning K'ung the Master) was proposing some theories that were similar to those advocated by Plato, particularly the need for rulers' main advisers to be selected by examinations. Confucius and his followers also advocated the need for training in "six disciplinatry arts": ritual, music, archery, charioting, writing and mathematics. But Confucius was also the first great Chinese teacher who sought to popularize education. We return to his influence on modern China in the final chapter of this book.

The world our kids are going to live in is changing four times faster than our schools.

DR. WILLARD DAGGETT
Director of International Center for
Leadership and Education*

*Address to Colorado school administrators, 1992.

The traditional British approach to schooling has always been based on the "essentialist" view: that a truly liberal education can best be produced through certain selected subjects. To that the great British universities of Oxford and Cambridge, and the great "public schools" such as Eton and Rugby, also added the responsibility for the moral training of future members of Britain's political and administrative classes, and those that would guide the British Empire.

Despite improvements in recent years, the hierarchy of Britain's class society has been inextricably linked with its streaming of education: "public schools" and Oxbridge for the "leaders", "industrial training" for tradesmen, and elementary "three Rs training" for the 50 percent who until recently ended up as farm or general laborers.

Elsewhere in Western Europe a different approach has predominated since the Moravian-born Czech bishop and educator John Comenius effectively introduced the modern textbook in 1658.

Some call this approach *encyclopedism:* the premise that the content of education should include all human knowledge, with illustrated "textbooks" on each subject.

Comenius also argued strongly that good education should flow from "natural laws"; and since learning takes place first through the senses, his curriculum was designed to develop these first.

Comenius's theories have strongly influenced some aspects of French education since the revolution there in the late 18th century: that, as all are created equal, society should not be divided into rulers and the ruled.

Since the 19th century, when Napoleon Bonaparte created a system of national education, France has concentrated on a curriculum of more than 10 compulsory subjects. Even today every child in France, in whatever school, is expected to be learning exactly the same body of information as other children of the same age, on the same day.

Germany has used many of Comenius's theories, but added them to its own Lutheran Protestant work ethic. Hence the continuing large percentage of Germans who undergo apprenticeships, linking together practical training with academic education.

Another European movement also owes its beginnings to Comenius and to Aristotle's philosophy that there is nothing in the intellect that does not first exist in the senses. The 18th century philosopher Jean-Jacques Rousseau took this further, proposing that the key to learning lies with developing each child's senses, starting with concrete experiences.

Children Learn What They Live

If a child lives with criticism, he learns to condemn.

If a child lives with hostility, he learns to fight.

If a child lives with fear, he learns to be apprehensive.

If a child lives with pity, he learns to feel sorry for himself.

If a child lives with ridicule, he learns to be shy.

If a child lives with jealousy, he learns what envy is.

If a child lives with shame, he learns to feel guilty.

If a child lives with encouragement, he learns to be confident.

If a child lives with tolerance, he learns to be patient.

If a child lives with praise, he learns to appreciate.

If a child lives with acceptance, he learns to love.

If a child lives with approval, he learns to like himself.

If a child lives with recognition,
    he learns that it is good to have a goal.

If a child lives with sharing, he learns about generosity.

If a child lives with honesty and fairness,
    he learns what truth and justice are.

If a child lives with security,
    he learns to have faith in himself and in those around him.

If a child lives with friendliness,
    he learns that the world is a nice place in which to live.

If you live with serenity, your child will live with peace of mind.
    With what is your child living?

Dorothy Law Nolte

The movement flowered into prominence as 19th century innovators linked *sensory and early childhood learning*. Paris physician Jean-Marc-Gaspard Itard and his student Edouard Seguin first devised graduated exercises to achieve dramatic results for youngsters previously thought mentally retarded. Johann Pestallozi, a Swiss follower of Rousseau, felt that the senses should be trained through successive stages of learning by formal exercise. And in the mid-19th century, the German Friedrich Froebel took both Rousseau's and Pestallozi's ideas, added his own, and established a school for very young children. He called it *Kindergarten*, based on the concept that young children grow like flowers.

Early this century Italy's first female doctor, Maria Montessori, put many of these theories into practice to show that the years from birth to age six are the most vital of all. She added her own revolutionary insights: that creating the right environment, at critical "sensitive periods" of early development, will enable children to "explode" into self-learning. Her results were equally revolutionary: with "retarded" preschool children learning to read, write, spell and do complicated mathematics, as we will cover later.

Starting mainly with America, but spreading quickly to other countries, has come the main countertrend to the British and Western European traditions. Some call it the *pragmatic* curriculum, or the *child-centered* concept of education.

Herbert Spencer was one of the first to ask anew this century: "What knowledge is of most worth?" His answer: "Knowledge which enables young people to tackle problems and prepares them to solve the problems they are likely to meet as adults in a democratic society."

American education professor John Dewey took this answer and turned it into a widely popular movement.

Inside that "progressive" theory, however, have developed two broad strands. One says education should be child-centered, and that the curriculum should be planned to build on the needs of each individual child.

The second is "society-centered"—promoted by educators such as Latin America's Paulo Freire who considers the main purpose of schools should be to reconstruct society.

New Zealand has also pioneered a succession of elementary school and preschool initiatives that generally fit under the heading of "child-centered" but which have been much more content-structured than many so-called "progressive" American ideas.

What should be taught?
*Five main theories**

 Essentialism: The 'essential core' needed for a sound education. Plato started it, and Britain carried on for its elite, with different systems for trades and laborers.

 Encyclopedism: Much broader base and available to all. Comenius started it with the first textbooks, and most European states still follow the same principles.

 The sensory-based early-start model: Aristotle first proposed that knowledge comes first through the senses. Itard, Seguin, Rousseau, Pestallozi, Froebel and Montessori have developed variations.

 The pragmatic child-centered movement: The original American breakaway, with Dewey the pioneer. Now two main strands: one around the individual child, and other to 'reconstruct society'.

 The common-sense aproach: as new insights emerge from research and practice, and as technology makes it easy to retrieve information, forget dogma, select the best from all, and keep an open mind.

* Plus the Confucian academic examination model,
still popular in Chinese societies, Hirsch's *Cultural Literacy,*
and Piaget's theories of phased intellectual development.

As a backlash against the appalling results achieved in many American schools, a new *Cultural Literacy* movement[13] has emerged, sparked by Professor H.D. Hirsch Jr. In his book of that name, he argues that there is a core of information that is essential for anyone to be able to sensibly discuss and understand the world. He and colleagues Joseph F. Kett and James Trefil have even produced *The Dictionary of Cultural Literacy:* subtitled *What Every American Needs to Know.*

Fortunately the emerging fifth alternative is one that combines the best of all. It is possible for all of us to absorb all that information that Professor Hirsch and the European tradition urges. It is now simple for that information to be available instantly, in easily accessible form, in a variety of interactive ways—whenever we want it.

It's also desirable that everyone should emerge from school able to read, write, spell and understand the basics of mathematics, history, geography, the physical sciences, music, and much, much more. It's vital that we continue to produce great academics and scientists. But, given the continual changes in society, it's even more important that everyone emerges from school with the ability to be self-acting, self-learning, self-managers of one's own future. And we can do that by linking the best of the systems that have been proven to work.

We prefer to think of it as *common sense.* But, given the way many theorists have elevated faulty theories into dogma, perhaps it's *uncommon sense.*

10. Learning on four levels

Whatever subject or subjects students tackle, the real test of tomorrow's education system will come from its ability to excite them with the utter joy of learning. That means encouraging every student to build the self-esteem that is vital for everyone to grow and develop.

In every successful system we have studied around the world, self-esteem ranks in importance ahead of course-content.

Equally important for those who would otherwise drop out is the need to learn the skills of coping with life. That means a four-pronged curriculum is needed—one that stresses:

❏ Self-esteem and personal development;

❏ Lifeskills training;

❏ Learning how to learn and learning how to think.

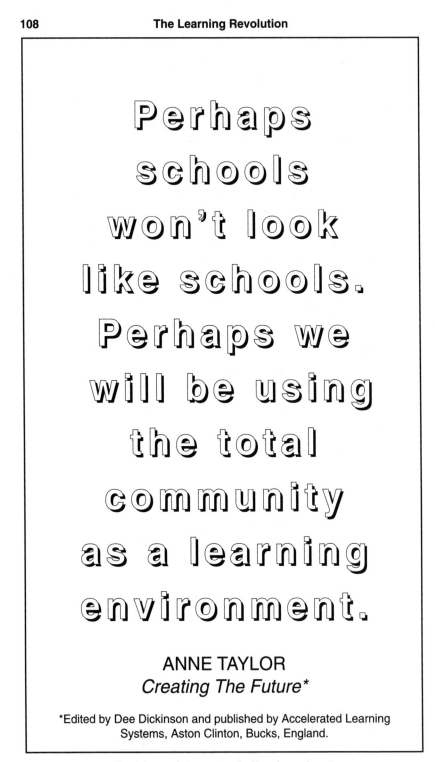

Perhaps schools won't look like schools. Perhaps we will be using the total community as a learning environment.

ANNE TAYLOR
*Creating The Future**

*Edited by Dee Dickinson and published by Accelerated Learning Systems, Aston Clinton, Bucks, England.

❏ As well as specific academic, physical and artistic abilities.

Fortunately, all aspects can be blended to reinforce each other.

11. A threefold purpose for study

Studying should generally also have a threefold purpose:

1. To learn skills and knowledge about the specific subjects—and how you can do that faster, better, easier.

2. To develop general conceptual skills—how you can learn to apply the same or related concepts in other areas.

3. To develop personal skills and attitudes that can also easily be used in everything you do.

12. Just where should we teach?

In the history of the world, classroom schooling is very new. And the time has come to ask if it is the best and if it should remain the main learning forum.

We see schools being changed into community resource centers for lifelong learning—and probably health and parent education centers as well. To use them for under 200 days a year for only a few hours a day is a tremendous waste of valuable assets, and amounts to less than 15 percent of total time. And to use them largely for one-sided lectures is largely to waste even that 15 percent. In later chapters we will explore the likely mix of future "schools". But for now it's vital to restress that most of us learn best by doing and participating through all our senses. It's also amazing what emerges when entire communities rethink their learning needs and start to redesign their schools around those needs.

13. Keep the mind open, the communication clear

We also make a strong plea to everyone involved in education, learning and schooling: to keep an open mind, and to communicate the results of breakthrough-research factually, honestly and clearly.

Millions of children's futures have been ruined by widespread educational theories since proven to be wrong.

Hitler and Mussolini closed down Montessori's brilliant preschools in Germany and Italy. But almost equal harm was done by her academic detractors in America, led by Professor William Kilpatrick who "felt that the teacher should be in total control of the students".[14]

To write simply, check your Fog Index*

To write clearly and well, generally use short words and short sentences.

To check your own clarity in writing:

 Count how many words you use in an average sentence.

 To do that, check any 100 words you have written, in a report or letter.

 Divide that 100 by the number of sentences used.

 Then count how many "complex" words you have used for every 100 words you have written (a "complex" word is one with three syllables or more—not counting words with capital letters).

Add the two totals together, and then take four-tenths of the total. That is your Fog Index.

For example: if you average 20 words to a sentence, and ten complex words in every 100 words, your total is 30. Four-tenths of this is 12. That is your Fog Index.

Reader's Digest has a Fog Index of between 8 and 9. *Time* magazine is about 11. If you're higher than 13 you're hard to read. Churchill's quote opposite has a Fog Index of 3.2. Except where quoting others, this book generally has a Fog Index between 8 and 10.

*Joseph Peart and Jim R. McNamara, in *The New Zealand Handbook of Public Relations,* published by Mills Publications, Lower Hutt, New Zealand (1987), attribute the invention of the Fog Index to Robert Gunning, an American businessman.

Probably the most influential theory of individual development this century is that of Swiss biologist and psychologist Jean Piaget. Using years of detailed research, he claimed that children everywhere in every culture grow through a fixed sequence of *intellectual* growth-stages from infancy to adulthood. "Yet many of Piaget's claims have been proven to be misleading, simplistic, and in some cases simply wrong." [15] That has not stopped their influence holding back the potential of children in the vital early years when their minds are wide open to flower into learning.*

The core of the scientific method is to test theories in practice against every possible alternative. The mark of good research, we believe, is also shown in the ability to clearly convey its results: and in not claiming, from one aspect of research, all-embracing panaceas for all of education.

Education is still suffering from the twin ills of bad practice based on invalid research and the inability to clearly communicate the break-throughs that are disproving the old myths.

Most good learning methods are common sense. Every infant learns naturally by many of these methods. Yet much educational theory is clothed in so much jargon that the parents and students, who most need that information, are instead "switched off".

This trend seems to be more rife in "education" than in any other profession, except perhaps medicine and law.

Nearly every professional writer is taught the Fog Index—to make his writing easy to read: to write using simple words, active verbs and short, clear, concise sentences.

Every good public speaker grows up with former British Prime Minister Winston Churchill as a model. He "hurled words into battle": "We shall go on to the end. We shall fight in France. We shall fight in the seas and oceans. We shall fight on the beaches, in the fields, in the streets, and in the hills. We shall never surrender."

So we make a sincere plea to those who have made or researched the changes that are needed in learning: please remember Churchill, and hurl your words into action—simply and crisply—to rally a world for change.

* *We hasten to agree there ARE definite stages of brain growth, physical growth and in the development of sensory-learning—which we will explore. Piaget's worst legacy is in the education systems using his theories to justify not exposing young children to experiences when their senses are ideally developed to benefit.*

Your magic brain:

❏ Has a trillion brain cells, including:
- 100 billion active nerve cells or neurons.
- 900 billion other cells that "glue," nourish and insulate the active cells.

❏ Can grow up to 20,000 "branches" on every one of those 100 billion neurons.

❏ Has four distinct brains in one:
- An instinctive brain.
- A "balancing brain".
- An emotional brain.
- And your amazing cortex.

❏ Has two sides that work in harmony:
- Your left "academic" brain.
- Your right "creative" brain.

❏ Runs a "telephone exchange" that shuttles millions of messages a second between the left and right sides.

❏ Has many different "intelligence centers".

❏ Operates on at least four separate wavelengths.

❏ Controls a transmission system that flashes chemical-electrical messages instantly to every part of your body.

❏ And it holds the key to your own personal learning revolution.

You're the owner of the world's most powerful computer

It's not much bigger than a large grapefruit.

It's much smaller than the heart of a lettuce. You could hold it easily in one hand. It generally weighs under three pounds (1,500 grams). Yet it's thousands of times more powerful than the world's most powerful computer. And it's all yours: the brain that makes you and other humans so unique.

A fruit fly has 100,000 active brain cells. A mouse has 5 million. A monkey: 10 billion. You've had about 100 billion[1] since birth.

And from the very earliest days of life those cells form new learning connections, or synapses, at the incredible rate of 3 billion a second.[2] Those connections are the key to brain power.

By comparison, in the first three days of the 1997 space journey over the surface of Mars, millions of users made 200 million Internet "hits" to follow its progress. Yet your brain can make 15 times as many new connections *in a second* as all the world's Internet users made in three days. No one is using more than a fraction of that amazing ability. And every day scientists are learning more about how to improve the process.

Ronald Kotulak, in *Inside The Brain,* summarizes the incredible pace of brain research in the past decade by quoting Jeri Janowsky, a neuro-psychologist: "Anything you learned two years ago is old information. Neuroscience . . . is exploding."

Says psychologist and memory expert Tony Buzan: "Your brain is made of a trillion brain cells. Each brain cell is like the most phen-omenally complex little octopus. It has a center, it has many branches, and each branch has many connection points. Each one of those billions

Your brain has 100 billion active cells, each with up to 20,000 connections

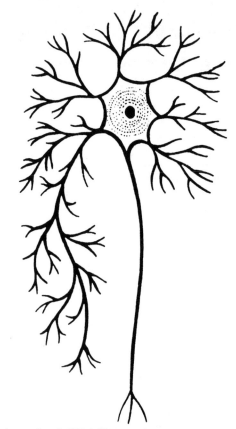

Your brain has about 100 billion active neurons or nerve cells.
Each one grows branches like a tree, to store information:
up to 20,000 branch-like *dendrites* with each cell.
Each neuron is like a powerful computer.
And each connects to other cells by sending
electrical-chemical messages along *axons*.

Illustration from *Make The Most Of Your Mind,* by Tony Buzan, published
by Pan, London, and reprinted here with permission from Tony Buzan.

of brain cells is many times more powerful and sophisticated than most of the computers around the planet today.   Each one of these cells connects, embraces, hundreds of thousands to tens of thousands of others. And they shuttle information back and forward.   It's been called an enchanted loom, the most astoundingly complex, beautiful thing in existence. And each person has one." [3]

Of those trillion brain cells, about one tenth consist of active neurons or nerve cells.   Each one is capable of making up to 20,000 different connections with other cells. Stanford University Professor Robert Ornstein says, in *The Amazing Brain,* that the possible number of connections is probably bigger than the number of atoms in the universe. [4]

Doubt it? Then consider what happens if you took only ten everyday items—like the first ten things you did this morning—and combined them in every possible sequence.   The result would be 3,628,800 different combinations. Take 11 items, connect them, and the number of possible combinations is 39,916,800! So now try combining 100 billion cells in every possible way—when each one can make up to 20,000 different connections—and you get some idea of the creative capacity of your own brain.

And how do you make the most of its great ability? Says Buzan: "You make the most of your mind by first studying what it is. The first thing you do is find out what it's made of. Then how it works. How does the memory work? How does concentration work? How does the creative thinking process work? So you literally start to examine and explore yourself." Start that exploration and you come up with some surprises:

Your four brains in one

First, you've got four brains in one—on three different levels, from top to brain-stem, and with the fourth tucked in behind.

Next, your brain has two sides. Each controls different functions and processes information in different ways. *These sides are linked by an amazing electronic and chemical relay-system that itself has 300 million operating nerve-cells.* This shuttles information around instantly like a multinational automatic telephone exchange.

We also now believe that each of us has many different "intelligence centers" in the brain. But very few of us develop more than a small part of that latent ability.

Your brain also works on at least four different electrical wave-

The five functions unique to humans

1 **The ability to walk upright.**

2 **The ability to oppose thumb and forefinger.**

3 **The ability to speak and write.**

4 **The ability to understand speech.**

5 **The ability to read.**

All these are functions of the brain's cortex, and when you see a damaged cortex you will see the loss of one of these functions.

GLENN DOMAN
*What To Do About Your
Brain-Injured Child**

* Published by The Better Baby Press, 8801 Stenton Avenue, Philadelphia, PA 19118.

lengths—like four different radio networks or television channels.

The most advanced part of your brain has six distinct layers.

You also have an active conscious brain and a subconscious brain. And much of the knowledge you take in is learned subconsciously.[5]

At the great risk of oversimplifying:

Your lower brain—or brain-stem—controls many of your instincts, such as breathing and heartbeat.

The central part of your brain controls your emotions. Scientists call it the *limbic* system—from the Latin word *limbus* for "collar" or "ring"—because it wraps around the brain-stem like a collar.

Your upper brain enables you to think, talk, reason and create. Scientists call it the *cortex*—the Latin word for "bark".

And tucked out the back you have the cerebellum, which plays a vital role in storing "muscle memory": the things you remember by actually performing tasks, such as riding a bike, or playing any sports.

You use many different parts of the brain together to store, remember and retrieve information.

Each one of these factors has an important bearing on how you use your inbuilt power that dwarfs that of any computer.

It is not the role of this book to indulge in religious debate. But the awesome power of your brain may well provide common ground for creationists and evolutionists. Those with deeply-held fundamental religious beliefs could well argue that the complexity of the human brain and mind, with the soul, represents a pinnacle of creation. All other creatures have brains that are puny by comparison.

Many scientists, on the other hand, say that humans are the end result of over four billion years of evolution.[6] They say that's how long the earth has existed. In this theory, the first primitive forms of life did not emerge for the first billion years.

Scientists now believe it wasn't until 500 million years ago that creatures started to develop brains, along with backbones and the nervous systems that link them. Even today, semi-primitive creatures like oysters or lobsters—without backbones—have very simple nervous systems, with only a few thousand nerve cells.[7] But in creatures with backbones the nervous-brain system is much more complex. Even a rat's brain has millions of cells: highly developed where they are linked to his whiskers.

If you dissected your brain, at the base of your skull you would find

The brain's levels

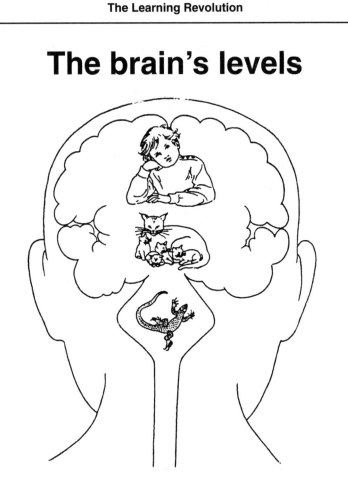

At bottom: Your brain-stem, near the top of your neck, is also called the "reptilian" brain—because it is similar to the brains of cool-blooded reptiles. It controls many of your body's instinctive functions, such as breathing.

In the center: Your "old mammalian" brain— which is similar to the brains of other warm-blooded mammals. It controls your emotions, your sexuality—and has a key role to play in your memory.

At top: Your "cortex" (bark), which you use for thinking, talking, seeing, hearing and creating.

Not illustrated here: the fourth "brain"or the cerebellum. See illustration, page 122.

The illustration is from *Your Child's Growing Mind,* by Jane M. Healy, published by Doubleday, 666 Fifth Avenue, New York, NY 10103.

a segment almost identical to that found in a lizard, a crocodile or a bird. Because of this, some scientists have dubbed it the "reptilian"[8] brain. This part of the brain controls very simple but important functions: like our breathing, heart rate and many basic instincts. Turn a light on and any insect nearby will stop dead still. The bright light will send an instant signal to its tiny reptilian brain. Drive toward a bird sitting on the road and it will fly off an instant before you hit it; its reptilian brain has an inbuilt program to flee. Think of that next time you go to swat a fly—and it escapes a split second before the swat lands.

Above your brain-stem is your second-tier brain. This limbic system is also often called the "old mammalian" brain—because it is similar to a major part of the brains of other mammals.

Scientists say it started developing with the first warmblooded mammals—or breast-feeding animals—between 200 and 300 million years ago. They say mammals still kept their "reptilian" brain, but added to it.

It's the part of the brain that is programmed to instruct a baby—or a lamb or pup—instinctively to suckle its mother almost instantly after birth. And, as we'll find out later, it's significant that the emotional and sexual center of your brain is very closely connected with parts of the brain that deal with memory storage. You can remember things better when you are emotionally involved—like your first love affair.

Sitting on top of the limbic system is the two-sided cerebrum and its cortex which caps everything else like a crumpled blanket. This cortex is only about 3 millimeters thick (about an eighth of an inch). But it has six layers, each with different functions; and several distinct "lobes", or centers, to process input from your individual senses and react to them. It is the part of our brain that makes humans a unique species.

Neurons, dendrites, glial cells and insulating system

Each of our 100 billion active neurons is a virtual computer in itself. Each is capable of sprouting between 2,000 and 20,000 branches, called dendrites—very much like the branches of a tree. Each of these stores information, and receives input from other cells.

Each neuron in turn transmits its own messages around the brain, and around the body, along major pathways known as axons. Each axon in turn is covered with a "myelin" sheath. This is much like insulation around electric wires. The better the sheathing or insulation, the faster messages will speed along the "wires": up to 100 meters a second.

The many types of intelligence

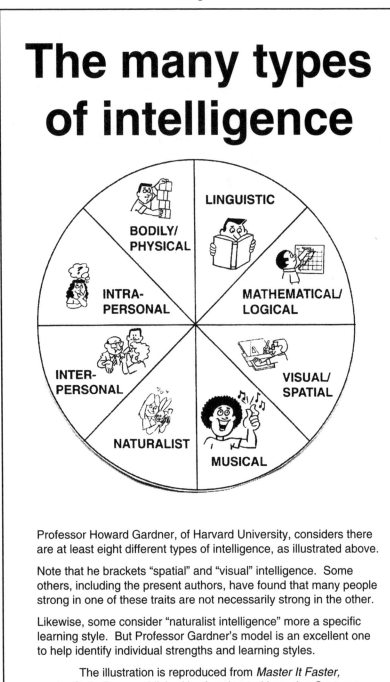

Professor Howard Gardner, of Harvard University, considers there are at least eight different types of intelligence, as illustrated above.

Note that he brackets "spatial" and "visual" intelligence. Some others, including the present authors, have found that many people strong in one of these traits are not necessarily strong in the other.

Likewise, some consider "naturalist intelligence" more a specific learning style. But Professor Gardner's model is an excellent one to help identify individual strengths and learning styles.

The illustration is reproduced from *Master It Faster,*
by Colin Rose, published by Accelerated Learning Systems,
Aston Clinton, Aylesbury, Bucks, England.

All the dendrites, in turn, are surrounded by up to 900 billion "glial" cells which "glue" the parts of the brain together.

And all these parts link to make up the most unique natural computer the world has ever known—if, in fact, we can call it that; it's more like a self-renewing ecosystem.

Learn how to use all parts of your amazing brain—and the results could astound you. "For a start," says Tony Buzan, "if you really set your mind to it you could easily read four books a day. And not just read them, but remember what you've read. Now four books a day is what the average student reads in a year—or is supposed to read in a year.

"Now imagine for a moment that four members of the one family start to study the same subject—and they each read four books on it in a day. Then they each put the main information together on a colorful Mind Map so the main points are easy to remember. They swap Mind Maps—and at the end of the day each of those four people could have absorbed the information from 16 different books: as many as the average student would read in four years."

And how hard is it to do that? Buzan again: "Not hard at all—if you learn how the brain works. It really is a fantastic tool.

"Let's take the human eye—only one small part of the brain. Like the brain itself, the eye is much more powerful than we've ever realized. We now know that each eye contains 130 million light receivers which can take in trillions of photons per second. It's like: bang! I see a new mountain scene, and I can take it in, in its entirety, in a second. So a single page in an ordinary old book is nothing for the eye-brain combination. It's just that we haven't been taught how to use those same visual skills for reading."

Your many different "intelligence centers"

Ask Harvard psychologist Professor Howard Gardner, and he'll tell you that visual ability is only one of your many "intelligences".[9] He's spent years analyzing the human brain and its impact on education. And his conclusions are simple but highly important.

Gardner says we each have several different types of intelligence. Two of them are very highly valued in traditional education.

He calls the first one linguistic intelligence: our ability to read, write and communicate with words. Obviously this ability is very highly developed in authors, poets and orators.

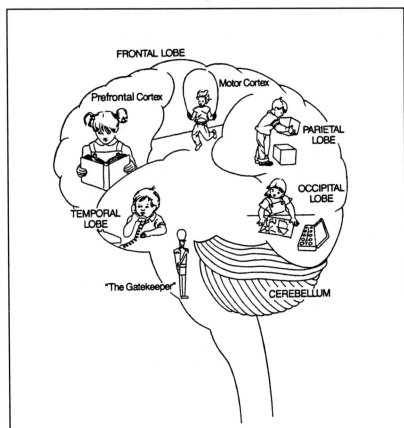

The parts of the brain that deal with different functions:

THE PREFRONTAL CORTEX, which deals with thinking.

THE MOTOR CORTEX: which controls activity.

THE TEMPORAL LOBE: the speech center of the brain.

THE PARIETAL LOBE: which handles your spacial ability.

THE OCCIPITAL LOBE: your visual center.

THE CEREBELLUM (or little brain), which plays a key part in adjusting posture and balance. It also acts like an "automatic pilot" when we perform learned functions like riding a bicycle or using a typewriter.

THE "GATEKEEPER": actually you have three "gatekeepers": the amygdala, the hippocampus and the caudate nucleus; all relay important messages to different parts of the brain.

Illustration from *Your Child's Growing Mind,* by Jane M. Healy, published by Doubleday, 666 Fifth Avenue, New York, NY 10103.

The second is logical or mathematical intelligence: our ability to reason and calculate. This is most developed in scientists, mathematicians, lawyers, judges.

Traditionally, most so-called intelligence tests have focused on these two talents. And much schooling around the world concentrates on those two abilities. But Gardner says this has given us a warped and limited view of our learning potential. In his early pioneering work he listed five other individual "intelligences":

Musical intelligence: obviously highly developed in composers, conductors and top musicians, from Beethoven to Louis Armstrong;

Spatial and visual intelligence: the kind of ability used by architects, sculptors, painters, navigators and pilots—what the current authors would argue are, in fact, two separate forms of intelligence.

Kinesthetic intelligence or physical intelligence: very highly developed in athletes, dancers, gymnasts and perhaps surgeons;

Interpersonal intelligence: the ability to relate to others—the kind of ability that seems natural with salesmen, motivators, negotiators.

And *intrapersonal intelligence* or introspective intelligence: the ability of insight, to know oneself—the kind of ability that gives some people great intuition. The kind of ability that lets you tap into the tremendous bank of information stored in your subconscious mind.

But these are not merely arbitrary functions that Professor Gardner has invented for a Ph. D. dissertation. He says brain surgery and research have shown that some of these "intelligences" or abilities are located in distinct parts of your brain. Severely damage that part and you could lose that particular ability. That is why strokes can affect the ability to walk or talk, depending on which part of the brain is affected.

Professor Gardner now considers there is another intelligence: "naturalist": the ability to work with and harmonize with nature. The two current authors consider this might better be grouped with several other types of learning styles, which we cover in chapter 10.*

* Professor Gardner's model does not cover what we consider one of the most important "intelligences" of all: the ability to create totally new concepts by linking together information from different parts of the brain—as we cover in chapter 5. Many modern thinkers, such as British Professor Charles Handy, say there are several other intelligences, such as plain common sense. But Professor Gardner's research is a brilliant starting point for designing schools that cater to different abilities and learning styles.

The two sides to your brain

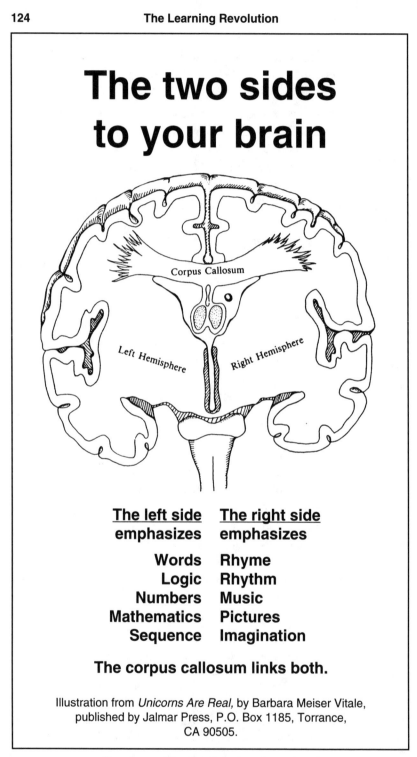

Corpus Callosum

Left Hemisphere

Right Hemisphere

The left side emphasizes	The right side emphasizes
Words	Rhyme
Logic	Rhythm
Numbers	Music
Mathematics	Pictures
Sequence	Imagination

The corpus callosum links both.

Illustration from *Unicorns Are Real,* by Barbara Meiser Vitale, published by Jalmar Press, P.O. Box 1185, Torrance, CA 90505.

The two sides of your brain

Look at an electronic scan of your brain and you'll see how parts of it process different types of information. We take in information through our five major senses: by what we see, hear, touch, smell and taste.

In general terms the left-hand side of your brain plays a major part in processing logic, words, mathematics and sequence—the so-called academic parts of learning.

The right-hand side of the brain deals with rhythm, rhyme, music, pictures and day-dreaming—the so-called creative activities.

The split is not, however, as simple as that. Both sides of the brain are linked by the corpus callosum. This is a highly complex switching system with its 300 million active neurons. It is constantly balancing the incoming messages, and linking together the abstract, holistic picture with the concrete, logical messages.

British businessman and researcher Colin Rose, author of *Accelerated Learning* and developer of several rapid-learning foreign language courses, gives a simple example of how different aspects of the brain can work together in an integrated way. "If you're listening to a song, the left brain would be processing the words and the right brain would be processing the music. So it's no accident that we learn the words of popular songs very easily. You don't have to make any effort to do that. You learn very quickly because the left brain and the right brain are both involved—and so is the emotional center of the brain in the limbic system."[10]

The emotional center of your brain is also very closely connected with your long-term memory storage system. That's why we all remember easiest any information with a high emotional content. Almost anyone can remember his or her first major sexual experience. Millions of people can also recall precisely where they were when they heard the news of the death of President John F. Kennedy or Princess Diana. Music and the words to songs trigger deep memories—if the music is associated with personal elation or pleasurable experiences. Discovering how the brain processes such information is a vital key to more effective learning.

Leading brain researcher Professor Marian Diamond[11] took a day out at the University of California at Berkeley to demonstrate precisely how the brain works; and how it's much more complex than any simple left-side-right-side explanation. Slicing into a human brain delivered from a nearby morgue, she starts with the stem or base. "This little area here

Your brain can keep learning from birth till the end of life.

MARIAN DIAMOND
co-author of *Magic Trees of the Mind**

* Published by Dutton, New York (co-authored by Janet Hopson).

is called the medulla," she explains. "It regulates your heartbeat and respiration, so it's essential to your life. It's only an inch long in the human brain, and the same length in a chimpanzee's brain." But the medulla in a human develops to three times the capacity of the chimp.

"Next to it is the cerebellum. Literally that means 'little brain'. It's responsible for coordination and balance. And only recently have we found out how important it is for learning and for speech."

She then holds up the top half of the brain, the part that looks like a giant wrinkled walnut: the cortex. "If it wasn't folded, it would be about two and a half feet square." Why is it folded? "Well, we believe it developed over thousands of centuries. Basically, to go through the human birth canal this part of the brain had to fold in upon itself." According to many scientists, the brain developed new capacities as our ancestors came down from the trees, started to walk upright, learned to use fire, started to use and make tools, and learned to speak.

Says Professor Diamond, the scientist who dissected part of the late Albert Einstein's brain: "You'll find the most recently-evolved part of the brain right behind your forehead: your frontal lobe. It's essential for your personality, for planning ahead, for sequencing ideas. It's this part primarily which makes modern man differ from his earlier ancestors."

Behind that she points to the area just behind the forehead. "For me to be talking to you right now, it's this part of my brain that's firing. We call it our motor speech area. For one to understand the words I'm saying [pointing to another area in the forebrain], this is the part of your brain that would be in action."

And not surprisingly you don't process sight only through your eyes. Professor Diamond points to the back of her head. "You'll find your visual cortex back here. When you're hit on the back of the head, that's why you see stars. You've jarred your visual cortex."

As she slices through the brain, she explains each part: the small areas that move your arms, legs and fingers; the parts that control feeling, pain, temperature, touch, pressure and hearing.

And as she moves down into the limbic system, Professor Diamond starts delving into even deeper secrets: the parts of the brain that deal with fear, rage, emotion, sexuality, love, passion. The tiny pituitary gland that secretes hormones. The ability of the brain to register and cut off pain. And the almost magical way the brain sends messages around itself and around your body: messages that are constantly changing from electrical

Six main pathways to the brain: We learn by . . .

 What we SEE

 What we HEAR

 What we TASTE

 What we TOUCH

 What we SMELL

 What we DO

GORDON DRYDEN

From slide presentation to World Book Encyclopedia
International Achievers' Conference,
Barcelona, Spain, August 1996.
See also Jeannette Vos's additions on page 32.

impulses to chemical flows. But to Dr. Diamond all these elements together simply prove the great untapped potential of the human brain.

We ask her what message she would communicate about the brain if she could talk individually with every person on earth. And her reply comes back clear and succinct: "I'd let them know how dynamic their brains are. And the fact that they can change at any age, from birth right to the end of life. They can change in a positive manner, if one is exposed to stimulating environments. Or they can change in a negative manner if they do not receive stimulation."

To her, humans' ability to communicate is a key element that separates us from other species. And especially our ability to communicate in so many ways: in speech, writing, pictures, songs, dance, rhythm and emotion.

Not surprisingly, scientists are now finding out what many societies seem to have known instinctively for thousands of years.

Over 2,000 years before Christopher Columbus sailed across the Atlantic to "discover" the New World, the ancestors of today's Polynesian societies sailed the much bigger Pacific.[12] They navigated by the sun, the moon and the stars—using what Professor Gardner would today call spatial intelligence. Not surprisingly, when his researchers tested Solomon Islanders they found the part of the brain dealing with "spatial intelligence" highly developed.

Those same Pacific explorers, with their fantastic navigational feats, would probably have failed a modern "intelligence test" because they never developed a written language. Even today Polynesian youngsters from their earliest years learn through dance, rhythm and song.

Language itself sets up different patterns in your brain—and different patterns in your culture.

If you grow up in China or Japan, you learn to write a "picture" language—and this is largely learned through part of the right-hand side of your brain.

Grow up in one of the Western "alphabet" cultures, and you learn how to take in information through all your senses but to communicate in *linear* writing.

The English language, for instance, has about 550,000[13] words, yet each one is made up of variations from only the 26 letters of the alphabet. Communicate in alphabet languages, and you will largely be using a section of the left-hand side of your brain.

The learning style of a typical student

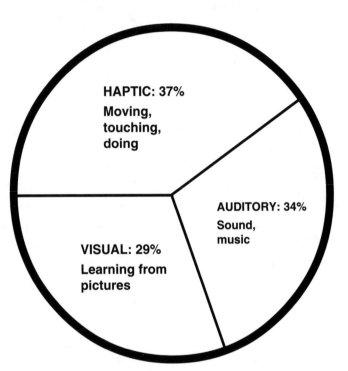

HAPTIC: 37%

Moving, touching, doing

AUDITORY: 34%

Sound, music

VISUAL: 29%

Learning from pictures

This is an average student "learning style profile" compiled by Specific Diagnostic Studies, of Rockville, Maryland, from 5,300 students, grades 5 through 12, who have undergone SDS's Learning Channel Preference Checklist, in the United States, Hong Kong and Japan.

SDS, however, stresses that it would be statistically incorrect to deduce from this that 37 percent of students are solely haptic (or tactile-kinesthetic) learners, that 34 percent are auditory and that 29 percent are visual.

Every student profile showed a certain percentage in each of the three categories, and the percentages in the graph above represented the mean average.[14]

But if you grew up in a traditional Polynesian, Melanesian or Micronesian culture in the Pacific, without either a picture or a "sequential" written language, then your main communication would be through sound alone—reinforced through rhyme, rhythm, song and dance, and of course by your holistic sense of sight.

Researchers will now tell you that there are at least three main learning-style preferences:

1. Haptic learners, from a Greek word meaning "moving along": people who learn best when they are involved, moving, experiencing and experimenting; often called kinesthetic-tactile learners.

2. Visual learners, who learn best when they can see pictures of what they are studying, with a smaller percentage who are "print-oriented" and can learn mainly by reading.

3. Auditory learners, who learn best through sound: through music and talk.

Lynn O'Brien, Director of Specific Diagnostic Studies Inc., of Rockville, Maryland, has found most elementary and high school students learn best when they are involved and moving, while most adults have a visual preference.[14] But most of us combine all three styles in different ways, as we explore later. We all learn best and fastest when we link together many of our brain's great abilities. Of those attributes, three are extremely important for learning:

1: How you store and retrieve information—quickly, thoroughly and efficiently.

2: How you can use it to solve problems.

3: How you can use it to create new ideas.

For the first two, you use the brain's unique ability to recognize patterns and associations. For the third, we learn how to break the patterns—how to recombine information in a new way.

How your brain stores information

As a patterning device, the brain almost certainly has no equal. It is capable of storing virtually every major piece of data it takes in.

Learn to identify and recognize a dog, for instance, and your brain sets up a storage file for dogs. Every other type of dog you learn to recognize is stored in a similar *patterning system.* And the same with birds, horses, cars, jokes or any other subject. Many scientists now believe we store

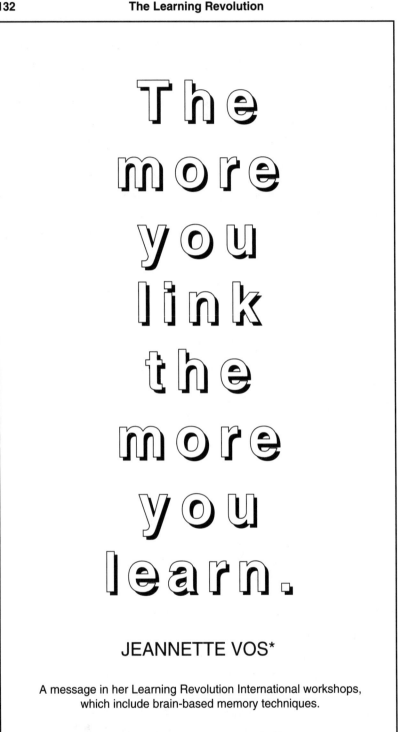

The more you link the more you learn.

JEANNETTE VOS*

A message in her Learning Revolution International workshops,
which include brain-based memory techniques.

many of those interconnected subjects like branches on a tree.

But it's much more complex than that. If we asked you to name the apples you know, you'd start to rattle them off: red delicious, golden delicious, Granny Smith and so on—from your "apple" memory-tree. If we asked you to list all the fruits you know, you'd have apples stored with oranges, pears and grapes on your "fruit" memory tree.

And if we asked you to name round objects, you'd include oranges from your "round objects" memory-tree. So your brain classifies information in many different storage-files—like a library, or a book-index, cross-references books.

It stores this information by making great use of associations. Every person's brain has an association cortex. It can link up like with like, from different memory banks.

As a simple experiment, take public speaking. Most people list it as one of their greatest fears. Ask anyone on the spur of the moment to make a spontaneous speech in public, and the first reaction will almost certainly be to clam up. Adrenalin flashes through the brain cells. The brain "downshifts" into a primitive mode. Fear blots out your memory banks. You're scared! Yet let someone else start by telling any sort of joke, and almost immediately each person in the group will start to remember an *associated* humorous story. Or gather round the piano at a party. As each person starts a song every one else remembers it almost instantly.

It's as if each of us has a tremendous ability to store information—and to remember it when we trigger the right *association*. And in fact that is exactly correct. Surgeons who have applied electrodes to parts of a brain during operations[15] have been amazed to find their patients, on awakening, have total recall of specific events, even right back to their early childhood. And that, of course, is what often happens under hypnosis. A hypnotist "unlocks our minds" and enables us to recall information that has been stored away for years.

Learning to store information in patterns and with strong associations is the first step toward developing your brain's untapped ability.

It's one of the first keys to improving your ability to remember anything: by *associating* it with a strong *image* and using one or more of your brain's abilities. How else do you easily remember that April has 30 days, if not by the rhyme that begins *Thirty days hath September, April, June and November*—all stored through the section of your right brain that deals with rhymes?

You are what you eat.

BRIAN AND ROBERTA MORGAN
Brain Food*

* While this quotation has been used many times before,
it forms a key theme of the Morgans' excellent book,
published by Michael Joseph Ltd., and by
Pan Books, London.

Your four separate wavelengths*

The second step is learning to use your subconscious mind.

And here's where we meet up with brainwaves. Link yourself up to an electronic scanner and you'll soon find out that parts of your brain can send and receive information on different frequencies. In one sense they're similar to television signals. Tune in your TV set to channel 2, or 22, and you'll be able to receive messages sent out on that wavelength.

Scan your brain when you're wide awake and it will be transmitting a certain number of cycles per second. Scan it when you're dozing and it will be transmitting on a "different frequency". Likewise when you're in the early stages of sleep and dreaming, and later when you're in deep sleep.

Many researchers are now convinced that we can absorb informa- tion much more quickly and effectively when our brains are in a state of "relaxed alertness".

That's the state we often achieve with certain types of meditation. Or listening to relaxing music. Some of the "accelerated learning" tech- niques to be explored later in this book are based on experiences with "baroque" music. The pace of many baroque compositions is similar to the "wavelength" you'll find in your brain when it's in that same state of "relaxed alertness". If information is read to you in time with that music, it "floats into your subconscious" and you can learn much faster.

But whether or not you use music, the logic is very simple. You'd find it impossible to make any sense out of a radio receiver if you were tuned in to four stations at once. Likewise in learning. You need to clear your wavelengths—and tune in to only one station.

That's why nearly every successful study session starts with relax- ation: clearing your mind so your subconscious can receive uncluttered messages—and store them in their right "file".

Your brain runs on oxygen and nutrients

Like any other complex machinery, your brain needs energy. Basi- cally, it gets that from the food you eat. If you're an adult, your brain makes up only about two percent of your total weight. But it uses about 20 percent of the energy you develop.

* See next chapter, page 168, for an illustration of brainwaves in action.
This subject is handled in much more detail in chapter 9.

How diet affects your transmission system

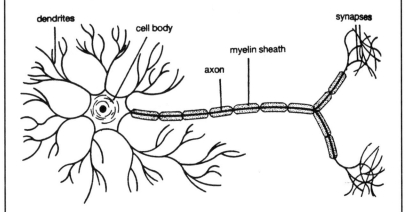

dendrites

cell body

synapses

myelin sheath

axon

Each of your 100 billion active neurons or brain cells stores information on its thousands of *dendrites,* like branches.

It then transmits that information to other cells, and other parts of the body, by electrical impulses, along a major pathway called an *axon* (for axle or axis).

When it reaches the synapse (connecting gap) to another brain-cell, each electrical impulse triggers a chemical reaction—a neurotransmitter which jumps across the gap to transfer the message.

Each axon is insulated by a myelin sheath, which acts as an insulator. The better the insulation, the more efficient the message is transmitted. The brain has at least 70 different types of neurotransmitter, and each is affected by diet.

The entire "communication system" is surrounded by *glial* cells (for "glue"), which lay down the myelin sheathing, and generally nourish the active nerve cells. The right diet is also vital for this nourishment (see more detail in chapter 6).

Illustration is from *Accelerated Learning,* by Colin Rose, published by Accelerated Learning Systems, of Aston Clinton, Bucks, England.

Feed it a low-energy diet, and it won't perform well. Feed it a high-energy diet, and your personal computer will work smoothly, efficiently.

For energy, the brain needs plenty of glucose. That's why fresh fruit and vegetables are so essential. They're rich in glucose.

Your brain also has a unique way of transmitting messages—around its billions of cells and to the rest of your body. Each message flows around your body *electrically* and *chemically,* and it keeps switching from one form to the other.

Each message travels like electricity along a brain cell's axon, then turns into a chemical flow when it jumps across the connecting-point to another cell. Scientists call these gaps *synapses.* These synaptic connections are another key to brain function. To send those messages, your brain first has to generate electricity. If you could test it now, you'd probably find it generating about 25 watts. That's the amount needed to run the smallest light-bulb in your home.

And the source of that brain-electricity: good food combined with oxygen. Obviously you get oxygen through breathing. That's why deep breathing is highly recommended before and during study: to oxygenate your blood. And that's why exercise is not only good for your body, it's good for your brain. It enriches your blood with oxygen.

Cut off the supply of oxygen and you destroy brain cells. Stop it completely and you die.

Your brain needs the right type of energy to produce those chemical flows—what the scientists call *neurotransmitters (neuro* meaning mind and *transmit* meaning send). And these in turn depend on a balanced diet, one that includes plenty of protein. Scientists have identified around 70 different types of neurotransmitters, including adrenalin and endorphins, the brain's natural painkillers or opiates. And, as Brian and Roberta Morgan point out in their excellent book *Brain Food:* "Any deficiencies in nutrients can reduce the levels of certain neurotransmitters and so adversely affect the types of behavior they are responsible for. Conversely, a physical or mental problem can be corrected by boosting the level of the relevant transmitter, and this can be done by making a simple alteration in the composition of your diet."

As an example, they point to the big increase in Alzheimer's disease among elderly people, and add: "Another characteristic of senility is the reduced ability of the brain—by as much as 70 or 80 percent—to produce acetylcholine, the neurotransmitter responsible for memory." Dr. Brian

Brain functioning depends very much on what you've eaten for breakfast.

RICHARD M. RESTAK
The Brain: The Last Frontier*

*Published by Warner Books, in arrangement with Doubleday & Co.,
245 Park Avenue, New York, NY 10017.

Morgan, formerly a Professor at the Institute of Human Nutrition at Columbia University in New York, recommends a diet rich in lecithin to help improve everyone's memory, but especially that of older people. Foods rich in lecithin include peanuts, soya beans and wheat germ. He also recommends lecithin and choline chloride dietary supplements to boost the neurotransmitters that are needed to improve your memory.

The Morgans also spell out other dietary deficiencies that impair mental performance, including a lack of polyunsaturated fat called *linoleic acid* which the body itself cannot manufacture. "Fortunately," say the Morgans, "it is also extremely easy to find: one teaspoon of corn oil a day is enough to supply an adult with all he needs. But that teaspoon is crucial for proper brain operation. Without it, the brain cannot repair its myelin sheaths, and the result may be a loss of coordination, confusion, memory loss, paranoia, apathy, tremors and hallucinations."

They say iron deficiency is a major cause of poor mental performance. It probably affects more people in Western society than any other single deficiency. It "decreases attention span, delays the development of understanding and reasoning powers, impairs learning and memory, and generally interferes with a child's performance in school".

The brain also needs a constant supply of other nutrients. Among the main ones are sodium and potassium. Each of your 100 billion neurons has up to one million sodium pumps. And they're vital for transmitting all your brain's messages. Sodium and potassium supply those pumps with energy. Like glucose, potassium is found mainly in fruits and vegetables. And sodium is found in most foods.

Put simply, reduce your sodium intake and you reduce the movement of electrical current around your brain; you reduce the amount of information the brain can receive. Reduce your potassium intake drastically and you risk anorexia, nausea, vomiting, drowsiness and stupor. All could be symptoms of your brain's vital pumps not working.

Simple tips on brain food

Fortunately, nearly all fruits are rich in potassium, especially bananas, oranges, apricots, avocados, melons, nectarines and peaches. So are potatoes, tomatoes, pumpkins and artichokes.

We'll deal with some aspects of diet in later chapters, particularly for pregnant women and children. But for now, if you want your brain to be working efficiently for all forms of learning and work:

At best, IQ contributes about 20 percent to the factors that determine life success, which leaves 80 percent to other forces: forces grouped as *emotional intelligence.*

DANIEL GOLEMAN
Emotional Intelligence *

* Summarized as the main theme of the book, published by
Bloomsbury, London.

1. Eat a good breakfast every morning, preferably with plenty of fresh fruit. Include half a banana for its potassium content—a whole one if you're pregnant—with an orange or kiwifruit for vitamin C, and any other fresh fruit in season. If you have children, make sure they do too.

2. Eat a good lunch, preferably including a fresh vegetable salad.

3. Make fish, nuts and vegetable "fats" key parts of your diet. Fish and vegetable oils have a vital role in nourishing the brain's billions of glial cells. And nuts and vegetable oils are major sources of that linoleic acid, which the brain needs to repair the myelin insulation around your brain's "message tracks".

4. Exercise regularly to oxygenate the blood.

5. Cleanse the toxins out of your body. One way to do that is to drink plenty of water. Coffee, tea or carbonated "soft drink" dehydrate the body, and fresh water reactivates it.

You are what you eat and drink. Knowing the correct "brain food" to fuel your brain is one of the first steps to better learning.

Your emotional intelligence is vital, too

You are also greatly influenced by your emotions and what you think.

In fact Daniel Goleman argues that "emotional intelligence" is of much greater importance than "academic intelligence" in developing a well-rounded person. He says that "at best, IQ contributes about 20 percent to the factors that determine life success, which leaves 80 percent to other forces". He summarizes these, in his best-selling book of the same name, as *Emotional Intelligence.*

Positive and negative thoughts can also cause major changes in the way your brain processes, stores and retrieves information: changes, in fact, to your learning ability.

Just as different foods can trigger your 70 neurotransmitters, so too can your "mental state". If you're on an emotional "high", for instance, your brain will release endorphins—those chemicals that are like natural opiates. These in turn trigger the flow of acetylcholine, the vital neurotransmitter that orders new memories to be imprinted in various parts of the brain.

Pulitzer Prize-winning science writer Ronald Kotulak describes acetylcholine as "the oil that makes the memory machine function. When it dries up, the machine freezes."[16] Not only is acetylcholine vital for

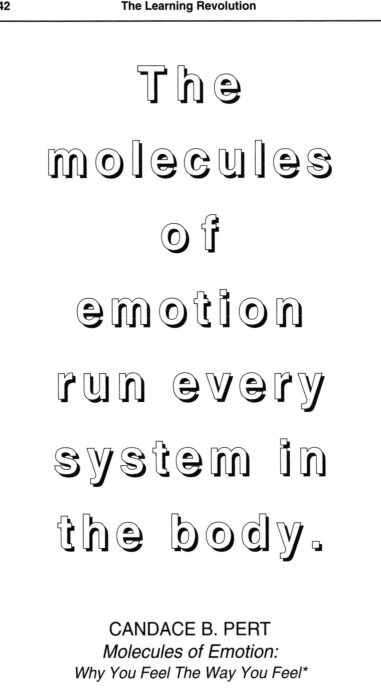

The molecules of emotion run every system in the body.

CANDACE B. PERT
Molecules of Emotion:
Why You Feel The Way You Feel*

* Published by Simon & Schuster, New York.

imprinting new memories, it is essential for retrieving old ones. When it dries up, Alzheimer's disease often results. The shortage of acetylcholine first robs Alzheimer's patients of their short-term memory and eventually their long-term memory as well.

The body and mind as one

Fortunately neuroscientists are regularly making important discoveries that will have enormous effects on learning, memory, health, and our ability to stay mentally active throughout life.

Recent research also confirms ancient religious beliefs that the body and the mind act effectively as one. Here Dr. Candace Pert's findings are particularly important. Professor Pert first came to prominence in the early 1970s for her discovery of the brain's *opiate receptor.* She describes receptors as "sensing molecules"—as microscopic, molecular *scanners.* Now her continuing research has revealed "the molecular basis of the emotions": the tiny *peptides* that lock into the mind's receptors. But the resulting *molecules of emotion* are not confined to the brain. They "run every system in our body". And "peptides are the sheet music containing the notes, phrases and rhythms that allow the orchestra—your body—to play as an integrated entity."

Thus memories—so vital for learning—are stored in all parts of the body. And wherever new information enters the body—through sight, sound, taste, touch or smell—memory-traces are stored not only in the brain, but in the body as well. In this way, she says, the body is "the unconscious mind". And the mind and body work as one for filtering, storing, learning, and remembering: key elements of learning.[17]

Little wonder that Oxford University Professor Colin Blakemore, in *The Mind Machine,* describes the human brain as "the most complex piece of machinery in the universe." Adds Bill O'Brien, former president of America's Hanover Insurance Company: "The greatest unexplored territory in the world is the space between our ears."

That challenging exploration starts with learning how the brain works. But it continues most effectively by using it regularly. And the words of the old axiom—"If you don't use it you lose it"—apply as much to your brain as your muscles. Use them together as an integrated whole, and learning will be easier and simpler.

20 easy first steps to better learning

1   Start with the lessons from sports.

2   Dare to dream.

3   Set a specific goal—and set deadlines.

4   Get an enthusiastic mentor—fast.

5   Start with the big picture first.

6   Ask!

7   Seek out the main principle.

8   Find the three best books written by practical achievers.

9   Relearn how to read efficiently.

10   Reinforce with pictures and sound.

11   Learn by doing.

12   Draw Mind Maps instead of linear notes.

13   Easy ways to retrieve what you've learned.

14   Learn the art of relaxed awareness.

15   Practice, practice, practice.

16   Review and reflect.

17   Use linking tools such as memory pegs.

18   Have fun, play games.

19   Teach others.

20   Take an accelerated learning course.

The first 20 steps to learn anything much faster, better and more easily

Try to forget everything you've ever thought about education.

If school was a bore, forget it. If you dropped out early, forget that too. If you flew through college exams, fine; this chapter should help you do even better. But even if you flunked school, accept that lifelong learning is now needed. And this chapter is an introduction to simple do-it-yourself learning methods—even if you don't have access to a teacher skilled in all aspects of accelerated learning.

If you're a professional teacher, we still think you'll pick up some new tips. But we handle new styles of teaching in later chapters. This is mainly for self-starters and those who'd like to be.

In brief, this chapter will help you develop new skills or abilities. It will pass on simple tips to absorb information more easily, retain it in your memory, and recall it when you need it. It will especially help you to use your new-found brainpower to achieve those results.

The 20 simple tips:

1. Start with the lessons from sports

Sports probably provide a much better learning model than many schools. There are at least eight lessons you can learn from it:

1. All sports achievers have a dream. They dream the impossible and make it happen.

The champion wants to break the 3 minute 50 second barrier for the mile. Or take the Olympic gold. Or be in a world series winning team.

All sports achievers, at every level, have dreams. It may be to break

Eleven steps to sporting success

1. **Have a vision**
2. **Develop a plan**
3. **Set goals**
4. **Select well**
5. **Induct well**
6. **Motivate**
7. **Continuously learn**
8. **Involve players**
9. **Value mistakes**
10. **Encourage flair**
11. **Use common sense**

JOHN HART
*The New Zealand international rugby coach**

* Summarized from *Success in New Zealand Business 2,* by Paul Smith, published by Hodder Moa Beckett, Auckland, New Zealand.

100 at golf, then 90, then 80. Or to become the club tennis champion. Or to run the New York marathon at age 65.

2. All have specific goals. And they break those goals down into achievable steps. So while the dream is always there, they build on their successes. You can't become a world champion overnight; you have to tackle hurdles regularly along the way—and celebrate each success as it is achieved.

3. All sports achievers combine mind, body and action. They know that their goals can be achieved when they link the right mental attitude, fitness, diet and physical skills.

4. They all have vision; they learn to visualize their goal. To *see* their achievements in advance. To play through their next football match like a video of the mind. Jack Nicklaus, possibly the greatest golfer of all time, says 90 percent of his success has come from his ability to visualize where every individual shot is going to land.

5. They all have passion. They have an overwhelming desire to succeed.

6. Each one has a coach, a mentor, a guide. In fact, we can probably learn more about real education from the success of the American college coaching system than we can from most school classes. If you doubt it, how many Olympic athletes, basketball and football stars have emerged from colleges—where the coaches are mentors, friends and guides?

7. All sports achievers have a fantastically positive attitude toward mistakes. They don't even call them mistakes; they call them *practice.* Even Bjorn Borg, John McEnroe and Martina Navratilova belted balls into the net thousands of times on their way to the top in tennis. No teacher marked those shots as failures. They were all essential parts of learning.

8. They all achieve by doing. Sport is a hands-on operation. You don't get fit by reading a book—although that may help with the theory. You don't develop the right muscles staring at a television set. You don't long-jump over 28 feet in a classroom. All sports achievements result from *action.*

Former American Olympian pentathlete Marilyn King says all astronauts, Olympic athletes and corporate executives have three things in common:

"They have something that really matters to them; something they really want to do or be. We call it *passion.*

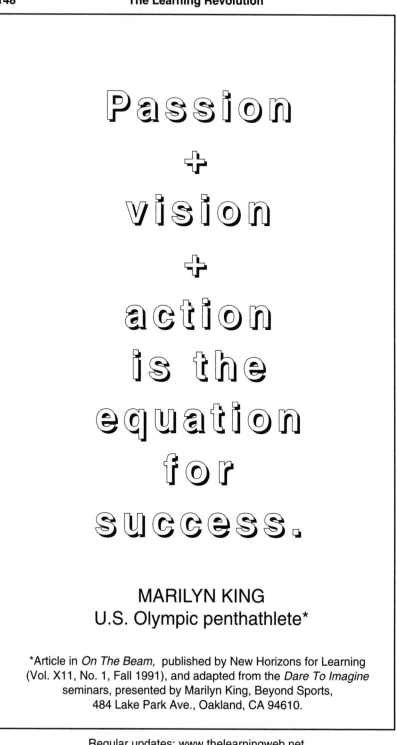

**Passion
+
vision
+
action
is the
equation
for
success.**

MARILYN KING
U.S. Olympic penthathlete*

*Article in *On The Beam,* published by New Horizons for Learning
(Vol. X11, No. 1, Fall 1991), and adapted from the *Dare To Imagine*
seminars, presented by Marilyn King, Beyond Sports,
484 Lake Park Ave., Oakland, CA 94610.

"They can see a goal really clearly, and the 'how to' images begin to appear like magic. While the goal may seem bold, they can imagine doing all these little steps on the road to that goal. We call it *vision.*

"Finally, they are willing to do something each day, according to a plan, that will bring them one step closer to their dream. We call it *action.*

"Passion + vision + action is our equation for success."[1]

Marilyn King runs courses and seminars teaching *Olympian Thinking* to corporate executives. She has also launched a *Dare To Imagine* project to pass on the same techniques to at-risk young people in her home city of Oakland, California.

So how can you apply the same principles to anything else you want to achieve and learn—and how can you do it faster, better, easier?

2. Dare to dream—and imagine your future

If, as we believe, nearly all things are now possible: what would you really like to do? What's your real *passion?* The thing you'd like to do more than anything else? Make great wine? Become the district golf champion? Get a doctorate? Start a new career?

Nearly every major achievement in the world has started with a vision: from Ford to Disneyland, Sony to Microsoft. So take up the King challenge—and *dare to imagine what you'd like to achieve.*

3. Set a specific goal—and set deadlines

Ask yourself first: What specifically do I want to learn? Why do I want to learn it?

If it's a new job, a new skill, a new hobby, a trip overseas, a new sport, a musical instrument or a new challenge, what will you need to know?

It's easier to learn anything if you have a set goal. When you've done that, break it down into achievable bite-sized pieces. Then set realistic deadlines for each step, so you can see your success from the start.

4. Get an enthusiastic mentor—fast

Whatever you want to learn, many others have already learned it. When you've set your goals, find an enthusiast you can come to for specific advice. And if you can swap skills, even better.

Let's say you're a printer who wants to learn word processing. Obviously you'll be skilled in typography. So find a word processing

An Olympian's challenge

If you have passion plus vision but no action

You're daydreaming

If you have vision plus action but no passion

You'll be mediocre

If you have passion plus action but no vision

You'll get there but find it the wrong goal

MARILYN KING*

* American pentathlete, from her *Olympian Thinking* program.

specialist in a computer publishing field. You teach them typography while they teach you word processing. If you're new to a firm, do the same thing. Find someone who can help, regularly. Someone in the office or only a phonecall away.

If you want to play golf, take professional lessons—certainly. But find a good player whose style you admire, and ask if you can play a game or two together.

The same principles apply if you're learning new technology. No one ever learned to operate a computer solely from a 700-page manual. Each student learned hands-on, with a coach.

5. Start with the big picture first

Learn from the marketers of jigsaw puzzles. If you started to assemble 10,000 pieces of a giant jigsaw puzzle one by one, it might take you years to finish. But if you can see the total picture on the package, you'll know exactly what you're building. Then it's much easier to fit each piece into place.

We're amazed at how often common sense disappears in educational systems. Subjects are taught in isolation. They're often taught in small segments, without students knowing the big picture first.

In real life, that's not the best way. It would take you years to discover New York by walking down every street. So what do you do as a tourist? You go to the top of the Empire State Building. Preferably with a New York guide. And you put yourself in the big picture. You can see Central Park, the Staten Island Ferry, the Statue of Liberty, Wall Street, the two main rivers, the key bridges, Broadway, Greenwich Village, the United Nations headquarters and the way the city is laid out in numbered avenues and streets. Then when someone tells you an address is 10 blocks south of Central Park on Sixth Avenue, or four blocks east of the Lincoln Tunnel, you have a mental picture of where to go. You can build on your overall image Mind Map.

Many traditional schools still introduce subjects through textbook lectures spread over months. You're taught to read each chapter slowly and deliberately—a week at a time—without ever having the "big overview". That's crazy. It's inefficient.

Instead, try this simple experiment. Next time you're planning anything, seek out the simplest overview. If you're visiting a new city, get the color tourist brochures in advance. They'll show you the main

Remember jigsaw puzzles: they're much easier when you can see the whole picture first.

GORDON DRYDEN*

* In *Back to Real "Basics":* program 4 in the *Where To Now?* New Zealand television series.

highlights.   Or go to your public library, seek out an encyclopedia summary and duplicate it. Then when you've got the big picture, build up the details.   You'll know where they fit.   Remember that jigsaw puzzle.

6. Ask!

It's the best three-letter word in the learner's dictionary.   Never be afraid to ask.   And never be afraid to ask the best experts you can find—even if you've never met them before.

We hope it won't be long before each of us has a home computer/video/Internet terminal linked with international databanks.   But even then you'll have to ask for what you want.   So begin now.

Start with your public library.   It's not merely a book center.   It's a learning resource.   Librarians are trained to help you.   Call them before you visit; tell them specifically what you want to do; and ask them for the best beginner's guide.   Use that for your overview; then build on it.   But be specific.   If you're a business executive planning a visit to Japan, ask them for simple guides to the country, its business, its culture, and the industry you're involved in.

If you learn easily by reading, that overview will probably be a book, a booklet or an article. If you learn best visually, seek out a videotape, or at least a book with plenty of colored pictures and graphics.   If you learn best by listening, get some audio tapes and play them in your car.

But don't stop at the library.   Find someone from college who's study-ing the field you're interested in.   Ask the name of the best professor—the one who's the best simplifier.   And phone him.

Or phone the university library, the nearest research institute, the best firm in the business. And don't be afraid to go to the top.   At the very least, ask for the Human Resources Manager or the person in charge of staff training and development. And ask for the company's most helpful simplifier.

If you want to learn about another country, call its embassy or con-sulate. Or its trade or tourist office.   Or one of its major companies.

To learn about radio, phone a radio station and ask if you can sit in on a recording session.   If you're a student and think you'd like a career in a specific field, ring the best company and ask if you can come in and work free of charge for a week during the holidays.

In fact, make asking a habit.   It's probably the simplest thing you can

I keep six honest serving men, they taught me all I knew: Their names are What and Why and When and How and Where and Who.

RUDYARD KIPLING
The Elephant Child

learn from journalism. How do you think all that information gets into newspapers, on to television and radio every day? By journalists calling "sources". And everybody else has the same right. Generally people love to help; they enjoy being asked about their specialty.

7. Seek out the main principle

In nearly every field you'll find one main principle for success. Or perhaps two or three. Find them out first—before you fill in the details.

In photography, the first principle for an amateur: never take a photo more than four feet from your subject. Second principle: preferably shoot without a flash, with a semiautomatic camera. On those two principles, one of the co-authors paid for a world trip by taking photographs!

In cost accounting, the main principle: there's no such thing as an accurate cost, unless your business is running 24 hours a day, 365 days a year, on automatic equipment and with a guaranteed market for all you produce. Second principle: find the break-even point. Below that you're losing money. Above it you're making a profit.

In talkback radio, the main principle: no matter how big or small the city, if the host asks only for *opinions* he'll get the same 30 uninformed callers every day; if he asks for *specific interesting experiences* he'll get new interesting callers, with stimulating new information.

In education, a main principle: people learn best what they passionately want to learn, and they learn fastest through all their senses.

In journalistic interviewing, the first principle: ask *what* and *why.*

How do you find main principles? First you ask. Then:

8. Find the best three books by practical achievers

Don't start with academic textbooks. In the area of your interest, find the three best books written by people who've *done it.*

If you want to study advertising, call Saatchi & Saatchi or a top agency and ask their creative director what to read. She'll almost certainly recommend *Ogilvy on Advertising* as an overview. And if you want to study copywriting: John Caples' *How To Make Your Advertising Make Money* and *Tested Advertising Methods.*

To practice new skills in thinking, start with the best book we know on the subject, Michael Michalko's *Cracking Creativity.* Then deal cards from Roger von Oech's *Creative Whackpack*—a brilliant ideas-starter.

The business revolution

❑ **Employees, acting as partners and associates, make all their own decisions.**

❑ **They evaluate their managers every six months.**

❑ **They're even encouraged to start their own companies.**

❑ **Potential managers are interviewed by the people who will be working for them.**

❑ **All have access to company books.**

❑ **No first-class and second-class citizens.**

❑ **Managers set their own salaries, bonuses.**

❑ **No formality: a minimum of meetings, approvals and memos.**

❑ **Shopfloor workers set their own productivity targets and schedules.**

❑ **Managers take turns to operate as chief executive.**

❑ **"The truly modern company avoids an obsession with technology and puts quality of life first."**

RICARDO SEMLER
Maverick*

* The story of Semco, the pace-settiing Brazilian company: an example of choosing a book by a practical achiever. Published by Arrow, London.

His first book, *A Whack On The Side Of The Head,* is also good.

To simplify business, try Robert Townsend's *Up The Organization,* Tom Peters' *Thriving on Chaos* and Ricardo Semler's *Maverick!*

For three books on effective learning, try one of Tony Buzan's many books, *Accelerated Learning For the 21st Century* by Colin Rose and Malcolm J. Nicholl, and *Maximizing Your Learning Potential,* by Jacqueline Frishknecht and Glenn Capelli.

If you're a teacher, maybe read *The Everyday Genius* by Peter Kline, *SuperTeaching* by Eric Jensen, and *The ACT Approach: the artful use of suggestion for integrative learning,* by Lynn Dhority.

For more about your brain, try *The Amazing Brain* by Robert Ornstein and Richard F. Thompson, *Inside The Brain* by Ronald Kotulak, and *Emotional Intelligence* by Daniel Goleman.

More books are suggested at the back of this book. But in your own field ask the nearest expert to suggest a beginner's guidebook.

9. Relearn how to read—faster, better, more easily

Amazingly, few people know how to read properly. And we're not talking about super reading techniques at thousands of words a minute.

Let's start with two questions: Do you think you could regularly read four books a day and absorb the main points?* Have you read a newspaper this week?

If you answered the first question no, and the second yes—think again. If you read a daily newspaper in any major city, you've read the equivalent of at least four books. And the Sunday editions of the *New York Times, Los Angeles Times* or any major British paper are equal to dozens of volumes.

And how do you read a newspaper? You read only those things you are interested in. And how do you know? Because newspapers are divided into sections, so you only read the sports pages if you're interested in sports, the business pages for business. But even then you don't read every sports story or every business article. Newspaper headlines highlight the main points, and make it easy for you to select. Even the writing style of newspapers makes it easy to glean the main

* In almost eight years as a radio talkshow host, Gordon Dryden read, on average, 15 new books a week—well over 6,000 in total—and generally skim-read two or three others a day, using the techniques covered here.

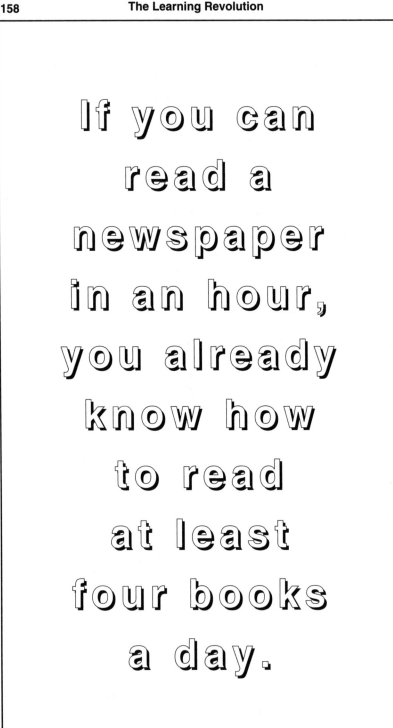

If you can
read a
newspaper
in an hour,
you already
know how
to read
at least
four books
a day.

points. After each headline, you'll generally find them summarized in the first paragraph. So you can either read the summary or devour the whole story.

Over half of a newspaper is advertising. But you don't read every ad. Advertisers flag your attention with headlines and pictures. Classified ads are in alphabetical order. So even if you want to buy a house, you don't read all the *Houses for sale* pages. You select those in your preferred suburb, listed alphabetically.

Very simply, *you've cracked the newspaper code.* You know the formula. You know how to skim-read a newspaper every day. So you already know how to skim-read four books or anything else in print. The secret is to crack each book's code, to find each publication's formula. Court reporters, for example, know the standard format for written judgments. The judge normally reviews the case and the main arguments for many pages, then delivers his or her finding in the last paragraph. So reporters never start reading a court judgment from the front. They start on the last page—generally at the last paragraph—because they are reading the judgment to report the verdict.

And the same principle applies to all nonfiction reading. First ask yourself: *Why am I reading this? What do I want to get out of it? What new information will I want to learn? Then find the book's formula.*

Nearly every nonfiction book will state its main purpose in an introduction—as this book has done. This will tell you whether the book can provide the answers you want. Then you have to decide whether you need to read every chapter. You've almost certainly come to the subject with some basic knowledge which you're looking to extend. So you don't have to read all the material unless you want to refresh your memory.

Generally, nonfiction authors write books like speeches: in the introduction, the speaker tells you what he's going to tell you; then he tells you; then he summarizes what he's told you. And often each chapter is written in a similar way: the chapter title and first paragraph or paragraphs indicate the theme, the chapter amplifies it, and it may end with a summary. If the book has subheadings, they'll help as well.

Many books have other pointers. With color pictures, skim them and their "captions". Tom Peters' *Thriving on Chaos* summarizes each chapter on a separate page at the start of each chapter. In the book you are now reading, key points are highlighted on every other page.

In brief, read every nonfiction book like a recipe book. If you want

How to skim-read a book*

❏ **First, define what information you are seeking.**

❏ **Then hold your book about 20 inches away from your eyes: far enough to see the whole page.**

❏ **Run your index finger down the center of the page, with your eyes looking just above your fingertip.**

❏ **Move the finger so fast that you do not have time to stop at each word and pronounce it to yourself.**

*Generally, this advice applies to nonfiction reading, where you are reading to gain information for a specific purpose. The same techniques can be used to read fiction, but even most good readers prefer to read fiction more slowly, so they can savor the atmosphere, the plot and the word-pictures.

to cook pork chow mein tonight, you don't read every page in *The 1,000 Recipe Chinese Cookbook.* You read only what you need to know. This tip alone will enable you to read four books in the same time it takes to skim a newspaper.

Another tip: do NOT read "slowly and deliberately". Look out your window right now. Then reflect on your brain's fantastic ability to take in all that information instantly. Remember those 130 million light receivers in each of your eyes, and their magic ability to flash that scene to your visual cortex. That's your brain's holistic ability to "photograph" a complete picture. Learn to use it.

Even those pages you think you need to read will include much information that can be skimmed. Remember your purpose, and the key answers you are seeking. For instance, school teachers, business executives and people approaching "retirement" are probably reading this book for different reasons.

So learn to skim for the points you want. Start by holding this book in one hand far enough from your eyes to see the entire page—generally about 18 to 20 inches: about 50cm. With your other hand use your index finger or a retracted ball-point pen. Practice running either your finger or the pen quite quickly down the center of each page, with your eyes looking just above the point of your pen or finger, following it down. You'll be amazed at what you can take in, if you know specifically what you are looking for.

This is not just speed-reading. It's sensible skim-reading and selective reading. If you're looking for main principles, then that skim-reading may be all you'll need. If you're looking for specific information and quotes to include in a report, article or book, you'll need to stop and note them. If you own the book, use it as a dynamic resource. Mark key information with a highlighter. If the book is not yours, write down page numbers. Return to them and write or type out the key points. The physical act of writing or typing will help embed them in your brain's memory-vaults—learning through the sense of touch as well as sight. Better still, highlighting will make it easy to refresh your memory when you want to retrieve the information later.

10. Reinforce with pictures and sound

Because you've read this far, you're obviously a print-oriented learner, and a linguistic learner. But you can also learn better if you

Just do it!*

- ❏ **You learn to talk by talking**
- ❏ **You learn to walk by walking**
- ❏ **You learn golf by golfing**
- ❏ **You learn typing by typing**
- ❏ **You learn best by doing it!**

* The slogan for Nike footwear.

reinforce the message with pictures and sound. So check out whether simple video or audio tapes are available on the subject you're studying.

And if you have family members who are not great readers, encourage them to *start* with their preferred learning style.

If one's an auditory learner, make her car into a university with a cassette-player. If one has a visual learning style, then seek out picture books, videos, digital video discs, and interactive computer programs.

11. Learn by doing

We can't stress enough the need to engage all your senses. We give practical suggestions in other chapters.

But for do-it-yourselfers, when you check out introductory courses—or advanced ones—make sure they provide hands-on experience.

You learn to cook by cooking. You learn to play tennis by playing tennis. And even when you take golf lessons, every good professional gets you right into action.

Education is generally ineffective when it separates theory from practice. So make an effort to learn through more than one sense. If you're learning a foreign language, try to picture the scene you're learning, try to imprint the information through other senses.

To learn to count to ten in Japanese, for instance, try miming the words with actions (see routine, page 34).

Good teachers and accelerated learning courses use many other techniques, as we'll explore later. But for do-it-yourselfers, interactive technology can now help greatly. Let's take two of the most complicated nonphysical games: bridge and chess. You can learn both by playing—especially with a good coach.

But bridge or chess masters don't really want to spend hours playing with a novice. So some of them have now worked with software programmers to put their knowledge into interactive computer games. So, as well as playing with your friends, you can "play the computer."

At bridge, you can see your cards on the screen and, if you win the bidding, you can see your partner's hand to play it. The computer will play your opponents' hands. And when each hand is over you have a choice of seeing all hands—and checking how the cards should have best been played.

In most computer chess games, you can choose your level of compe-

Draw Mind Maps instead of taking linear notes

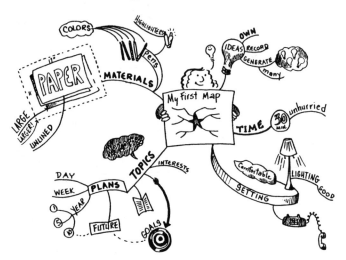

An adaptation of the Mind Mapping principle originated by Tony Buzan, and drawn here by Nancy Margulies,* of St. Louis, Missouri, U.S.A. Note how:

1. The main theme is in the center.

2. There is a main branch for each sub-theme.

3. Single words are used for each concept.

4. Where possible, each concept has a picture.

In the accompanying text, Nancy Margulies also recommends setting aside 30-minute periods of uninterrupted time to practice Mind Mapping— and her illustration summarizes that reminder.

* Taken from *Mapping InnerSpace,* by Nancy Margulies, published by Zephyr Press, P.O. Box 13448-C, Tucson, Arizona 85732-3448, and reprinted with permission. A videotape is also available.

tency, from novice to advanced; the computer will play at the same level.

12. Draw Mind Maps instead of taking linear notes

There's no use taking in important information if you can't recall it when you need it. And here traditional schooling methods are archaic. Tens of thousands of students around the world right now are taking notes. They're writing down words line by line. Or in some languages, column by column. But the brain doesn't work that way. It does not store information in neat lines or columns. The brain stores information on its treelike dendrites. It stores information by *pattern and association.* So the more you can work in with the brain's own memory-method, the easier and faster you'll learn.

So don't take notes, make Mind Maps. And make them with trees, with pictures, with colors, with symbols, with patterns and associations. Mind Mapping is a method devised by Tony Buzan. Singapore-based author and Buzan facilitator Dilip Mukerjea has written and illustrated an excellent introduction to the subject, entitled *Superbrain.*

Swedish publisher Ingemar Svantesson has produced *Mind Mapping and Memory.* And in the United States the finest book on a similar theme is Nancy Margulies' *Mapping InnerSpace.* Margulies has also written a great accelerated-learning book *Yes, You Can Draw!* and produced a first-class video to go with it.

Those books, and some of the Mind Maps in this one, demonstrate the principles in practice. The main points are simple:

1. Imagine your brain-cells are like trees, with each one storing related information on its branches.

2. Now try arranging the key points of any topic on a sheet of white paper in the same treelike format.

3. Start with the central topic—preferably with a symbol—in the center of the page, then draw branches spreading out from it. If you're Mind Mapping New York, use the Statue of Liberty as the centerpoint. If it's Sydney, use the harbor bridge. If it's our chapter on the brain, sketch a two-sided brain.

4. Generally record only one word and/or symbol for each point you want to recall—one main theme to each branch.

5. Put related points on the same main branches, each one shooting off like a new subbranch.

The principles of smart reading in map form

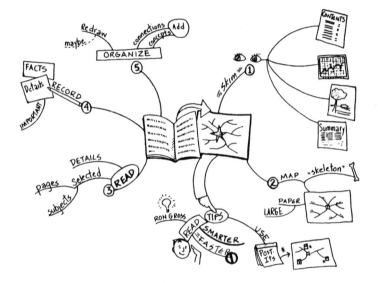

In her book, *Mapping InnerSpace,* Nancy Margulies* draws this map to illustrate the key concepts of "smart reading":

1. Skim-check the main points first.

2. Prepare a large map skeleton.

3. Read not merely faster, but smarter.

4. Record key facts and important details on your map.

5. Organize concepts together, and when you've finished the book or other reading matter, redraw your Mind Map if you feel it needs to be simplified.

* From *Mapping InnerSpace,* by Nancy Margulies, published by Zephyr Press, Tucson, Arizona, and reprinted here with permission.

6. Use different colored pencils or markers for related topics.

7. Draw as many pictures and symbols as you can.

8. When you've completed each branch, enclose it in a different colored border.

9. Add to each map regularly. In this way it's easy to start with the overview and then build up your Mind Map as you learn more key points about each subject.

13. Easy ways to retrieve what you've learned

Since the brain stores information by patterns and associations, and Mind Maps record it in the same way, then it's sensible to use the same methods for easy recall.

Here some more brain-knowledge will come in handy. Your brain has both a short-term and a long-term memory. And that's fortunate. You come to an intersection as the traffic light is turning red, and you stop. The lights turn green and you go. Your long-term memory has learned and remembered the rules about traffic lights. But your short-term memory doesn't have to remember each of the thousands of times you stop for the red light.

So how do you store and retrieve the information you need for long-term use? Partly by patterns and associations.

Mind Mapping is just one method. Another is to use all your intelligence-centers, including those involved with rhyme, rhythm, repetition and music. You don't have to spend hours on boring rote memory. As you've read this book, highlighted key phrases and subheadings and made a Mind Map of the main points, we suggest you do two things immediately you've finished:

1. Immediately reskim the key points you've highlighted.

2. Redo your Mind Map. This will also help you link your main lessons: by pattern and association. Almost certainly, if you're new to Mind Mapping, you'll have found it difficult to list each key point in only one word. But try to do so. It's very important.

Then tonight, not too long before you're thinking of sleeping, play some relaxing music. Take another look at your Mind Map. Try to think of the main lessons you have learned; try to visualize them.

Think of the associations—because that state of almost reverie, just before sleep, is a vital part of the learning process.

Your brainwaves

1. Beta

2. Alpha

3. Theta

4. Delta

These are actual recordings of human
brainwaves—from top:
1. When wide awake—the conscious mind,
operating at 13 to 25 cycles per second,
the so-called beta state.
2. The ideal learning state of "relaxed alertness,"
8 to 12 CPS— alpha.
3. The early stages of sleep, 4 to 7 CPS—theta:
the mind is processing the day's information.
4. Deep sleep, 0.5 to 3 CPS—delta.

14. Learn the art of relaxed alertness

Up to now, most points we've summarized are logical, "left brain" activities. But to make use of the extraordinary powers of your right brain and your subconscious, *the real key to effective learning can be summed up in two words: relaxed alertness—your state of mind, especially when you start any learning session.*

We've already mentioned brainwaves. Now let's start to put them to use. Your brain operates, much like a television or radio station, on four main frequencies or waves. We can measure them with an EEG machine (electro-encephalograph).

If you're wide awake and alert at the moment, or if you're talking, making a speech or working out an involved problem in logic, your brain is probably "transmitting" and "receiving" at 13 to 25 cycles per second. Some call this the beta level.

But that's not the best state for stimulating your long-term memory. Most of the main information you learn will be stored in your subconscious mind. Many researchers and teachers believe that the vast bulk of information is also best learned subconsciously. And *the brainwave activity that links best with the subconscious mind is at 8 to 12 cycles per second: alpha.*

Says British accelerated learning innovator Colin Rose: "This is the brainwave that characterizes relaxation and meditation, the state of mind during which you daydream, let your imagination run. It is a state of relaxed alertness that facilitates inspiration, fast assimilation of facts and heightened memory. Alpha lets you reach your subconscious, and since your self-image is primarily in your subconscious it is the only effective way to reach it."[2]

When you start getting sleepier—the twilight zone between being fully awake and fully asleep—your brainwaves change to between 4 and 7 cycles per second: theta.

When you're fully into deep sleep, your brain is operating at between .5 and 3 cycles per second: delta. Your breathing is deep, your heartbeat slows and your blood pressure and body temperature drop.

And the impact of all this on learning and memory? American accelerated learning pioneer Terry Wyler Webb says beta waves—the very fast ones—are "useful for getting us through the day, but they inhibit access to the deeper levels of the mind. Deeper levels are reached in the

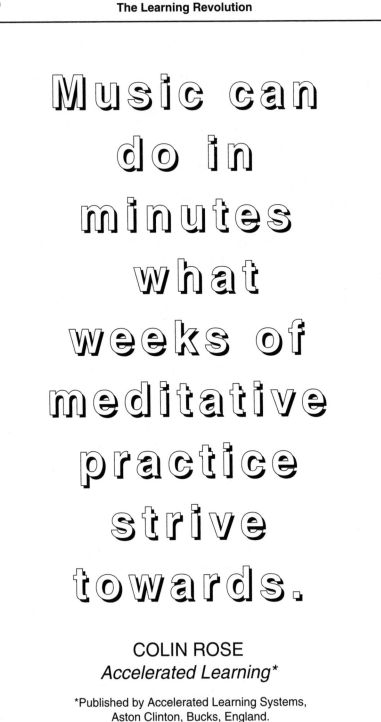

Music can do in minutes what weeks of meditative practice strive towards.

COLIN ROSE
*Accelerated Learning**

*Published by Accelerated Learning Systems,
Aston Clinton, Bucks, England.

alpha and theta brainwave patterns, which are characterized by subjective feelings of relaxation, concentrated alertness and well-being. *It is in the alpha and theta states that the great feats of supermemory, along with heightened powers of concentration and creativity, are achieved."* [3]

And how do you achieve that state? Thousands of people do it with daily meditation, or relaxing exercises, especially deep breathing. But more and more teachers are convinced that some types of music can achieve the results much quicker and easier. Says Webb: "Certain types of musical rhythm help relax the body, calm the breath, quiet the beta chatter and evoke a gentle state of relaxed awareness which is highly receptive to learning new information."

Of course many types of music can help you remember messages when the music is accompanied by words—as television and radio advertising prove every day. But researchers[4] have now found that some baroque music is ideal for rapidly improving learning, partly because its main 60-to-70 beats-to-the-minute is identical to the alpha brainwaves.

Skilled teachers are now using this music as an essential ingredient of all accelerated-learning teaching. But for do-it-yourself learners, the immediate implications are simple: play the right type of music at night when you want to review your material, and you'll dramatically increase your recall.

In part that's because of how your brain works most efficiently when you're dropping off to sleep. Some call it R.E.M. sleep. The initials stand for *rapid eye movement.* And EEGs tell you why: it's almost as if your mind—even with your body asleep—is using its visual cortex to take quick frame-by-frame photographs of the day's main events.

Many researchers believe that in this state the brain is sorting out new information and storing it in the appropriate memory banks. And quiet relaxation as you review your Mind Maps, and reflect on the day's main points, opens up the pathways to those subconscious storage files.

That probably also explains why you dream: your subconscious is "dialing up" your old memories to collate the new information. And if you're thinking through a problem, your subconscious sifts through some alternative solutions, as we'll discuss in the next chapter.

The alpha state is also ideal for starting each new specific study period. Quite simply, it makes great sense to clear the mind before you start. Take your office problems on the golf course and you'll never play great golf. Your mind will be elsewhere. And the same applies to study. Come

Music suggestions

Use different music for different purposes.

For creating a calm atmosphere

Relaxing music, like *Watermark* by Enya; most of Corelli's 12 concertos, from op. 6; and specialized, sequenced baroque music in OptimaLearning Classics, 303 and 601, from Barzak Institute.

For getting in the mood

Especially for cooperative learning activities, *Deep Breakfast* by Ray Lynch.

For "clustering" and fast writing

Antarctica by Vangelis or *Brazilian* in the *Invisible Touch* album by Genesis (the latter is especially popular with teenagers).

For "poetry writing"

December by George Winston.

For putting poems and whole language to raps

Hammer's tapes, but just the instrumental part.

For "state changes"

Vary the music depending on the age groups, but generally any upbeat instrumental music, such as *Planet of Light* by Deuter; and, for teenagers, songs like *Run Away* by The Real McCoy, or *I Need You,* by Savage Garden; and Elvis Presley music for those from an earlier era.

For getting started with teenagers

Right after a break, *Strike It Up* by Black Box, or *Sweet Harmony* by Beloved Conscience.

For goal setting

Chariots of Fire by Vangelis.

For "visualizations"

Waterfalls by Paul Lloyd Warner; Michael Jones' *Sunsets,* and George Winston's *December.*

These are from selections used by Jeannette Vos. See also page 180 for specific selections of music for "passive" and "active" concerts, terms covered in later text.

straight from a high school French class to a mathematics lecture and it can be hard to "switch gears". But take a few moments to do deep breathing exercises, and you'll start to relax. Play some relaxing music, close your eyes and think of the most peaceful scene you can imagine— and soon you'll be in the state of relaxed alertness that makes it easier to "float information" into your long-term memory.

15. Practice, practice, practice

If you're learning to speak French, speak it. If you're learning about computers, use them. If you've taken a course in Asian cooking, cook an Asian feast for your friends. If you're studying shorthand, write it. If you want to be a public speaker, join Toastmasters—and speak publicly. If you want to be a writer, write. If you want to be a bartender, mix drinks.

Remember the sporting maxim: it's not a mistake, it's practice.

16. Review and reflect

When you're learning a physical-mental skill, like typing or cooking, you can practice it with action. But in gaining other types of knowledge, make sure you review regularly. Look again at your Mind Map and review the main points immediately you've finished it. Do it again in the morning. And again a week later. Once more a month later. Then review it, and other associated data, before you have specific need for it: for an examination, an overseas trip, a speech or whatever. Before reading a new book, for instance, many people find it helps to first look at their existing Mind Maps on the subject, or skim-read the highlighted parts of three of four books that they've already read on the subject.

17. Use linking tools as memory pegs

Since the memory works best by association, develop your own "memory pegs". Associate newly acquired knowledge with something you already know.

The association can be physical: such as learning to count in Japanese by scratching your knee (see exercise, page 34).

It can be visual: like visualizing scenes to remember names—forging gold in a blacksmith's shop to remember Mr. Goldsmith, a picture of a crocodile under a McDonald's arch to remember founder Ray Krok.

It can be a strong visual story: like picturing a sequence to remember,

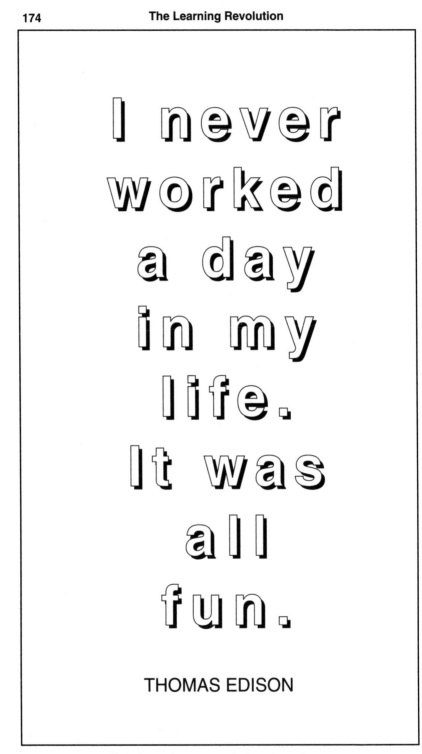

I never worked a day in my life. It was all fun.

THOMAS EDISON

say, the planets in order from earth—the hot sun shining so strongly it breaks a thermometer, and all the Mercury spills out; this runs outside where a beautiful woman, Venus, is standing on the Earth; it keeps running over the earth into the next-door neighbor's red-earth garden; a warlike neighbor, Mars, appears and starts hurling abuse. But just then a smiling giant appears, Jupiter—the biggest planet—and on his super-man-type chest he has the word SUN emblazoned, for Saturn, Uranus and Neptune, and running alongside him is a happy dog, Pluto.

It can be rhyming and visual: like memorizing numbers with rhyming pictorial words, and linking them up with the items to be memorized: so that **one** becomes **sun; two, shoe; three, tree; four, door; five, hive; six, sticks; seven, heaven; eight, gate; nine, mine;** and **ten, hen.** To remember ten items, such as on a shopping list, link each one *visually* with the numbered sequence—so that if your first three items are butter, cheese and milk, you visualize butter being melted with the sun (one), cheese in a shoe (two), and milk being poured over a tree (three).

It can use the initial letter principle: as marketing people remember the key elements of advertising by AIDA: *attract Attention, arouse Interest, create Desire,* and *urge Action.*

But whichever association method you use, *try to make it outlandish, funny and preferably emotional—because the "filter" in the brain that transfers information to your long-term memory is very closely linked with the brain's emotional center. And link your associations with as many senses as you can: sight, sound, smell, touch and taste.*

18. Have fun, play games

Ask a friend what images flash to mind when you mention education or study. Now see how they tally with Tony Buzan's experience. He says: "In my 30 years of investigating people's associations with the word 'study,' ten major words or concepts have emerged. They are: boring, exams, homework, waste of time, punishment, irrelevant, detention, 'yuck,' hate and fear."[5]

But ask a four-year-old fresh out of a good preschool center and she'll talk about the fun she had. So nearly all progressive educators now stress the need to recapture the fun-filled joy of early learning. And humor itself is a great way to learn. So try to link humor with study. Think up games to play to reinforce the key points with someone who's studying the same subject—even *Trivial Pursuit*-type quizzes can be great aids.

Philip arrives in Paris (Monday).	**Philip arrive à Paris (Lundi)**
Philip looks at the house.	**Philip regarde la maison.**
It is big and beautiful.	**Elle est grande et belle.**
Philip goes up to the front door.	**Philip s'approche de la porte d'entrée.**
He rings the bell and waits.	**Il sonne et attend.**
An old lady opens the door.	**Une dame âgée ouvre la porte.**
What do you want, young man?	**Qu'est-ce que vous voulez jeune homme?**
Hello.	**Bonjour madame.**
Is this Mr Dubois' house?	**C'est ici la maison de Monsieur Dubois?**
Yes it is.	**Oui, c'est ici.**
I have an appointment with Mr Dubois.	**J'ai rendez-vous avec Monsieur Dubois.**
Who shall I say it is, please?	**C'est de la part de qui, s'il vous plaît?**
Mr West.	**Monsieur West.**
Ah yes, Mr West.	**Ah oui, Monsieur West.**
Please come in.	**Entrez, s'il vous plaît.**
Thank you.	**Merci madame.**
Philip goes into the house.	**Philip entre dans la maison.**
Madame Brossetout calls Mademoiselle Dubois.	**Madame Brossetout appelle Mademoiselle Dubois.**
Who is it?	**Qui est-ce?**
It's Mr West.	**C'est Monsieur West.**

This is a typical written page from a good accelerated learning language course. Note:

1. Each "act" is written like the act of a 12-act play, so you can visualize what you are doing.
2. Your own language version and the foreign version are written side by side, line by line.
2. You can read the foreign language version, accompanied by music, while listening to it through headphones—and still be aware of the translation.
3. No sentence is longer than seven words, a good "chunking" principle as it is easier to remember concepts with no more than seven items.

*Reprinted from a French course for English-speakers, produced by Accelerated Learning Systems, Aston Clinton, Bucks, England, and reprinted here with permission. Turn the next page to see a pictorial version of the same material.

19. Teach others

"Each one—teach one." That's the recommended theme for the nineties from California brain-researcher Marian Diamond.

As well as being professor of neuroanatomy, she's Director of the Lawrence Hall of Science, a fun-filled resource and learning center attached to the University of California at Berkeley.

"I want to introduce the concept," she says, "that everyone can learn to be a teacher. One has to be accurate with the facts as a teacher, yet imaginative with creative ideas for new directions in the future. As we learn the facts, we can turn around and share with the next person so that the 'association cortices' can create the new ideas."[6]

Diamond believes that even a child in kindergarten can learn to be a teacher. And she asks: "Why spend the next 12 to 15 years in only being taught? What one learns the first day of school can be shared not only with other schoolmates but with parents as well."

And whatever your age there are few better ways to crystallize what you've learned than to teach the principles to others, to make a speech or to run a seminar.

20. Take an accelerated learning course

This chapter has concentrated on simple, do-it-yourself tips. But the best way to learn all the principles is to take a specific accelerated learning course. Inquire what's available at your school or college. Or take a do-it-yourself course, preferably one based on the breakthroughs by Bulgarian psychiatrist Georgi Lozanov, whose work we detail later.

Many of these courses are now available for learning a new language. Some of the best do-it-yourself courses we have seen are from Accelerated Learning Systems in England.[7] An Australian high school that covered a three-year French course in eight weeks' part-time study also used the same methods. Here are the basic principles, and how they're used in a typical foreign language learning kit:

a. There are 2,700 languages in the world. English has about 550,000 words. German has under 200,000.[8] But linguists agree that about *90 percent of all speech uses only about 2,000 to 3,000 words.[9] Understand these fluently, speak them fluently, and you'll be able to converse reasonably well in your new language. In fact, even 1,000 words learned fluently may enable you to get by.*

Illustrations from a typical accelerated learning foreign language course* workbook. Each picture depicts the same sequence as the written dialog. Students are encouraged to duplicate and enlarge the illustrations, to use them as posters and to color them in. The illustration above is the pictorial version of the wording reproduced on page 176.

*Published by Accelerated Learning Systems, Aston Clinton, Aylesbury, Bucks, England, and reprinted here with permission.

b. An accelerated learning language course therefore builds the basic 2,000 words into, say, 12 different "plays" or scenes—like a 12-act drama.[10]

c: An attractive workbook helps. On some pages *the script for each act is written in both English and, say, French line by line. But no sentence is longer than seven words*, because your short-term memory can absorb information easiest in "seven bit" bites. That's why phone numbers are generally easy to remember; over seven digits, and they switch to a separate area code. Teachers call this principle "chunking."

d. Many acts involve you as a visitor to a new country, and weave a story around the typical events a tourist would find. So *the workbook also illustrates each act with pictures—stimulating the visual sense.*

e. Each scene is also recorded on an audio tape, in the foreign language, so the student can learn by listening while reading the foreign language and visualizing it.

f. Before starting each lesson, the student plays relaxing music from a special tape—through headphones—and follows suggestions for breathing and relaxation exercises. The aim is to tune out other distracting thoughts, and to place the brain in a state of "relaxed alertness"—so the new language can "float" into the brain.

g. That's where *music plays its three-part role: (1) it helps you relax; (2) it activates your right-brain to receive the new information; and (3) it helps move the information into your long-term memory-storage banks.* Lozanov* teachers believe a well-orchestrated music concert can in effect do most of the teaching in a greatly-reduced time.[11] The student first listens to the words of the foreign language while reading the text, with specific music in the background—and the words read in time and tone to the music. The first "active concert" is then followed by a so-called "passive" concert, in which the student sits with

---

* There is much more depth to the Lozanov method of teaching and learning than we can cover in this brief introduction to the technique. Music selection, in particular, is critical for the "active" and "passive" concerts. In chapter nine, we link the main principles of Lozanov with many other proven techniques. But for those experimenting with music in preparing their own accelerated learning programs, we strongly recommend studying the music principles first. In a new program, The Music Revolution, for publication in 1999, Dr. Jeannette Vos has selected scores of tracks for a complete guide to using music in education. These are are grouped under six headings, and the associated workbook gives detailed instructions on to how to use each track.

Georgi Lozanov's music for improved learning

The Georgi Lozanov method uses music in three distinct ways to accelerate learning:

1. Introductory music to relax participants and achieve the optimum state for learning.
2. An "active concert," in which the information to be learned is read with expressive music.
3. A "passive concert" in which the learner hears the new information read conversationally against a background of baroque music, to help move the information into the long-term memory.

Here are a few typical selections:*

FOR ACTIVE CONCERT	FOR PASSIVE CONCERT
Beethoven, Concerto for Violin and Orchestra in D major, Op. 61.	Corelli, Concerti Grossi, Op. 6, No. 2, 8, 5, 9.
Tchaikovsky, Concerto No. 1 in B flat minor for Piano and Orchestra.	Handel, The Water Music.
Mozart, Concerto for Violin and Orchestra, Concert No. 7 in D major.	J.S. Bach, Fantasy in G major, Fantasy in C Minor and Trio in D minor; Canonic Variations and Toccata.
Haydn, Symphony No. 67 in F. major; Symphony No. 69 in B. major	Corelli, Concerti Grossi, Op. 4, No. 10, 11, 12.
Beethoven, Concerto No. 5 in E flat major for Piano and Orchestra, Op. 73 ("Emperor").	Vivaldi, Five Concertos for Flute and Chamber Orchestra.

*Selections are from *Language Teacher's Suggestopedic Manual,* by Georgi Lozanov and Evalina Gateva, and *Suggestology and Outlines of Suggestopedia,* by Lozanov, both published by Gordon and Breach, New York.

eyes closed while more music is played in soft tones and the language is effectively "surfed" under it. This is a key element of the Lozanov technique, and the music is almost invariably baroque to maintain, and synthesize with, the most effective learning state: alpha.

h. Students are also encouraged to replay the baroque music before they go to bed at night, and to look through their workbook pictures of the "act" they're studying. In that way, the subconscious keeps filing the new information overnight.

i. Next day the student plays games, supplied in his kit, to reinforce some of the main words learned.

j. The kit* includes other suggestions, including pictures and words for common clothes and household items—and a physical learning video. This teaches you in the same way you learned your own language as an infant—although much faster. The presenter mimes each word or phrase, while you learn to say "sit" *(asseyez-vous* in French), "walk" *(marchez)* or "touch your elbow" *(touchez votre coude).*

k. Apart from the 2,000 main words, *most other words can be worked out if you understand the "keys".* In Japanese, for example, most female first names end in "ko," so if you see the name "Michiko" you know the person is probably female. *So a typical do-it-yourself kit includes a guide to all the main principles of the new language.*

*

These simple methods will help you remember anything much more effectively, even without making a detailed study of integrative accelerated learning techniques. But the real challenge is to use your ability to create new solutions. To use your brainpower to think for successful new ideas. And here, too, The Learning Revolution provides some easy answers.

*Not all foreign language programs are the same. With the development of these techniques, some language programs around the world have merely been "put to music". The method we have outlined here is that used by Accelerated Learning Systems, of Aston Clinton, Aylesbury, Bucks, England, which is the system we have found most effective for "teaching yourself". We acknowledge, with thanks, their permission to summarize their main points, and to use illustrations from one of their language courses. But we stress that these courses are basically intended for do-it-yourself study. Teachers using the same material in classrooms are recommended to link it directly with the teaching methods covered in chapter nine.

Your checklist for producing ideas

1 Define your problem.*

2 Define and visualize the ideal solution

3 Gather the facts: specific, general.

4 Break the pattern.

5 Go outside your own field.

6 Try new combinations.

7 Use all your senses.

8 Switch off — let it simmer.

9 Use music or nature to relax.

10 Sleep on it.

11 Eureka! It pops out.

12 Recheck it.

* Note: You can also reverse steps 1 and 2—start with your dream, next define where you are now, and then proceed to bridge the gap.

New program to teach yourself or students creative thinking

Amazingly the most important "subject" of all is not taught at most schools: how to invent your own future, how to create new ideas.

Yet the world today needs a diet of revolutionary new ideas as never before. As Roderic Gorney says in *The Human Agenda:* "For the first time in our two million or more years we have the possibility of enough to go around." But most of the world's political leaders are driving into that future through a rear-vision mirror fixed on a bygone era.

In education, the contrast between past and future is even more marked. As Robert Gross puts it: "We live in the first era in human history when our species' entire heritage of knowledge, wisdom and beauty is available to each of us virtually on demand."[1]

That gives us the opportunity to reinvent education and usher in a golden age of discovery and innovation: to reinvent they way we think, learn, work, live, enjoy ourselves and create. The models already exist.

Thomas Edison held 1093 patents,[2] and electrified the world. Walt Disney and Apple Computers' Steve Jobs[3] each founded giant commercial empires on the power of a new idea—and a different make-believe mouse. Ray Krok[4] was a middle-aged milk-shake machine seller when he first visited the California hamburger bar of Dick and Maurice Mc-Donald. He was to take their basic concept, mix it with others, and turn the result into the world's biggest fast-food chain. Georgi Lozanov, the Bulgarian psychologist, linked yoga, meditation and music to revolutionize the teaching of foreign languages. The Internet and World Wide Web have completely changed the way the world communicates.

Bill Gates is the the world's richest person firstly because he and his

An idea is a new combination of old elements.

There are no new elements.
There are only new combinations.

GORDON DRYDEN
Out Of The Red*

*Published by William Collins, Auckland, New Zealand.

partner, Paul Allen, had a dream to put a computer on every desk and in every home.

The two richest men in Europe[5] owe their wealth to their father, Richard Rausing. While watching his wife prepare homemade sausages, he became intrigued by how she peeled back the skins to insert the ingredients. That idea, when reversed, turned into the system of pouring milk from cartons. And his heirs still receive royalties every day from millions of Tetrapak milk cartons.

All the great ideas in history, all the great inventions, obviously have one thing in common. All have come from the human brain. Just as the brain has fantastic ability to store information, it has an equal ability to reassemble that information in new ways: to create new ideas.

And very simply, *an idea is a new combination of old elements.* Write that down, underline it, reinforce it. It could be the most important sentence you ever write. It contains the key to creating new solutions. There are no new elements. *There are only new combinations.*[6]

Think for a moment of the thousands of different cookbooks around the world. Every recipe in every book is a different mixture of existing ingredients. Think of that example whenever you tackle a problem.

And all the breakthroughs everywhere—radio, television, the internal combustion engine—are new combinations of old bits. A push-button shower combines at least three "old" elements: hot and cold water and a mixing valve. Nylon and other "new" synthetic fibers are new combinations of molecules that have existed for hundreds of centuries. In nylon's case: recombined molecules from coal.

Since an idea is a new mixture of old elements, *the best ideas-creators are constantly preoccupied with new combinations.*

In most management courses, you learn the overriding need to define correctly the problem you want solved. *But now a new revolutionary element has emerged. We can now define the ideal solution in advance—and start creating it.*

This is a revolutionary change. Whereas previously we organized our existing knowledge to solve a problem, within the limits of that knowledge, today we start by defining what we would like to achieve. And then we organize the things we don't know in order to achieve it.

Seventy years ago clothing manufacturers were stuck with such basic yarns as wool, cotton and silk. Then Wallace Corothers synthesized

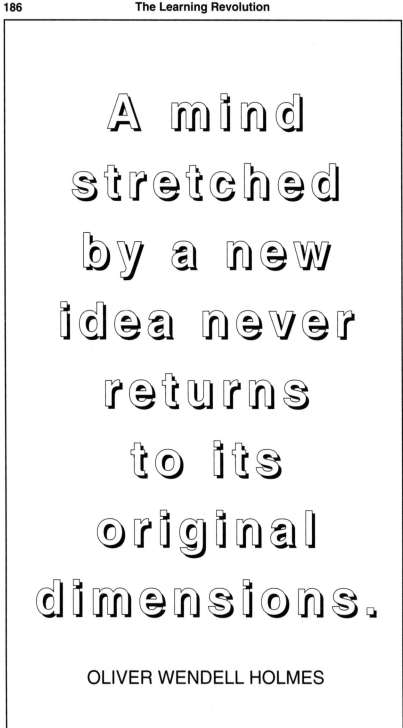

A mind stretched by a new idea never returns to its original dimensions.

OLIVER WENDELL HOLMES

nylon in 1935. Today we can define the ideal garment, and then produce the fibers and mixtures to create it.   Families became tired of darning socks, so science created a blend of nylon and wool to give us the benefit of both: a new mixture of old elements. Iron-weary mothers wanted shirts that would drip-dry without creases. So science created polyester fibers: a new combination of old elements. Fashion-conscious women liked the easy-care properties of nylon but pined for the fluffiness of wool. So science created acrylics—by recombining the elements of natural gas.

Peter Drucker, in *The Age of Discontinuity,* has crystallized the new innovative technique in a graphic way.   He calls it "a systematic organized leap into the unknown". Unlike the science of yesterday, he says, "it is not based on organizing our knowledge, it is based on organizing our ignorance".

Amazingly these techniques are not taught in most schools, yet in many ways they are the key to the future.

Even worse: school tests are based on the principle that every question has one correct answer.   The great breakthroughs in life come from entirely new answers. They come from challenging the status quo, not accepting it.

Courses in thinking should be a top priority in every school. Otherwise, as American educator Neil Postman has suggested in *Teaching As A Subversive Activity:* children may "enter school as question marks but leave as periods".

California creative consultant Roger von Oech says, in *A Whack On The Side Of The Head:* "By the time the average person finishes college he or she will have taken over 2,600 tests, quizzes and exams. The 'right answer' approach becomes deeply ingrained in our thinking. This may be fine for some mathematical problems, where there is in fact only one right answer. The difficulty is that most of life isn't that way. Life is ambiguous; there are many right answers—all depending on what you are looking for. But if you think there is only one right answer, then you'll stop looking as soon as you find one." So how do you use your own brainpower to make Drucker's systematic organized leap into the unknown? These are the steps we've found most useful:

1. Define your problem

One first step is to define in advance your problem—specifically but not restrictively.

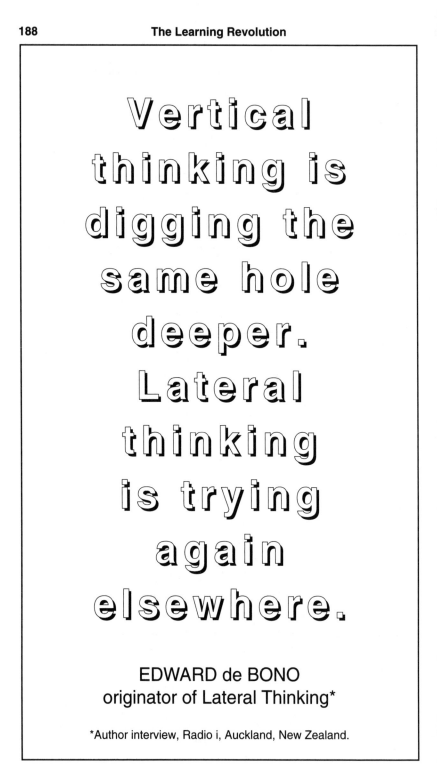

Vertical thinking is digging the same hole deeper. Lateral thinking is trying again elsewhere.

EDWARD de BONO
originator of Lateral Thinking*

*Author interview, Radio i, Auckland, New Zealand.

2. Define your ideal solution and visualize it

Step 2 is to define what you would like to achieve—ideally. And then you organize your 100 billion active brain neurons to bridge the gap between where you are and where you want to be. It also helps greatly to visualize the ideal solution, to picture "in your mind's eye" the best possible result.

Let's use a world-famous industry as a typical model: the watch industry. Up to 1970, the entire industry was dominated by Switzerland. But its business model had not changed in half a century. By 1970 it was still making sales of $10 billion a year. But "by the early 1980s, most of that value had migrated away from the traditional Swiss business model to new business designs owned by Timex, Citizen, Seiko and Casio. Employment tumbled in parallel with the drop in value. From the mid-1970s to the early 1980s, the number of workers in the Swiss watchmaking industry contracted from 90,000 to 20,000."[7]

So the industry called in consultant Nicolas Hayek. His experience in the industry: nil. But even as a boy "Hayek was always asking his family and teachers, 'Why do we do things the way we do?' He was born with an innate and incurable curiosity about the way things work and where we come from. He consumed every book he could find on physics, astronomy, the Big Bang, and Einstein's theories of mass and speed."[8]

And as an adult he applied that same curiosity to his newest challenge—and ended up reinventing an entire industry. Until he arrived on the scene, most people bought a watch to last a lifetime. And those flocking to the new Japanese brands were also doing so because of their low cost. But Hayek started with a new series of questions: What did people want from a watch? Fun? Spirit? Style? Variety? Fashion?

Those questions were to lead directly to the invention of the Swatch watch—not solely as a timekeeper but as an ever-changing fashion accessory. And with it, Hayek launched a marketing program to persuade customers to wear a different-colored watch with every dress or suit.

From 1983 to 1992, Swatch sold 100 million watches. By 1996 he had sold his 200 millionth.

Even the name itself emerged as typical of the innovation process. As Adrian J. Slywotzky and David J. Morrison recount in their excellent business book, *The Profit Zone:* "Hayek differentiated his watches by giving them a soul. He created a message, an emotional sense that appeals to everyone, conveying a sense of fun, of style, and of lightheartedness.

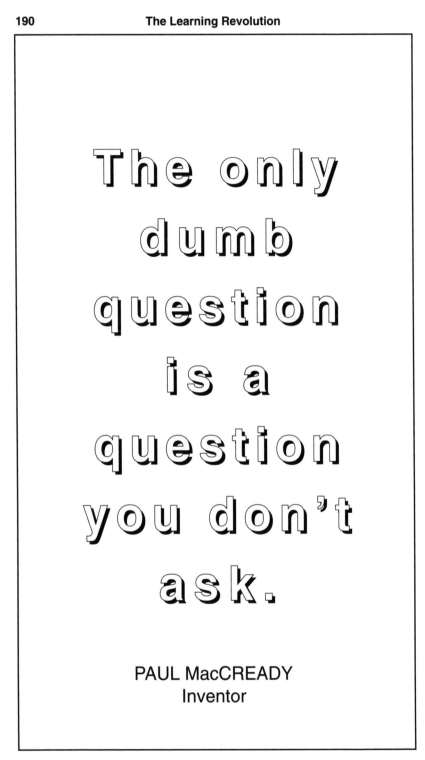

The only dumb question is a question you don't ask.

PAUL MacCREADY
Inventor

Then he wrapped it around indisputable high quality and low cost.

"All Hayek's new product lacked now was a name. 'We were working with an American advertising company,' Hayek says. 'We had the craziest names in the world and none pleased me. Finally, we went for lunch and this woman wrote on the blackboard "Swiss watch" and "second watch"' Then she wrote "Swatch". It helped that we were not very strong in English. We didn't know that "swatch" in English meant a cleaning towel. If we had known, we wouldn't have started the company with such a name!'" Problem defined. Vision set. And the two linked by new mixtures of old elements.

3. Gather all the facts

Since a great idea is a new combination of old elements, then the next step is to *gather all the facts* you can. **Unless you know a big array of facts on any situation or problem, you're unlikely to hit on the perfect new solution.**

Facts can be *specific:* those directly concerned with your job, industry or problem. And they can be *general:* the facts you gather from a thousand different sources. You will only be a great ideas-producer if you're a voracious seeker of information. A questioner. A reader. A challenger. And a storer of information, in notebooks and dendrites.

There is no substitute for personalized, purposeful homework. What comes out must have gone in. The key is to somehow link information filed in, say, "brain-cell number 369,124" on "dendrite 2,614", with another stored on "cell number 9,378,532"—or wherever.

Here your brain's patterning ability creates both problems and opportunities. Each one of us uses our brain for every waking minute to take action in a pre-patterned way —from walking to running, from driving a car to stopping at red lights. Your brain tends to store information in narrow channels, on associated "branches" for easy and quick retrieval, so we normally come up with the same answers.

4. Break the pattern

To solve problems creatively, however, you've got to *open up new pathways, find new crossover points, discover new linkages. You've got to break the pattern.*

And the easiest way to do that is to *start with questions that redirect your mind.* What would happen to your problem if you doubled it, halved

Go outside your own field

- [ ] The inventors of Kodachrome color film, Leopold Mannes and Leopold Godowsky, were musicians.

- [ ] George Eastman (of Eastman Kodak) was originally a book keeper in a bank.

- [ ] Ladislo Biro, the inventor of the ballpoint pen, was in turn a sculptor, a painter and a journalist.

- [ ] King Camp Gillette (the inventor of the safety razor) was a traveling salesman in bottletops.

- [ ] John Boyd Dunlop (inventor of the air-inflated tire) was a veterinary surgeon.

GORDON RATTRAY TAYLOR
in *The Inventions That Changed The World**

*Published by Reader's Digest, 26 Waterloo Street, Sydney, NSW 2010, Australia.

it, froze it, reconstituted it, reversed it, adapted it, rearranged it, combined it? What if you eliminated it—or part of it? If you substituted one of the parts? If you made it smaller, shorter, lighter? If you recolored it, streamlined it, magnified it? If you repackaged it? Distributed it in a different way? What if you applied all your senses—and added scents or fragrances, added sounds or made it different to see or touch?

5. Go outside your own field

Put your existing preconceptions aside. The elements you use to solve problems should not only be those that are specific to the industry or process you're involved in. Use only those and you'll come up with the same old solutions.

Ask a teacher to redefine education, and generally he'll start thinking about school, and not about interactive videodiscs or life in 2010. Ask your brain to add 1 plus 1 and it will automatically answer 2. It's programmed that way.

But your brain has also stored facts about thousands of different interests: from recipes to football. The answers to problems in farming may well come from meanderings in space research. So all good inventors, innovators and creators develop an insatiable appetite for new knowledge. *Always remember to ask.*

6. Play with various combinations

Next: since an idea is a new combination of old elements, play with various combinations. Jot them down as they come to you. Try different starting points. Choose anything at random—a color, an animal, a country, an industry—and try to link it up with your problem and solution.

Work at it. Keep your notepad full. But a word of caution: don't concentrate too closely on your specific field or you'll be limited by your own preconceptions.

Read as widely as you can—particularly books on the future and challenging writings away from your own speciality. Keep asking: *What if?* "What if I combined this with that? What if I started from here instead of there?" And keep asking.

7. Use all your senses

It also helps greatly to consciously try to engage all your senses. If

Who said this?

1. "The horse is here to stay, but the automobile is only a novelty—a fad."

2. "Heavier-than-air flying machines are impossible."

3. "Video won't be able to hold on to any market it captures after the first six months. People will soon get tired of staring at a plywood box every night."

4. "Everything that can be invented has been invented."

5. "Who the hell wants to hear actors talk?"

ANSWERS:

1. President of the Michigan Savings Bank, advising Henry Ford's lawyer not to invest in the Ford Motor Company.

2. Lord Kelvin, 1895.

3. Daryl F. Zanuck, head of 20th Century Fox movie studio, commenting on television in 1946.

4. Charles H. Duell, commissioner of the U.S. Office of Patents, in a 1899 report to President McKinley, arguing that the Patents Office should be abolished.

5. Harry M. Warner, president of Warner Bros., the movie company, in 1927.

your problem has been defined mathematically, try to visualize some answers. Remember how Albert Einstein's theory of relativity came to him after he'd been daydreaming, imagining that he was traveling through space on a moonbeam.

Mind Mapping, too, is an excellent creative tool—to link information together in new ways, on new branches, in new clusters, so your ideas are not merely listed in one-dimensional lines.

Work at it until your head swims. Then . . .

8. Switch off—let it simmer

Like good food after you've eaten it, let your digestive juices take over and do the work—in this case the digestive juices of your own subconscious. Note the relaxation techniques we've touched on in accelerated learning, to put your brain into its most receptive and creative mode.

9. Use music or nature to relax

Many people find it pays to play relaxing classical music, visit an art gallery or go for a walk by a river or the sea. Anything that opens up the mind to new combinations.

Different techniques work for different people. One of the present authors has always found chess a positive creative stimulant—mainly because of the way every move opens up new possibilities. Other people find chess too focused. The other co-author finds swimming and walking more effective.

10. Sleep on it

Just before going to sleep at night, remind yourself of the problem— and the ideal solution. If you have a set deadline, feed that into your "brain-bank" too. And then *your subconscious mind will take over.* It never sleeps.

But as advertising leader David Ogilvy puts it: "You have to brief your subconscious. Then you have to switch off your thought processes and wait for something, for your subconscious to call you and say, 'Hey, I've got a good idea!' There are ways to do that. A lot of people find that to take a long hot bath produces good ideas. Other people prefer a long walk. I've always found that wine produces good ideas—the better the wine the better the idea."[9]

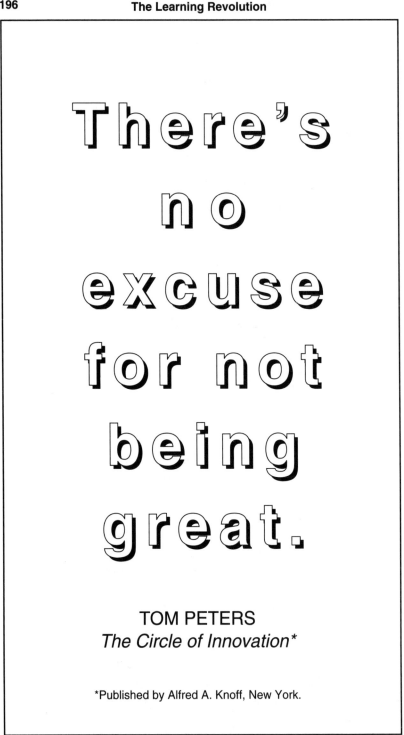

There's no excuse for not being great.

TOM PETERS
The Circle of Innovation*

*Published by Alfred A. Knoff, New York.

11. Eureka! It pops out

The next step is the easiest of all: it pops out. You'll be shaving, or taking a shower, or sleeping—and suddenly the answer is there.

In part the process works because it's similar to the way your brain processes information in the first place. Just as you can use your subconscious to file information in patterns, so you can use your subconscious to deliberately break up those patterns and find new combinations. But only if you state your vision and your goal *specifically. It also pays to set a deadline, so your subconscious can feed that, too, into its data banks.*

12. Recheck it

When the new answer has popped out, *recheck it.* Does it fully solve your problem? Can you amend it or improve it?

The system we've just highlighted could be called the problem-solving way to creativity.

An alternative is a vision or mission approach. That's the same as problem-solving—except you don't start with the problem. You start with a vision of a future where virtually every dream is now possible.

Australian futurist Dr. Peter Ellyard is one of many who favor this approach. He feels that starting with a problem often limits the solution. "The dangers of a problem-centered approach can be best seen," he says, "in the inappropriately named 'health care' industry. In most first-world countries 'health care' is virtually out of control. The words 'health care' actually mean 'illness cure.' The industry consists of the activities of doctors, hospitals and pharmacies. The size of our health care budget has become an index of the nation's sickness, rather than its health. This forgets that the basic state of humans is to be healthy, not ill. We have adopted a problem-centered approach to health, largely defining health as an absence of illness, and a healthy future as an illness-free one. A *mission-directed* approach to promoting and maintaining health would be very different. It would concentrate on nutrition, exercise, good relationships, stress management and freedom from environmental contamination. This is a totally different agenda. However, the current problem is that we now pour so much money and effort into the problem-centered, technology-driven approach that there are very few resources available for a mission-directed approach."[10]

SCAMPER

is a checklist
of ideas-spurring questions.
Some of the questions were first
suggested by Alex Osborn,
a pioneer teacher of creativity.
They were later arranged
by Bob Eberle into this mnemonic:

S	=	Substitute?
C	=	Combine?
A	=	Adapt?
M	=	Modify? Magnify?
P	=	Put to other uses?
E	=	Eliminate or reduce?
R	=	Reverse? Rearrange?

To use SCAMPER:

1. Isolate the challenge or subject
you want to think about.

2. Ask SCAMPER questions about
each step of the challenge
or subject and see what new ideas emerge.

MICHAEL MICHALKO
Thinkertoys*

**Published by Ten Speed Press, Berkeley, California.

The current authors certainly wouldn't disagree with this analysis—except to say that the "problem" was not correctly defined. And Ellyard makes a vital point: generally we all try to define a problem too narrowly. Define your problem as "unemployment", for example, and you may restrict your answers to new jobs—and not consider retraining leave or the desirability of leisure and study-time.

When consulting engineer William J. J. Gordon was given the task of finding a new way to open cans, he deliberately didn't use the word "can-opener" when briefing his engineers and designers. Instead they toyed with such notions as a banana and its easy-peel abilities. Their eventual solution: the ringpulls you now see on most teartab cans. A "canopener" approach would have limited the result.[11]

Whether you use the problem-solving or mission-directed approach, you generally won't come up with a great idea unless you define a specific goal in advance.

There are, of course, many exceptions. Bacteriologist Alexander Fleming stumbled on penicillin when confronted with a strange mould growing at St. Mary's Hospital in London.

And when Massachusetts inventor Percy Spencer was working on a novel radar system in 1945, it struck him that the radiation it emitted could have a culinary use. So he hung a pork chop in front of the magnetron machine he was working on. And, as British BBC presenters Peter Evans and Geoff Deehan report, he "produced the first microwave meal in history".[12] In another of history's quirks, it was the Japanese who capitalized on the invention. "When a Japanese firm started to manufacture magnetrons, it was forbidden under the peace treaty to undertake military contracts. Therefore it concentrated on peaceful uses of microwave technology; now Japan leads the world in microwave sales." Or at least it did until the Koreans caught up.

But most breakthroughs come from a firm vision of the future: a specific goal. Many of those creative techniques can be adapted from other fields. Advertising, for example, has given us "brainstorming"[13]—the original idea of Alex Osborn, one of the founders of Batten, Barton, Durstine and Osborn, the giant advertising agency.

Here are some specific examples of how you can apply the brainstorming, ideas-creation process in practice:

When you're looking for a new idea, can you:

Double it: like London's double-decker buses? *Halve it:* like bikinis

Eureka!

Some of the innovations that have built Nike

Phil Knight, a University of Oregon athlete, chose running-shoes as the project for a marketing essay at Stanford University: and pondered whether Japanese methods might be able to do for that industry what they'd done to Germany in watches and cameras.

He and U.S. Olympic coach **Bill Bowerman*** formed a company by contributing $500 each—on a handshake. Watching his wife make waffles, Bowerman then poured liquid urethane into the waffle iron—and, after gumming up the works, conceived the famous nipple-soled shoe.

Invited by Knight to design a shoe-stripe for the company, art student **Carolyn Davidson** came up with a curved line that looked like the swoosh of a check-mark. Said Knight: "I don't love it, but I think it will grow on me." Davidson charged only $35 for the design.

Pondering a brand name, **Jeff Johnson,** another Bowerman runner and Knight's first commission salesman, slept on it—and woke up with *Nike:* the winged Greek goddess of victory. Said Knight when he considered the alternatives: "I don't like any of them. I guess we'll go with the Nike thing for now."

Phil Knight is now one of America's ten richest men.

Information extracted from *Swoosh: The unauthorized story of Nike and the men who played there,* by J.B. Strasser and Laurie Beckland, published by Harper Business, New York.

* Author Dryden writes about Bowerman with a wry smile. Dryden arranged the 1960s American track team visit to New Zealand where the U.S. coach discovered jogging from Auckland coach Arthur Lydiard. Non-writer Bowerman was so impressed with Lydiard's stamina he co-authored a book on jogging—and it sold over a million copies in the U.S.

or the miniskirt? *Expand it:* like one-stop shopping centers or the Boeing 747? *Dry it:* like packet soup? *Slice it:* like bread? *Stretch it:* like denims or stretch limousines?

What could you substitute?

Ladislo Biro substituted a ball for a nib, and the ball-point pen was born. *The fax machine* has substituted electronic transmission for posted mail—and the Internet has superseded the fax. *Clarence Birdseye*— after finding frozen fish in Canada's Arctic Circle—substituted freezing for canning, to invent the frozen food industry. *Supermarkets* substituted self-service and trolleys for shop assistants. Xerox's Palo Alto Research Center substituted the "point and click" method of running a computer; Apple adapted it commercially, and the world's simplest computing system was born. *Bed-and-breakfast homes* in Ireland have substituted for hotels and become the core of that country's tourist industry. *Compact discs* have replaced vinyl recordings for music.

What new combinations can you make?

Sony combined earphones with a transistor radio to invent the *Walkman.* Pressure-cooked chicken and a special sauce gave us *Kentucky Fried Chicken.* Nylons combined with panties to make *pantyhose.* Walt Disney combined Mickey Mouse with tourism to invent *Disneyland.* Shops and carparks linked together to produce *shopping centers.* General Motors combined hire purchase with a choice of colors and built *the world's biggest car company.*

How can you adapt it?

Rollerblades are now a multimillion-dollar seller—realigning skate-wheels into one line. *Rugby football* has been adapted from soccer, *rugby league* from rugby, *softball* from baseball.

What could you magnify or increase?

McDonald's magnified hamburgers to produce the *Big Mac. Prince* has made a fortune by enlarging the tennis racket. So has Calloway with its *Big Bertha* golf clubs. *Wal-mart* has become the world's most profitable retail chain, selling through giant discount stores. *JVC* invented *three-hour videotape* and beat off Sony to establish the world standard —because the extra length enabled buyers to record complete sports events.

What could you reduce, reverse or eliminate?

Frank Whittle reversed wind and invented the *jet engine. Bill Ham-*

Have you ever thought of this?

 All the literature that has ever been written in the modern English language consists of patterns of only 26 letters.

 All the paintings ever made are patterns of only three primary colors.

 All the music ever written consists of patterns of no more than 12 notes.

 All the arithmetical expressions we know of consist of only 10 symbols.

 And for the vast computations of digital computers, everything is made up of patterns of only two components.

 Thus, whenever we speak of something as being "new" we are really talking about original patterns of already existing components.

DON FABUN
*Three Roads To Awareness**

*Published By Glencoe Press, Beverly Hills, California.

ilton adapted the principle further and gave us the *jet boat. The vacuum cleaner* is based on a similar principle. In Australia, *Kerry Packer* of the Nine TV Network, reduced the time of test matches to invent *one-day cricket,* and a very profitable new summer television feature. *Computer spell-checkers* have reduced printing mistakes.

What new forms can you create?

Can you make it: *Hard,* like frozen ice blocks? *Soft,* like easy-spread butter or margarine? *Quiet,* like a Rolls Royce? *Loud,* like rock music? *Thick,* like Doc Marten bootsoles (a profitable fashion industry, based on the initial choice of unfashionable"skinheads")? *Fun,* like *Trivial Pursuit? Vertical,* like rocket takeoffs? *Horizontal,* like reclining chairs?

Can you: *Blend it,* like shampoo and conditioner? *Glue it,* like Glue Stick? *Shake it,* like a milk shake? *Cover it,* like umbrella cocktail decorations? *Uncover it,* like the miniskirt or split skirts? *Color it,* like new lipsticks, cosmetics or blue-packed Pepsi Cola? *Compress it,* like CD-ROMs? *Liquefy it,* like shoecleaners? *Squeeze it,* in plastic bottles? *Spread it,* like pate? *Raise it,* with self-raising flour?

Can you repack it: *In teartab cans,* like premixed drinks? *In plastic containers,* like cask-wine? *In aerosol cans,* like hairspray? *As roll-ons,* like deodorant? *Sleek,* like Apple iMac and Acer Aspire computers?

Business innovations like these —and hundreds more —are changing the face of society. *Dell Computers* have gone from a $60,000-a-month business to $18-billion-a-year in 16 years because of the revolutionary way they have customized individual computers and sold them by direct marketing and great telephone service. *Lego* has developed into a $1.5 billion business, since started by an out-of-work Danish carpenter, Olo Christiansen, as small wooden toy company. Sweden's *IKEA* has become the world's biggest home furniture retailer, with 79 outlets in 19 countries, through brilliant catalog selling and simple home assembly.

Yet where is the same innovation in the vital field of education and learning? For this book we've selected breakthroughs from around the world. But generally they've been chosen from isolated pockets.

Come up with a new idea in electronic communication—and it will be carried to a million enthusiasts immediately on the Internet and World Wide Web, and within a week or a month by scores of personal computing magazines. Inventors and early-adaptors are making fortunes by cashing in on the new third-wave of economic development. Why not the same verve in education?

If you learn only one word of Japanese make it KAIZEN

**KAIZEN strategy is
the single most important
concept in Japanese
management—the key to
Japanese
competitive success.
KAIZEN means improvement.
KAIZEN means *ongoing*
improvement
involving *everyone:*
top management,
managers
and workers.**

MASAAKI IMAI
*Kaizen: The Key To
Japan's Competitive Success**

*Published by Random House, 201 East 50th St., New York, NY 10022.

We suspect that overwhelmingly it is because of the way schools and curricula are structured. *From the very moment of starting school, most children are taught that the answers have already been found.* Even more: they are taught that success is learning a limited range of those answers—absorbed from a teacher—and feeding them back correctly at exam time. Yet that is not the way the real world innovates. The simple questions on the past three pages are typical of the queries posed in businesses every day as they strive to do things "better, faster, cheaper".

Don Koberg and Jim Bagnall, in their book *The Universal Traveler,* have suggested other words to encourage innovation: multiply, divide, eliminate, subdue, invert, separate, transpose, unify, distort, rotate, flatten, squeeze, complement, submerge, freeze, soften, fluff-up, bypass, add, subtract, lighten, repeat, thicken, stretch, extrude, repel, protect, segregate, integrate, symbolize, abstract and dissect.

Stanford University engineer James Adams[14] suggests thinking up your own favorite "bug list"—the things that irritate you—to start you thinking. And he lists among his own: corks that break off in wine bottles, vending machines that take your money with no return, bumper stickers that cannot be removed, crooked billiard cue sticks, paperless toilets, dripping faucets and "one sock". "If you run out of bugs before ten minutes," says Adams, "you are either suffering from a perceptual or emotional block or have life unusually under control."

Another technique is to focus on 1,000 percent breakthroughs. What can you do ten times faster, better, cheaper? What is the "killer application" in your field: the big "Aha!" that can take your company, your school or your industry to new peaks of excellence? That's what Microsoft has achieved in computer software; what Netscape has done in Internet browsers; what Canon has achieved in color copiers.

Given the tremendous increase in technology, in almost any field 1,000 per cent improvements are possible: in some operations. Learning to typeset magazine advertisements and newspapers, for instance, once took a six-year apprenticeship. To "makeup" pages took five years of training. Today, with desktop computerized publishing, any competent typist can compress much of that 11-year training into a week. What would it take to achieve similar breakthroughs in your field?

At the other extreme, *if you learn only one word of Japanese in your life, make it Kaizen. It means continuous improvement.* But it means much more than that. *It means a philosophy that encourages every*

A hexagon
Kaizen
Think Kit

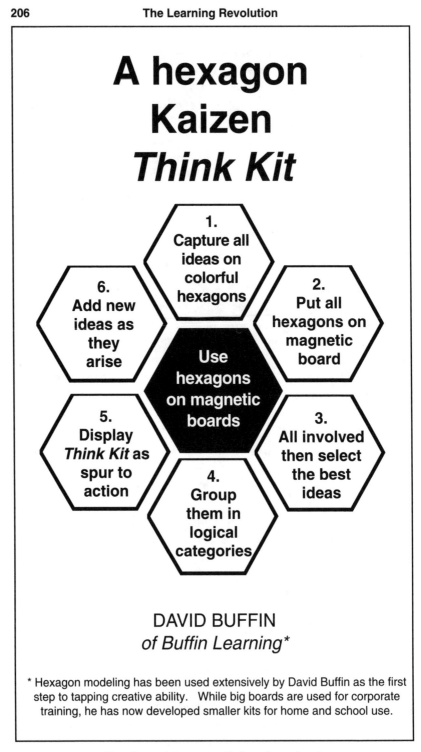

DAVID BUFFIN
of Buffin Learning*

* Hexagon modeling has been used extensively by David Buffin as the first
step to tapping creative ability.   While big boards are used for corporate
training, he has now developed smaller kits for home and school use.

person in an industry—every day—to come up with suggestions for improving everything: themselves, their job, their lunchroom, their office layout, their telephone answering habits and their products.

Says Toyota Motor chairman Eiji Toyoda: "One of the features of the Japanese workers is that they use their brains as well as their hands. Our workers provide 1.5 million suggestions a year, and 95 per cent of them are put to practical use."[15] And at Nissan Motors "any suggestion that saves at least 0.6 seconds—the time it takes a worker to stretch out his hand or walk half a step—is seriously considered by management."[16]

Matsushita, the giant Japanese electronics company, receives about 6.5 million ideas every year from its staff.[17] And the big majority are put into operation quickly.

It is beyond the scope of this book to cover the total secret of Japan's Total Quality Management and Kaizen movements. But to test, in part, the effectiveness of their method, try an introductory *Kaizen* on anything you're involved in. One excellent method is to use David Buffin's hexagon *Think Kit.* Staff or students are encouraged to fire in new ideas. The teacher or facilitator writes each on a colored magnetic hexagon and attaches the hexagons to a large magnetic board. The group then arranges the hexagons around various themes or activities, and agrees on the main priorities. These are then left on display as a continual spur to agreed action (see diagram opposite).

For business we prefer to marry the two methods together: to look for the big *Aha!* idea for strategic planning (what is the really big breakthrough that will change the future of your company or industry?) and *Kaizen* (how can you involve all your staff in continuously striving to upgrade every aspect of that performance?). In oversimplified terms, many would describe *Aha!* as the key to American business success, and *Kaizen* as the Japanese secret weapon. Their "marriage" is *The Third Way.* And an excellent way to display them is on another David Buffin innovation, the arrowed action kit (see illustration next page): again a good permanent and colorful visible reminder of agreed goals and actions.

Many universities, of course, would say they have always taught thinking as part of logic, psychology and philosophy. But most schools don't teach what Edward de Bono[18] has termed *lateral thinking:* the ability to open-mindedly search for new ideas, look in new directions.

Roger von Oech thinks even the terms logical and lateral thinking are

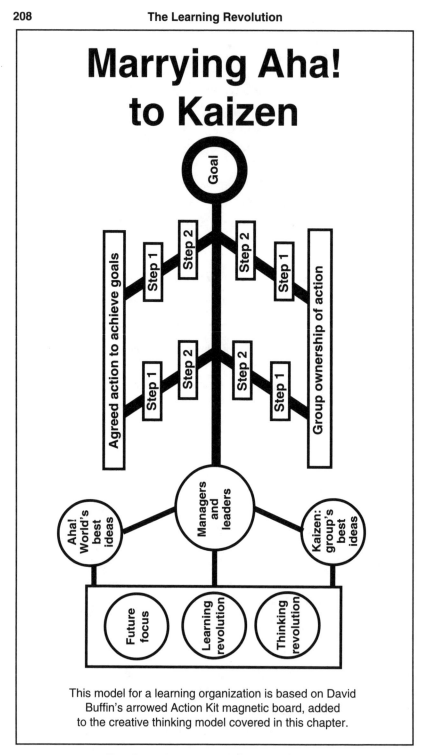

Marrying Aha! to Kaizen

This model for a learning organization is based on David Buffin's arrowed Action Kit magnetic board, added to the creative thinking model covered in this chapter.

too restrictive. He says we're also capable of conceptual thinking, analytical thinking, speculative thinking, right-brain thinking, critical thinking, foolish thinking, convergent thinking, weird thinking, reflective thinking, visual thinking, symbolic thinking, propositional thinking, digital thinking, metaphorical thinking, mythical thinking, poetic thinking, nonverbal thinking, elliptical thinking, analogical thinking, lyrical thinking, practical thinking, divergent thinking, ambiguous thinking, constructive thinking, thinking about thinking, surreal thinking, focused thinking, concrete thinking and fantasy thinking.[19]

But most people unwittingly limit their thinking potential. One reason is the brain's ability to file material inside existing patterns. When a new problem is tackled, we're conditioned to go down the track of previous answers. We all have preconceptions, taboos and prejudices, though few of us ever admit to them. They can be emotional, cultural, religious, educational, national, psychological, sexual or culinary.

We are also preconditioned from school to come up with "the right answer"—not the open-minded challenge for a better way. Almost every adult who has succeeded at high school or college will have firm ideas on the best educational system. And it will generally be the system that he succeeded in. Listen to anyone praise a "good school" and you will almost certainly find a school that suits that particular person's learning style.

Now that's not unusual. You could probably go through life and never find a person totally objective about everything. And fortunately no one system of education, or religion, or health, suits all. So perhaps the first step in "conceptual blockbusting"—to use James Adams' term[20]—is to accept that we all have fears, we all have biases. The best way we know to start overcoming them is to combine fun and humor. That often works for students in particular. A fun-filled atmosphere can lead to high creativity.

If you're not used to "far-out" brainstorming sessions, probably a good warm-up exercise is to start with a humorous challenge. Try inventing a new golfball—one that can't get lost. Or planning what you'd do with a holiday on the moon or underwater. Or ask some "What if?" questions. Like what would happen if pets became school teachers? Or if computers ran the government? Then use some of de Bono's techniques, such as PMI, CAF, C&S, APC and his "Six Thinking Hats."[21]

PMI standards for Plus, Minus and Interesting. Here the students

Do a "PMI" on this proposition:

That all teaching should be done by computers

Write three separate columns,
one headed Plus, one Minus
and one Interesting.

Now list all the "plus" points
(All study could be
interactive; you'd get
instant feedback)

Then all the "minuses"
(No personal relationships;
and how could a computer be
a field-trip guide?)

Then all the "interesting" ideas
that occur to you
(How would a computer handle
discipline? How would a
computer be paid?
Could you make computer study
a joint venture between
home and school?)

PMI is one of Edward de Bono's
suggestions for teaching thinking.

are asked to choose a fairly outlandish statement, and in three columns write down all the points they can think of to be "plus" factors, then all the "minuses," and lastly all the reasons the proposition could be "interesting."

CAF means Consider All Factors. And again write them down, searching for new factors that don't spring immediately to mind.

C & S stands for Consequences and Sequel. Logically, both should be listed under CAF, but de Bono says that most people just do not consider all the consequences unless their attention is specifically drawn to them.

APC stands for Alternatives, Possibilities and Choices. And again the reasons are obvious: a list that encourages you to speculate.

As de Bono summarizes one of his other techniques: "The theme of my book *Six Thinking Hats* is simple. There is the white hat for neutral facts, figures and information. There is the red hat to allow a person to put forward feelings, hunches and intuitions—without any need to justify them. The black hat is for the logical negative, and the yellow hat for the logical positive. For creativity there is the green hat. The blue hat is the control hat, and looks at the thinking itself rather than at the subject—like an orchestra conductor controlling the orchestra. The purpose is to provide a means for rapidly switching thinkers from one mode to another—without causing offence." [22]

All are excellent techniques. Especially the "six hats"—when you go to the trouble to obtain some bizarre models, in colors and odd shapes, and pass them around so each person can act the part.*

But the simple ideas we have suggested earlier in this chapter are the ones we have found to work effectively in virtually any situation: in advertising, business, marketing, selling, exporting, market research and all aspects of learning and education. They work, we believe, because they show the logical links between sequential and creative thinking. Your critical "left-brain" logic sees the common-sense in the step-by-step link-up to the "right-brain's" creative ability.

They start, of course, by tapping into the outstanding power of the brain. And the brain's potential, as we'll turn to next, is grounded in processing which goes back to the start of life—even before birth itself.

* A restaurant in Sydney, Australia, has all its main walls covered with amusing hats. Each customer chooses one on arrival—and it sets the tone for an hilarious evening, as each diner fits into an acting role.

Checklist for new mothers

 1 Most of the active brain cells a child will ever have are present by birth.

 2 A well-nourished fetus during pregnancy will develop an average of 250,000 new brain cells every minute.

 3 Smoking, alcohol and drugs can severely affect that brain-growth.

 4 Poor diet during vital periods can cause lifelong learning disabilities.

 5 Eat plenty of fish, green-leaf vegetables, fruit, nuts and vegetable oil.

 6 Have a banana a day when pregnant, for potassium and folic acid.

 7 Iron- and zinc-rich foods are essential for baby's brain-growth.

 8 Breast-feed if possible—to add the vital "coating" to the main brain cells.

 9 After birth, make sure to get baby's hearing and eyesight checked regularly.

A sensible guide to producing better, brighter babies

Your body is more fascinating than any machine.

Every day about two million of its cells wear out. But the body replaces them automatically.

Every 15 to 30 days your body completely replaces the outermost layer of your skin. What you see in the mirror today is not the same skin you had a month ago.

But some cells your body will never replace: the 100 billion active nerve cells, or neurons, that make up your brain's cortex.[1]

Every one of them was present the day you were born. In your mother's womb you were growing them at an average of 250,000 cells every minute.

Each one continues to grow in size over the first few years of life. Each one, as we've seen, is capable of sprouting up to 20,000 dendrites. But after birth you never gain another *cortical* neuron as long as you live.*

What happens to each brain in the nine months before birth is therefore vital to later learning ability. When pregnant women are severely undernourished, their children can be born with fewer than half the brain cells of a healthy child.

As we've seen, neurons are not the only cells in the brain. We each have up to 900 billion *glial* cells to nourish the neurons. These glial cells also develop *myelin,* the sheathing that wraps around our *axons* . These are the nerve pathways that speed messages from neuron to neuron and

---

* *You do, however, grow new brain cells in the cerebellum, the "little brain" that plays such a big part in storing "muscle memory"; hence the vital importance of learning by doing.*

213

Within the next minute an average of 250,000 brain cells will have multiplied in each and every well-nourished growing fetus in the world.

RICHARD M. RESTAK
The Infant Mind*

*Published by Doubleday & Company, 666 Fifth Avenue, New York, NY 10103.

around our bodies—like electrical transmission wires. Both of these cell groups start growing in the womb, and continue during the first few years of life.

If the baby is poorly fed in those vital early years, it will not produce all the nourishing glial cells it needs. *And if some foods are missing from the expectant mother's diet, the nerve pathways around the brain and body will not be efficiently insulated.*

As American researchers Brian and Roberta Morgan put it in their highly-recommended book *Brain Food:* "The human brain begins growing in the womb, and the majority of this development does not slow down until the age of six. Growth in the brain of the fetus, infant and young child is time-dependent. This means that the brain grows in specific stages at specific times. If it does not have all the nutrients essential for its growth at those times, damage or malformation can result which cannot be corrected at a later date. A developing infant who is fed poorly during its period of brain growth may be left with learning disabilities which will remain for the rest of its life, no matter what is done at a later date to correct the nutritional deficiency."

Scottish Professor Michael Crawford sums up ten years of research into the impact of nutrition on infant and fetal brain growth: "Wherever we've found low birth-weight babies, small head circumference and intellectual deficits in infants, we've found that right across the board the mothers concerned had diets before and during pregnancy that were deficient in a large number of nutrients."[2]

Even in developed societies such as Britain, the United States and New Zealand, at least ten percent of babies continue to arrive with low birth-weights. Generally that results from the mother's poor diet, smoking, taking drugs or being affected by toxic substances such as lead.

Crawford is amazed at the lack of education on diet and nutrition. And he says poor diet before birth affects more than the brain. Seven separate studies indicate that later heart problems, high blood pressure and many strokes have their roots in poor diet before birth.

One of the major deficiencies is fat. But a special kind of fat. "Unfortunately," says Crawford, "we've come to think of fat as lard and dripping. *But what the fetus really needs is a highly specialized fat— the essential fats we call them. They're the fats you need to build cells, especially brain cells, and not the sort of fats that animals and humans dump on their waistlines.*

If a pregnant woman smokes one cigarette, her fetus will stop breathing for five minutes.

RICHARD M. RESTAK
The Infant Mind*

*Published by Doubleday & Company, 666 Fifth Avenue,
New York, NY10103.

"Many of those fats come from marine life. Now of course it's an old wives' tale that fish is good for the brain. It happens to be that we now have absolute scientific evidence for this. *We find that the fats found in fish and seafood of all sorts are especially relevant to the growth and development of the brain." And those same fats are vital for developing the body's immune system.*

They are also needed to build and maintain the myelin insulation.

Crawford wishes everyone would return to "the unsophisticated foods of nature": plenty of green leafy vegetables, fruit, nuts and vegetable oil.

If Crawford and his dietician, Wendy Dole, could get one message through to every potential mother in the world, it would be simply this: *the most important time for your child's brain-growth is before you become pregnant.*

Women who have used oral contraceptives should be especially careful of their diet before pregnancy. "The pill" reduces your body's stores of pyridoxine (one of the B vitamins) and folacin or folic acid, a vitamin needed for neural development. Severe folic acid deficiencies can cause serious malformations of the brain and other organs.

Crawford says pregnant women in particular should include bananas in their regular daily diet. "Not only are they a good source of potassium, they also contain good supplies of folic acid."

Zinc and iron are minerals essential for early brain growth. Where pregnant monkeys have been fed a diet low in zinc, their infants later play less with others, act withdrawn and have difficulty learning complex tasks. Iron is needed for all cell growth and multiplication. It also influences the oxygen supply to the blood.

Most dietary experts say that a simple, sensible diet is best before and during pregnancy: three meals a day, plenty of fruit, vegetables, nuts, fish and lean meat. An iron supplement during pregnancy is highly recommended. The diet should be high in foods that are rich in iron and zinc, such as beans, peas, broccoli, carrots, whole wheat bread, berries and brown rice. And don't try any special diets to keep you slim.

The other "no-no's" during pregnancy? "Smoking, alcohol and drugs,"[3] says New York researcher Ian James, Professor of Paediatrics, Obstetrics and Gynecology at Columbia University's Presbyterian Medical Center. *He says "for every one cigarette the mother smokes, the baby smokes two". Smoking starves the fetal brain of oxygen—at a time when oxygen is vital for cell formation.*

Drugs are most dangerous to the fetus during the first three months of pregnancy, when the heart, brain, limbs and facial features are forming.

The Reader's Digest Body Book*

*Published by The Reader's Digest.

Pregnant women who smoke 15 to 20 cigarettes a day are twice as likely to miscarry as nonsmoking mothers. In the first few weeks after birth, smokers' infants die at a rate 30 percent higher than nonsmokers' infants. Babies also absorb poisonous nicotine through breast milk. And they are later more prone to respiratory infections, and they also have a higher rate of pneumonia.

Alcohol can also damage the growing brain. Heavy drinking can cause what has become known as "fetal alcohol syndrome", which results in reduced brain size, distorted facial features, poor coordination and hyperactive behavior.

James describes the effects of cocaine or heroin as devastating, especially for young pregnant women and their babies. Educational psychologist Jane M. Healy, of Vail, Colorado, says research estimates show that at least one of every nine babies born in the United States is drug-affected. "Many authorities warn," she adds, "that growing cocaine use by pregnant women will soon flood the schools with children who have attention, learning and social problems. And these children are not even included in our already declining test scores."[4]

Because of the caffeine content, heavy coffee and tea-drinking during pregnancy is also not recommended.

After birth, diet is still vital for all cell growth. And the importance of myelination cannot be stressed too much. Some of it is in place before birth: around the nerve pathways that enable a newborn baby to suck, cry and move its fingers. But at birth the pathways needed for walking, talking and bladder control are not yet myelinated.

"Common sense tells us that it is useless to try and get a newborn to walk alone," says Healy, "but at about one year, when those connections have myelinated, it may be difficult to prevent."

About 75 percent of myelin comes from fat—from what Crawford calls "essential fats." And the other 25 percent comes from protein. Breast feeding by a healthy mother is the best source of both. And of zinc, which is also vital to form glial cells. Breast milk also contains specific antibodies which coat the baby's intestines and respiratory tract and fight off infection. It also helps protect the baby from ear infections, eczema and other allergies. And it provides calcium and phosphorous needed for rapidly growing bones. In fact, the only thing lacking in a healthy mother's breast milk could be vitamin D. That's why many doctors recommend a vitamin D supplement. A well-balanced milk

Conception can be impaired when women consume more than 300 mg. of caffeine a day. That's 3 cups of coffee, 6 cups of tea or more than 7 sodas.

USA Today*

December 19, 1995.

"formula" can also be used in place of breast milk—but it must be one that tries to duplicate the essential elements of mothers' milk.

All this sounds like elementary common sense. But many mothers can't cope without some form of help. And around ten percent of mothers, even in developed countries, are at "high risk".

Researchers at the Otago University School of Medicine in New Zealand, for instance, have completed a ten-year study of women having babies at the nearby Dunedin maternity hospital. Before a baby is born, hospital staff ask the mothers some simple questions, such as age, marital status, employment and home addresses over the previous year. And the figures have been consistent year by year: 78 percent of mothers can cope adequately. But 22 percent need some form of help. And nine percent of all babies are considered high risk.[5] They could be seriously abused or maltreated unless their mothers are helped.

It's not hard to identify the risk factors: young, single mothers, moving around a lot. No job. Parents who've already split up. A history of foster homes. Maybe a background of drugs. Mother suffered parental violence as a child.

Unfortunately, a similar pattern exists in many countries. The United States has 22 million children under six.[6] Five million of these are living in poverty and about two and a half million are just above the poverty line.[7] And guess who'll be the educational failures of the new century unless that poverty trap is broken?

That's why we've listed parent education and early childhood health programs as vital first priorities in any sensible education system.

Many research projects show the vital connection between nutrition and other brain-developing activities in the first five years of life.

Ideally most early brain development happens in sequence. A child learns to see before it learns to talk. It learns to crawl and creep before it walks. Walks before it runs. Learns to identify simple objects before it learns to reason. If an infant misses out on one of those steps—like walking without ever crawling or creeping—learning problems can result. To use computer terms, that's because the early activities lay down the "hard-wiring" or "hardware" of the brain—in a set sequence. When the hardware is in first-class condition, it can be used to "run" any software program: like learning a foreign language or a new subject. But if any of the "hard-wiring" has been skipped, the brain could have difficulty running some programs.

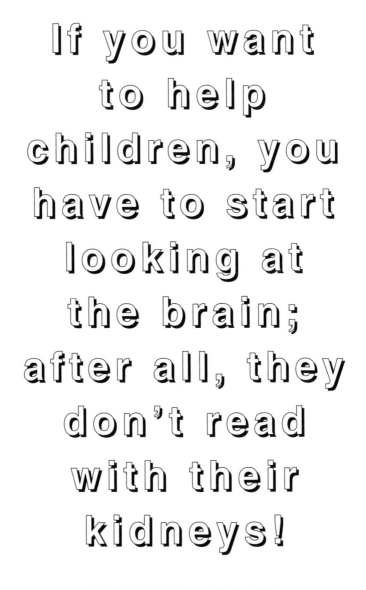

If you want to help children, you have to start looking at the brain; after all, they don't read with their kidneys!

DR. DEBORAH WABER
of Harvard University*

*Quoted by Jane M. Healy, in *Endangered Minds,*
published by Simon & Schuster, 1230 Avenue of the Americas,
New York, NY 10020.

The early-development timetable is set in part by the sequence of myelination. A thin spiral of sheathing around axons is present at birth, but the full insulation is then laid down around the body, and the brain, in sequence. Overall, in the body that starts at the top and works down. That's why you can make sounds before you learn to walk—the long axons transmitting messages to your toes and calf-muscles take longer to coat than the axons to your tongue and larynx.

In the brain, full myelination starts at the back and moves to the front. That's why you learn to see before you learn to talk and reason: your optical nerve-center is at the back of the brain, your speech-center is further forward, and your reasoning-center is at the front. The process is completed in the center of the brain—what some scientists call the "association cortex": the part you use to sort incoming information and blend it with data already in your storage files.

When axons are fully covered by their myelin sheath, they can transmit messages around the body up to 12 times faster than they could before. In fact, the speed of transmission around the body can vary from one mile an hour to 150 miles.[8]

Just as the fetus grows in spurts, so does the new infant brain. And the timing of those bursts can be vital.

Close one eye of a two-year-old for as little as a week, for instance, and you will almost certainly damage its ability to see. This is because the growing brain is laying down its main visual pathways from the eyes to the vision-center at the rear of the brain. The two separate pathways are competing for dominance. Shut one eye for any length of time and the other one will lay down the dominant pathway. Close one eye for a week when you're 20 and it won't matter, because by then your basic pathways have been laid down.

Says Stanford University human biology professor Robert Ornstein: "The critical period during which the two eyes establish their zones of dominance seems to be about the first six years in humans, six months in monkeys, and perhaps three months in cats. It is a very sensitive period. If one eye of a kitten is kept closed for only one day, it will have poor vision in that eye as an adult.

"There is a very important practical lesson from this basic work on the visual brain. Do not ever keep *one* eye of a human infant closed for an extended period of time. Keeping both eyes closed is better; after all, infants sleep a good bit of the time."[9]

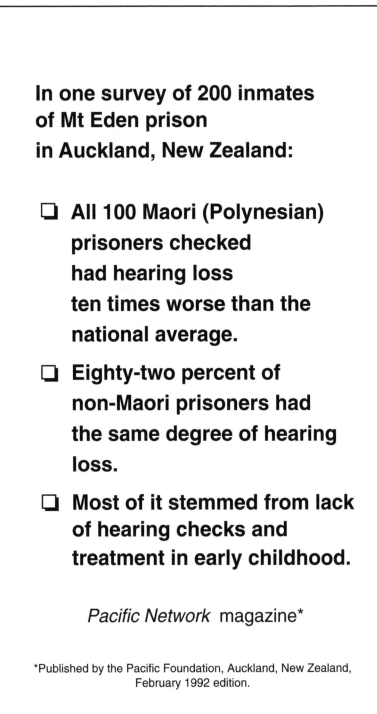

In one survey of 200 inmates
of Mt Eden prison
in Auckland, New Zealand:

❏ All 100 Maori (Polynesian)
prisoners checked
had hearing loss
ten times worse than the
national average.

❏ Eighty-two percent of
non-Maori prisoners had
the same degree of hearing
loss.

❏ Most of it stemmed from lack
of hearing checks and
treatment in early childhood.

Pacific Network magazine*

*Published by the Pacific Foundation, Auckland, New Zealand,
February 1992 edition.

It is the same with hearing. Your inner ear is no bigger than a small nut, but it contains as many circuits as the telephone system of many cities. The ear also contains another tiny vital structure called a cochlea. It looks like a snail shell and works like a piano keyboard. But a piano has only 88 keys, while the cochlea has 20,000 hairlike sensory cells which pick up sound impulses and transmit them to the brain.

The whole intricate hearing mechanism is obviously vital for learning language. As with sight, the basic language pathways are also laid down in the first few years of life. English-language dialects, for example, have only beween 40 and 44 different sounds. And all the world's main languages about 70. Hear all those sounds clearly in the vital first few years of life, learn to pronounce and use them, and you'll be able to pronounce other languages much better if you learn them later in life.

Most healthy children in a well-rounded environment also learn to speak fluently at least the 2,000 basic words of their language in the first four years of life. But if they can't hear, they'll find it much more difficult to speak fluently. And if they can't hear or speak, they'll have difficulty learning. Several surveys in New Zealand, for instance, found 20 percent of preschool children with hearing problems in one ear, and ten percent with severe hearing loss in both.[10]

That's just one more reason that the most effective early childhood development programs include regular hearing and sight checks, along with major attention to nutrition and parent education.

We are indeed what we eat—and what our mothers ate. We are also very much the result of what we do and what we think. And just as the right nutrition and exercise can provide the nourishment for a young brain's "nerve highways" and developing dendrite branches, so the right activity, involving all five senses, can produce more dendritic connections. All future learning will be based on those connections—and the early nourishment that went into their development.

All the best educational programs around the world combine elements that stimulate both a child's physical and mental development— for in truth there is no split between the two.

We are all a combination of what we eat, think and do. And, after good care in the nine months before birth, the best programs concentrate next on the most vital years of life: from birth to ten.

How to make the most of the vital years: from birth to ten

❏ Fifty percent of a person's ability to learn is developed in the first four years of life.

❏ Another 30 percent is developed by the eighth birthday.

❏ Those vital years lay down the pathways on which all future learning is based.

❏ After age ten, the branches that haven't made connections die off.

❏ Youngsters are their own best educators, parents their best first teachers.

❏ Youngsters learn best by what they experience with all their senses, so stimulate these senses.

❏ Our homes, beaches, forests, play grounds, zoos, museums and adventure areas are the world's best schools.

❏ Simple physical routines can help infants explode into learning.

❏ Infants grow in a patterned way, so learn to build on that growth pattern.

❏ Learning anything, including reading, writing and math, can and should be fun.

How to enrich your child's intelligence from birth to ten

Every country's educational priorities are completely back to front.

Researchers have proved beyond doubt that you develop around 50 percent of your ability to learn in the first four years of life. And you develop another 30 percent of that ability before you turn eight.[1]

This does not mean that you absorb 50 percent of your *knowledge* or 50 percent of your *wisdom* or 50 percent of your *intelligence* by your fourth birthday. It simply means that in those first few years you form the main learning pathways in your brain. Everything else you learn in life will be built on that base. You also take in a fantastic amount of information in those early years. And all later learning will grow from that core.

Yet nearly every country spends well under ten percent of its educational budget on the years where 50 percent of development takes place.

Says British psychologist Tony Buzan: "At the moment a child is born it's already really brilliant. It picks up language, much better than a doctor of philosophy in any subject, in only two years. And it is a master at it by three or four."[2]

Buzan says every child born, unless it has severe brain damage, is a budding genius. He demonstrates that early built-in urge to learn with a piece of paper. "Imagine I am now a three-month-old baby," he smiles. "You've given me this piece of paper. You know it's not going to last long. Now do I do it like this? (He mimes a small child looking passively at the paper and then ignoring it.) Or do I do it like this?" (He then tries to tear the paper, crumple it, rattle it, and even stuff it in his mouth.) "It's obviously the second way. And what that little baby was doing was being

Male and female brain differences

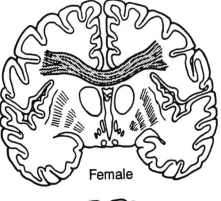

Female

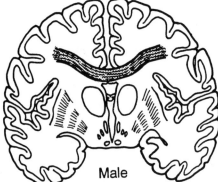

Male

Baby girls generally develop their corpus callosum
(the shaded area in the brain at top)
earlier than boys (same area in lower brain).
Girls generally develop language skills faster than boys,
but boys seem to develop distance vision
and space perception better than most girls,
giving them an advantage at some sports.

Illustrations from *The Learning Brain,*
by Eric Jensen, published by Turning Point for Teachers,
P.O. Box 2551, Del Mar, CA 92014, USA.

a little Isaac Newton—the perfect scientist. What kind of musical instrument can I make from this material (shaking it)? What is the sociological, economic value of this material (putting it in his mouth)? Anybody want some (offering it around)? What is the engineering, mechanical, tensile strength of the material (pulling it apart)? Stick it in the chemical laboratory (chewing it)? Check the musical instrument— and on to the next experiment. Now the baby is using all of its brain. Logic? Yes. Analysis? Yes. Rhythm? Yes. Everything? Yes."

Scientists have tested this infant ability in many ways. In 1964, Benjamin S. Bloom, Professor of Education at the University of Chicago, published a summary of major research findings. In it, he studied five main human characteristics between birth and age 17 and 18: height, general learning ability, school achievement, aggressiveness in males and dependence in females.[3]

Overwhelmingly, he found that development soared in the first few years—then tapered off. Generally it reached its halfway point before the fifth birthday. He found boys reached 54 percent of their maximum height by their third birthday, another 32 percent between three and 12, and the last 14 percent by the 18th birthday.

He also concluded that among both girls and boys, about 50 percent of intelligence, as measured in tests at 17, took place between conception and age four, about 30 percent between four and eight, and the final 20 percent between the ages of eight and 17. Even researchers who question the validity of standardized intelligence tests would probably endorse this overall finding—so long as the words *learning ability* are substituted for *intelligence.*

Bloom also analyzed vocabulary, reading comprehension and general school achievement between birth and age 18. This convinced him that 33 percent of an 18-year-old's academic skills are achieved by age six, 42 percent between six and 13, and 25 percent between 13 and 18.

Since Bloom's study, much other research has shown, however, that several differences between male and female brains do show up early in life.

The corpus callosum in baby girls, for instance, is generally thicker than in boys. This helps most girls to read earlier than boys. Generally girls speak earlier and learn languages more quickly. Males seem to have better distance vision and depth perception than females, making them more adept at certain sports.[4]

If I had my child to raise over again

If I had my child to raise all over again,
I'd finger paint more, and point the finger less.
I'd do less correcting, and more connecting.
I'd take my eyes off my watch,
    and watch with my eyes.
I would care to know less,
    and know to care more.
I'd take more hikes, and fly more kites.
I'd stop playing serious, and seriously play.
I'd run through more fields, and gaze at more stars.
I'd do more hugging, and less tugging.
I would be firm less often, and affirm much more.
I'd build self-esteem first, and the house later.
I'd teach less about the love of power,
And more about the power of love.

DIANE LOOMANS
Full Esteem Ahead*

* Published by Kramer, Tuburton, California.

Two of the most thorough analyses since Bloom's have been done in the South Island of New Zealand. The first is through the Otago University School of Medicine in Dunedin, a city of around 100,000 people. In 1972, 1,661 babies were born in Dunedin. Their progress has been checked regularly ever since. And more than 1,000 of them are still being surveyed.

Research director Dr. Phil Silva says that the survey underlines the vital importance of the first few years of life.[5] "That doesn't mean that the other years are unimportant, but our research shows that children who have a slow start during the first three years are likely to experience problems right through childhood and into adolescence."

He says it's also vital to identify any special problems in the first three years, such as hearing or eyesight defects, "because if we don't help them at the early stages then it's likely that they are going to experience long-lasting problems throughout their lives".

The other survey has checked the progress of 1,206 infants born in the city of Christchurch in 1977. One of its key findings: between 15 and 20 percent of youngsters fall behind because they don't get the necessary early-childhood health-checks and developmental experience.[6]

Buzan agrees. "Make sure that the child, from as early as possible, gets as much exercise as its wants, with as much of a free body as possible: hands free, feet free, able to crawl a lot, climb a lot. Allow it to make its own mistakes so that it learns by its own trial and error."

There are six main pathways into the brain, the five senses of sight, hearing, touch, taste and smell, and the sixth step of what we do physically. Youngsters obviously learn through all the senses. Every day is a learning experience. They love to experiment, to create, to find out how things work. Challenges are there to be accepted. Adults to be imitated.

Most important, a child learns by doing. He learns to crawl by crawling. He learns to walk by walking. To talk by talking. And each time he does so he either lays down new pathways in the brain—if his experience is new—or he builds on and expands existing pathways—if he is repeating the experience.

Youngsters are their own best educators, parents their best first teachers. And our homes, beaches, forests, playgrounds, adventure areas and the whole wide world our main educational resources—as long as children are encouraged to explore them safely through all their senses.

Researchers stress the need for positive encouragement. Says British

The unstimulated and stimulated brain

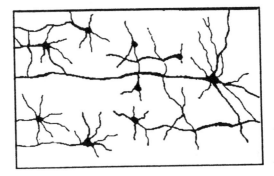

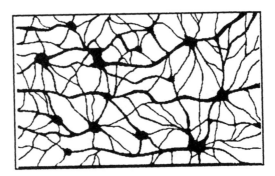

**At top: a model of an unstimulated brain, with few interacting connections.
Lower: a young brain rich in connections, from stimulating activities.**

These illustrations have been adapted from
Professor Marian Diamond's book
Enriching Heredity, published
by Macmillan, New York.

accelerated learning pioneer Colin Rose: "It's true throughout life that if you think you are a poor learner, you'll probably be a poor learner." But the real question is how that thought pattern is programmed. American research has shown that most children, from a very early age, receive at least six negative comments to every one of positive encouragement.[7] Comments like "Don't do that," or "You didn't do that very well," are where the problem starts.

Research has also established beyond doubt the importance of every child growing in an enriched environment.

Berkeley scientists in California have been experimenting for many years with rats—and comparing their brain growth with humans. "Very simply," says Professor Marian Diamond, "we've found with our rats that all the nerve cells in the key outer layers of the brain are present at birth. At birth the interconnecting dendrites start to grow. For the first month the growth is prolific. Then it starts to go down.

"If we put the rats in enriched environments, we can keep the dendrite growth up. But if we put them in impoverished environments, then dendrite growth goes down fast.

"In enrichment cages, rats live together and have access to toys. They have ladders, wheels and other playthings. They can climb, explore and interact with their toys. Then we compare them with rats in impoverished environments: one rat to a cage, no toys, no interaction. Again very simply: we've found that the rat brain cells increase in size in the enriched environment—and the number of dendrites increases dramatically. In the impoverished environment, the opposite."

The rats then take an "intelligence test": they're put in a maze, and left to find food in another part of the maze. The "enriched" rats do so easily. The others don't.

Obviously, scientists can't cut up human brains to test the impact of early stimulation. But they can check with radioactive glucose. "And these checks," says Diamond, "show that the vital glucose uptake is extremely rapid for the first two years of life—provided the child has a good diet and adequate stimulation. It continues rapidly until five years. It continues very slowly from five to ten. By about ten years of age, brain-growth has reached its peak—although the good news is this: the human brain can keep on growing dendrites till the end of life, so long as it is being stimulated. Very simply, the human brain cell, like the rat's, is designed to receive stimulation—and to grow from it."

Even 15 minutes of rocking, rubbing, rolling and stroking a premature baby four times a day will greatly help its ability to coordinate movements and therefore to learn.

RUTH RICE*

*Summarized from her dissertation, *The Effects of Tactile-Kinesthetic Stimulation on the Subsequent Development of Premature Infants*, University of Texas (1975).

That doesn't mean turning an infant's home into a formal school classroom. The reverse, in fact: infants learn by play and exploration. It's the formal classroom that needs redesigning.

"We used to think that play and education were opposite things," say Jean Marzollo and Janice Lloyd in their excellent book *Learning Through Play.* "Now we know better. Educational experts and early childhood specialists have discovered that play *is* learning, and even more, that play is one of the most effective kinds of learning."

The key: turning play into learning experiences—and making sure that most learning is fun.

In fact, activities that good parents take for granted provide some of the best early learning. But we don't mean "academic" studies. *Scientists have proved, for instance, that regularly rocking a baby can help greatly in promoting brain growth.* It stimulates what they call *the vestibular system.* This is a nerve-system centered in the brainstem and linked very closely with the cerebellum and a baby's inner-ear mechanism, which also plays a vital part in developing balance and coordination. Scientists say this is one of the first parts of the brain to begin to function in the womb—as early as 16 weeks after conception.

"It is this early maturity that makes the vestibular system so important to early brain development," says Richard M. Restak, M.D., author of *The Brain: The Last Frontier* and *The Infant Mind.* "The fetus floating in its amniotic fluid registers its earliest perceptions via the activity of its vestibular system. In recent years evidence has accumulated that the vestibular system is crucial for normal brain development. Infants who are given periodic vestibular stimulation, by rocking, gain weight faster, develop vision and hearing earlier, and demonstrate distinct sleep cycles at a younger age." [8]

Dr. Ruth Rice, of Texas, has shown in controlled tests that *even 15 minutes of rocking, rubbing, rolling and stroking a premature baby four times a day will greatly help its ability to coordinate movements and therefore to learn.* [9]

And Dr. Lyelle Palmer, Professor of Education at Winona State University in Minnesota, has completed extensive studies at kindergarten level* to demonstrate the vital importance of such simple stimulation for five-year-olds. [10] Every day youngsters have attended a gymnasium as a

* In the United States, kindergarten starts at age five. In New Zealand and some other countries, it is for children aged three and four.

Helicopter spin

For ages three years and above, provided they can walk and run

Have children stand and extend their hands out from the sides of their bodies.

Invite them to spin as fast as possible,* in a standing position, for 15 seconds. Say: "We are helicopters flying to the airport." Play loud music while spinning.

Then say: "STOP and close your eyes. Keep your balance. Remain standing." (Do not say: "Don't fall down." Emphasize what to do, not what not to do.) The children stand for 25 seconds until they no longer feel dizzy. The process is then repeated.

Spin ten times. This will take about five minutes. Spin 15 seconds, rest 15 seconds, spin 15 seconds and so on. Speed is important. It keeps the ear fluid moving.

Eventually children will spin with eyes closed, opening them occasionally in order to check on safety. (Do not spin one way and then immediately spin the other way because it is important that the fluid in the semicircular canals of the ear keeps moving. When you start spinning the other way, the fluid movement stops and stimulation is reduced.)

For children having difficulty, the adult stands over the child and assists by grasping one hand and quickly pulling the child's arm around the body and to create a continuous spinning action.

This is one of the routines used by Professor Lyelle Palmer with great success to improve the learning ability of young children.

Mats and Irene Niklasson, of Vestibularis, in Sweden, have children do this exercise by spinning much slower than Professor Palmer recommends—but, they say, with similar beneficial results.

key part of early schooling. There they are encouraged to carry out a simple series of routines: spinning, rope jumping, balancing, somersaulting, rolling and walking on balance beams. In the playground, they are encouraged to swing on low "jungle gyms", climb, skate, perform somersaults and flips. And in classrooms they play with a wide range of games, also designed to stimulate their sense of sight, hearing and touch. All activities are designed to increase in skill-level during the year, and thus help stimulate ever-increasing brain development.

At the end of each year, many of the children undergo the Metropolitan Readiness Test to measure whether they've developed enough to start first-grade schooling. Nearly all have passed the tests in the top ten percent for the state—and most have been in the top five percent. Nearly all of them come from working-class backgrounds.

Palmer, a former president of the Society for Accelerative Learning and Teaching, emphasizes that the children are not simply walking, running and skipping—the normal "motor" activities. "The stimulation activities we recommend," he says, "are specifically designed to activate the areas of the brain we know will promote their sense of sight, touch and hearing—as well as their ability to take in knowledge."[11]

Most parents, for instance, seem to learn instinctively that infants love to be held firmly by their hands and spun around like a helicopter blade. Palmer's Minneapolis public school research at New Vision School has shown that such activities result in important brain growth. And the greater the intensity of the activity the greater you see the results of the brain-growth in areas that are receptive to further learning.

The overall result is a big gain in competence and self-confidence, increased attention, faster responses and the ability to tackle learning activities of increasing complexity.

Palmer stresses that the activities are not what many schools would regard as "academic." But any classroom visit shows the youngsters "exploding" into true learning. Early reading is taught with word-card games. The youngsters get an early introduction to mathematics by playing with dominoes and big cards with dots instead of numbers. And they play games to develop pre-writing skills.

Does it help "academic development"? You bet! In another study of at-risk youngsters who were not doing well at school, Palmer's methods produced dramatic gains in reading ability. The children of the experimental group read three to ten times faster than the control group.[12]

How physical activity builds a child's mental abilities

What a child does *physically* in the first few years of life plays a major part in how well he or she will develop other abilities. Here's a simple model of how it works:

1. The instinctive reptilian brain

The activity:		Leads to:
Grasping	Touching	Hand-eye coordination
Crawling	Arm-leg	Big-motor skills
Walking	movements	Prewriting ability
Reaching	Pushing	
Turning	Pulling	

2. The balancing cerebellum

The activity:		Leads to:
Spinning	Tumbling	Balance
Balancing	Dancing	Sporting ability
Listening		Bicycle riding
Swinging		Writing skills
Rolling		Fine motor coordination
		Reading skills

3. The emotional brain

The activity:	Leads to:
Stroking	Love
Cuddling	Security
Playing	Bonding
together	Social skills
	Cooperation
	Confidence

4. The thinking brain or cortex

The activity:	Leads to:
Stacking toys	Math, logic
Assembling puzzles	Problem solving
Recognizing patterns	Fluent reading, spelling
Making patterns	Writing, painting
Playing word games	Good vocabulary
Repetitive play	Memory
Appreciating music	Musical ability

Reproduced from *FUNdamentals Guidebook,* by Gordon Dryden and Colin Rose, published by Accelerated Learning Systems, England. Chart compiled on recommendations by Jerome and Sophie Hartigan, of Jumping Beans, Auckland, New Zealand.

Regular updates: www.thelearningweb.net

Two Swedish vestibular-stimulation experts, Mats and Irene Niklasson, have also achieved great results using techniques similar to Palmer. At their Vistabularis organization, they've found that slow spinning and slow movement is ideal for many children, particularly those diagnosed as having severe learning problems. Says Mats Niklasson: "Most learning problems, I found, relate to lack of balance and difficulty with the reflexes." Through spinning and other motor activities, the Niklassons "rewire the brain".[13]

They also agree that effective learning starts from the moment of birth. Again, the main points are simple:

1. The vital importance of step-by-step movement

Infants grow in a patterned way. They're born explorers. So encourage them to explore in a safe, environment.

In New Zealand two Irish migrants, Jerome and Sophie Hartigan, have combined their talents to introduce a parent-involvement program based very much on children's natural physical development. Jerome is a former Olympic pentathlete, has a masters degree from Ithaca College, New York, and is a scientist and physical training specialist. Sophie is an accomplished music teacher. Their *Jumping Beans* child-development centers, now springing up around New Zealand, involve parents in regular one-hour sessions.

Jerome Hartigan says "physical, motor learning" forms the basis for all learning, including reading, writing, arithmetic and music. "Without motor learning," he says," the brain simply will not develop."[14] He says specific movement patterns "wire up" the whole brain.

The Hartigans say it's important that physical routines should link in with the way the brain grows.

Janet Doman, director of The Institutes for the Achievement of Human Potential, in Philadelphia, agrees. And those routines should start from day one. "Give children the chance to crawl from as early an age as possible," she says. "Babies can actually crawl from birth, but generally they are restricted by so much clothing that they don't develop this ability till later."[15]

So long as children are warm, she says, parents should not limit their movements with too much clothing.

"Very simply, the more they crawl the sooner they're going to creep, and the more they creep the more they'll be able to walk. And each of

Nature has built the brain in such a way that during the first six years of life it can take in information at an overwhelming rate and without the slightest effort.

GLENN DOMAN
author of *Teach Your Baby To Read**

*Author interview, Philadelphia, PA.

these stages ensures that the next stage comes at the right moment—and that they have completed the neurological maturation that goes with it.

"If babies are bundled up for so long that they don't really crawl much at all, but go straight to creeping, then they may well pay a price for that five years later when they get to the point where they need to be able to converge their vision perfectly."

But how on earth can creeping affect a baby's *eyesight?* "Basically, a newborn baby has no ability to converge its two eyes," says Janet Doman. " But when the baby starts to crawl, the need to use two eyes together is born—because all of a sudden the baby is moving forward in space and he begins to hit the sofa or the chair. Nature's a little bit of a tough teacher, and whenever this happens the baby says: 'Wait a second; I'd better see where I'm going.' And that's when the baby begins to pull in those two roving eyes and begins to say: 'Where am I?' After that, every time the baby is moving he will turn on his vision, look to see where he's going, and bring those two eyes together. As they converge their vision, it gets better and better. But if you miss that vital stage of development you're missing out a vital stage of brain development."

Part of the reason is very simple: to creep and crawl, a baby needs to use all four limbs. And this movement strengthens the 300 million nerve-cell pathways that link both sides of the brain through the corpus callosum. Children who skip creeping or crawling—common in youngsters with severe brain damage from birth—thus find it impossible to fully coordinate both hemispheres.

2. Use your common sense

Almost everything we learn about the world comes in through our five senses. Very early in life, infants try to touch, smell, taste, hear and look at whatever surrounds them. So encourage them from the outset.

Says Janet Doman: "A baby is born into a world in which, essentially, he is blind, can't hear very well and his sensation is far from perfect. And that's a very uncomfortable place for a baby to be. He's trying to figure out: 'Where am I? What's going on? What's gonna happen next?' Because he can't see, he can't hear and he can't feel very well. So I think the job of a parent is very clear: to give enough visual, auditory and tactile stimulation so that the baby can get out of this dilemma of not being able to see, hear or feel.

"That doesn't have to be complicated. For example, often new

Why a baby needs to see sharp contrasts

In its earliest months a baby's brain lays down its main "visual pathways".

Its cortex has six layers of cells which transmit different signals from the retina in the eyes along optic nerves to the back of the brain.

One layer, for example, transmits horizontal lines, one vertical.

Other layers or columns handle circles, squares and triangles.

If a baby was to see only horizontal lines, for example, then when it crawled or walked it would continually be banging into the legs of tables and chairs because its "visual pathways" could not process vertical lines.

American scientists Torstein Wiesel and David Hubel won the Nobel prize for showing that such early sensory experience is essential for teaching brain cells their jobs.

Says Ronald Kotulak: "Even if a person's brain is perfect, if it does not process visual experiences by the age of two the person will not be able to see, and if it does not hear words by age ten, the person will never learn a language."*

That is why Glenn Doman has for more than 30 years recommended exposing babies to strong black-and-white contrasting shapes from birth, rather than using bland pastel wall coverings.

* RONALD KOTULAK
Inside The Brain
Published by Andrews and McMeel (1996),
4520 Main Street, Kansas City,
Missouri 64111, USA.

Regular updates: www.thelearningweb.net

parents put children in a pastel environment. And this for baby is a disaster. The baby needs to see contrast, needs to see outlined shapes and images, needs to see black-and-white contrasts.

"If you put him in a room of pale pinks and pale blues, it's like putting him in a world where there's nothing to see—so he can't see it."

Or take taste. Doman says it is one of the most neglected senses. "In the normal course of events, a baby in his first few months of life would probably taste only two things: milk and vomit. Now that's not a very interesting taste variety! So we encourage our mothers to introduce some variety: a little taste of lemon or orange or nutmeg."

And sound: "Mothers intuitively speak in a slightly louder, clearer voice to babies—and that's great," says Doman. "And it's even better if you constantly tell baby what's happening: saying, 'Now I'm dressing you,' 'I'm putting your right sock on,' 'Now I'm changing your diaper.'"

Playing soothing background music is also recommended, both before and after birth. It's significant that youngsters in the Pacific islands of Polynesia, Melanesia and Micronesia almost invariably grow up with the ability to sing in harmony—an almost perfect sense of pitch. Every Polynesian also seems to be a natural dancer. Every New Zealand Maori seems to be able to sing in perfect tune. Again, experts will tell you it's because of what they did well before they went to school. They grew up in a culture where singing and dancing play a major part. And they patterned all that information in the vital early years.

In a similar way thousands of three- and four-year-olds around the world can now play the violin—many in their own orchestras—thanks to programs pioneered by Japan's Shinichi Suzuki.

3. Build on the five senses

As an infant gets older, many parents feel it's even easier to encourage learning through all the senses—because you see the instant feedback.

In *Learning Through Play,* Marzollo and Lloyd stress that children learn from experiences that are concrete and active. "For a child to understand the abstract concept of 'roundness', he must first have many experiences with real round things. He needs time to feel round shapes, to roll around balls, to think about the similarities between round objects, and to look at pictures of round things. When children are at play, they like to push, pull, poke, hammer and otherwise manipulate objects, be they toy trucks, egg cartons or pebbles. It is this combination of action

The simple start to learning English

 It has a total of 550,000 words

 But 2,000 words make up 90% of most speech

 400 words make up 65% of most writing

English has 26 letters and only 44 sounds

There are only 70 main spelling combinations

 Half the key words are phonetic, half are not

GORDON DRYDEN

* Adapted from slide presentation to The Peoples Network Mastermind conference, Dallas, Texas, June 1996.

and concreteness that makes play so effective as an educational process."

4. Use the whole world as your classroom

Turn every outing into a learning experience.

You can search for shapes

"They're all around you," say Marzollo and Lloyd. "Point them out to your child and soon he'll point them out to you." Circles, such as wheels, balloons, the sun, the moon, eye glasses, bowls, plates, clocks, coins. Rectangles, such as doors, windows, apartment houses, cereal boxes, books, beds and delivery trucks. Squares, like paper napkins, handkerchiefs, windows and tabletops. Triangles, like rooftops, mountains, tents, Christmas trees and sails.

You can see opposites everywhere

And this is a great way to learn words—by association: if a ball goes up it must come down. So do seesaws at the park. Lights go on and off, doors get open and closed, night turns into day.

Every supermarket trip is a learning journey

Before you shop, ask your youngster to help you check through the refrigerator and pantry to see what you need: for your infant and the rest of your family. Then in the supermarket, the search is on: to find what the child needs and talk about where it comes from. But again, make it a game: "See who's first to see the cornflakes."

Learn to count with real things

Start with the things your child can touch: "This is one spoon; and these are two spoons." Then make it a natural fun game: "You've got one nose but how many eyes? You've got one mouth but how many ears? And how many fingers?" Involve him as you set the table for two, three or four people. Let him count the money at the shopping counter.

Make it fun to classify

As we've already discussed, the brain stores information by association and patterns. So start the process early. On laundry day, perhaps, he can sort socks into pairs, shirts for ironing, shirts for folding and storage.

5. The great art of communication

Language, of course, is a unique human ability. And infants learn by listening, imitation—and practice. So talk to them from the start. Tell

First step to reading

Show your child brightly-colored books from the day you first bring her home.
And read to her every day.

Summarized from
DOROTHY BUTLER
Babies Need Books*

* Published by Penguin, London.

them what you're doing. Introduce them to their relatives. Read to them regularly. Above all, remember the importance of positive encouragement. If she says "I goed to the store," don't tell her that's wrong. Instead, try: "You went to the store, didn't you? And I went too. Tomorrow we'll go to the store again."

Again: make everything a fun language lesson by introducing a subject, then turning it into a guessing game: "These are my eyes, and this is my nose. Have you got eyes? Where are they? Have you got a nose? Where is it?"

Nursery rhymes are great—simply because they do rhyme, and rhymes are easy to remember. Every child should be exposed to colorful books from the start—and should be read to regularly.

Says New Zealand reading expert and author Dorothy Butler: "Keep the baby's books within reach, and make a practice of showing them to her from the day you first bring her home. The covers will be brightly illustrated, and at first you can encourage her to focus her eyes on these pictures. You can teach your baby a lot about books in the first few months."[16] Butler suggests showing even very young babies successive pages of suitable books: "Babies need people: talking, laughing, warm-hearted people, constantly drawing them into their lives, and offering them the world for a playground. Let's give them books to parallel this experience; books where language and illustration activate the senses, so that meaning slips in smoothly, in the wake of feeling."

Learning to read should be a natural and fun-filled process.

Again the principles are simple. English has about 550,000 words.[17] But 2,000 to 3,000 words make up 90 percent of most speech.[18] And only 400 to 450 words make up 65 percent of most books.[19] Introduce those words to children in a natural way, and reading develops as naturally as speaking. In fact the principle is so simple it's amazing there is any debate. Words, like pictures, are only symbols of reality. A picture of an apple is a symbol of a real fruit. So is the sound "apple". And so is the written word "apple". So if children can hear and see the word apple, and can taste it, smell it and touch it, they soon learn to speak and read it.

Glenn Doman has been proving this since before he first wrote *Teach Your Baby To Read* in 1964. He's also had many critics. Yet most of the critics actually recommend many of the same techniques, and often they criticize Doman for things he has never recommended.[20]

Says Doman: "It's as easy to learn to read as it is to learn to talk. In

Second step to reading

If an infant can see it, touch it, taste it, hear the word and see the word, she can learn both to speak and read it. So link reading with all the senses.

apple

GORDON DRYDEN

From a slide presentation on *The Learning Revolution* to World Book International Achievers' Conference, Barcelona, Spain, August 1996.

fact it's probably easier—because the ability to see is developed before the ability to talk. But don't take my word for it. Ask any producer of television commercials. They use the same simple communication techniques. Look at TV any night, and you'll hear someone screaming COCA COLA, or McDONALD'S—and at the same time the brandnames appear in large colored words, often tied in with a jingle that's easy to remember. And two-year-olds have broken the code. Now they can read because the message is large enough to be interpreted."[21]

So Doman-trained parents not only talk new words to their youngsters—loudly and clearly—they show them the words in big type, just like TV commercials or company billboards do.

In many parts of the world parents have found it simple common sense to label as many things as possible, so children can recognize written words as well as those spoken, starting with all the names of important things: from baby's own name to mommy (in America, or 'mummy' in Britain) and daddy, parts of the body and everything around the house. Printed letters, three inches high (about 7 cm.), are recommended.

When preschools were combined with parent education centers in the Pacific island of Rarotonga over 20 years ago, they labeled everything in English as well as their native Polynesian language. They found it a great way to encourage youngsters to read and speak in two languages.

In Malaysia, the Nury Institute has trained hundreds of parents to teach their three- and four-year-olds to speak and read in both Malay and English—specifically using the Doman technique.[22]

English-born teacher and author Felicity Hughes has used similar methods to teach young Tanzanian children to read in both English and Swahili.[23] Many of those children have then helped their parents read.

Felicity Hughes and the current authors agree—but Glenn Doman disagrees—that phonetics have an equal part to play with the "whole word" method of learning. Of the key words in English, about half are phonetic—written approximately as they sound: *hat, sat, mat, hit, fit, sit.* The other half are not phonetic, including such difficult spellings as *through, tough, cough, where, tight, weigh* and *bridge.*

Learn only "phonetics" and you'll be able to spell *set, bet, get* and *met.* You'll also quickly learn prefixes and suffixes such as *un, de, dis, re, ing* and *ed.* But you won't be able to read *Once upon a time* (phonetically: *Wunce upon uh taim).* And you won't be able to read the words from one to ten (phonetically pronounced *wun, tu, three, for, faiv, six, seven, ait,*

Third step to reading: label what she can see

nose	**bath**
toes	**bed**
eyes	**plate**
coat	**shoe**

GLENN DOMAN
Teach Your Baby To Read Kit

* Published by Better Baby Institute, Philadelphia, PA, USA.
Similar word labels are contained in *FUNdamentals,* published
by Accelerated Learning Systems, Ltd., England.

nain, ten). You won't even be able to read *phonetically!* The long "e" in English, for instance, can be written 12 different ways: *On the quay* we could see one of these people seize the key to the green machine and give it to the chief officer who threw it in the sea.* So word-cards should include the most-used words, whether spelled phonetically or not.

The first cards should contain "labeling" words—the nouns of the things children first see as their parents are telling them: "That's your bottle. This is your dress. And these are your toes." Then when they can crawl, roll over and walk, they can start learning the action words, both spoken and written: "Let me see you roll over. Good boy, you can walk." Then come the adverbs: "Roll over slowly." "See how quickly you can walk." And the adjectives, too: "What a big, black dog."

But is too much early learning robbing infants of their childhood? Glenn Doman gives the simple answer:

"We have a fail-safe law. We teach all mothers this law. When teaching your child, if you aren't having the time of your life, and the child isn't having the time of his life, stop, because you're doing something wrong. That's the fail-safe law."

The early years are also the ideal time to pick up more than one language, especially if you live in an area where other languages are spoken regularly. Says Doman: "All children are linguistic geniuses— witness their ability to learn to speak a language in the first three years of life. If they live in a bilingual house, they learn two. And if they're born in a trilingual household, they learn to speak three."

Neuroscientist Professor Diamond cautions that "love" is the most essential ingredient in early childhood education. "I think that warmth and affection is the prime consideration for healthy brain development. But from then on, expose them to a great variety of experiences. Let the child choose what interests her—and then move out from there."[24]

6. Parents as first teachers

So how can any parent become a better "first teacher"? Or better still, a first coach and mentor? Obviously you can read books on the subject, as you're doing now. But, like any other learning, hands-on experience with a mentor helps. And again the world provides many models.

* In "English English" the word "key" as in waterfront is spelled "quay".
Dr. Seuss 'Beginner Books' are excellent for rhyming words that sound the same but are spelled differently, such as 'fun' and 'done'.

Fourth step to reading: label what she can do

walk	sit
run	dance
roll	talk
slowly	quietly

GORDON DRYDEN & COLIN ROSE
FUNdamentals*

* Published by Accelerated Learning Systems, England. The program includes cards, with large blue letters, for key early verbs and adverbs.

In the United States, the Missouri Parents As Teachers program has been an important trailblazer.[25] It started in 1981 as a pilot program—under the Parents as First Teachers title—and its early results were thoroughly researched. When all children in the pilot reached age three, a randomly-selected group was tested against a carefully-matched comparison group. In all significant areas—language, problem-solving, health, intellectual skills, relating to others and confidence—the PAT group scored much better.

PAT is now a state-funded service provided by all 543 public school districts in Missouri. On average in recent years, 60,000 Missouri families, with children from birth to three, have taken part in the program. They're being helped by about 1500 trained part-time "parent-educators". Every month, each parent is visited by a parent-educator, who offers information about the next phase of each child's development and suggests practical ways parents can encourage sound growth. Parent-educators also offer tips on home safety, effective discipline, constructive play and other topics.

At each visit, the parent-educator takes along toys and books suitable for the next likely phase of development, discusses what parents can expect, and leaves behind a one-sheet series of tips on how to stimulate the child's interest through that next stage.

"Families receive three types of service," says parent-educator Joy Rouse.[26] "The primary part is the monthly home visit. We also provide group meetings—a chance for parents to come together with other families who have children in the same age-group. Sometimes it will be for parent-child activities, others to hear a consultant talk about child development or parenting, and sometimes it's just a fun time. The third component is screening, and this is a key component. We screen for language development, general development, hearing and vision. We also have a network where we can refer families with special needs."

Many Missouri schools link their PAT work with other programs. The Ferguson Florissant School District, in St. Louis county, is one of the leaders.[27] It runs six separate preschool programs: PAT; a LINK program, with parents and infants together on courses; "Saturday School"—a half-day for four-year-olds, with group visits at home; a program for three-year-olds; a child-care center, with youngsters from two to five, where parents pay; and an education program for preschoolers with special needs. The day-care center operates at the local high school, and is used as part of a training program for teenage high-school pupils.

Fifth step to reading: play phonetic games

FUNDAMENTALS

bat	got	train
cat	pot	brain
sat	hot	drain
mat		

GORDON DRYDEN & COLIN ROSE
FUNdamentals*

* Published by Accelerated Learning Systems, England. The program includes two sets of *Phonic Fun* cards, the first for simple "short" vowels, and the others for "combinations" such as "ai". The cards can be used for *Phonic Snap* or for the board game indicated above.

Note: Approximately half the core-words in English are phonetic; they are written approximately as they sound.

Thirty percent of Missouri families with youngsters under three were on the PAT program at the start of the 1990s. The cost per family was approximately $250 a year, of which the state provided $180 and the school district found the rest. So to provide that service to every American family with children up to three would cost $3-billion a year for 12 million youngsters. That's only about twice what tiny Singapore (with Oregon's population) is spending equipping its schools with computers.

But Former Harvard Professor Burton L. White, who played a big part in establishing the program, has ended his involvement with PAT because he says it is "hopelessly underfunded".[28] To do the job properly, he says, would require much higher spending—and it should be top priority. *He says not more than one American child in ten gets adequate development in the vital first three years of life.* "This state of affairs may be a tragedy," he says, "but it is by no means a twentieth-century tragedy. In the history of Western education there has never been a society that recognized the educational importance of the earliest years or sponsored any systematic preparation and assistance to families or any other institution in guiding the early development of children."[29]

Professor White says the period from when a child starts walking up to two years is most important. "Every one of the four educational foundations—the development of language, curiosity, intelligence and socialness—is at risk during the period from eight months to two years."

He says bluntly that "our society does not train people to raise children". Today he runs a model program at his Center for Parent Education in Waban, Massachusetts, and dreams of the day when nations make similar projects the top educational priority. So do we.

Professor Diamond, however, sounds a note of caution: "I do worry when people say things like 'Well, if you don't do something by three years of age forget it; you've closed the opportunity to stimulate that brain.' We don't want to give the impression that all of cortical input is essential that soon, though it is true for certain functions to reach optimal development, such as vision, hearing, and beginning language."[30]

Adds Professor Robert Sylwester: "The best time to master a skill associated with a system is just when a new system is coming on line in your brain. Language is a good example. It's very easy for a two- or three-year-old to learn any language. But if that person waits until 18 or 30, learning a new language will be more difficult because the systems governing this have been used for something else. Many skills, like

Sixth step to reading: play with key words

FUNDAMENTALS

an	any	been	best
but	can	do	even
fun	hand	hat	must
none	now	once	slow

GORDON DRYDEN & COLIN ROSE
FUNdamentals*

* Published by Accelerated Learning Systems, England. The program includes all the 450 most-written English words and three sets of *Key Word Bingo* cards.
An adult or older child shows one bold word at a time, and younger children try to find a matching word on their card.
The first child to complete a line across or down wins the game.

learning to play a musical instrument or developing fine and gross motor skills, are best done as early as possible."[31]

Another home-based parent-education program, which has had excellent success for children from age four to six, is called HIPPY: Home Instruction Program for Preschool Youngsters.

It started in Israel in 1969, and is now operating in over 20 other countries or states, servicing about 20,000 families a year outside Israel. It has probably been given its biggest initial boost in America through its success in Arkansas, with the support of the former Governor and now President Clinton and Hillary Clinton. President Clinton is warm in his praise for HIPPY: "This program, in my judgment, is the best preschool program on earth, because it gives parents the chance to be their children's first teachers, no matter how meager the education of the parent." [32]

HIPPY was designed by Professor Avima Lombard, initially for the nearly 200,000 refugees who came to Israel from Africa and Asia in the 1960s. They were poor and unsophisticated, and their children were sometimes neglected as their parents struggled to establish themselves in their new home. Like PAT, HIPPY takes training directly into the home, but for parents of children aged four and five. Mothers in the program receive one visit every two weeks, and they meet with other mothers in group meetings every second week.[33]

Again, the results have been excellent—and in Arkansas not only have children benefited but the program has increased literacy among parents.[34]

In Malaysia, a parent-education program has been taken out into the villages by Dr. Noor Laily Dato' Abu Bakar and Mansor Haji Sukaimi. They call it the Nury program—from a word that means "shining light". In the first ten years they had trained 20,000 parents in Malaysia and 2,000 in Singapore.[35]

7. Parents in preschool centers

New Zealand again has shown the way by piloting and researching both the Missouri PAT program and HIPPY. In Missouri, PAT is very much linked with schools, but in New Zealand the government has associated it with that country's Plunket program (named after a former head of state), which has pioneered infant health-care checks, parent education and family assistance for most of this century. For many years

Children's work IS their play. Children learn from everything they do.

CAROLYN HOOPER
New Zealand Playcenter Movement*

*Interviewed by Gordon Dryden in *Where To Now?* television series,
reprinted in *Pacific Network,* February, 1992. Playcenter is a
parents' cooperative movement in New Zealand that for over
50 years has been a world pioneer in combining parent education
with early childhood development.

the Plunket program played a major part in achieving for New Zealand the world's lowest infant death rate.

An even more thorough program has been piloted and researched by New Zealand's Pacific Foundation.[36] Early in the 1990s the foundation designed and built a combined preschool and parent-training center at Kelvin Road School, Papakura, in the heart of an area with major deprivation problems. The center also links in closely with most other district health and social services. The preschool centrer also provides a full HIPPY-based development program for infants and their parents. Foundation executive director Lesley Max describes the total project as a "one-stop shopping center for parent and preschool services".[37] Results have been so outstanding that the government is now financing similar centers in other parts of the country.

Again in innovative New Zealand, a parents' cooperative Playcenter movement has been operating since 1941. It was started as a project to provide support for mothers whose husbands were away at the war. The women would take turns looking after a group of children to free the others for shopping or recreation. The movement quickly spread, and one of the early pioneers, Gwen Somerset, organized wider programs to train the young mothers in child development skills. Today there are 600 playcenters throughout the country, catering to 23,000 children. And parent involvement is the key. They take turns in helping a trained, part-time supervisor run each center. And their own training helps make them more competent parents.

Sweden is another country with highly advanced early childhood development programs—but with a tax-rate that most countries might find too high. For every child born in Sweden, one parent can have a year off work on almost full pay to be a fulltime parent.[38]

Later, Sweden offers excellent preschool development centers. It also has one of the world's best refugee-support programs, with migrants from 114 different countries. By law, each preschool center must employ adults who can speak both Swedish and the native language of each child. And generally they speak English as well.

But the prize for excellence in early childhood education could well go to aspects of a movement that was started over 90 years ago by Italy's first woman medical doctor, Maria Montessori.[39]

Most Montessori preschools are private, and often have high fees. But at French Camp near Stockton, California—an hour's drive from San

The 24 first steps to fluent writing

1. Play with big balls from crawling stage
2. Stack plastic cups from 9 to 18 months
3. Use pegboards from 12 to 18 months
4. Simple puzzles with big knobs from 18 to 24 months
5. Thread large beads at 18 to 24 months
6. More complex hand puzzles from 2 years
7. Pour rice from one jug to another, then switch to water
8. Early scribbling
9. Tons of water play
10. Hand, sponge and finger-painting
11. Switch to small balls
12. Small blackboard
13. String macaroni between ages 2 and 3
14. Fold paper napkins from 30 months
15. Big jigsaws from third birthday
16. Draw inside big writing templates from age 3
17. Then use smaller writing templates
18. Finger-trace over stippled letters
19. Polish shoes between 3 and 5
20. Copy own name by fourth birthday
21. You write her first story, and child writes over it
22. Help her write shopping lists
23. Play writing games on home computer
24. She 'explodes' into writing before age 5

GORDON DRYDEN & COLIN ROSE
*FUNdamentals Guidebook**

* Published by Accelerated Learning Systems, England.
Note: Most activities are to develop prewriting skills.

Francisco—a New Zealand television crew, videotaping the world's best learning ideas in 1990, found a Montessori center catering to America's poorest working families, Mexican fruit and vegetable pickers.[40] Both parents were working the fields from 4:30 or 5:00 each morning—for a family income of around $7,000 a year.

Yet their children were benefiting from preschool education that ranks with the top in the world. Their center was one of 18 set up as a research experiment by the California-based Foundation Center for Phenomenological Research.* In the grounds of the French Camp center the TV crew videotaped migrant youngsters dancing, singing and playing. Inside, others were engrossed in a wide variety of activities adapted from Montessori's original ideas.

They sat in child-sized chairs, at child-sized tables, use tools and implements specially designed for small hands. They also were learning advanced mathematics the Montessori way, using wooden rods of different lengths and colors to do decimals and numbers up to 2,000.

Among many other innovations, Montessori pioneered cutout sandpaper letters so infants could learn by touch as well as sight. And French Camp children were involved in a full range of similar sensory experiences. Each room had a variety of live animals and fish to help the learning process. Well-trained parents were always on hand to assist, but overall the youngsters were encouraged to be self-learners.

As one of the Foundation's then organizers, Antonia Lopez, told the TV audience: "The major job of the adult is to provide the children with as many opportunities in all of their areas, whether it's cultural, or science, art, music, mathematics or language—to provide as many opportunities that are age-appropriate and sequentially developed."[41] Something to eat was being served every two hours, with each meal a lesson in diet and nutrition: low-fat soups, whole-wheat tortillas instead of white-flour tortillas. Children set the tables as they learned to count the spoons and forks and plates. Each meal was a cultural delight.

And it didn't stop with nutrition. All family members—male, female, siblings and children—were physically examined each year.

Like so many effective pioneering ventures, lack of finance has since forced the Foundation Center to close many of its preschool centers, including the one visited at French Camp. Some have been taken over by other groups. And in mid-1999 the Foundation Center was building four new centers in Sacramento: based on the same principles outlined here.

A five-year-old writes

*Vogliamo augurare
la buona Pasqua all'in-
gegnere Edoardo. Talamo
e alla principessa Maria?
Diremo che conducano
qui i loro bei bambini.
Lasciate fare a me:
Scriverò io per tutti
7 Aprile 1909.*

A sample of hand-writing, done in pen, by a five-year-old
student of Italian educator Maria Montessori in 1909.
Translation: "We would like to wish a joyous Easter
to the civil engineer Edoardo Talamo and the Princess Maria.
We will ask them to bring their pretty children here.
Leave it to me: I will write for all. April 7, 1909."*

*Reprinted from *The Montessori Method,* by Maria Montessori,
published by Schocken Books, Inc., New York.

Those who criticize Glenn Doman's early *reading* program would probably gasp with amazement when they hear that French Camp children were *writing* fluently before they reached their fifth birthday. As Lopez put it: "Montessori tells us that children at about four and a half literally seem to explode into writing. Now that's the official 'I can-write-a-sentence-and-a-word' version of writing. But our children are really being introduced to writing and to reading much earlier. Even as young as two and a half, they're being introduced to prewriting experiences: they're doing things left to right, top to bottom; learning relationships. And they're obviously exposed to rhymes and story-telling and all kinds of talking—so they're ready to explode into writing well before they are five."

It's perhaps significant that both Montessori's and Doman's initial research began with youngsters who were severely brain-damaged—and they then realized that these children, after multisensory stimulation, were often performing much better than "normal" children.

Montessori set out to fashion materials and experiences from which even "intellectually handicapped" youngsters could easily learn to read, write, paint and count before they went to school. She succeeded brilliantly; her brain-damaged pupils passed standard test after test.[42]

Under the Montessori method, however, a small child is not "taught" writing; she is exposed to specific concrete experiences that enable her to develop the "motor" and other skills that lead to the self-discovery of writing. Montessori specialist Pauline Pertab, of Auckland, New Zealand, explains: "As early as two-and-a-half years of age, a child will be encouraged to pour water and do polishing, developing hand and eye coordination; to paint and draw, developing pencil control; and later to work with shapes and patterns, tracing the inside and outside of stencils and to work with sand-paper-covered letters about nine centimeters in depth—three to four inches—to get the feel of shapes."[43] The "explosion" occurs when a youngster discovers, by himself, that he can write.

As Maria Montessori was proving in the early 1900s, the key to early childhood deprivation lies overwhelmingly in providing a total supportive environment for all children to develop their own talents.

She demonstrated conclusively that if children can grow up in an environment structured to encourage their natural, sequential development, they will "explode" into learning: they will become self-motivated, self-learners, with the confidence to tackle any problem as it arises in life.

Two developmental theories compared

Maria Montessori, the Italian early childhood educator, and Jean Piaget, the Swiss developmental psychologist, both proposed that children develop in sequence. But they disagreed on timing. Piaget believed children had specific periods of "cognitive" or intellectual development, with children not reaching their "concrete operational" stage until age seven. Montessori believed, however, that while children had specific "sensitive periods" for development, they should be encouraged to develop all of their senses from a very early age, and that self-learning would be based on the way the senses develop. In summary:

Montessori:

Birth to 3 years:
Absorbent mind.
Sensory experiences.
18 months to 3 years:
Coordination and muscle development.
Interest in small objects
2 to 4 years:
Refinement of movement.
Concern with truth and reality.
Awareness of order sequence in time and space.
2.5 to 6 years:
Sensory refinement.
3 to 6 years:
Susceptibility to adult influence.
3.5 to 4.5 years:
Writing.
4 to 4.4 years:
Tactile sense.
4.5 to 5.5 years:
Reading.
Overall:
The prewriting steps on page 260 are a good example of a modern-day adaptation of Montessori in action.

Piaget:

Sensorimotor period, from birth to age 2:
Obtain basic knowledge through the senses.
Preoperational period, from about age 2 to 7:
Develop language and drawing skills, but self-centred and cannot understand abstract reasoning or logic.
Concrete operational period from 7 to 11 years:
Begin to think logically, organize knowledge, classify objects and do thought problems.
Formal operations period from 11 to 15:
Children begin to reason realistically about the future and deal with abstractions.
Overall:
Piaget claimed reading, writing and mathematics should be left until the period from 7 years onwards: Montessori: much earlier.

Yet almost 100 years later we've found only two early-childhood centers that combine nearly all the key principles outlined in this chapter. The first is Montessori International in the sparsely-populated American state of Montana.[44] No ludicrous arguments there about which method of teaching English is more important: phonics or "whole language". Their children learn by both methods: Montessori, Doman—whatever works. And they learn them early. They know that the sounds of English can be written in 70 different letter-combinations, so they play games with those sounds and combinations.

They know that the main steps to fluent writing include dozens of prewriting activities, so their children get plenty of practice in those steps. They know that music and rhythm are essential to learning, so those, too, are key ingredients of a balanced program. They know that physical routines, based on the Doman-Palmer-Hartigan approach, are vital for brain development, so their youngsters go through them each day.

Before starting grade one, every one of the children can speak confidently, read fluently, write well, construct stories, spell, count, add, subtract and multiply. *

In England, too, the Montessori movement is showing the way in early-childhood development—a movement driven by the energetic head of the London Montessori Center, Lesley Britton. The Montessori Farm School, run by South African-born Helen Watkins, in Bracknell, Berkshire, is one of the best in Britain.[45] But Britain overall shares with the United States one of the developed world's worst records for early-childhood education.

In New Zealand 82 percent of all three and four-year-olds are in early childhood education programs, and the government's stated aim is to lift this total to 95 per cent by 2001.[46] Many European countries have similar high percentages of children in preschool centers. But America's overall performance in early childhood education is appalling. In California, for

---

There are now about 6,000 different preschools and schools in the United States operating under the "Montessori banner" but most do not follow the Montana model. Montessori International, for instance, follows the Doman philosophy of introducing reading much earlier than Maria Montessori recommended, and certainly much earlier than schools that follow the Piaget model (see comparisons opposite). Montessori International is also part of a religious community. And while neither current author would claim sufficient expertise to comment on the community's religious philosophy, its approach to learning is superb.

Brain development in the early years*

By birth: most children have 100 billion active brain cells, and these have made about 50 trillion connections with other brain cells and other parts of the body.

In first month of life: As a baby's senses react to her environment, she develops new "synaptic" connections at the phenomenal rate of up to 3 billion a second.

In the first six months: Baby will babble using all the sounds in all the languages of the world, but she will then learn to talk using only the sounds and words she picks up from her environment, particularly from her parents. Her brain will discard the ability to speak in languages she does not hear.

By eight months: A baby's brain has about 1,000 trillion connections (1,000,000,000,000,000)! After that the number of connections begins to decline—unless the child is exposed to stimulation through all her senses.

By age ten years or so: about half the connections have died off in the average child, but that still leaves about 500 trillion that last through most of life.

Up to age 12: "The brain is now seen as a super-sponge that is most absorbent from birth to about the age of 12. It is during this period, and especially the first three years, that the foundations for thinking, language, vision, attitudes, aptitudes and other characteristics are laid down. Then the windows close, and much of the fundamental architecture of the brain is completed."**

* Summarized from various sources, many of them quoted by Ronald Kotulak in *Inside The Brain,* published by Andrews and McMeel, Kansas City, Missouri.

** The exact quote is from Robert Kotulak's own summary.

instance, only 41 percent of English-speaking children and 15 percent of Mexican-American children come into kindergarten at age five with any experience of preschool centers.[47]

8. Continue the same fun-filled approach at school

Even worse: in many states "formal academic education" is the norm from the first elementary-school years. Children don't get the chance for the fun-filled, experience-rich learning that is the basis for real growth. And all too often the joy of learning fades. They learn not to learn.

The alternatives are shown in yet another school which follows successful fun- and activity-filled lessons from preschool into its primary school. It's called The Classical Academy, formed by the Maxin Learning Institute at St. Louis Park, in Minnesota. A small group of teachers and parents got together in 1991 and analyzed some of the world's best teaching methods. They came to similar conclusions as the present authors, and to favor what they now describe as Maxin's "Best of the Integrated Learning Systems" program. By 1994 their Academy had grown to encompass students from preschool through ninth grade.

Four of the key founders—Nancy Nicholson Terry, Nora Flood, Janet Oliver and Amira Sewell—have had extensive Montessori training. Now they have broadened out from that sound beginning, using many models from our first edition and content from Jeannette Vos workshops.

The Classical Academy uses Romalda Spalding's *The Writing Way to Reading*—an integrated phonics program which the Academy has linked with many Doman methods (as does Montessori International), the Japanese Kumon math program; Paul Dennison's Brain-Gym methods (which we cover in chapter 11); the Marva Collins Classical Literature program—a multimedia program linking history and art; and a wide range of other stimulating accelerated learning methods.

The Upper School administered the Iowa Test of Basic Skills for all students in 1993 and then again in May 1994. Students averaged an increase of 1.6 years over that six-month period. Several students achieved four and five years' growth in major academic areas.[48]

Fortunately other examples also abound of what can happen when common sense is linked to good research and dedicated principals and teachers; and when schools program for success instead of failure.

SELF-ESTEEM:

The secret heart of learning

1 Program for success, not failure, for everyone.

2 Learn the lessons from the big achievers.

3 Concentrate on the six vital ingredients:*

- ■ **Physical safety**
- ■ **Emotional security**
- ■ **Identity**
- ■ **Affiliation**
- ■ **Competence**
- ■ **Mission**

*From Bettie B. Youngs, *The 6 Vital Ingredients Of Self-Esteem: How To Develop Them In Your Students,* published by Jalmar Press, P.O. Box 1185, Torrance, CA 90505.

How to program for success
in education as in business

Sometimes a great truth sears itself into your brain.

Or one crisp sentence telegraphs a truism more effectively than a thousand books.

Or you feel a mask has been whipped from shrouded eyes—as you see something so simple you wonder why you've never seen it before.

And the simplest truths have emerged from every success story we've analyzed for this book:

❏ *The best systems in the world are programmed to succeed.*

❏ *Most current educational systems are programmed to fail.*

They're not programmed to fail everybody. But they are programmed to fail a large percentage of students. In some cases up to 50 percent. And whatever you program you'll generally achieve.

The world's airlines plan to land their planes with 100 percent safety every time. A one-in-a-million failure rate would rightly be regarded as a tragedy.

The world's top car companies spend a fortune to reduce their manufacturing fault-rates from 2 percent to 1 percent.

But most school systems actually expect and plan for a reject rate that would send any business bankrupt.

Businesses use spell-checking computers so that every letter they write can go out word-perfect. Accounting firms use electronic calculators and computer programs to help make sure their clients' financial reports and tax returns are 100 percent accurate. Anyone in the real world who is learning a computer turns to a friend for advice when stumped.

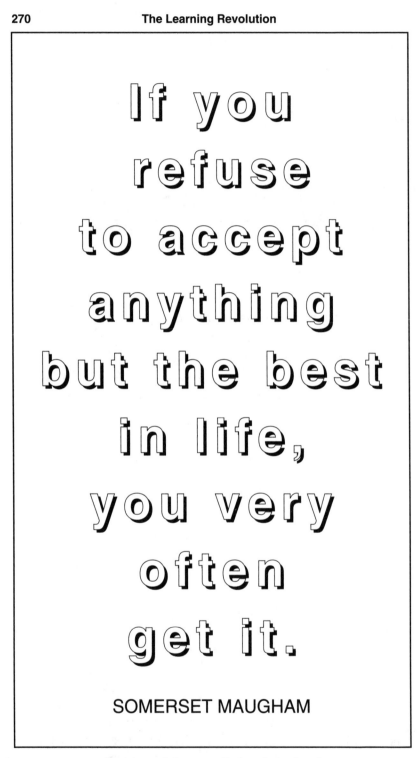

If you refuse to accept anything but the best in life, you very often get it.

SOMERSET MAUGHAM

But in school examinations students using the same common sense techniques for excellence would be disqualified for cheating.

We stress that we are NOT opposed to evaluations and qualifications. Far from it. In our view, most school achievement standards are absurdly low.

A 20 percent product failure rate in any business, anywhere in the world, would be regarded as a financial disaster.* Schools are the only organizations to regard that result as a success.

❏ More than half of America's young people "leave school without the knowledge or foundation required to find and hold a good job", says the SCANS** report on *What Work Requires of Schools*.[1] If you're an American reader, please stop and read that last sentence again—and weep for the future of half the children of the world's richest nation who can move out of a school system unfit to find a decent job.

❏ "These young people will pay a very high price. They face the bleak prospects of dead-end work interrupted only by periods of unemployment"—from the same report.

❏ "SCANS estimates that less than half of all young adults have achieved these (required) reading and writing minimums; even fewer can handle the mathematics; and schools today only indirectly address listening and speaking skills."

❏ "Britain's workforce is under-educated, under-trained and under-qualified," says a major similar study by Sir Christopher Ball, entitled *More Means Different*.[2]

❏ Forty-seven percent of potential British employees in industry are unable to meet the skill needs required, Ball reports. If you're a British reader, please stop and read that sentence again—and weep.

The economic results are bad enough. But even worse, the angry human rejects of this crazy system often wear their rejection-slips as

---

The only business exception we know to this rule: the production of raw silicon chips. As each of these can be mass-produced for a few cents, some companies plan for a higher reject rate as the trade-off for speedy production. But they then test every chip to make sure that it works perfectly as the brain of the multi-thousand-dollar computer it will operate.

** *The Secretary's Commission on Achieving Necessary Skills, commissioned by the U.S. Secretary of Labor under the former President Bush's America 2000 Program.*

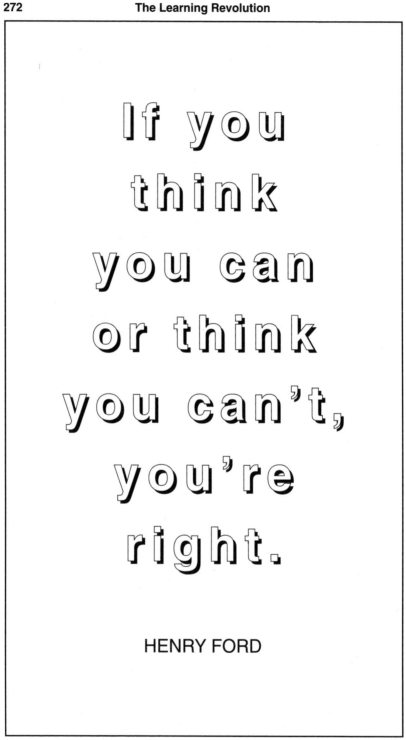

If you think you can or think you can't, you're right.

HENRY FORD

lifelong badges of under-achievement, shame, despair and anger.

But the answer, we're convinced, is not in more of the same. It is certainly not in a system that is actually programmed to produce failure.

And it would be a confidence trick of the worst type to suggest that even brilliant new learning techniques at school can completely compensate for a society that itself is also programmed for many of its members to fail. There is no way optimal learning can take place without physical safety and emotional security. And even the world's richest country is not providing that security for millions of its youngsters.

Of the 65 million Americans under 18, fully 13 million live in poverty—one in five. Around 14.3 million of them live in single-parent homes. Almost three percent live with no parents at all.[3]

Children of single parents are most at risk. In America three-quarters of them live in poverty during at least part of the crucial first eight years of their lives. And single-parent children are, on average, at least twice as likely to have behavioral and emotional problems, and 50 percent more likely to have learning disabilities, than two-parent children. They are also twice as likely to drop out of high school. Fully 3.4 million American school-age children are left to care for themselves after school each day.[4]

America has one of the developed world's highest rates of teenage pregnancy. America and New Zealand also have a high percentage of children born to unmarried parents. The proportion soars in minority groups: two-thirds of African-American and New Zealand Maori babies are born to unmarried parents.[5] And most grow up in single-parent families. The self-perpetuating cycle of deprivation rolls on.

Bulgarian psychiatrist and accelerated learning pioneer Dr. Georgi Lozanov calls it the "social suggestive norm"—the total social environment that conditions us all for success or failure.[6]

Henry Ford summarized part of the equation many years ago in simpler terms: "If you think you can, or think you can't, you're right." Others have restressed the message regularly: We are what we think we are. We become what we think we'll become.

And here we're not talking about the "touchy, feely, all-you-have-to-do-is-think-and-you'll-grow-rich" brand of fantasy. In our view, all self-esteem has to be firmly grounded in positive achievement. And real achievement is grounded in self-esteem. You have to achieve something specific to achieve full potential. "Feeling good about yourself" is not enough, although it's part of the secret. You have to ground your feelings

The challenge lies in creating a workplace in which people can be the best they can be.

FREDERICK W. SMITH
in *The Book of Leadership Wisdom**

* Edited by Peter Krass, published by John Wiley & Sons, New York.

in something you can do well: math, science, cooking, sewing, reading, karate, playing the piano, sports, singing, dancing—whatever.

But, as Lozanov argues, another aspect is equally vital: *too often we become what others expect.* And when those expectations are telegraphed daily by parents and teachers through word, attitude, atmosphere and body language, then *their expectations* become *students' limitations.*

Sports provide countless examples of the opposite effect. In the early 1960s three athletes living in one area of Auckland, New Zealand, won Olympic gold medals or broke the world record in every middle-distance event: 800 yards, 800 meters, 1,000 meters, 1,500 meters, one mile, 5,000 meters and three miles. Only one of them, triple gold medal-winner Peter Snell, was a natural athlete. One of them, Olympic 5,000 meters champion Murray Halberg, had a crippled arm. They succeeded because their coach, Arthur Lydiard, helped develop their confidence—and provided the training—to lead the world. "The talent wasn't exceptional," says Lydiard. "Anyone could do it. Motivation is the key."[7]

And sure: not every athlete can become a Carl Lewis, a John Walker or a Michael Jordan. But no one should be programmed to fail. Maybe— just maybe—society could tolerate such failure-based school systems 50 years ago. Then the world was a different place. Our schools served a different society.

In most developed countries they did a good job of preparing the people who would become our future managers and professionals: our accountants, lawyers, doctors, teachers, administrators, academics— perhaps 20 to 30 percent of the population.

They did a reasonable job of preparing those who would become the skilled or semiskilled craftsmen and tradesmen, or the generally-female typists and accounts clerks who would support the mostly-male management teams. Many countries skimmed several groups off early into "technical education", to become the apprentice carpenters, plumbers, electricians, printers, engineers and other tradesmen.

At its best, the mid-20th-century elementary school also trained the rest of its youngsters to cope in the unskilled jobs that were then required. It taught them the basics of reading, writing and arithmetic—the so-called three Rs. Our schools were programmed to produce the citizens needed for an industrial economy. And they produced what they programmed— what they expected. Their examination systems, too, were designed to produce the right professional-technical-laboring mix.

A well-developed mind, a passion to learn, and the ability to put knowledge to work are the new keys to the future.

SCANS REPORT*
What Work Requires of Schools

* U.S. Labor Secretary's Commission on Achieving Necessary Skills.

Even a much-praised early-education leader like New Zealand for years deliberately "scaled" the main high school examination to ensure that 50 percent of students failed. Even if the overall national average rose dramatically, 50 percent of students who lasted even three years at high school had built-in failure as a guaranteed result. Future generations will look back on that guarantee with horror and dismay.

But at least most of the "failures" could then get unskilled jobs, often highly paid. Today a soaring number can't. They're unemployed, disheartened, frustrated—often violent.

Every reliable "futures" forecast we have studied convinces us that this is not the only alternative. We live in a world where almost anything is now possible, where excellence is achievable. But for the vast majority of people to benefit from this new age demands from our educational systems *the same kind of educational results for most people that were previously guaranteed to the "top" 20 to 30 percent of students.*

As Ball puts it in his British report: "The nature of work is changing. It is becoming increasingly brain-intensive, value-laden and unpredictable. Skilled brain power is replacing disciplined muscle-power. Unskilled and low-skilled work is rapidly diminishing. In its place employers call for more people with professional, technical and managerial skills. Competitive economies in future will depend on the success of the education system in producing a high average level of education and training, rather than just a small leadership elite."

The Ball Report has called for Britain to increase the number of students in higher education—college, polytechnic and university—by a whopping 50 percent. And it has called for linking much more hands-on training with academic education.

Like Ball, we're convinced that "more means different." In later chapters we spell out many ways to achieve that type of result. But it will not be achieved in any school system that is programmed to fail even one person. As in sports, this does not mean that everyone will end up with first-class academic honors. But it does mean that *everyone should have the chance to excel at something—and to succeed regularly at something.*

Now obviously we're not criticizing the great schools that exist at every level around the world. We are talking about the norm. And what societies or schools *expect*—what they program to *achieve*—they will normally get. Plan for "Ds"—for failure—and you'll get them.

Existing systems produce existing results. If something different is required, the system must be changed.

SIR CHRISTOPHER BALL
More Means Different*

* British report on Widening Access to Higher Education, published by Royal Society for the encouragement of Arts, Manufactures and Commerce, 8 John Adam Street, London, England.

Compare this with other systems that are programmed to succeed—
and where excellence results:

❏ The U.S. armed forces, for instance, where a 50 percent failure rate
would never be tolerated. Whatever your views on the 1991 Gulf War,
the electronically-controlled rockets that rained down on Saddam
Hussein's armed forces spelled out a message of excellence in military
technology, planning, efficiency and competence.

❏ Disneyland, where even a novice cleaner can't get to sweep a floor
without a one-week extensive training course in the theme-park's philosophy, values and attractions.[8] And where every visitor is regarded as
a guest and every employee as a partner committed to being a vital part
of a daily extravaganza that smiles excellence at every corner.

❏ Silicon Valley pioneer Hewlett-Packard, where the lower-skilled
computer assemblers work, eat, exercise and play alongside the Ph. D.
systems-designers; where all, without exception, are encouraged to take
computers home to explore new ideas with their families; where all are
partners in achieving excellence; and where most even have full authority
to work their weekly hours at any time to suit them, without punching
timeclocks.[9]

❏ Japan's Matsushita-Panasonic, with its six million staff suggestions a year: 90 percent of them put into action in a day-by-day search to
encourage all to share in a continuously-improving result.[10]

❏ McDonald's, with its $40-million hamburger university, the train-
ing ground for the world's biggest fast-food chain.[11]

❏ Japan's Sony, with its policy of disregarding every employee's
former educational qualifications after he or she has been employed,
because it wants everyone to be seen as an achiever, an innovator, a
"seeker of the unknown" as part of a joint contribution to building a better
world.[12]

❏ Andersen Consulting, the world's largest management consulting
firm, which at its own company university in St. Charles, Illinois, each
year spends more than $400 million to retrain the 10,000 new MBAs it
employs annually from the world's top university colleges.[13]

❏ Or General Electric, the world's biggest company, which spends
$800 million a year on its various training and educational programs. Ask
CEO Jack Welch what he thinks GE will be in 20 years, and he replies:
"I hope it will be the greatest learning institution in the world." [14]

Or take any computer system as an example of striving for *excellence*

Create an institution where people aren't *allowed* to be curious, and people *won't* be curious.

TOM PETERS
*Liberation Management**

*Published by Alfred A. Knopf, New York.

as the norm. The program that's being used to typeset this page, for example. This comes complete with an automatic "spell-checker." When each chapter is finished, the computer program, if asked, automatically scans every word—and questions every possible mistake. The *expectation* is 100 percent excellence. And because of that expectation—and the system that produces it—nearly all books are printed with perfect spelling. Better still, the computerized spell-checker is a built-in, self-correcting educator. Even poor-spelling authors using it can check mistakes, and see correct or alternate versions instantly on the screen. They expect 100 percent achievement. And because they expect it, and know how to get it, they succeed. They know they're a success by the final results they produce—and not the mistakes they learn on the way. Thus they learn to spell the successful way.

As Thomas Edison put it when a friend tried to console him when about 10,000 experiments with a storage battery had failed to produce results: "Why, I have not failed. I've just found 10,000 ways that won't work."

In most of today's school systems, Edison would have been graded a failure. In fact, he had only three months of formal schooling—but became probably the greatest inventor in history, with 1,093 patents to his credit.

Maybe not all of us can be an Edison. But each warmly-encouraged infant seems to have the same insatiable sense of adventure and exploration that motivates the great inventors and scientists.

Dr. Thomas Armstrong, author of *Awakening Your Child's Natural Genius,* talks about the child's "extraordinary" openness to new learning during the preschool years. At two or three, says Armstrong, the average child "explodes" into language and learning.

The infant learns best in an ideal atmosphere, with affection, warmth, encouragement and support. Where that same attitude continues in school, the same fun and speed of learning continues.

There are many ways to achieve this for major improvements in learning, as we'll cover later. But more important than all: every positive educational turnaround we've examined around the world starts with self-esteem—or self-image. That esteem is nurtured where a school, like the leading businesses, is also in search of excellence—where every student is encouraged to succeed.

Says Colin Rose, the British-based entrepreneur who has produced

Many of life's failures are people who did not realize how close they were to success when they gave up.

THOMAS EDISON

the world's fastest-selling accelerated-learning foreign-language training programs: *"Of all the things thrown up by our research, probably the most vital is this: our self-image is probably the most important thing in determining whether we are good learners — or, frankly, whether we are good at anything else."[15]*

Every school leader featured in this book would agree. All use a variety of techniques to make sure each youngster's self-image flowers and is grounded in practical achievement:

❏ When Dr. Dan Yunk* arrived as new principal at Northview Elementary School in Manhattan, Kansas, in 1983, he found low test scores, little discipline and a dispirited staff.

A PBS television crew seven years later found a complete change in atmosphere—and results. Fourth-graders were learning fractions by making pizzas, learning Spanish by singing, learning American history through plays and songs. Fourth-graders were paired with kindergarten buddies, acting as teachers themselves, and putting into written words the five-year-olds' stories.

Youngsters were active in the school gymnasium from 7 a.m. In class, teachers were catering to all different learning styles: with plenty of sight, sound and action; a school where most pupils were playing musical instruments, and the curriculum was rich with the arts.

In a workstyle that most teachers in other countries would find bewildering, in 1983 Yunk found teachers who "in 20 years had never been in each other's classrooms".[16] He made teacher cooperation the norm.

When he first arrived, "parents didn't feel comfortable. Now they act as tutors, aides and mentors; one is even head of the computer club." Of all elementary schools in the state in 1983, only about a third of Northview's fourth graders reached the expected competency levels. By 1990: 97 percent—in the top three percent. And in some areas in the top 1 percent. Yunk's recipe for success? The same as Bill Hewlett and Dave Packard's in business: "Management by walking around." "Empower pupils, parents and teachers; they have to feel that they own it."

❏ The City Magnet School in Lowell, Massachusetts, is at the heart of a traditional Old England industrial town. It was set up early in the 1980s—planned by parents and educational leaders as one of the most unusual schools in the world.

For the school is much more than a school: it is a society in miniature.

* *Since then Dr. Yunk has moved on to more senior supervisory roles.*

Imagine
a school
with its own
bank, currency,
shops, traders,
lawyers,
courts and
newspaper:
a complete
micro-society.*

*The City Magnet School in Lowell, Massachusetts: a "normal" school
in the morning, a "society in miniature" in the afternoon — as
covered in a special PBS television report.

It has its own central bank, trading bank, courts, currency, lawyers, publishers and businesses. It publishes its own newspaper, magazines and yearbook, so its "staff" learn to write as reporters and editors, to produce as publishers and computer operators. Its "citizens" use their own currency to sell and buy each other's goods and services. And they learn all about interest rates, bank deposits, profit and loss accounts.

Parents are closely involved. One computer consultant is there two hours a day. But he doesn't think of it as a school. "We're a family," he says, "school and parents and students together."[17]

As principal Sue-Ellen Hogan told the PBS special television report in 1990: "We want it to be an interactive society." Regular classes take up four hours a day, before the school turns into a "Micro Society". But even the classes are geared to the real world. Says one teacher: "I teach publishing, not English." But the students learn both. Discipline? Not surprisingly, the students handle that mostly themselves: run their own court cases, with charges, prosecution, defence and juries. Civics as a subject? "It's not just part of the curriculum; it's part of everyday life."

Its students perform well above grade levels on all standardized tests. But its parents, teachers and students think that's a minor part of the achievement. The school is based firmly on the principle that experience is the best teacher. And that education is grounding achievement and self-esteem in practice.

❏ An even faster dramatic improvement in standards has come at the Emerald Middle School in the Cajon Valley Union School District, San Diego county, since principal Nancy J. Girvin introduced a wide-ranging program of values education, character-development and brilliant innovation.

Ten years ago co-author Vos found Emerald School so poor she refused to allow her second daughter to attend it. But today Emerald is a national model. Thanks to a $1.2 million renovation in 1994-95, the campus has 45 beautifully upgraded classrooms, including seven fully-equipped science labs, five computer labs and a school-wide computer network with Internet access. Every school day begins with an interactive television show run by the students. And not only do the classrooms and corridors glow with colorful posters, but students add HyperStudio Stack graphics to their daily TV presentations that publicize the school's values and character-building program.

Emerald has its own space shuttle laboratory, run by teacher Jim

The six vital ingredients of self-esteem

Self-esteem is a composite of six vital ingredients that can empower or detract from the vitality of our lives: The six are:

 PHYSICAL SAFETY
Freedom from physical harm.

 EMOTIONAL SECURITY
The absence of intimidations and fears.

 IDENTITY
The "Who am I?" question.

 AFFILIATION
A sense of belonging.

 COMPETENCE
A sense of feeling capable.

MISSION
The feeling that one's life has meaning and direction.

BETTIE B. YOUNGS
The 6 Vital Ingredients of Self-Esteem
How To Develop Them In Your Students*

*Published by Jalmar Press, P.O. Box 1185, Torrance, CA 90505.

Hamilton, where students simulate their own space probes. Students run their own office and business. They even provide 30 percent of the clerical needs of the entire school. And students work with Emerald's business partner, Home Depot, in a wide-ranging program to beautify the school. The values program is integrated into all aspects of the curriculum. And many students volunteer for regular community service.

"Because the Emerald staff is committed to using technology, we model its applications constantly," says Mrs. Girvin. "All teachers, instructional aides, office and support staff, the assistant principal and principal have their own desktop computers that are used throughout the day for email, word processing and data retrieval. Our students use technology to research on the Internet, word process assignments, access desktop publishing to create our yearbook, student newspaper business cards and stationery, create data bases and graphs for math projects and compile electronic portfolios." And the extensive multimedia facilities are used after hours by parents, teachers and students and as part of Emerald's role as one of San Diego's Model Education Centers for Student Teachers.

Emerald has developed two concepts that are now being taken up by many other schools: an *Emerald Way* Teacher Curriculum Notebook, and a *Powerful Learners* program that encourages rigorous academic and behavioral goals through the widespread character-building program. And all this in a school where 74 percent of students come from poor families, and those families speak 20 different languages.

❑ Cross the Pacific from San Diego and you'll find similar breakthroughs in the New Zealand city of Palmerston North, at Monrad Intermediate School. Only a few years ago the school and its district featured in a scathing television expose on glue-sniffing, drugs and social despair.

Visitors today would hardly recognize the same school. It has one of the most sophisticated computer systems in the country. Eleven-year-olds are learning every day to master computer skills like advanced desktop publishing, scanning pictures from videotape and photography on to a computer-produced school newspaper. Others are using computer programs to create music, solve problems and catch up if behind. Students turn up early each day to work at the computers and may, if they wish, stay in at lunchtime to continue.

But probably the main changes at the school stem from a change of

Motivation and productivity skyrocket when students reach their goals.

BETTIE B. YOUNGS
The 6 Vital Ingredients Of Self-Esteem
How To Develop Them In Your Students*

**Published by Jalmar Press, P.O. Box 1185,
Torrance, CA 90505.*

attitude, and from building close links with parents and their community. Of all the new technologies at the school, the most important is a minibus. With it come weekly visits to local senior-citizens' retirement homes and other community activities.

Every pupil now takes part in lifeskills programs. From the Red Cross they learn how to handle babies. They learn the basics of car repair, how to mend their own clothes, to bake, and the principles of good nutrition. The school caretaker even teaches a class where the youngsters learn cleaning. And all these activities are hands-on. They learn to bath real babies, change tires on real cars.

Monrad is also a multicultural school—and so is its curriculum. About 25 percent of its students are Maori—and its cultural enrichment programs have played a big part in bringing Maori parents into the school.

Monrad, in fact, is a classic case study of the links between self-esteem, lifeskills study, and an overall curriculum that is also deeply imbedded in a wide range of activities at the school and around the community.

❑ To complete "the Pacific triangle", travel north-west to Japan for some equally interesting models.

Japanese schools have some of the world's highest math and science test scores. More than 90 percent of students graduate from high school. And Japan has almost no illiteracy. Yet Japan spends proportionately less on public education than most other developed countries: only 5.3 percent of the gross national product, as compared with 7.8 percent in Canada, 6.2 percent in Britain and 6 percent in the United States.[19]

Many "back to basics" Westerners attribute this success to an extremely rigid school system of long hours and rote learning. This is the major method of teaching at junior and senior high school, but visit any elementary school and you'll find the opposite.[20] In the primary grades there's an almost kindergarten atmosphere. In one second-grade classroom we found children on the floor playing with big globs of clay, beautiful artwork on the walls, and children who appear relaxed, physically safe and emotionally secure.

Visit the children's lunchroom in Mito Municipal Oda Elementary School, and again comes the sense of social and emotional well-being: the beautiful classical music in the background, the children wearing hygiene masks as they serve lunch to other children in the line.

In fact, from kindergarten through third grade, one of the main

As Japanese teachers see it, their concern extends to the totality of their students' lives.

ROBERT C. CHRISTOPHER
The Japanese Mind

*Published by Pan.

Japanese school goals is social: teaching youngsters to be part of a group. After surveying 13 Tokyo elementary schools, American researcher Katherine Lewis reports that of all the goals and objectives displayed in classrooms, only 12 percent referred to academic work. The rest covered procedural skills, peer socialization, how children feel, personality development, physical energy, hygiene and personal habits. "The whole experience," says Lewis, "was at times more reminiscent of a scout meeting or a Sunday School than of a first-grade classroom." [21]

An overwhelming impression remains of early Japanese kindergarten and elementary schooling: that it is there *to lay the emotional and social groundwork for later academic learning.* In this way it may be one of the world's best bases for later accelerated learning.

Japanese elementary schools also delegate class control to small groups of children, to encourage group self-discipline and responsibility. For example, children take collective responsibility for cleaning up any graffiti. Result: no graffiti—and a great saving in janitor costs.

There is also no "tracking" in Japanese elementary schools. In every grade, slower learners are mixed with the more gifted. And promotion is automatic from grade to grade. Japan is very homogeneous—with a cultural climate that encourages a sense of community and family. So to "fail" youngsters at elementary school, to separate them according to ability, or any other criterion, would be regarded as antisocial.

Japan's teachers, too, enjoy, a public esteem that is missing in many countries. They also have a cultural tradition that sees them giving "life guidance" to students with special problems. Says former *Newsweek* foreign editor Robert C. Christopher, who lived in Japan for many years: "As Japanese teachers see it, their concern extends to the totality of their students' lives. If a Japanese youngster suddenly slumps academically, is caught smoking a cigarette or otherwise appears to be sliding into delinquency, his teacher will almost automatically call on the student's parents to find out what is troubling the child and to devise means of straightening it out." [22]

Japan, of course, is a consensus society—a land with few extremes of rich and poor. Many outside its borders would say it is too conformist: that "the nail that sticks up gets pounded down," in the words of one of its most famous proverbs. But, says Christopher, "the manner in which consensus is achieved is known as *nemawashi,* or 'root-binding'—a term taken from *bonsai* culture, in which, whenever a miniature tree is re-

Caring for people, caring for mother earth, and caring for tomorrow.

*New Paradigm Pioneer**

*The guiding principles of the China Productivity Center, laid down by its former President, Dr. Casper Shih. CPC is Taiwan's leading provider of business training programs, specializing in automation and total quality management.

potted, its roots are carefully pruned and positioned in such a way as to determine the tree's future shape." Obviously that "root-binding" has a big bearing on Japan's early-education system.

Unfortunately, that system changes in upper elementary and high school to one heavy with rote learning. English is taught by methods that would be regarded as old-fashioned even by school systems who have not attained anywhere near the accelerated-learning results we detail in the next chapter. As a result, Japan's foreign language ability generally lags well behind the Dutch and Swedes. But criticism of those methods should not blind outsiders to the positive benefits that can come both from root-binding and the priority placed on family and cooperative values.

As former Singapore Prime Minister Lee Kuan Yew puts it: "The fundamental difference between Western concepts of society and government and East Asian concepts . . . is that Eastern societies believe the individual exists in the context of his family." [23]

While American leaders talk strongly at election time of "family values", many Asian leaders think the breakdown of the family in the West is leading to its social decay. "Since 1960," says Kishore Mahbubani, permanent secretary in Singapore's Foreign Ministry, "the U.S. population has grown by 41 percent. In the same period there has been a 560 percent increase in violent crime, a 419 percent increase in illegitimate births, a 400 percent increase in divorce rates, a 300 percent increase in children living in single-parent homes, a more than 200 percent increase in teenage suicide rates, and a drop of almost 80 points in Scholastic Aptitude Tests." [24] With this sort of record, says Mahbubani, the West should "stop lecturing Asia".

In *Megatrends Asia* — mainly covering the area outside China — John Naisbitt lists "hard work, respect for learning, self-discipline, self-reliance and honesty" as top Asian personal values—in that order. The family unit has long been the foundation of Asian society. "In Asia," says Naisbitt, "families take care of themselves, above all else, and personal responsibility is emphasized. For Asians, the very idea of a central government being involved in family life is culturally unthinkable, horrifying. The idea of taking care of family first is why the savings rate in Asia is 30 percent or more in almost every country. Asia lives family values and self-sufficiency, and not only do Asians believe the cost of the welfare state is a heavy burden on competitiveness; they also contend that it undermines the importance of family and leads to out-of-wedlock children (in the United States, 30 percent of children are born out of

The effective development of brain power within a nation will decide the prosperity of the country in the future.

STAN SHIH
Me-Too Is Not My Style*

* Published by The Acer Corporation, Taiwan.
Mr. Shih is the Chairman and CEO of Acer.

wedlock, whereas in Malaysia it is 2 percent), high divorce rate, loss of self-reliance and lower academic achievement."

By contrast, the Chinese family networks that are now the dominant economic force in Asia also add, to their Asian and family values, their traditional emphasis on learning as a key goal for every child. Inside that nurturing cultural web, Asian countries have already shown how they can take the world's best technical breakthroughs and improve on them, without changing their own core values.

The Acer Group, Taiwan's leading computer manufacturer, has already contributed $7 million as seeding finance to set up the Acer Foundation to popularize new business methods. Acer has also set up its own children's computer and electronic games magazine—in Chinese. And it will not surprise us if satellite educational programs, in Mandarin, linking sites around Asia, play a bigger part than politicians in solving differences between Taiwan and the Chinese mainland.

Significantly, when *The Learning Revolution* was first published, it was one of Singapore's leading international schools that led the overseas demand by airfreighting in copies for every member of its staff.

And at Beijing's 21st Century Experimental School you'll find an excellent blend of traditional values and interactive technology. Go into one typical class, and eight-year-olds will be holding a wide-ranging discussion on behavioral values: a daily "subject". Next door nine-year-olds will be learning English by playing games. Elsewhere others will be working with computers or studying history through fossils in a school museum, learning classical music, or entertaining parents and foreign visitors in a completely unconscious and friendly way.

Even the school's establishment reflects the changing era. It is headed by Professor Zhang Fuqi, a Director of China's Senior Professors Association; the buildings financed by a donation from his entrepreneurial son; the land donated by the local government: all this in the main city of the world's biggest "communist-led" state.

No problems here with self-esteem and self-confidence as the school strives to link great methods of learning and teaching: some as ancient as Chinese civilization, others as tomorrow-geared as an electronic beep.

Six steps to teaching

1. THE RIGHT "STATE"

* Orchestrating the environment.
* Positive mood of teacher, student.
* Affirming, anchoring and focusing.
* Outcome and goal-setting: What's In It For Me?
* Visualize your goals.
* Regard mistakes as feedback.
* Peripheral posters.

2. THE RIGHT PRESENTATION

* Getting the Big Picture first, including field trips.
* Using all learning styles and all intelligences.
* Drawing, Mind Mapping, visualizations.
* Active and passive music concerts.

3. THINK ABOUT IT

* Creative thinking.
* Critical thinking—conceptual, analytical, reflective.
* Creative problem solving.
* Deep memory techniques for permanent storage.
* Thinking about your thinking.

4. ACTIVATE TO DRAW OUT

* Use it and practice it.
* Games, skits, discussions, plays, including all learning styles and all intelligences.

5. APPLY IT

* Use it outside school.
* Do it.
* Turn students into teachers.
* Combine it with what you already know.

6. REVIEW, EVALUATE AND CELEBRATE

* Know that I know.
* Self/peer/instructor evaluation.
* Ongoing review.

This is a Jeannette Vos checklist for teachers and trainers to set up a model integrative accelerated learning program.

New-century guideposts for tomorrow's teachers, trainers

Bright teachers and trainers around the world are now preparing for the challenges of the 21st century.

And they're doing it simply: by combining lessons learned from early childhood, brain research, show business, advertising, television, music, dancing, the movies, sports, art, and electronic multimedia.

Above all they're restoring fun to the learning process.

At Simon Guggenheim School, 11-year-old students from the poorest district of Chicago, Illinois, have learned to speak fluent Spanish, through visualization, puppet shows and songs.[1]

In southeast Asia non-accountants are learning the principles of accountancy in a two-day accelerated-learning game.[2]

In Australia, secondary school students have appeared as French actors in their own videotape production— as a vital part of learning a three-year foreign-language course in eight weeks.[3]

In the tiny European State of Liechtenstein, one trainer has created over 240 games to teach virtually anything—from patent law to geography, history and physics.[4]

In Auckland, New Zealand, aspiring Polynesian company managers have learned the main principles of marketing in only 90 minutes— playing the Great Pacific Century Marketing Game, with pineapples, bananas and gambling dice.[5]

Intel, IBM, Apple Computers and Bell Atlantic in the U.S., The Burton Group and British Airways in the United Kingdom, Shell Oil and Air New Zealand are among the major companies using similar tech-

To learn anything fast and effectively, you have to see it, hear it and feel it.

TONY STOCKWELL
*Accelerated Learning
in Theory and Practice**

*Published by EFFECT (European Foundation for Education,
Communication and Teaching), Liechtenstein.

Regular updates: www.thelearningweb.net

niques to slash staff training time and costs: from teaching German and Japanese to aircraft crews to training telephone linesmen—using music, relaxation, visualization and games.

In Scandinavia more than 30,000 teachers, parents, business trainers and managers have so far been through accelerated-learning workshops and seminars run by coauthor Vos.[6]

In New Zealand, all primary schools are using brightly colored puzzles and games to learn elementary mathematics. And managers from a wide range of businesses are learning in one day how to prepare a complete marketing plan with the Accelerated Planning Technique.[7]

At Cambridge College in Massachusetts, teachers are gaining a Masters Degree in education after only two semesters, including a five-week summer "intensive" that involves them directly in integrative accelerated learning techniques. Better still, they are seeing modeled in the classroom the techniques they're absorbing to earn their degree in record time.[8]

Some of the new techniques go by a variety of names: suggestopedia, neuro linguistic programming and integrative accelerated learning. But the best all combine three things: they're fun, fast and fulfilling. And the best involve relaxation, action, stimulation, emotion and enjoyment.

Says outstanding West Australian teacher and seminar leader Glenn Capelli: "Forget all the jargon. Forget all the big names. What we're really coming to grips with can be summed up in two words: true learning."[9]

Says British-born, Liechtenstein-based educational psychologist Tony Stockwell: "We now know that to learn anything fast and effectively you have to see it, hear it and feel it."[10]

Later we'll look at using the world as our classroom. But obviously much education will continue to revolve around schools, colleges and company training seminars.

And from our own research around the world, and practice in schools, colleges and business, all good training and educational programs involve six key principles. As a lifelong learner of any age, you'll learn quicker, faster and easier if all six are organized brilliantly by a teacher who is an *involver*—not a *lecturer*—who, acting as a *facilitator,* orchestrates these factors:

    1. The best learning "state";

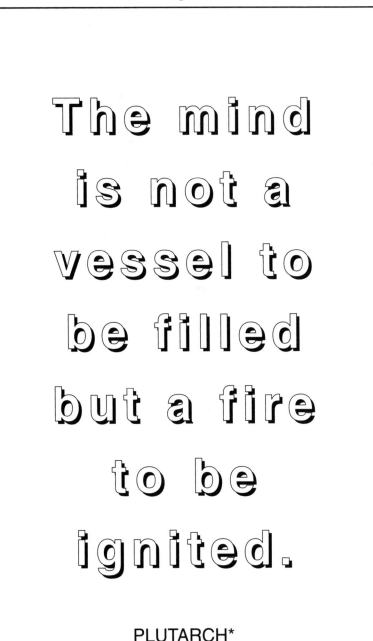

The mind is not a vessel to be filled but a fire to be ignited.

PLUTARCH*

* Greek biographer and essayist, written almost 3,000 years ago.

2. A presentation format that involves all your senses and is both relaxing, fun-filled, varied, fast-paced and stimulating;

3. Creative and critical thinking to aid "internal processing";

4: "Activations" to access the material, with games, skits and plays, and plenty of opportunity to practice;

5: The transfer to real-life applications and connections;

6: Regular review and evaluation sessions; and with them opportunities to celebrate learning.

1. The best learning "state"

Not surprisingly, each of those principles works best for an adult in almost the same way it works early in life, when learning develops quickly and easily through exploration and fun.

Orchestrating the environment

Can you imagine a two-year-old youngster learning by sitting still on a classroom seat all day? Of course not. She learns through doing, testing, touching, smelling, swinging, talking, asking and experimenting. And she learns at a phenomenal pace.

She is highly suggestible, and absorbs information from everything that goes on around her—her total environment.

But once she gets past kindergarten, too often education starts to become boring. The fun disappears. In many classrooms around the world, youngsters are told to sit still, in straight rows, listening to the teacher and not exploring, discussing, questioning or participating.

Good teachers know that's not the best way to learn. So they plan a classroom setting that facilitates easy learning. They use fresh flowers for scent and color. They cover the walls with colorful posters, highlighting all the main points of the course to be covered, in words and pictures—because it seems highly likely that most learning is subconscious.[11] Students absorb the lesson-content even without consciously thinking about it.

More and more teachers have music playing to establish the mood as students enter the classroom. Many use balloons and swinging mobiles to create an almost-party atmosphere.

"The total atmosphere must be nonthreatening and positively welcoming,"[11] says Mary Jane Gill, of Maryland, U.S.A., formerly in charge

When I taught new safe-driving techniques to truck drivers, we welcomed them with Dolly Parton music—and they loved it. It immediately told them they were welcome.

CHARLES SCHMID
founder of the LIND* Institute

*Learning in a New Dimension. Comment in author interview,
San Francisco, California.

of staff training for Bell Atlantic. Her techniques on one accelerated learning course cut training time by 42 percent, on another 57 percent. And the very first thing they did was change the atmosphere.

Top Swedish teacher, the late Christer Gudmundsson, agrees: "The atmosphere from the time your students enter the classroom must be thoroughly welcoming."[12] And the late Charles Schmid, of San Francisco, California—a world pioneer in new teaching methods—found mood-setting music one of the major keys to achieving learning rates at least five times better than before. "And that applies everywhere, from preschool to a business seminar teaching computer technology."[13]

Liechtenstein's Stockwell—one of Europe's leading new-style trainers in both schooling and business—says the importance of well-designed colorful posters cannot be overstressed. "Overhead projector slides, 35mm slides and flipcharts are fine," he says, "but posters are miles better—and all should be up around the walls before any learning session begins. They're peripheral stimuli. Their constant presence engraves their content into your memory, even when you're not consciously aware of them." He also says color psychology is important. "Red is a warning color; blue is cool; yellow is seen as the color of intelligence; green and brown have a pacifying effect and are warm and friendly. Never forget that effective posters make a strong impression on the long-term memory. They create memory pictures which can be called on when required although they were never consciously learned."[14]

Stockwell even brings his own specially-designed chairs—ideal for relaxed learning—to seminars he runs in the United States.

It's also the kind of lesson that all educational institutions can learn from the best businesses:

❏ The Seattle-based Nordstrom chain of clothing stores is used in dozens of management seminars as a model in profitable service—and it always has freshly-cut flowers in its customer changing rooms.

❏ Every international airline welcomes passengers on board with soothing, calming music—before presenting safety demonstrations.

❏ Visit Hawaii, the tourist capital of the mid-Pacific, on a package tour and you'll soon slip into a welcoming vacation mood as you're greeted with a lei of island flowers.

❏ Visit Disneyland or Disneyworld and you're immediately struck by the cleanliness and total atmosphere.

Since the brain cannot pay attention to everything . . . uninteresting, boring or emotionally flat lessons simply will not be remembered.

LAUNA ELLISON
*What Does The Brain Have
To Do With Learning?**

*Article in *Holistic Education Review*, Fall 1991.

Think of that the next time you visit a school or company seminar-room that persists with uncomfortable straight-backed wooden chairs and an atmosphere that is cold, lifeless and often colorless.

Setting the right mood and getting students' attention

Canadian teachers Anne Forester and Margaret Reinhard, in their excellent book, *The Learners' Way,* talk of "creating a climate of delight" in every school classroom. They say variety, surprise, imagination and challenge are essential in creating that climate. "Surprise guests, mystery tours, field trips, spontaneous projects (old-fashioned days, pet displays, research initiated by the children) add richness to reading, writing and discussion. The production of plays and puppet shows is stimulated by the children's reading and is masterminded more and more fully by the children themselves.

"Your classroom will rarely be totally silent. Sharing and interaction are the vital components of a climate of delight. Discoveries, new learning, the sheer joy of accomplishment demand expression."

If that "climate of delight" sweeps over you as you enter a well-planned seminar room or classroom, it's the first step in setting the right mood for more effective learning.*

Early activity is vital

The next step is activity: precisely what students or trainees are encouraged to *do.* The colorful setting, posters and mobiles will already have started to stimulate those who are mainly *visual learners.* The music will have "touched base" with the mainly *auditory learners.* And early activity makes the *kinesthetic learners* feel instantly comfortable. Interspersing all three learning styles also makes sure that all three levels of the brain are activated: our *thinking* brain, our *feeling* brain and our *doing* brain. But there are other good reasons for instant activity:

Jazzercise-type exercises to music encourage an increased flow of

* Before starting any teacher-training session, co-author Vos spends at least an hour putting out props, covering the walls with colorful posters, and making sure that all audio-visual equipment is working—including the CD-player for the music that will welcome the audience. Co-author Dryden always urges participants to have a brain-jogging breakfast of bananas, kiwi fruit, oranges and other fresh fruit before spending time at one of his innovation seminars. Then, at the start of a seminar, after a warm-up exercise to music, he may throw out "brain-food" bananas to those who have forgotten breakfast.

Human Bingo

Find someone who has done the following
and write each name in the square

A kinesthetic learner	Owns a rowboat	Uses graphics in their workshops
Has a piece of the Great Wall	Plays an harmonica	A visual learner
Slept in an airport overnight	Has been to Bulgaria	Has taken part in a funny business luncheon
An auditory learner	Has taken a Dale Carnegie course	Is a good singer
Loves music	Is a great high school teacher	Is a fabulous cook

A Human Bingo Game: the type used by Libyan Labiosa-Cassone and Philip Cassone to break the ice in a seminar session at an annual conference of the International Alliance for Learning.

Jeannette Vos uses the technique regularly, for example in social studies classes. Each student may receive a duplicated page of questions on a subject such as China or Japan, and each is encouraged to wander round the room at the start of class to find the answers from fellow students.

She also uses it to bring out the importance of rapport and relationship as the foundation of teaching and learning.

oxygen to the brain—and the brain runs largely on oxygen and glucose.

Other exercises to music—*such as simple juggling and left-foot/ right hand, right foot/left-hand movements*—*can stimulate instant communication between the "right brain" and the "left-brain,"* as we cover in more detail in chapter 11.

Others can loosen students up—mentally and physically: to help them relax. Canadian psychologist and astronomer Tom Wujec covers many in *Pumping Ions*—*Games and Exercises to Flex Your Mind.*

Other activities can break the ice and help participants get to know each other—*and the talents that are available to be tapped, inside and outside the specific setting.*

Minneapolis accelerated learning trainers Libyan Labiosa-Cassone and Philip Cassone often start international seminar sessions with a game of "Human Bingo" (see opposite). Participants have two minutes to meet as many people as possible.

Other activities can put you in a positive mood. Australia's Capelli often gets his learners to:

❑ Sit in pairs—with someone they've never met before—and spend 45 seconds recounting the most interesting aspect of their background; so that each person starts the session by focusing on projects that have been personally successful (reinforcing self-esteem).

❑ Massage each other's neck and shoulder muscles to encourage relaxation.

❑ All sing a specially composed *Attitude song*—"The Big A in my life (students spell out each letter of A-T-T-I-T-U-D-E with their arms in time with the music)."[15]

Obviously the techniques will depend on whether you are taking a regular school class, running a specific-topic seminar, or introducing an international symposium.

Eric Jensen, author of *SuperTeaching* and co-founder of SuperCamp, believes two core elements affect learning: they are *state* and *strategy.* The third is obviously *content.* "State" creates the right mood for learning. "Strategy" denotes the style or method of presentation. "Content" is the subject. In every good lesson you have all three.

But many traditional school systems ignore "state". Yet it is the most critical of the three. The "door" must be open to learning before true learning can happen. And that "door" is an emotional one—*the*

Is it possible to learn 1,200 foreign words a day?

The most remarkable claims for accelerated learning in foreign-language training have come from Dr. Georgi Lozanov.

He reports* that Bulgarian students have actually found it easier to remember between 1,000 and 1,200 new foreign words *a day* than 500 words.

Here are the results he records from 896 "suggestopedic" language-training sessions:

Number of of words given in session	Number of students in session	% of words memorized per session
Up to 100	324	92.3%
100 - 200	398	96.8%
201 - 400	93	93.1%
401 - 600	53	90.4%
1000 - 1200	28	96.1%

*Dr. Lozanov's results are reported fully in his book, *Suggestology and Outlines of Suggestopedy,* published by Gordon and Breach, New York (1978).

Both the current authors were present during Dr. Lozanov's keynote presentation to the Society for Accelerative Learning and Teaching in Seattle, Washington, in 1991.

It is fair to report, however, that in all our research we have not encountered results outside Bulgaria that come anywhere near matching the ones reported above. Dr. Charles Schmid, in San Francisco, has reported students being presented with 400 foreign words in a day and being able to use them in conversation within three days (see page 323), a remarkable enough feat.

"gatekeeper to learning", part of being in a fully resourceful state.

The right brain wavelength

One of the main steps to achieve this is to get everyone working on the "right wavelength." *And here probably the most ironic contradiction occurs: to learn faster you slow down the brain.* One of your brain's "wavelengths" is obviously most efficient for deep-sleep. Another is more efficient for inspiration. And another, the one you're most conscious of: the wideawake alertness of daily living. But many studies now reveal that a fourth brainwave is the most efficient "frequency" for easy, effective learning: what some call the alpha state.[16]

Bring on the music

Dozens of research projects have found that music is a very efficient dial to tune into that alpha frequency.[17]

"The use of music for learning is certainly not new," Californian accelerated-learning innovator Charles Schmid told us not long before his death. "We learned our alphabet to music—ABCD—EFG—HIJK—LMNOP. But in the last 25 years we've expanded our music knowledge tremendously. We've found out that in a special kind of relaxation, which music can induce, our brain is most open and receptive to incoming information. That type of relaxation is *not* getting ready to fall asleep. It's a state of *relaxed alertness*—what we sometimes call *relaxed awareness.*"[18]

Much of our recent knowledge in this field has been built on the pioneering research started in the 1950s by Bulgarian psychiatrist and educator Georgi Lozanov. Lozanov set out to determine why some people have super-memories.

After years of research, he concluded that we each have an "optimum learning state". This occurs, he says, "where heartbeat, breath-rate and brainwaves are smoothly synchronized and the body is relaxed but the mind concentrated and ready to receive new information."[19]

In putting that research into practice, Lozanov achieved some amazing results, particularly in foreign-language learning. By the early 1960s Berlitz, then the world's largest language-training school, promised students could learn 200 words after several days' training—a total of 30 hours.

But Lozanov's research reported Bulgarian students learning 1,200

Music reduces stress, relieves anxiety, increases energy and improves recall. Music makes people smarter.

JEANNETTE VOS
*The Music Revolution**

*Published by The Learning Web Ltd.,
Auckland, New Zealand.

words *a day* and remembering a remarkable 96.1 percent of them.[20]

Many others have built on his research. According to Schmid: "We now know that most people can achieve that ideal learning state fairly easily—and quickly. Deep breathing is one of the first keys. Music is the second—specific music with a certain beat that helps slow you down: anywhere from 50 to 70 beats a minute."

The most common music to achieve that state comes from the baroque school of composers, in the 17th and early 18th centuries: the Italian Arcangelo Corelli, the Venician Antonio Vivaldi, France's Francois Coupertin and the Germans, Johann Sebastian Bach and George Frideric Handel.

Lozanov found baroque music harmonizes the body and brain. In particular, it unlocks the emotional key to a super memory: the brain's limbic system. This system not only processes emotions, it is the link between the conscious and subconscious brain.

As Terry Wyler Webb and Dougles Webb put it brilliantly in *Accelerated Learning With Music: A Trainer's Manual:* "Music is the interstate highway to the memory system."[21]

Vivaldi's *Four Seasons* is one of the best-known pieces of baroque music used to start the journey along that highway. It makes it easy to shut out other thoughts and visualize the seasons. Handel's *Water Music* is also deeply soothing. And for teachers trained in new learning techniques, Johann Pachelbel's *Canon in D* is a favorite to relieve tension.

Most of those teachers also use specially-prepared tapes to start each learning session—with soothing word-pictures to match the music and encourage relaxation. Tapes can be either self-made, if you're competent in music, or bought. Their key first use in education is to put students into a relaxed, receptive state so they can focus on learning.

Break down the learning barriers

Lozanov says there are three main barriers to learning: the *critical-logical* barrier ("School isn't easy, so how can learning be fun and easy?"); the *intuitive-emotional* barrier ("I'm dumb, so I won't be able to do that"); and the *critical-moral* barrier ("Studying is hard work—so I'd better keep my head down"). Understand where a student "is coming from" and you gain better rapport. Step into his world and you break resistance quickly, smoothly.

STEPPING OUT

MY OWN ACTION PLAN

1. **GOAL:**

2. **ECOLOGY CHECK:**

   What resources do I have? What's in it for me?

   What's in it for my world?

3. **COMMITMENT:**

   Am I willing to put forth all the effort needed to achieve my goal?

4. **ACTION:**

   First step:

   Next step:

   Follow-up:

5. **ANTICIPATED ROADBLOCKS:**

6. **MONITOR:**

   How do I monitor? How am I doing?

   Who can mentor me?

7. **SUPPORT:**

   What support do I need?

8. **REVIEW:**

   Do I need to adjust anything to achieve my goal?

9. **SELF ASSESSMENT:**

   To what degree did I achieve my goal?

A simple checklist used by Jeannette Vos to help students set and focus on their goals.

Encourage personal goal-setting and learning outcomes

Encourage students to set their own goals—and to plan their own future. If they know where they are going, then their path is focused. In our experience, *most people will over-achieve personal targets that they set themselves*—possibly the soundest principle in management.

In classroom settings, we both encourage the "Station WIIFM" game—to focus on "What's In It For Me?" Not in a selfish sense, but to get participants, perhaps in pairs, to tell each other and teachers what they specifically hope to get from the session, the day or the year.

The way this is introduced is vital, especially in school. Many at-risk students get very angry with the traditional "You-will-learn-this today" introduction. Instead, good teachers invite students to set their own goals, right from the outset, and the outcomes they would like from the session.

Often students come with "hidden agendas"—and they don't always "buy in" to the instructor's agenda. The key is to make learning a partnership, where the instructor prepares a smorgasbord of possible "curriculum pieces" and the students get a big say in what they want out of it.

Try visualizing your goal

Visualizing is a powerful learning tool. An ineffective teacher might well say: "Don't forget to study or you might do poorly in the upcoming test"—a negative reinforcer.

Eric Jensen suggests two better ways. One is to encourage students to visualize precisely how they would be using their new-found knowledge in the future. The other is to plant a positive thought that will encourage students to browse through their study-book looking for specific answers that might be used in the future.

We cannot stress this point too strongly: many teachers do not realize how damaging negative suggestions can be.

Trigger the emotions

Nor can we overstress that the emotional "limbic" part of the brain is the gateway to long-term memory, so all good teaching encourages warm emotions. This fuses what you have been learning into deep memory.

2. The keys to good presentation

Positivity and linking are the first ones

All good presentations must be learner-centered and linked to stu-

Your most valuable asset [in learning] is a positive attitude.

BOBBI DePORTER
*Quantum Learning**

*Published by Dell Publishing, 666 Fifth Avenue,
New York, NY 10103.

dents' own goals and existing knowledge. "The more you link, the more you learn." The flower is the perfect metaphor to link to positive imagery: "What does it take to make your flower grow?"

Another technique to guarantee involvement from the start is for the learners and the instructor to toss a squashy, brightly colored Koosh ball to volunteers to tell one main point they already know about a topic, and to draw Mind Maps covering the same points—from a pre-prepared map that lists the main "learning branches".

The sequence is designed to encourage the learners of every subject to start by identifying what they want to know, and then proceeding from what they already know—generally an amazing amount.

The entire presentation must also be positive. The facilitator should never suggest in any way that the session is anything but fun—no "now the break's over, let's get back to the hard work" talk.

Lozanov called his fast-learning process "suggestopedia," from "suggestology"—but that is an unfortunate translation into English. Says Stockwell: "The name is rather unusual, but if you see 'to suggest' in the sense of 'to propose' or 'to recommend' then it is easier to understand the relationship."[22]

As we've touched on in the previous chapter, the power of suggestion is paramount in learning: we all do best when we think we can do it; we fail if we expect to fail. Every adult has seen how infants' learning abilities soar in a favorable, positive atmosphere. All good Lozanov-style facilitators try to recreate the same kind of positive fun-filled atmosphere in the classroom. And like all good advertising copywriters, they go out of their way to stress how easy the project is. Japanese-language teachers may well use the "Itchy knee; sun, she go rock!" exercise we've covered on page 34.

Business-seminars may well start with the story of Ray Krok, the 52-year-old seller of milkshake machines, who first visited a Californian hamburger restaurant in 1952 and saw the start of an idea that ended up as McDonald's—an example to show how great projects can grow from very modest beginnings.

Lozanov stresses the important links between conscious and subconscious presentation. He believes each of us has an enormous reserve of brain power waiting to be tapped. He believes that by far the most important part of all learning is subconscious; and that good teachers remove the barriers to learning by making their presentations logical,

Try this balloon test to match your abilities with others

To demonstrate to any group their individual learning and working strengths, provide each with four different colored balloons. And get each one to select, from the boxes below, his or her eight main strengths.

Creativity (red)	Communications (blue)
Open minded **Lateral thinking** **Brainstorming** **Visionary**	**Writing** **Speakng** **Listening** **Visualizing**
Administration (yellow)	Organization (green)
Financial **Structured** **Logical** **Sequential**	**Leader** **Simplifier** **Delegator** **Self starter**

Then get each person to blow the four balloons to match his or her main strengths. Thus, if you selected all four in the red box and only one in the blue, you'd blow your blue balloon up to a quarter the size of the red one. Then split your team into groups of four so they combine strengths from each quartile.*

The balloon-match, as used above, adapted from original concept from Alistair Rylatt, Director, Excel Human Resource Development, P.O. Box 164, Newtown 2042, NSW, Australia.

ethical, enjoyable and stress-free. Hence the importance of posters and "peripherals" as part of the total presentation.

Getting the big picture first

A major presentation technique is to present "the big picture" first—to provide an overview, like the total jigsaw puzzle picture, so that all the later pieces can then fall into place. Again, posters or other classroom peripherals may well present the big picture—so it's always there as a focusing point.

Telling a story is also a great preview technique.

And field trips are highly recommended at the start of any study—to see the big picture in action.

Drawing Mind Maps at the start of study, including all the main "limbs", allows students to draw in the smaller branches later.

Involve all the senses

All good presentations also appeal to all individual learning styles.

The most neglected learning style in nearly every school system is kinesthetic—or movement. Every good learning experience has plenty of verbal stimulation, plenty of music, plenty of visuals—but the really great teachers make sure to have plenty of action, plenty of participation, plenty of movement. Even though students may be visual learners, everyone embeds information by doing.

Step out of the lecturing role

This is probably the major personal change required in teaching styles. All the best "teachers" are activators, facilitators, coaches, motivators, orchestrators.

Always orchestrate "non-conscious" processing

Since Lozanov practitioners say most learning is "subconscious", the room setting, posters, body language, tone of speech and positive attitude all are vital parts of the learning process.

Plenty of role playing and "identities"

Lozanov teachers also encourage students to "act the part". There are few faster ways to learn science than to act out the roles of famous scientists; or to learn history by putting yourself in the historical setting.

Organize plenty of "state changes"

The best teachers organize plenty of "state changes" so that students

Because music can both calm and stimulate, it offers one of the quickest ways to influence the mood of a group.

JEANNETTE VOS
The Music Revolution*

* Published by The Learning Web Ltd.,
Auckland, New Zealand.

switch from singing, to action, to talking, to viewing, to rhyme, to Mind Mapping, to group discussions. This has a two-fold purpose:

1. It reinforces the information in all learning styles; and

2. It breaks up the lesson into chunks for easy learning.

Both have a major bearing on how well the information is absorbed. For example, it is now well proven that, in any presentation, students can generally remember easiest the information at the start, the end and any "outstanding" examples that gripped their imagination. Regular "state changes" provide the opportunity for many more "firsts", "lasts" and graphic examples.

Make learning-how-to-learn a key part of every course

This is probably the main overall desired result from all learning. So the techniques should be blended into all activities.

The Lozanov "concerts"

Possibly Lozanov's greatest contribution to education has again been in the sphere of music: not only to relax your mind and put it into a highly receptive state—but to use music to float new information into your amazing memory system.

Lozanov recommends two *concerts*. And again, Charles Schmid has summarized the theory and practice neatly: "If, say, a class is learning a foreign language, as the first step the teacher sets out the new vocabulary in the form of a play, and with an overview of it in pictures. The student sits there taking a 'mental movie' of it. Immediately following this comes the first concert—what Lozanov called the *active concert*. With the student looking at the text, the teacher turns on some selected music, and he reads the foreign language in time to the music. He deliberately acts out the words dramatically in time to the music.

"Now there's no magic to this; it's precisely why it is easier to learn the lyrics of a song, rather than remember all the words on a page of notes. The music is somehow a carrier and the teacher surfs along with the music—almost like catching a wave."[23]

Lozanov's second learning phase is called a *passive concert*.

Charles Schmid again: "The second concert follows immediately after the first. And here we use very specific slow baroque music—around 60 beats to the minute—very precise. And while the first reading of the language was very dramatic, the second is in a more natural intonation. Now the students are invited to close their eyes if they want—

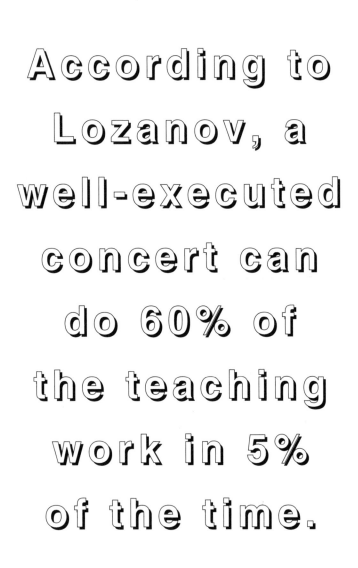

According to Lozanov, a well-executed concert can do 60% of the teaching work in 5% of the time.

TERRY WYLER WEBB with DOUGLAS WEBB
Accelerated Learning With Music:
A Trainer's Manual*

**Published by Accelerated Learning Systems,
Norcross, Georgia 30092.

although they don't have to. They put the text aside, and imagine, say, that they are in a theater in the country they're studying, and somebody is acting a story in the background. Generally this will be the last part of a particular language session—and the students will then go home—and probably skim through their foreign-language 'play' just before they go to sleep." Overnight the subconscious goes to work—and the seemingly automatic start of the transfer to long-term memory storage. Lozanov fans claim the use of music in this way can accomplish 60 percent of learning in 5 percent of the time.[24]

We hasten to add that even great Lozanov enthusiasts do not recommend using his full "concert" technique in every session. Even in something as clearly defined as learning a foreign language, perhaps only three "concert" sessions might be held in a week. But all the other key principles of learning would be used in other sessions.

3. Thinking about it, and deep memory storage

Education is, of course, not only about absorbing new information. It involves thinking about it and storing it into deep memory as well.

Learning how to think is a major part of every educational program, and good facilitators use "thinking games" and "mind games" as part of synthesizing information—as well as providing "state changes". In business seminars we've found it best to introduce this by fun projects: designing "a golf ball that can't get lost" or playing the "What if?" game on subjects well divorced from the activities of each group.

For deep memory storage, Lozanov's active and passive concerts are tops. They are designed to access the long-term memory system in order to link new information subconsciously with data already stored.

4. Activate to draw out the learning

Storing information is also only one part of the learning process. The information also has to be accessed. So the next step is "activation".

And here games, skits, discussions and plays can all be used to "activate" the memory-banks—and reinforce the learning pathways.

Again, this needn't make more work for the teacher. The opposite, in fact. Students love to organize their own plays, presentations, debates and games. Give them the chance to present their new-found information to the rest of the class or group—any way they prefer.

Lozanov's music for the two "concerts"*

ACTIVE CONCERT

Beethoven, Concerto for Piano and Orchestra No. 5 in B-flat major.

Mozart, Symphony in D major, "Haffner," and Symphony in D Major, "Prague."

Haydn, Concerto No. 1 in C Major for Violin and Orchestra; Concerto No. 2 in G Major for Violin and Orchestra.

Haydn,Symphony in C Major No. 101, "L'Horioge;" and Symphony in G Major No. 94.

Mozart, Concerto for Violin & Orchestra in A Major No. 5; Symphony in A Major No. 29; Symphony in G Minor No. 40.

Brahms, Concerto for Violin and Orchestra in D. Major, Op. 77.

PASSIVE CONCERT

Vivaldi, Five Concertos for Flute and Chamber Orchestra.

Handel, Concerto for Organ and Orchestra in B-flat Major, Op. 7, No. 6.

J. S. Bach, Prelude in G Major, "Dogmatic Chorales."

Corelli, Concerti Grossi, Op. 6, No. 4, 10, 11, 12.

J.S. Bach, Fantasia for Organ in G. Major; Fantasia in C Minor.

Couperin, Sonatas for Harpsichord: "Le Parnasse" (Apotheosis of Corelli); "L'Estree;" J.F. Rameau, Concert Pieces for Harpisichord "Pieces de clavecin" No.1 and No. 5.

*From *The Foreign Language Teacher's Suggestopedic Manual,* by Georgi Lozanov and Evalina Gateva, published by Gordon and Breach, New York,1988. See other selections on page 180.

Schmid explains a typical activation session, after French-language students have slept on a concert-session: "The next morning, or within 48 hours, the students come in; they haven't said a word of French yet—or at least not in the new vocabulary. Now comes three or four hours of what we call activation.

"Now we play games with the vocabulary. We're feeding their brains in different ways. We've already done it consciously in showing them the words and pictures of their French play. Then we've fed it into their subconscious, with the aid of music. And now they're activating their brains in different ways to make sure it's stored. And I tell you: now I wouldn't teach in any other way"

Schmid, who unfortunately died not long after our interview, had degrees in music, psychology and foreign language instruction. He taught at the University of Texas and New York University for many years with traditional methods before "getting hooked" on the new techniques.

"I started to teach French and German and sometimes Italian with these new techniques; I wanted to see if the system worked, if it really was all it was cracked up to be. And I was amazed. I would teach students in a three and a half hour class. I'd give them 400 words of French, say, the first day. And by the end of the third day they were able to repeat them in forms of conversation. And that had never happened before.

"Previously at the university, if I gave students 25 words a day in the old way, they'd be lucky to remember ten the next day. I was convinced.

"In fact, when I first started using the techniques myself, I started dreaming in the language after about the third day. And I had never had that feedback before."

Schmid's experience left him no doubt as to the benefits of the new learning methods: "I would say the speedup in the learning process is anywhere from five to 20 times—maybe 25 times—over what it was in traditional methods. But it's not only the acceleration; it's the quality of learning that goes on. And the feedback. They say: 'This is fun. Why didn't I learn this way in high school?'

"Recently at a New England telephone company students were using these methods to study optic fibers and some technical telecommunications work. The trainees were sitting on the floor, playing with wooden blocks, fitting them together and understanding what goes on in an optic fiber. The trainer said: 'OK, it's time for a break.' And the trainees said:

Sample design for a learning game

Getting students to design their own learning game can in itself be an effective learning tool.

Here's one designed by Gordon Dryden to teach the basic principles of innovation: *The Aha! Game.**

 A brief but graphic color-slide presentation introduces creative thinking and problem-solving, using examples from chapter 4.

 The game is based around eight segments of a pineapple, with each segment an aspect of the marketing cycle: the product or service; the customers; presentation; pricing and profitability; distribution; promotion; building satisfied customers; and taking on the world through niche marketing.

 In one version of the game, 11 key marketing tips are numbered in a workbook under each segment. Students roll two dice, and, whatever the total, they discuss the implications or run quiz shows to find telling examples.

 Another version is a board game, with cards similar to *Trivial Pursuit* **and Roger von Oech's** *Creative Whack Pack.*

5 *The Aha! game* **generally takes students through a mythical product-problem (such as selling surplus bananas)—and the eight segments provide plenty of "state changes" and breaks—between graphic visual presentation, group workshops, discussion in pairs and quiz shows. It teaches thinking and problem-solving skills along with marketing principles.**

* The Aha! Game is copyright The Learning Web Ltd., Auckland, New Zealand.

'You take a break; we're having fun; we're learning; and we're getting this finally.' That's what I mean. It works and it's fun."

5. Apply it

In our view, the real test of learning is not a written examination through multiple-choice questions. The key is to use the learning and apply it to purposeful situations, preferably real-life.

The real test of a French course is how well you can speak French. The real test of a sales course is how well you can sell.

You learn to play a piano by playing a piano, you learn to type by typing, to ride a bike by riding a bike, to speak in public by speaking in public. So the best teachers and business seminar organizers plan plenty of action sessions to back up the theory so students can purposefully use and apply the learning.

Turn your students into teachers

As in the activation phase, it makes sound sense to have students work in pairs or teams, with a free hand to prepare their own presentations of main points. Groups in a teacher-training class, for example, may each be asked to crystallize a specific aspect of educational psychology. And more and more schools are using the "buddy" system, where an older or more qualified student helps another, and both benefit.

Encourage Mind Mapping

We've already covered the principles of this and suggested you use it to preview the learning, but it is also a remarkable way to review and make notes. *It really is what it says: a map that records main points in the same way the brain stores information—like branches on a tree.* It's also a major tool in the next process.

6. Review, evaluate and celebrate

Even highly efficient learners will not always be conscious of whether they "know what they know". One way to bring the learner to that awareness is through a quick Koosh-ball throw at the end of a lesson. This will jog students' memories of all the important learnings of the day. Another way is a "passive concert" review, which also covers all the points handled.

And then comes one of the most crucial steps: the self-evaluation. This is where a student truly "digs within" to uncover those precious gems

Novel ways to end seminars

Here are two of the many "accelerated learning" ways* to end a seminar or learning session on a high note, with plenty of fun while encouraging participants to crystallize the main points they have learned:

a. Ask each participant to write, on one sheet of paper, a sentence summing up the main message learned.

b. Participants then pair-off, and each has 45 seconds to convince the other that his or her main point is the key one.

c. Those two then pair off with another two, with the same conditions.

d. Those four participants then line up with another four, and so on until finally half the gathering appoint a spokesperson to argue their agreed main point with the other half.

Allowing about two minutes for each segment, and a little longer for the all-in debate at the end, a conference of 300 people can complete the process in under 20 minutes.

a. Give all participants five minutes to write single-sentence summaries of all the main points they have learned—each on a separate sheet of paper.

b. Each one then attaches his or her sheets to a giant noticeboard.

c. They each then start moving the sheets about, matching like with like, discussing the reasons.

The size of each selection of main points will then help crystallize the group's conclusions—and enable the facilitator to sum up.

* Both examples here observed at workshop sessions at International Alliance for Learning conferences in America.

of the day. Self-evaluation is a tool for higher thinking: reflecting, analyzing, synthesizing, then judging.

Peer-evaluation and instructor-evaluation are also important parts in culminating a lesson, but the most important is self-evaluation.

Another way to review is to skim over your Mind Maps or "highlighted" notes, or both:

* Before you go to sleep on the day you've been studying;
* The next morning;
* A week later;
* A month later;
* And just before you need to use it—or before an exam.

If you're on a one-week course with an examination at the end, spend at least 15 minutes a night on that day's Mind Map and highlights, and at least five minutes on each of the previous days.

Or if you're writing an article or even a book, it's amazing how much you can recall by skimming your Mind Maps and underlined books.

And always remember to celebrate every victory—just as any sporting achiever would celebrate. Praise the entire class effort, and whenever possible turn that praise into a recap of the main points learned.

Putting it all together

And how does all this theory work in practice? Let's look at four examples: an entire school that has switched to integrative accelerated learning techniques; a high school class that has done the same for one subject; a special foreign language project in the army; and a teacher who's made the change, with outstanding results.

The Simon Guggenheim School experiment

The first is an example of the great potential changes that can come from innovative schooling. It is also a sobering example of how that potential cannot be fully realized unless the entire social climate of a community changes, too.

Simon Guggenheim K-8 School is in one of the poorest districts of Chicago, Illinois. Nearly all families are African-American, 85 percent are officially below the poverty line, with annual incomes between $9,000 and $11,000 and a large proportion live on social welfare.

Our aim is still for our school to be the best . . . a school without failure, where all children leave school having identified a talent, a skill, an intelligence, through which they can become whatever they want to be.

MICHAEL ALEXANDER
Former Principal, Simon Guggenheim School*

*Author interview, in Chicago, Illinois.

Fifteen years ago their children's futures were bleak. Their school had one of the worst scholastic records in all the United States. Today a great deal has changed. Guggenheim School is now regarded as a model on how school disasters can be turned into success.

When Michael Alexander first arrived there as principal in 1984, the school was a failure and in danger of being shut down by the local Board of Education. Alexander's first decision was to upgrade the morale and skills of a demoralized staff. Using some State Title 1 funds, for schools with special needs, he offered all staff members a 30-hour retraining course with Peter Kline, the man he now describes as "the genial dynamo of integrative learning". Half the teachers went at one time, while substitutes filled their places; then the other half.

"To put it mildly," Alexander recalls, "they were sceptical at first. We agreed there would be no pressure on them to use the principles and techniques of integrative accelerated learning. It was up to them to apply what they found valuable."[25] The rest, he says, is pleasant history.

Walk into one class, and you'll find 11-year-olds learning Spanish—at their own request—by taking part in puppet shows and singing to music. Walk into another and 13-year-olds will be learning American history by actually taking over the roles of Abraham Lincoln or Thomas Jefferson. Walk into the computer room and parents and students will be learning together. Go into another and a happy bunch of young African-Americans are learning about hygiene through a "rap session". The corridors are a blaze of colorful posters. Photos of black achievers adorn the walls of many classrooms.

Ask Alexander what's so unusual about the school, and his reply is direct: "This school is a fun place to be—and it's a place where people throw aside all the roles that are generally germane to education—where teachers act one way and students act another. Everybody is now focused on creating an atmosphere of joy and learning for children—and people move in any role that's necessary in order to facilitate that."[26]

That change doesn't end in the classroom. The school runs its own breakfast and lunch program—with meals high in nutrition. At its simplest, you can't learn if you're hungry.

"Students walk through the hall now, very polite, very respectful," says Alexander. "Overhearing children on the playground, they talk about their school becoming the school of the future. 'We use accelerated learning. We're gonna be the most sophisticated school in the city with

**The richest component of one
of our learning courses
is the activation phase.
This takes about 75 to
80 percent of the time.
We play board games,
card games, we play with
a ball, we play with
paper dolls, we play
musical chairs, we play
with construction paper.
Much like the games you
would buy in a toy shop
but adapted to
make learning fun.**

LIBYAN LABIOSA-CASSONE*

*Second-language and accelerated learning consultant to
Simon Guggenheim School; author interview, Chicago, Illinois.

computer technology. We have Spanish in our school. We have tai chi in our school.' They tell their friends, and they're very excited about it."

So are the parents. An average of 20 turn up each day to help out.

What about the results?

"Academically, the performance changed dramatically," says Alexander. "The year prior to our teachers being trained in integrative, accelerated learning techniques, only 27 percent of our kids were making a year's growth in a year's instruction. A year subsequent to that, the rate went up to 54 percent, and in math it went to 58 percent."*

Dr. Larry Martel, President of Interlearn Integrative Learning Systems in Hilton Head, South Carolina, surveyed the results after that year. And he reported a 103 percent increase in reading scores and an 83 percent increase in math and reading combined. In two years Guggenheim went from being at the bottom of Chicago's Subdistrict 16 schools to second from the top.

It would be great to report that its efforts have completely turned around a whole community. But the district still has one of the highest homicide rates in the country. The poverty still remains. For those students who stay on at Guggenheim, the overall achievements remain high. But many transient students are there for too short a time to have other than a glimpse of their true potential. And the surrounding neighborhood bears daily testimony to America's urgent need for the same kind of innovative approaches to social problems that Guggenheim has brought to schooling.

Fluent French in eight weeks

For a class demonstration of accelerated learning in action, an excellent example comes from Beverley Hills Girls' High School in Sydney, Australia.

In the early 1990s they introduced an accelerated learning course that successfully compressed a three-year French course into eight weeks. Says teacher Sylvia Skavounos: "I was amazed. We'd had a standard French course for two-thirds of a year before we started. Yet in the two weeks after we began, the students had learned at least 200 new words, and they could say them fluently"—much better in two weeks than the previous several months.[27] The course they chose was produced by

---

Michael Alexander is no longer principal at Guggenheim, but new principal Nancy Ellis has continued with an expanded program.

Learn a language in record time

In 1993, Bridley Moor High School in Redditch, England, tested the effectiveness of accelerated learning methods for studying a foreign language.

One group of students' German study included ten weeks of accelerated learning methods, and their examination results were compared with others studying at the same level by conventional methods.

On July 16, 1993, BBC television broadcast the examination results:

	Using new methods	Using normal methods
80% pass mark or better	65%	11%
90% pass mark or better	38%	3%

Thus, using new techniques, more than ten times as many students achieved a 90 percent pass mark.

Sources:

School examination results from Mrs Val Duffy-Cross, Assistant Head, Bridley Moor High School, Redditch, U.K. Television program on BBC Midland TV, July 16, 1993. Course materials and methods from Accelerated Learning Systems, Aston Clinton, Bucks, England: the course outlined on page 177, and used also by the Sydney high school with its French results reported on pages 331 to 333. The course is designed for do-it-yourself home study, but can be supplied with an optional kit for teachers.

Accelerated Learning Systems of England, mainly for self-help learning. It also comes with a teacher kit for classroom use. When a crew from Australia's Channel 7 television network visited the Beverley Hills French class, they found students doing exactly what Charles Schmid has described: starting with relaxation exercises; clearing their mind for the session to come; learning through *active* and *passive* concerts; reactivating their learning through games and even acting out and producing their own videotape.

TV brought in Jean-Philippe de Voucoux, an expert from Alliance Francais, to check progress. And he was amazed "at how quickly they were able to speak without reading" and how easy it was to have a conversation with them.

As Channel 7 summed up: it's an experiment that could have turned Australia's education system "on its head".　　Unfortunately the rival Channel Nine Network later followed up with a program highly critical of some claims for "accelerated learning", and the New South Wales Government reacted by stopping many of these new methods.

The army learns a foreign language in record time

In any event, a journalistic story is not scientific evidence. For that we turn in brief to the American army and one of the best users of the new teaching techniques, Professor Freeman Lynn Dhority, of Boston.

Dr. Dhority was already a highly successful German teacher before he studied the *suggestopedia* method with Lozanov. He then had the opportunity of testing the method and comparing it with other measured results using standard-style German teaching. All materials for the course were prepared thoroughly in advance according to Lozanov guidelines: "peripherals", including posters, music, games, songs, activities and scripts. And because of Dr. Dhority's academic training, he was able to ensure that the results could be documented.

His "control group" of 11 students studied basic German, using accelerated learning techniques, for 108 hours over three and a half weeks (18 days) at Fort Devens army base. The results were then compared with another group of 34 army students, not taught by Dr. Dhority, learning basic German under regular "audio drill" methods over a period of 360 hours, spread over 12 weeks.

The comparative results recorded levels of "listening, comprehension, reading and speaking". And they were then checked by Dr. Lyelle

How to increase the learning rate 661% with these techniques

Former Boston Professor of Education Freeman Lynn Dhority specializes in teaching second languages by many of the creative learning techniques outlined in this book.

In one well-researched study:

❏ **Three groups of American soldiers studied basic German for 12 weeks using standard educational methods (60 days, 360 hours).**

❏ **Another group studied the same subject, using "accelerated learning" techniques, for 18 days (108 hours).**

❏ **Only 29 percent of the "standard groups" reached the required level of understanding in 360 hours.**

❏ **But 64 percent of the "accelerated learning" group achieved the same ability to read German in 108 hours; and 73 percent reached the required level of understanding spoken German.**

❏ **Statistically, that is a 661 per cent better learning rate: more than twice the results in one-third the time.***

*These results are summarized from: *The 661% Solution: A statistical evaluation of the extraordinary effectiveness of Freeman Lynn Dhority's U.S. Army accelerated learning German class,* by Lyelle L. Palmer, Professor of Education and Special Education Chair, Winona State University, Minnesota, in a joint paper with Professor Dhority.

Palmer, Professor of Education at Winona State University, Minnesota. They disclosed that only 29 percent of the "regular course" students reached the required "level one" of basic German in the 360 hours, while 73 percent achieved the required level of "listening understanding" and 64 percent the required level of reading ability in the 120 hours.

Dr. Palmer recorded the results statistically in a joint paper headed: *The 661% Solution: A statistical evaluation of the extraordinary effectiveness of Lynn Dhority's U.S. Army accelerated learning German class.*[28] And for us he summed them up even more succinctly: "Lynn Dhority achieved more than twice the results in less than one-third the time. Statistically, that was a 661 percent increase."[29] Major savings were also achieved, of course, in instructor time and expenses, daily expenses for trainees, and time away from the job.

An accelerated integrative learning teacher

For a glimpse at a new-style teacher in action, visit a Leo Wood's chemistry class at Tempe High School in Arizona, at the start of a typical year. Walk into the room and you're struck first by the paintings and photographs: a Monet, a mountain scene, portraits of Albert Einstein and Linus Pauling, and graphics on chemistry and the miracle of life. From the ceiling hang posters and models of molecules and polyatomic ions. Relaxing baroque music fills the room. The classroom is colorful, interesting and relaxing.

Wood uses techniques brought to the United States by another Bulgarian, Dr. Ivan Barzakov, and perfected with his actress partner Pamela Rand. Like Lozanov, Barzakov experimented early with yoga and relaxation techniques. Later he was the star teacher at Lozanov's experimental school in Sophia before fleeing Bulgaria. Since then he and Rand have built on Lozanov's basic principles, making great use of many types of music, visual art and metaphorical stories. In 1978, with a group of teachers and psychologists, they formed the Barzak Educational Institute in Novata, California. The Barzakov team have since trained more than 10,000 people in 17 countries.

Ivan Barzakov calls his method OptimaLearning. While Lozanov used his techniques mainly for foreign language-learning, Barzakov applies his principles to any subject. Effectively he combines Lozanov's "two concerts" into one. And he's developed a careful selection of music tapes which are used not just for learning and memory, but for imagination, creativity, problem solving and decision making. He carefully

Recommended music guides

The multimedia revolution has enormous potential for music in learning.

It enables those teachers highly skilled in the use of music, art and drama to make their talents widely available to the world.

The first breakthrough came in October 1989, when Voyager Company launched *Ludwig van Beethoven: Symphony No. 9 CD Companion*—the first consumer release to link audio CDs and computer software to create multimedia.

It owed its beginnings to a UCLA classical music class run by Professor Robert Winter in 1982 and attended by Voyager co-founder Bob Stein. Winter used slides, tapes and performances to demonstrate the art of the great composers.

Seven years later, Stein was able to turn teacher Winter's ability into a ground-breaking CD-ROM.

It uses a recording of the Vienna Philharmonic, with soprano Joan Sutherland and contralto Marilyn Home, plus superb commentary by Winter. The CD-ROM includes an essay on *The Art of Listening,* a glossary of musical examples, audio samples and the ability to pause the music at any point and link to related materials elsewhere on the disc. Winter has since produced several other masterpieces for Voyager, and in 1994 co-founded his own interactive company, Calliope Media.

Accelerated learning teachers wishing to explore the potential for interactive musical CD-ROMs are urged to read *Entertainment In the Cyber Zone,* by Chris McGowan and Jim McCullaugh, Random House, New York (1995).

There are now many other excellent music teachers specializing in accelerated learning, among them: in Australia, Glenn Capelli of the True Learning Center; and in the United States Ivan Barzakov and Pamela Rand of the Barzak Educational Institute; Don Campbell of the Institute for Music, Health and Education; Chris Brewer; and Dr. Arthur Harvey of the LIND Institute in San Francisco.

The newest program available is *The Music Revolution,* by co-author Dr. Jeannette Vos, for publication in 1999. The total program outlines the six main ways to use music for teaching and training, and then provides a full list of music tracks for each way, along with recommended activities.

blends different types of music together for contrast, "because variety stimulates our minds and keeps us alert".[30] He also changes the "texture" of the music, from violin to flute through to mandolin and clavichord and piano. The result is a unique sequence that brings serenity, relaxation and anticipation. Taking part in a class with OptimaLearning music is very much like sitting through a classic movie, where the music is a powerful subconscious carrier of the total theme, and the visual art blends with it.

In a Leo Wood chemistry class, you'll very soon be caught up in that same type of drama. As part of a typical demonstration, the teacher may switch the lights off, turn up a special tape for creativity and imagination, and start mixing chemicals together in a test tube. As the suspense mounts with the music, sparks of light begin popping in the test tube, one at a time. Wood begins talking about light and life and their interaction. The popping becomes more rapid and the sparks much brighter. The teacher introduces the theme: "Life is a miracle, and you and I are part of that miracle." Wood walks to a demonstration table, pours the test tube contents into a large beaker, and says: "We will learn how miraculous life really is." A big burst of fire flashes from a beaker and into the test tube as the music reaches a climax. The lights go on, the music stops, and the students are silently processing what has just happened.

Says Wood: "The theme for the year has been introduced, properties of three compounds and density are discussed, and the relationship and interaction of light and life have been demonstrated and revealed—all in about 15 minutes."[31]

Then he may take the students outside, to stand facing the sun with their eyes closed, before returning to class to write their impressions as Debussy music plays in the background.

Then in the teacher's finale the students learn of the fusion reaction that occurs on the surface of the sun. But not as a lecture: they actually become the hydrogen atoms as their bodies become a circle, and their fists are brought together in a clasping position to indicate the fusion of the nuclei.

"We have a little oral quiz at the end of the class," says Wood, "and everyone always gets 100 percent." And in later examinations, the results are spectacular. ***Before introducing these accelerated learning techniques, 52 percent of Tempe chemistry students achieved A, B and C grades. With the new methods: 93 percent.***[32]

A full selection of Barzakov music tapes are now readily available.

School should be the best party in town.

PETER KLINE
The Everyday Genius*

*Published by Great Ocean Publishers, 1823 North Lincoln Street, Arlington, VA 22207.

What's held up the big breakthroughs?

Given the proven results of the new techniques, in many ways they have been slow to spread. This is probably as much a result of the "cold war" atmosphere of the 1960s and 70s as it is of any conservatism in the educational establishment. Early incorrect reports of "sleep learning" in the then Communist bloc countries also conjured up illusions of "brain-washing".

Lozanov's accelerated learning techniques made their biggest early impact in foreign-language training for adults. The reasons were simple:

1. His first published international results were in this field.

2. Probably more than in any other subject, the spectacular results were easy to assess. People with no knowledge of another language were obviously learning much faster and more effectively.

Sheila Ostrander and Lynn Schroeder publicized some of these feats early in the 1970s with their book *Psychic Discoveries Behind the Iron Curtain.* And their use of the word "psychic" probably turned-off as many people as "Iron Curtain". Soon afterwards, Lyall Watson answered much of the scepticism with *Supernature.* In it he mounted fact after fact to prove that what many people regard as "supernatural" is really "supernature;" that we all have hidden reserves of talent.[33]

In North America, some of the first interest came from Canada, with its concentration on bilingual education. Dr. Jane Bancroft, Associate Professor of French at the University of Toronto, brought Lozanov to Canada in 1971. And a year later Dr. Donald Schuster, Professor of Psychology at Iowa State University, and a colleague, Ray Benitez-Bordon of Des Moines, began some of the first United States experiments. By 1975 Benitez-Bordon was reporting classes learning more than a full year's Spanish in 10 days—with four hours' study a day.[34]

But many of the early American results did not live up to the pre-publicity, largely because of misunderstanding over the role of music in the process. Many early enthusiasts thought any relaxing music would do. And the cause of good learning was not helped by many early spurious claims of spectacular results.

Fortunately the early development of the techniques coincided with some major breakthroughs in brain-research, as we've covered earlier.

They have also been accompanied by other research into the vital importance of individual learning styles.

Key points on learning styles

Every human being has a learning style and every human being has strengths.[1]

It's as individual as a signature.[2]

No learning style is better– or worse—than any other style.[3]

All groups—cultural, academic, male, female—include all types of learning styles.[4]

Within each culture, socio-economic strata or classroom, there are as many differences as there are between groups.[5]

Quotations from research by
Professors Ken and Rita Dunn*

*The sources for the quotations on this page are cited in the
chapter notes for chapter 10, to which they refer.
To obtain details of the Dunns' learning and working style checks,
contact Learning Styles Network, School of Education and
Human Services, St. Johns University, Grand Central and
Utopia Parkways, Jamaica, NY 11439.

How to find your own learning style and use your many intelligences

Albert Einstein was a daydreamer. His teachers in Germany told him he would never amount to anything, that his questions destroyed class discipline, that he would be better off out of school. Yet he went on to become one of the greatest scientists in world history.

Winston Churchill did poorly at schoolwork. He talked with a stutter and a lisp. Yet he became one of the greatest leaders and orators of the 20th century.

Thomas Alva Edison was beaten at school with a heavy leather strap because his teacher considered him "addled" for asking so many questions. He was chastised so much that his mother took him out of school after only three months' formal education. He went on to become probably the most prolific inventor of all time.

Fortunately Edison's mother—a former school teacher herself—was a pioneer in true learning. Says *The World Book Encyclopedia:* "She had the notion, unusual for those times, that learning could be fun. She made a game of teaching him—she called it exploring—the exciting world of knowledge. The boy was surprised at first, and then delighted. Soon he began to learn so fast that his mother could no longer teach him." But he continued to explore, experiment and teach himself.

Einstein, Churchill and Edison had learning styles that were not suited to their school styles.

And that same mismatch continues today for millions of others. It is possibly the biggest single cause of school failure.

It's also obvious that everyone has different talents. Pablo Picasso

Multiple intelligences
Personal and professional uses

1. Linguistic intelligence.

Commonly found in: Novelists, poets, copywriters, scriptwriters, orators, political leaders, editors, publicists, journalists and speech writers.

Example of famous person: Winston Churchill, British journalist turned orator, political leader and writer.

Likely traits:

* Sensitive to patterns
* Orderly
* Systematic
* Ability to reason
* Likes to listen
* Likes to read
* Likes to write
* Spells easily
* Likes word games
* Has good memory for trivia
* May be good public speaker and debater, although some linguistic specialists may prefer either oral or written communication

How to strengthen for learning:

* Tell stories
* Play memory games with names, places
* Read stories, jokes
* Write stories, jokes
* Do vocabulary skits
* Use journal writing
* Interviewing
* Do puzzles, spelling games
* Integrate writing and reading with other subject areas
* Produce, edit and supervise class magazine
* Debate
* Discussions
* Use word processor as introduction to computers

ACKNOWLEDGEMENT:

This page and pages 344, 346, 348, 350, 352 and 354 have been based on and adapted from the original research of Howard Gardner, David Thornburg, Thomas Armstrong, David Lazier, Linda Campbell, Bruce Campbell, Dee Dickinson and Jeannette Vos.

was obviously a great painter, William Shakespeare a phenomenal writer, Joe Louis and Babe Ruth great sportsmen, Enrico Caruso a brilliant tenor, Anna Pavlova an outstanding ballet dancer and Katharine Hepburn a fine actress.

Every person reading this page has a different *lifestyle* and a different *workstyle*. Successful businesses depend on their ability to cater to those different lifestyles. And human-resource consultants spend their lives matching workstyle talents to jobs.

Yet many of our schools operate as if each person is identical. Even worse: most operate with an evaluation or testing system that rewards only a limited number of abilities. And those rewards early in life often separate the allegedly gifted and intelligent from those who are claimed to be less intelligent and underachievers.

Possibly the worst educational innovation of this century was the so-called intelligence test. Two French psychologists, Alfred Binet and Theodore Simon, developed the first modern tests in 1905. Two American psychologists, Lewis M. Terman and Maud A. Merrill, both of Stanford University, later adapted the French work into what became known as the Stanford-Binet tests.

These did a good job of testing *certain* abilities. But they didn't test *all* abilities. And, worse, they gave rise to the concept that intelligence is fixed at birth. *Intelligence is not fixed.*

Better still: we each have access to many different "intelligences" or intelligence traits.

And if the current authors had to choose any one step needed to transform the world's high-school systems in particular it would be this: find out each student's combination of learning styles and talents—and cater to it; and at the same time encourage the well-rounded development of all potential abilities.

The major fault with so-called I.Q., or intelligent quotient, tests is that they *confuse logic with overall intelligence*—when logic, as we've seen, is only one form of thinking or learning skill. Some tests also confuse linguistic ability with overall ability.

In recent years Harvard Professor of Education Howard Gardner has been one of many who have made pioneer breakthroughs in shattering the "fixed I.Q." myth. For more than 15 years Gardner has used prolific research to prove that each person has at least seven different "intelligence centers", probably more. As we've touched on, he's defined:

Multiple intelligences
Personal and professional uses

2. Logical-mathematical intelligence.

Commonly found in: Mathematicians, scientists, engineers, animal trackers, police investigators, lawyers and accountants.

Example of prominent person: Marian Diamond, Professor of Neuroanatomy at the University of California at Berkeley.

Likely traits:

* Likes abstract thinking
* Likes being precise
* Enjoys counting
* Likes being organized
* Uses logical structure
* Enjoys computers
* Enjoys problem-solving
* Enjoys experimenting in logical way
* Prefers orderly note-taking

How to strengthen for learning:

* Stimulate problem solving
* Do mathematical computation games
* Analyze and interpret data
* Use reasoning
* Encourage own strengths
* Encourage practical experiments
* Use prediction
* Integrate organization and math into other curricular areas
* Have a place for everything
* Allow things to be done step-by-step
* Use deductive thinking
* Use computers for spreadsheets, calculations

Linguistic intelligence as the ability to speak or write well—highly developed in such people as Winston Churchill, John. F. Kennedy and all brilliant writers.

Logical-mathematical intelligence as the ability to reason, calculate and handle logical thinking—highly developed in such people as Bertrand Russell and Chinese Prime Minister and economics leader Zhu Rongji.

Visual-spatial intelligence as the ability to paint, take great photographs or create sculpture.

Bodily-kinesthetic intelligence as the ability to use one's hands or body—epitomized in sports achievers and great actors.

Musical intelligence as the ability to compose songs, sing and play instruments.

Interpersonal intelligence—what we would prefer to call "social" intelligence—as the ability to relate to others.

And intrapersonal intelligence as the ability to access one's inner feelings.*

The difference is much more than semantics. Children early in life are still being herded into the mythical "gifted" and "non-gifted" streams or tracks based largely on testing in only two traits.

We believe Gardner's findings[6] have vital importance in planning the future of education. *Every child is a potentially gifted child—but often in many different ways.* Every person, too, has his or her own preferred learning style, working style and temperament. Back in 1921, Swiss psychiatrist Carl Jung outlined how people perceived things differently. He classified them as feelers, thinkers, sensors or intuitors. Jung was, as far as we know, the first to classify people also as either introverts or extroverts. It's unfortunate that many of Jung's perspectives were dropped by 1930 and relatively ignored until recently.

We all know people who embody many of the concepts he defined, and New Zealand professor of theology Lloyd Geering has summarized them in his excellent book *In The World Today,*[7] which seeks to bridge the gap between religion and science:

The extroverted thinkers, who abound in management, military

* *As touched on elsewhere, Howard Gardner has more recently postulated an eighth intelligence: "naturalist" intelligence. Other writers, including British management consultant and professor Charles Handy, say there are many more "intelligences", including "common sense".*

Multiple intelligences
Personal and professional uses

3. Visual-spatial intelligence*.

Commonly found in: Architects, painters, sculptors, navigators, chess players, naturalists, theoretical physicists, battlefield strategists.

Example of famous person: Pablo Picasso, painter.

Likely traits:	**How to strengthen for learning:**
* Thinks in pictures	* Use pictures to learn
* Creates mental images	* Create doodles, symbols
* Uses metaphor	* Draw diagrams, maps
* Has sense of gestalt	* Integrate art with other subjects
* Likes art: drawing, painting and sculpting	* Use Mind-Mapping
* Easily reads maps, charts and diagrams	* Do visualization activities
* Remembers with pictures	* Watch videos or create your own
* Has good color sense	* Use peripheral stimuli on the walls; signs such as the posters in this book
* Uses all senses for imaging	* Use mime
	* Change places in the room to gain a different perspective
* As mentioned elsewhere in this book, the present co-authors consider that visual and spatial traits do not always coincide. Some highly visual people may have difficulty, for instance, in following the directions from maps, even though the maps may be visually accurate.	* Use advance organizers or goal-setting charts
	* Use clustering
	* Highlight with color
	* Use computer-graphics

strategy and some forms of science. People such as automotive path-finder Lee Iacocca or British wartime military leader Bernard Montgomery.

The introverted thinkers, often interested in ideas for their own sake: philosophers such as Charles Darwin, Rene Descartes and Jung himself.

The extroverted feeling types, interested deeply in other people—the Mother Teresas of the world.

The introverted feeling types, including those who agonize over the world's problems but internalize them and assume them as a burden.

The extroverted sensation types, the sports-loving, thrill-seeking, pleasure-seekers.

The introverted sensation types "who find the outer world uninteresting and unsatisfying and turn inwardly to seek fulfillment"—including some of the great mystics.

The extroverted intuitive people "who enter new relationships with great gusto but do not always prove dependable. They can move quickly from one new interest to another, especially if it is not immediately fruitful. They have visions of new worlds to conquer or to build. They are promoters of new causes. We may name as examples Alexander the Great, Julius Caesar, Napoleon, Hitler, Henry Ford and builders of today's economic empires."

The introverted intuitive people, including the visionaries and dreamers who draw from their own hidden resources.

Geering says "the acknowledgment of psychological types is an essential first step if we are to appreciate Jung's concept of individuation, the process by which each of us becomes the one unique and whole human person we have the potential to become".

Many educators have now built on these concepts. Rudolph Steiner schools, for instance, place great emphasis on identifying and catering to individual temperaments.

Determining your learning style

There are currently about 20 different methods of identifying learning styles. And research by Professors Ken and Rita Dunn, from St. Johns University, New York, provides one of the most comprehensive models. But overall your learning style is a combination of three factors:

❏ **How you perceive information most easily**—whether you are

Multiple intelligences
Personal and professional uses

4. Musical intelligence.

Commonly found in: Performers, composers, conductors, musical audiences, recording engineers, makers of musical instruments, piano-tuners, cultures without traditional written language.

Example of famous person: Mozart.

Likely traits:

* Sensitive to pitch, rhythm, timbre
* Sensitive to emotional power of music
* Sensitive to complex organization of music
* May be deeply spiritual

How to strengthen for learning:

* Play a musical instrument
* Learn through songs
* Use active and passive concerts for learning
* Study with baroque music
* Workout with music
* Join choir or choral group
* Write music
* Integrate music with other subject areas
* Change your mood with music
* Use music to get relaxed
* Image/make pictures with music
* Learn through raps such as timetables, whole language poems, choral reading
* Compose music on computer

mainly a visual, auditory, kinesthetic or tactile learner; whether you learn best by seeing, hearing, moving or touching. (The ability to taste and smell can be important in some work-styles, such as wine-tasting and perfume-blending, but these two senses are not major ones in most learning styles.)

❏ **How you organize and process information**—whether predominantly left-brain or right-brain, analytical or "global", using "global" in the sense that you are more "a broadbrush" person than a systematic thinker.

❏ **What conditions are necessary to help you take in and store information**—emotional, social, physical and environmental.

❏ **How you retrieve information**—which may be entirely different to the way you take it in and store it.

How you take in information

In the Dunns' research, they discovered that:

❏ Only 30 percent of students remember even 75 percent of what they *hear* during a normal class period.

❏ Forty percent retain threequarters of what they *read* or *see*. These visual learners are of two types: some process information in word-form, while others retain what they see in diagram or picture-form.

❏ Fifteen percent learn best *tactually*. They need to *handle* materials, to write, draw and be involved with concrete experiences.

❏ Another 15 percent are kinesthetic. They learn best by *physically doing*—by participating in real experiences that generally have direct application to their lives.

According to the Dunns, we each usually have one dominant strength and also a secondary one. And, in a classroom or seminar, if our main perceptual strength is not matched with the teaching method, we may have difficulty learning, unless we can compensate with our secondary perceptual strengths.

This has major implications for solving the high-school dropout problem. *In our experience, kinesthetic and tactile learners are the main candidates for failure in traditional school classrooms.* They need to move, to feel, to touch, to do—and if the teaching method does not allow them to do this they feel left out, uninvolved, bored.

Neuro linguistic programming specialist Michael Grinder says that of

Multiple intelligences

Personal and professional uses

5. Bodily-kinesthetic intelligence.

Commonly found in: Dancers, actors, athletes and sporting achievers, inventors, mimists, surgeons, karate teachers, racing car drivers, outdoor workers and the mechanically gifted.

Examples: Basketball star Michael Jordan, golfer Tiger Woods.

Likely traits:

* Exceptional control of one's body
* Control of objects
* Good timing
* Trained responses
* Good reflexes
* Learns best by moving
* Likes to engage in physical sports
* Likes to touch
* Skilled at handicrafts
* Likes to act
* Likes to use manipulatives
* Learns by participating in the learning process
* Remembers what was done rather than what was said or observed
* Very responsive to physical environment
* Plays around with objects while listening
* Fidgety if there are few breaks
* Mechanically minded

How to strengthen for learning:

* Use physical exercises wherein you become the object you are learning about
* Use dancing to learn
* Use movement to learn
* Act out the learning
* Use manipulatives in science, math
* Take lots of "state changes" and breaks
* Integrate movement into all curricula areas
* Mentally review while you are swimming, jogging
* Use models, machines, Technic Lego, handicrafts
* Use karate for focusing
* Use field trips
* Use classroom games
* Use drama, role-plays
* Finger snapping, clapping, stamping, jumping, climbing

a typical class of 30 students, 22 will be fairly balanced in their ability to take in information in a variety of ways. They will generally be able to cope when the information is presented in either visual, auditory or kinesthetic ways.

Two to three of the youngsters will have difficulty learning because of factors outside the classroom. And the remaining youngsters—up to six in a class of 30, or 20 per cent—will be "visual only," "auditory only" or "kinesthetic only" learners. They have great difficulty in absorbing information unless it is presented in the favored style.

Grinder dubs them VO's, AO's and KO's. And he says, "It's not just a coincidence that the initials 'KO' stand for 'knockout.' These kids are 'knocked out' of the educational system. In every study I have seen regarding 'kids at risk,' kinesthetics make up the vast majority of the 26 percent dropout rate."[8]

How you organize and process information

People with strong left-brain traits take information in logically— they can absorb it easily if it is presented in a logical, linear sequence.

People with right-brain dominance generally like to take in the big global picture first; they're much more comfortable with presentations that involve visualization, imagination, music, art and intuition.

And if you can link together the powers of both hemispheres, and tap into those "multiple intelligence centers", you'll obviously be able to absorb and process information more effectively.

The conditions that affect your learning ability

The physical environment obviously affects learning. Sound, light, temperature, seating and body posture are all important.

People also have different *emotional needs.* And emotion plays a vital part in learning. It is in many ways the key to the brain's memory system. And the emotional content of any presentation can play a big part in how readily learners absorb information and ideas.

People also have different *social needs.* Some like to learn by themselves. Others prefer to work with a partner. Still others, in teams. Some children want an adult present or like to work with adults only. The Dunns say most underachievers are very peer-motivated.[9]

Multiple intelligences
Personal and professional uses

6. Interpersonal or "social" intelligence.

Commonly found in: Politicians, teachers, religious leaders, counsellors, sales people, managers, public relations and "people people."

Example of famous person: Oprah Winfrey, talk-show host.

Likely traits:

* Negotiates well
* Relates well, mixes well
* Able to read others' intentions
* Enjoys being with people
* Has many friends
* Communicates well, sometimes manipulates
* Enjoys group activities
* Likes to mediate disputes
* Likes to cooperate
* "Reads" social situations well

How to strengthen for learning:

* Do learning activities cooperatively
* Take lots of breaks to socialize
* Use "pair and share" learning activities
* Use relationships and communication skills
* Do "partner talks" on the phone
* Have parties and celebration of learning
* Make learning fun
* Integrate socialization into all curricular areas
* Use "People Search" activities where you have to talk to others to get answers
* Work in teams
* Learn through service
* Tutor others
* Use cause and effect

Physical and biological needs that affect learning

Eating times, time-of-day energy levels and the need for mobility can also affect learning ability.

Try learning, for instance, when you are hungry. It's hard for most of us. And some people need to constantly nibble.

Some people are morning people. Others are night owls. Again, the Dunns have found that students do better when their class-times match their own "time-clocks." [10] Significantly, they've found that most school and college students are not morning people. "Only about one-third of more than a million students we have tested prefer learning in the first part of the morning," they report. "The majority prefer late morning or afternoon. In fact, many do not begin to be capable of concentrating on difficult material until after 10 a.m." For daytime learning, the Dunns recommend 10 a.m. to 3 p.m. But who says high schools shouldn't be open evenings for the night-owls?

The Dunns confirm that "the tactile-kinesthetics" face most learning difficulties in traditional schools.[11] They often drop out because they can't focus well sitting down hour after hour. Those that stay often "get into trouble" and get suspended. Others are often unfortunately classi-fied as "learning disabled" and put into "special education" classes—where they do more of the same: lots of seatwork activity, paying little attention to their true strengths and learning styles.

Every top learning environment we have seen caters to a variety of intelligence-traits and a variety of learning styles. But many high schools in particular still seem geared to "academic" two-dimensional teach-ing—directed mainly at linguistic and logical learners. Not surprisingly, many of the people involved in school administration were themselves high-achievers in logical-mathematical and linguistic ability—so to them that type of environment naturally seems best.

How to determine students' preferred learning styles

Again, one simple way is to ask. A simple request and discussion on learning styles and preferences is also often one of the simplest ways to break down barriers between teacher and students. You can also often tell people's preferred style by listening to them talk.

Ask a visual learner for instructions and she'll tend to draw a map. If she is starting to grasp an otherwise difficult subject, she'll say: "I see

Multiple intelligences
Personal and professional uses

7. Intrapersonal or intuitive* intelligence.

Commonly found in: Novelists, counsellors, wise elders, philosophers, gurus, persons with a deep sense of self, mystics.

Example of famous person: Plato, philosopher.

Likely traits:

* Self-knowledge
* Sensitivity to one's own values
* Deeply aware of one's own feelings
* Sensitivity to one's purpose in life
* Has a well-developed sense of self
* Intuitive ability
* Self motivated
* Deeply aware of own strengths and weaknesses
* Very private person
* Wants to be different from mainstream

* The core capacity of "intrapersonal" intelligence is the ability to access one's inner self. Some feel intuition is a separate intelligence trait: a seemingly innate ability to know about others or events.

How strengthen for learning:

* Have personal "heart-to-heart" talks
* Use personal growth activities to break learning blocks
* Debrief activities
* Think about your thinking through "Pair and Shares" and "Think and Listen"
* Take time for inner reflection
* Do independent study
* Listen to your intuition
* Discuss, reflect or write what you experienced and how you felt
* Permit freedom to be different from the group
* Make "My Books" and journals of life story
* Take control of own learning
* Teach personal affirmations
* Teach questioning

what you mean." Read her a menu in a restaurant and she'll have to look at it herself. Buy her a present and you can't go too wrong with a book—but check to see whether she's print oriented or prefers pictures. If the latter, she might even prefer a videotape. Most visual learners, but not all, tend to be organized, tidy and well dressed.

An auditory learner generally couldn't care less about reading a book or an instruction manual. He'll have to ask for information. He doesn't buy a car for its looks—he buys it for its stereo system. In a plane he'll immediately strike up a conversation with his new neighbor. And when he grasps new information, he says something like: "I hear what you're saying." If you buy him a present, make it a tape recorder, not a book.

A kinesthetic, tactile learner always wants to be on the move. If she bumps into you accidentally, she'll want to give you a reassuring hug. When she grasps a new principle, "it feels right" to her. And for her Christmas present: a laptop computer?

Your unique working style

Since the early 1990s New Zealand-based Barbara Prashnig, who heads the Creative Learning Company, has introduced the Dunn and Dunn model with great success in New Zealand primary and secondary schools and among MBA students at the University of Auckland.

"People of all ages can learn virtually anything if allowed to do it through their unique styles, through their own personal strengths," she says in *Diversity Is Our Strength: the learning revolution in action.*

She has also built on the Dunns' research base to build a practical program for analyzing individual students' learning styles, anyone's individual working style, plus individual teaching styles and training styles.

"Working style," she says, "can be defined as the way people in the work force usually absorb and retain new and difficult information, think or concentrate, generally do their daily work, and effectively solve problems." [12]

By inquiring through the World Wide Web, anyone can quickly receive a computer printout showing strengths to build on and weaknesses to overcome. [13] "It's therefore ideal," she says, "for both individuals and companies looking at applications for any position."

Her learning-style, working-style and teaching-style programs are

The key to successful learning and working is knowing one's unique personal learning or working style.

BARBARA PRASHNIG
The Power of Diversity *

* Published by David Bateman, Auckland, New Zealand.

now being used effectively in New Zealand, Britain, Finland, Sweden and several other countries.

Four types of thinking style

Not only do we have preferred learning and working styles, we also have favorite thinking styles. Anthony Gregorc, professor of curriculum and instruction at the University of Connecticut, has divided these into four separate groups:[14]

❏ **Concrete sequential.**

❏ **Concrete random.**

❏ **Abstract random.**

❏ **Abstract sequential.**

We're indebted to SuperCamp consultant John LeTellier for adapting the Gregorc model and providing the checklist on the next three pages.[15]

We stress, however, that no thinking style is superior; each is simply different. Each style can be effective in its own way. The important thing is that you become more aware of which learning style and thinking style works best for you. Once you know your own style, you can then analyze the others. This will help you understand other people better. It will make you more flexible. And perhaps we can all pick up tips from each other on how to be more effective.

Once you've made a graph for yourself on page 360, consider these explanations to improve your own ability to learn, think, study, work and enjoy life:

Concrete sequential thinkers are based in reality, according to SuperCamp co-founder and president Bobbi DePorter. They process information in an ordered, sequential, linear way. To them, "reality consists of what they can detect through their physical sense of sight, touch, sound, taste and smell. They notice and recall details easily and remember facts, specific information, formulas and rules with ease. 'Hands on' is a good way for these people to learn."[16] If you're concrete sequential—a CS—build on your organizational strengths. Provide yourself with details. Break your projects down into specific steps. Set up quiet work environments.

Concrete random thinkers are experimenters. Says DePorter: "Like concrete sequentials, they're based in reality, but are willing to take more of a trial-and-error approach. Because of this, they often make the

To test your own thinking style
read each set of words and mark the two that best describe you

1.
   a. imaginative
   b. investigative
   c. realistic
   d. analytical

2.
   a. organized
   b. adaptable
   c. critical
   d. inquisitive

3.
   a. debating
   b. getting to the point
   c. creating
   d. relating

4.
   a. personal
   b. practical
   c. academic
   d. adventurous

5.
   a. precise
   b. flexible
   c. systematic
   d. inventive

6.
   a. sharing
   b. orderly
   c. sensible
   d. independent

7.
   a. competitive
   b. perfectionist
   c. cooperative
   d. logical

8.
   a. intellectual
   b. sensitive
   c. hardworking
   d. risk-taking

9.
   a. reader
   b. people person
   c. problem solver
   d. planner

10.
   a. memorize
   b. associate
   c. think-through
   d. originate

11.
   a. changer
   b. judger
   c. spontaneous
   d. wants direction

12.
   a. communicating
   b. discovering
   c. cautious
   d. reasoning

13.
   a. challenging
   b. practicing
   c. caring
   d. examining

14.
   a. completing work
   b. seeing possibilities
   c. gaining ideas
   d. interpreting

15.
   a. doing
   b. feeling
   c. thinking
   d. experimenting

After completing the test at left:

In the columns below, circle the letters of the words you chose for each number. Add your totals for columns I, II, III and IV. Multiply the total of each column by 4. The box with the highest number describes how you most often process information.

	I	II	III	IV
1.	C	D	A	B
2.	A	C	B	D
3.	B	A	D	C
4.	B	C	A	D
5.	A	C	B	D
6.	B	C	A	D
7.	B	D	C	A
8.	C	A	B	D
9.	D	A	B	C
10.	A	C	B	D
11.	D	B	C	A
12.	C	D	A	B
13.	B	D	C	A
14.	A	C	D	B
15.	A	C	B	D

TOTAL: _____

I ___ X 4 = ☐ Concrete Sequential (CS)

II ___ X 4 = ☐ Abstract Sequential (AS)

III ___ X 4 = ☐ Abstract Random (AR)

IV ___ X 4 = ☐ Concrete Random (CR)

Now graph your results on the chart on next page.

After you have completed your personal thinking-style test on the previous page chart your results below

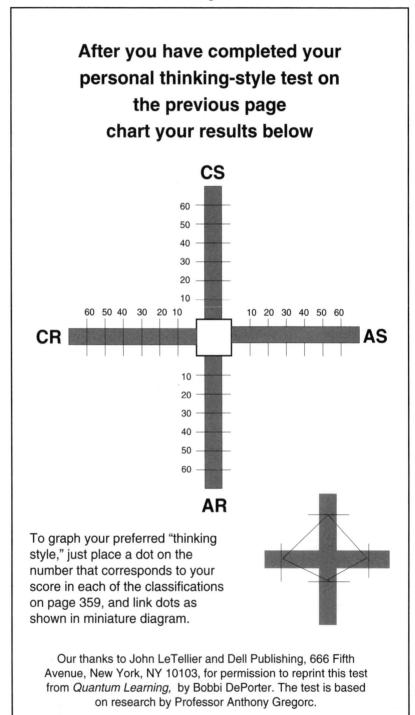

To graph your preferred "thinking style," just place a dot on the number that corresponds to your score in each of the classifications on page 359, and link dots as shown in miniature diagram.

Our thanks to John LeTellier and Dell Publishing, 666 Fifth Avenue, New York, NY 10103, for permission to reprint this test from *Quantum Learning,* by Bobbi DePorter. The test is based on research by Professor Anthony Gregorc.

intuitive leaps necessary for true creative thought. They have a strong need to find alternatives and do things in their own way." If you're a CR, use your divergent thinking ability. Believe that it's good to see things from more than one viewpoint. Put yourself in a position to solve problems. But give yourself deadlines. Accept your need for change.

Abstract random thinkers organize information through reflection, and thrive in unstructured, people-oriented environments. Says De-Porter: "The 'real' world for abstract random learners is the world of feelings and emotions. The AR's mind absorbs ideas, information and impressions and organizes them through reflection. They remember best if information is personalized. They feel constricted when they're subjected to a very structured environment." If you're an AR, use your natural ability to work with others. Recognize how strongly emotions influence your concentration. Build on your strength of learning by association. Look at the big picture first. Be careful to allow enough time to finish the job. Remind yourself to do things through plenty of visual clues, such as colored stickers pasted up where you'll see them.

Abstract sequential thinkers love the world of theory and abstract thought. They like to think in concepts and analyze information. They make great philosophers and research scientists. DePorter again: "It's easy for them to zoom in on what's important, such as key points and significant details. Their thinking processes are logical, rational and intellectual. A favorite activity for abstract sequentials is reading, and when a project needs to be researched they are very thorough at it. Generally they prefer to work alone rather than in groups." If you're an AS, give yourself exercises in logic. Feed your intellect. Steer yourself toward highly structured situations.

The implications for schools and individuals

We believe every aspect of this research can greatly improve learning and schooling.

For personal home study, it makes great sense to know your own strengths, know your family's learning styles and build on them. If it's hard for you to sit still for a long time, you're almost certainly a kinesthetic learner. So consider starting to study by previewing your material with a giant Mind Map—on a big sheet of paper. Put it on the floor and use your body while you're working. After previewing the material, play some classical music—and move with its rhythm. Then do something

How to tell learning styles by the eyes

Teachers skilled in neuro linguistic programming (NLP) say that they can often tell students' preferred learning styles by looking at their eye movements and listening to them speak.*

A student who sits still and looks straight ahead, or whose eyes look upwards when accessing information, and who is a fast talker, is generally a visual learner.

A student who looks from side to side when accessing information, or looks down to his "offside" (right-handed student looking to the left), is probably an auditory learner. He will generally speak with a rhythmic voice.

A right-handed student who moves a lot, looks to the right and downwards when accessing and storing , and is a slow speaker, will probably be a kinesthetic learner.

*Illustrations are from an inexpensive filmstrip cassette, *Teaching to Modality Strengths: A Common Sense Approach to Learning,* by Walter B. Barbe and Raymond H. Swassing, available through Zaner-Blozer, Inc., Columbus, Ohio. Copyright 1979.

*Similar points are covered in extensive detail in *Righting The Educational Conveyor Belt,* by Michael Grinder, published by Metamorphous Press, P.O. Box 10616, Portland, Oregon 97210.

Note: Barbara Prashnig says strong tactile learners can generally be identified by the way their eyes tend to look up when pondering a question.

physical. Go for a walk, a swim, or move your body while you practice mentally, through visualization, what you've just put into your brain.

Especially if you're kinesthetic, feel free to get into your favorite learning atmosphere and position. If you are an auditory learner, record your notes on to a cassette tape over baroque music. And if you are a visual learner, be sure to draw Mind Maps, doodles, symbols or pictures to represent what you are learning. For a visual learner, a picture represents a thousand words.

For taking control of your life, all people have what Dr. Robert Sternberg, Yale Professor of Psychology and Education, calls *styles of managing.* "The ways in which students prefer to use their intelligences," he says, "are as important as ability. Children—in fact, all people—need to 'govern' their activities, and, in doing so, they will choose 'styles of managing themselves with which they are comfortable.' The mind carries out its activities much as a government. The *legislative* function is concerned with creating, functioning, imagining and planning. The *executive* function is concerned with implementing and with doing. The *judicial* function is concerned with judging, evaluating and comparing. Mental self-government involves all three functions, but each person will have a dominant form."[17]

For school teachers and seminar leaders, we would hope the lessons are equally obvious: analyze each student's learning style, and cater to it. You won't be able to do this for everyone all the time. But you can make sure that every style is catered for regularly throughout every learning sequence. If you do, you'll be amazed at how easily people can learn—and how much less resistance you will find.

One of the first American schools to be based almost entirely on Howard Gardner's principles is the Key Elementary School in Indianapolis. Walk into the Key School and you'll find youngsters learning in all the different "intelligences". Sure, you'll find all the traditional subject areas, such as reading and math, being covered. But you'll also find everyone involved in music, painting, drawing, physical activity and discussion. For four periods a week, children meet in multi-aged groups called pods, to explore a whole range of interests such as computers, gardening, cooking, "making money", architecture, theatre, multicultural games and other real-life skills.

"Once a week," says Gardner, "an outside specialist visits the school and demonstrates an occupation or craft. Often the specialist is a parent,

How body language indicates learning styles

For intaking information

A visual learner usually sits up very straight and follows the presenter around with her eyes.

An auditory learner often softly repeats to herself words spoken by the presenter, or nods her head a lot when the facilitator is presenting spoken information. An auditory learner often "plays a cassette in her head" when she is trying to retrieve information so she may be staring off into space when she does this.

A bodily-kinesthetic learner often slumps down when she listens.

A tactual person loves to play with objects while she listens: flicking her pen or fiddling with papers, or playing with a koosh ball while she listens to someone talk.

JEANNETTE VOS*

* Six-day training on 21st Century Techniques for Learning and Teaching: Summer Institutes.
For further details of training, write to P.O. Box 13006, La Jolla, CA 92039-3066, USA, or see website at www.learning-revolution.com

and typically the topic fits into the school theme at the time."[18]

The school is also closely involved with the Center of Exploration at the Indianapolis Museum. "Students can enter into an apprenticeship of several months, in which they can engage in such activities as animation, shipbuilding, journalism or monitoring the weather."

Key School is also alive with projects. Says Gardner: "During any given year the school features three different themes, introduced at approximately ten-week intervals. The themes can be quite broad (such as 'Patterns' or 'Connections') or more focused ('The Renaissance— then and now' or 'Mexican heritage'). Curriculums focus on these themes; desired literacies and concepts are, whenever possible, introduced as natural adjuncts to an exploration of the theme."

All projects are also videotaped so that eventually each student has a portfolio of videos to show both the work done and to reveal each one's strengths.

In brief, the Key School encourages all students to learn through all their intelligences, those where they're strong and those where they need building; it focuses on their learning styles; it encourages thinking and experimentation; and it builds apprenticeship and mentoring models.

The New City School, in St. Louis, Missouri, has gone even further. Since basing school activities around multiple-intelligence principles, its staff have collectively written a definitive book on the subject. *Celebrating Multiple Intelligences: Teaching For Success* is a practical resource guide to teachers at every level on how to cater to all individual "intelligence-strengths" while teaching all major subjects.

Better yet, both New City and the Indianapolis school show precisely what can happen if a country finally uses its tremendous academic research skills and blends them with well-planned schools, innovative teachers, tremendous community resources and a focus that sees all children as gifted.

Great catch-up programs

1. Specialized kinesiology.
2. Physical routines.
3. Ball/stick/bird teaching.
4. Catching up at spelling.
5. Back-writing for letter recognition.
6. Four-minute reading program.
7. Finger phonics.
8. Tape-assisted reading program.
9. Peer tutoring.
10. "Look, Listen" method.
11. Reading Recovery.
12. Personal key vocabularies.
13. Beginning School Mathematics.
14. Computerized catch-ups.
15. The SEED mathematics program.
16. 3 "medical-educational" programs.

The world's greatest catch-up programs—and why they work

Until she was 10, Helen Keller was deaf, blind and mute.

But by 16 she had learned to read in Braille, and to write and speak well enough to go to college. She graduated with honors in 1904.

Fortunately her first teacher had never heard of the term "learning disabled".

Unable to use her sense of sight or hearing, Helen Keller learned first through touch. And the good news is that modern breakthroughs have now provided the tools for all of us to "switch on" to easier learning, even those who may have been labeled "backward" or "slow".

Almost a century after Keller's graduation, her message to the world is still clear: everyone is potentially gifted—in some way.

Obviously, the earlier you start to develop those talents the better. One *Fortune* survey has concluded that every dollar spent on good care before birth saved $3.38 on intensive care in a hospital neonatal unit. And every $1 spent on the best head-start programs before school "lowers expenditures for special education, welfare, teen pregnancy and incarceration of criminals by $6".[1]

But even if experience in infancy is poor, can children still catch up at primary school? Fortunately the evidence gives an overall "yes." This is not to deny that some people have learning difficulties. But labeling them "learning disabled" must rank with I.Q. tests as one of the great educational tragedies of the century. The very act of labeling often adds to the stress. *Our research convinces us that any person can learn— in his or her own way. And those ways are many and varied.*

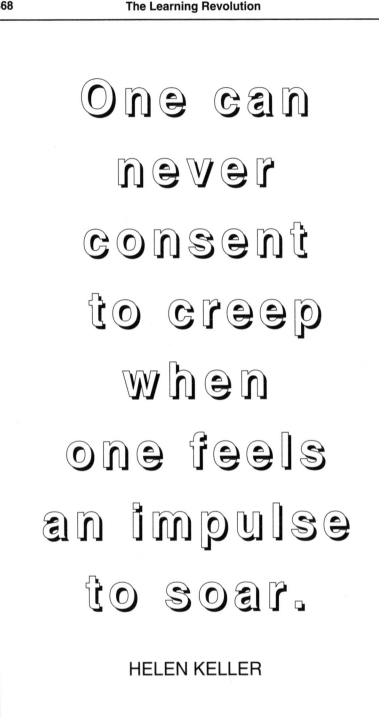

One can never consent to creep when one feels an impulse to soar.

HELEN KELLER

Two key principles: the mind-body connection and the mind-brain connection

The first principle to restress is that learning is not only an *academic* process. Just as an infant develops his brain by sucking, grasping, crawling, creeping, walking, climbing, rocking and spinning, so too with children and adults. You may never develop another cerebral cortical brain cell after you are born, but you can keep growing those dendrites—the brain's connecting and "storage" branches—throughout life.

Professor Diamond and her co-researchers at Berkeley have proven conclusively that the more effective the physical and mental stimulation, the bigger and better the dendritic brain growth.[2] Professor Palmer has proven in Minnesota that *physical* routines at kindergarten can dramatically improve five-year-olds' *academic* performance, because those concentrated physical activities actually grow the brain.[3] Secondly, the brain and the mind are not the same. To oversimplify: if you were to compare them to a computer, the brain would be the *hardware* and the mind the *software.* The brain is biological and neurological: it has neurons, glial cells, dendrites and myelin sheathing that together provide the biological *mechanism.* In the context of this book, the mind is the *content* of the brain. It is not only possible but highly desirable to stimulate the mind through the body as well.

Again, Helen Keller is a classic case-study.[4] It took her three years merely to learn the alphabet. Her teacher, Anne Sullivan, was able to communicate with the girl's brain and mind through a sense of touch. She later spelled out words on her hand. Helen then learned to read and write in Braille, but in her own time.

Five main factors influenced Keller's *ability* to learn: time, culture, context, support and the freedom to choose.

Time was obviously vital. Her first learnings took a long time. But once she made her initial gains she was able to build on them rapidly. Learning had nothing to do with being "disabled"; it had everything to do with having handicaps and needing *her own time-clock* to overcome them. She would never have succeeded by starting in today's regimented graded classrooms.

Culture was also important. Helen Keller's culture esteemed the ability to talk and read. By comparison, in a culture without a written language, navigation might rate much higher than reading; thus culture determines the context of learning—and learning problems. "Special

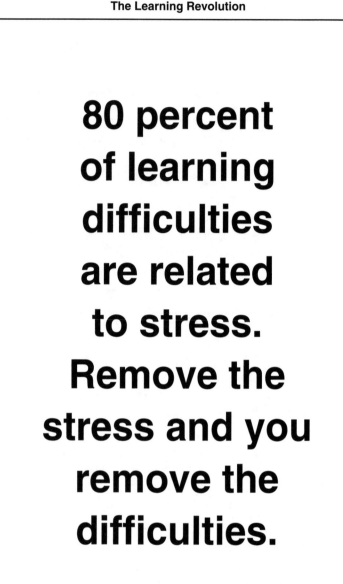

80 percent of learning difficulties are related to stress. Remove the stress and you remove the difficulties.

GORDON STOKES
President, Three in One Concepts*

*This quotation is a major theme of the book *One Brain: Dyslexic Learning Correction and Brain Integration,* published by Three In One Concepts, 2001 W. Magnolia Blvd., Suite B., Burbank, CA 91506-1704. It is highly recommended as a guide to specialized kinesiology.

education" teacher and author Thomas Armstrong puts it succinctly: "Culture defines who's 'disabled' . . . a child labeled dyslexic, hyperactive or learning-disabled in our society might excel in another culture."[5]

Keller's plight was being blind, deaf and mute. She had to learn within that limited context. Had she taken an I.Q. test, with its linguistic base, her rating would have been extremely low, if she had scored at all. Without Sullivan, she may have been placed in an institution for the retarded, instead of developing as a highly gifted person.

The support of a caring and able teacher is equally essential. Sullivan never gave up on Helen, even though the girl had wild temper tantrums.

Helen Keller also had the freedom of choice. At ten she chose to want to learn to talk. There was no rush. She did it in her own time and context. Again the message is obvious: too many people in traditional education are put in no-choice situations in both conscious and subconscious ways.

Anne Sullivan discovered the brain-body and mind-body connection because she, too, had experienced difficulties in learning. Fortunately, there is now a wealth of other research to back up those discoveries.

Specialized kinesiology

Some of the most interesting research and practical applications have come from the field of specialized kinesiology. Just as *kinesthetics,* or movement, is an important aspect of many learning styles, so is *kinesiology* the science of motion, and *kinesthesia,* the sensation of position, movement and tension of parts of the body.

Kinesiology has become well known in some countries because of the way it has helped peak performance in sports. Brigitte Haas Allroggen, of the Munich Institute of Kinesiology, talks about the effectiveness of the science with Olympic teams: "All of a sudden things exploded. We began working with top Austrian athletes who later won Olympic medals and worldwide competitions. Then the Norwegian Olympic team came to us, and the Italians too. All had remarkable results."[6]

Similar techniques are now helping in education, and not just for people with learning difficulties. Says kinesiologist Kathleen Carroll, of Washington D.C., who links her training with accelerated integrative learning strategies: "Kinesiology improves academics for *anyone.*"[7]

This is, in part, because of the way the brain transmits messages both *electrically* and *chemically,* and the way in which stress causes block-

How to improve your spelling, writing, reading and listening with this simple brain exercise:

1.   Stand up and, by raising your knees alternately, touch each hand to the opposite knee.

2.   Do this about ten times whenever you are stressed.

Variations:

1.   Do it with your eyes closed.

2.   Do it by raising each foot, alternately behind you; touching each foot with the opposite hand.

This is a typical exercise recommended by educational kinesiologists to integrate both sides of the brain, reduce stress and make learning easier. If you have difficulty with exercises like this, the authors recommend repatterning by a certified kinesiologist.

Exercises like this are covered in the highly-recommended books, *Brain Gym,* published by Edu-Kinesthetics Inc., P.O. Box 3396, Ventura, CA 93006-3396, and *One Brain: Dyslexic Learning Correction and Brain Integration,* published by Three In One Concepts, 2001 W. Magnolia Blvd., Suite B., Burbank CA 91506-1704.

We acknowledge the assistance of certified kinesiologist Kathleen Carroll, Three In One Concepts facilitator of Washington DC, in compiling this section of the book.

ages. In simple terms, educational kinesiologists say that when stress overwhelms us our brain is short-circuited—the "wiring" becomes fused. They say this is a major cause of learning problems—and labeling those problems "dyslexia" or anything else generally adds to the stress and the fusion. Often the answer lies in simple exercises which "defuse" the blockage between the left and right sides of the brain. Get rid of the blockage and you often get rid of the problem.

Some of the most outstanding work has come from specialized kinesiology researchers and practitioners Gordon Stokes and Daniel Whiteside through their Three In One Concepts organization based in Burbank, California. They say 80 percent of learning difficulties are related to stress. And this can be released by kinesiology.[8]

They have developed body exercises—using pressure-points, muscle testing and coordination patterns—to reorient the electrical patterns of the brain and thus *defuse* stress, clear the "blocked circuits" and turn on the ability to learn. By working through the body they've been able to change the state of both the brain and the mind.

Since the brain operates most effectively when both left and right sides are working in harmony, many of those kinesiology exercises can help you become more *centered,* more coordinated, less stressful and can make learning easier and natural—in the same way that Olympic athletes use centering exercises to prepare for competition.

Many of the best and simplest exercises have been developed by educational kinesiologists Paul and Gail Dennison and illustrated in *Brain Gym,* a highly-recommended handbook.[9]

These exercises were originally developed by Dr. Paul Dennison for people labeled "dyslexic"—people who supposedly see writing in reverse, like a mirror-image. But they help more than people with handicaps: they can be used at any age level and even for people who don't think they have learning problems. They're excellent, for instance, for classroom "state changes"—for any age group.

Unfortunately most schools are not yet using these tools, but where they are the results are outstanding. A typical example comes from the Sierra Vista Junior High School in California, where Three In One Concepts worked with 11 "special education" students who were three to seven years behind their grade level. All were considered to be handicapped by "dyslexia". A kinesiology specialist worked with the students one afternoon a week for eight weeks. And at the end of that time 73

If we insist on looking at the rainbow of intelligence through a single filter, many minds will erroneously seem devoid of light.

RENEE FULLER
inventor of ball/stick/bird teaching method*

*The quotation above is the subheading of an article entitled *Beyond IQ,* by Renee Fuller, *In Context* magazine (winter 1988).

percent of the students showed "significant improvement" (at least one year's growth in eight weeks) in three of six learning abilities tested, 50 percent in one and 27 percent in two others.[10]

The world abounds with other excellent catchup programs. Among the best we have found:

Doman-Palmer-Niklasson-Hartigan models

Variations of the physical routine programs developed by Glenn Doman, Lyelle Palmer, Irene and Mats Niklasson, and Jerome and Sophie Hartigan are now being used effectively in many parts of the world. Montessori International, in Montana, puts its older preschool children every day through a routine of log rolls, alligator crawls, rapid spinning and swinging on bars. In the Hartigans' *Jumping Beans* program children as young as 18 months go through a series of routines to music, starting with gentle rolling, and balancing, then moving up to brachiating exercises: swinging from their hands on 'jungle gyms' or 'monkey bars'.

Before age three, the Hartigans recommend plenty of fun and dance to music. After three, the more structured program can begin.[11]

In Shidchida, Japan, you'll also now find more than 100 centers where parents can do advanced developmental activities with their children.

The ball/stick/bird method

In Maryland, USA, outstanding results have been achieved by Dr. Renee Fuller while on the staff at Rosewood Hospital Center Psychology Department. She worked with 26 persons who were institutionalized for retardation—ranging in age from 11 to 48 and in I.Q. tests from 28 to 72.

Fuller taught them to read. And that achievement greatly increased both their learning ability and their self-esteem. "Not only did they learn to read advanced story material with comprehension," she reports, "they also showed some unexpected emotional and behavioral changes."[12] By learning to read they learned to think. And when they learned to think, their behavior changed and their appearance changed.

Fuller provided them with a tool to break the reading code: the ball/ stick/bird method. In this method, the ball represents all the parts of letters of the alphabet having a circle; the stick represents the parts of letters with a line; and the bird the "wings" of letters, such as an "r."

Helpful hints on spelling

Try this with children having difficulty with "problem words" in English or alphabet languages. Get them to:

a. Picture the word in their favorite color.

b. Make any unclear letter stand out by making them look different to the others in some way, for example, bigger, brighter, closer or a different color.

c. Break the word into groups of three letters, and build your picture three letters at a time.

d. Put the letters on a familiar background. Picture something like a familiar object or movie scene, then put the letters you want to remember on top of it.

e. If it is a long word, make the letters small enough so that you can easily see the whole word.

f. Trace the letters in the air with your finger and picture in your mind the letters that you are writing.

ROBERT DILTS and TODD A. EPSTEIN
*Dynamic Learning**

* Published by Meta Publications, P.O. Box 1910, Capitola, California 95010, USA.

She showed her students how all the letters of the alphabet consisted of just these three simple concrete forms. With that "code" and fast-paced stories, even the most retarded students were soon learning and thriving.

Catching up at spelling

Other children are catching up at spelling using methods outlined in three excellent books, *Catchwords,* by Charles Cripps and Margaret L. Peters; *Alpha to Omega,* by Beve Hornsby and Frula Shear; and *The Writing Road to Reading,* by Romalda Bishop Spalding.

Alpha to Omega provides a particularly good introduction to the ways in which words are grouped both phonetically and in similar patterns— as pattern-recognition is particularly important to improve spelling.

Catchwords takes the core words in the Australian, New Zealand and British primary school curriculum and shows both teachers and parents how to introduce them in a natural, logical and active way.

Spelling, in fact, is one of the big casualties of the nonsensical phonics-versus-nonphonics debate. Obviously phonics can help any child learn words and syllables based on the "short" vowels: *get, set, bet; sit, hit, fit.* And simple games and blackboard lists can help children identify the most common word and syllable patterns: *fate, mate* and *plate (the magic 'e'); light, might* and *sight; bridge, ridge, sledge* and *dredge.*

But problem words are, by their very definition, not simple ones: *spatial* and *facial; session* and *faction; cough, through* and *bough.* And even such often quoted "principles" as "i before e except after c" don't, in fact, work: as with *ancient, conscience, deficient, glacier, science, society, financier, sufficient* and many more.

Most good teachers now feel that spelling is best taught through writing. As Cripps and Peters put it: "Spelling is best remembered in the fingertips, and it is the memory of the moving pencil writing words that makes for accurate spelling." That's because "muscle memory", processed by the cerebellum, is one of the most effective forms of memory.

Non-phonetic spelling is also a visual skill, rather than a listening skill. Most children find it hard to learn non-phonetic words from spoken examples alone. So encourage them to learn by both the look and feel of words. Encourage them, too, to write words from memory, rather than copying them. By doing this, they are calling on their visual and muscle-memory ability, rather than spelling out the sounds.

Robert Dilts and Todd A. Epstein, in their excellent N.L.P. book,

How back writing solves problems

Back writing, the method recommended by Peter Young and Colin Tyre in *Teach Your Child To Read*—for children who have difficulty distinguishing between some letters. Place a large sheet of paper on a smooth wall at your child's shoulder height. Give him a thick crayon or felt-tipped pen, so he can write on the paper at arm's length. Then, with your child facing the paper, write the first letter on his back, with your index finger, as if you were printing a 'lower-case' non-capital letter. Make sure he can feel it, tell him what it is, and ask him to write it on the paper. But do only one letter at a time. The system works because of the power of "muscle memory": the ability to memorize through bodily actions.

The illustration is from *FUNdamentals*,
by Gordon Dryden and Colin Rose.

Dynamic Learning, also make many first-rate suggestions for teaching those who find spelling difficult. In particular, they recommend using "visual imagination" in tackling tough words: visualizing each word so that the difficult letter-combinations stand out, either by making them bigger, brighter or a different color (see hints, page 376).

Back writing for mirror writing problems

For school-age children who continue to have problems distinguishing letters such as *b* and *d,* and *p* and *q,* British educators Peter Young and Colin Tyre, in their excellent book, *Teach Your Child To Read,* recommend "back writing". The principles are simple: place a large sheet of paper on a wall at your child's eye-level; with the child facing the poster, you use your index finger to "print" the letter *b* on his back, repeating something like, "B says buh; first down for the bat and round for the ball;" and get him to write the letter on the poster, using a thick felt pen and repeating your wording. Teach only one letter at a time.

Young and Tyre say that "over very many years we have not known this to fail".

Running fingers over the shape of Montessori sandpaper letters also helps children distinguish "similar but opposite" letters. Sets of stippled plastic letters are now available.

New Zealand breakthroughs

Other breakthroughs are often blends or developments of techniques covered in our True Learning chapter.

New Zealand's catchup programs, for instance, have become so successful that groups of American and Swedish teachers now fly across the Pacific regularly to see how they work. New Zealand teachers are amazed to find that many American elementary schools still shuffle children around to several different teachers during a day: a reading teacher, for example, and a music teacher.

American visitors "down under" are impressed by what they call whole-language teaching. But that term is too restrictive. Whole life may well be better. The whole structure is based around the principle that students come first.

New Zealand has "a national curriculum" but that paints only in broad strokes the educational philosophy and teaching goals. Individual teach-

Wherever possible, students should be given choices and responsibility for their own education.

ELIZABETH SCHULZ*

* Writing in the *American Teacher* Magazine,
February 1993, on her visit to New Zealand schools.

ers are regarded very much as self-acting professionals, graduates of Colleges of Education which specialize in teacher training. Large blocks of all three-year teacher-training programs are also spent in practical hands-on school experience.

Even the term *national curriculum* is probably a misnomer in that it suggests a French-style system where every year each child is learning the same set body of knowledge.

"The new national curriculum doesn't tell teachers how to run their classes," reports *American Teacher* Magazine's Elizabeth Schulz, "but it does emphasize that schools are for the students and should be organized to give them access to the skills and understanding they need to participate effectively and productively in society. School learning is meant to be relevant. Class projects should illuminate for students the interconnectedness of subjects. And, whenever possible, students should be given choices and responsibility for their own education."[13]

Four other factors play a big part in the country's highly successful catchup programs:

1. While New Zealand education is financed by central government and the funds are distributed to schools on the basis of roll-numbers, extra money is provided for schools in low-income areas or areas with special ethnic needs.

2. The Ministry of Education funds a world-renowned *Reading Recovery* program (although many individual schools say their own programs are much more effective).

3. Its Learning Media division also provides to all schools an outstanding selection of free material. This includes a *Beginning School Mathematics* program; a fast-paced, colorful *Ready To Read* series of beginner books; and a regular *School Journal,* which includes top-notch writing for children on a wide range of topics. These *Journals* have been published for years. All writing has been indexed for age groups and subjects. And that makes them ideal source-material for thematic study.

4. Teachers are also encouraged to use their own initiative.

Among the resulting breakthroughs:

The four-minute reading program

Like many countries, New Zealand has a large number of migrant families for whom English is a second language. Not surprisingly, many

All it takes is four minutes a day at school, four minutes at home, and a great link between home and school.*

* The key to New Zealand's "four-minute reading program",
as reported in the television series, *Where To Now?*
produced by Gordon Dryden for The Pacific Foundation
and broadcast on the Television One network.

of them starting school at age five have an English reading equivalent of three or four. Now many of them are catching up within a few weeks. All it takes is four minutes a day and a great link between school and home.

The entire scheme is common sense and simple. When each child starts school, teachers check his or her level of understanding. If Bobby can recognize his own name and other words starting with "B," but he can't manage those starting with "P" or "W" or "K," then the teacher works out a personalized daily list of words—beginning with those letters. Those will include the recommended first 300 most-used words in the language, and others well-known to the child, such as family and local street names.

A new list of words is provided each day, handwritten on note paper. The list is taken home for study, and a carbon copy kept at school. Each morning, the teacher spends only four minutes with each child to check progress—and provide encouragement.

But the big extra ingredient is the home involvement. A "school neighborhood worker" takes home the first list with each child, and explains to the parents, grandparents or brothers and sisters just what Bobby needs to learn—and how only four minutes a day is needed for him to flourish. If the parents have difficulty with English, a neighborhood volunteer is found.

Educational psychologist Donna Awatere, now a Member of Parliament, played a big part in developing the program. She says the home-link is the real key. "It's only half as good without that."[14] Another key is the "positive reinforcement" that comes from daily success. While the program started over 18 years ago for five-year-old new entrants, it is now being used successfully in other schools for older children. As well as sending a new reading list home to parents each night, some have brought parent-helpers into the school. At Bruce McLaren Intermediate School in Auckland, for instance, 12 parents help out part-time.

Even senior reading teacher Beth Whitehead was a bit reluctant when asked by her principal to introduce the program, saying "What can you do in four minutes?" But she tried it out. "I soon thought I'd show it wouldn't work. But when I started it, the children just zoomed in their reading. They were absolutely amazing."[15]

Whitehead stresses that the program is built "on praise and positive reinforcement of everything that the child does correctly, however small".

The key ingredients of TARP: Tape-Assisted Reading Program*

1 Provide a full range of books and stories graded by age-group reading levels, with interesting photos or pictures.

2 Encourage each child to choose stories on subjects that interest him.

3 Have those stories recorded on audio tape, by parents, teachers or older students.

4 The student reads the story as he listens, at home and at school, on a Walkman.

5 When he feels confident, he reads the story without the tape.

6 Then he reads parts of it to his teacher, some parts from his selection, some from her choice.

On average, children on this program are making three years' progress in eight to ten weeks.

*Details are covered fully in *TARP: The Tape Assisted Reading Program* by John Medcalf, Training Coordinator, Special Education Service, Hastings, New Zealand. Email: medcalfj@ses.org.nz

Finger-phonics program

At nearby Don Buck Elementary School in West Auckland, teacher Mary Ashby-Green, colleague Lynne Hailey and principal Jennice Murray have achieved outstanding success with a British-based *Finger Phonics* program. Created by Sue Lloyd of Woods Lake School, Suffolk England, the program is known internationally as *Jolly Phonics.*

This takes the extremely simple approach of teaching phonetic reading by linking each sound of English with a specific action and finger movements. And it works. Kinesthetic children who have been way behind at reading early in school are now zooming ahead, proving once again the strength of "muscle memory"—and catering to different learning styles.

Before the program was introduced at Don Buck, 40 percent of its six-year-olds were not reading. With a few months all six-year-olds were reading, and the brightest were reading 12 to 18 months above their chronological age.

Mary Ashby-Green says the program also has children beginning to write in the first couple of weeks at school. But she stresses that the school does not use *Jolly Phonics* in isolation. All teachers are particularly strong in identifying individual learning styles and catering to them. She says similar results from the system are being reported from around the world.

TARP—the tape-assisted reading program

In another part of New Zealand, schools have successfully linked together one of the simplest Japanese electronic innovations with the New Zealand *School Journal*[16] library—and used it to make spectacular progress in overcoming reading difficulties at primary school.

The innovation is the Sony Walkman cassette tape player. And in the small New Zealand suburb of Flaxmere, educational psychologist Dr. John Medcalf has taken the Walkman and used it to solve major reading problems.

The method is called TARP: tape-assisted reading program. Each child is encouraged to read stories of his own choice—based on his own interests. But when he reads each book, at home or at school, he can hear the same story on a cassette tape, through a set of Walkman headphones.

"The readers are actually selecting stories they want to read," says Medcalf, "about subjects they're interested in: reading them when they

Principles of Peer Tutoring:*

 Students' reading levels should be checked first.

 Students should be matched in pairs, with the tutor only a slightly better reader.

 Books should be chosen for the right reading and interest levels.

 Tutors are trained with a simple checklist, which shows them how to use "pause, prompt and praise" techniques.

 Parents are fully informed, books taken home each night, and a list kept of books mastered.

 Tutoring should be done daily or at least three times a week.

 Each pair should record their efforts on a tape-recorder provided.

 The teacher monitors the recordings to check progress in both reading and tutoring.

Over six months the average reading gain for tutors has been four years and for slower learners just over two years.

* Details are fully covered in *Peer Tutoring in Reading,* by John Medcalf, Training Coordinator, Special Education Service, Hastings, New Zealand.
email: medcalfj@ses.org.nz

want to read them—as many times as they like before they actually try to read them to somebody else."[17]

When the student feels confident enough, the teacher checks progress. "Some of the best results," says Medcalf, "have been four to five years' reading gain over approximately eight weeks on the program." Overall documented results show a three-year reading gain in eight to ten weeks.[18]

The program is helped greatly in New Zealand through the graded *School Journal* material, backed by a regularly updated catalog covering content, subjects and age-levels. Students may choose from a selection of taped stories that the school has built up, or may ask a teacher or parent to record on to a tape a story or article of special interest.

Where a similar program has been used in America, the results have also been striking. Marie Carbo, Director of the National Reading Styles Institute, refers to it as "the recorded book" method. As a strong advocate of matching reading methods and materials to learning styles, she says it can even be adapted for use with highly kinesthetic youngsters: reading a book on a music stand attached to a stationary bike while listening to the tape and pedaling. If that sounds "far out", listen to the answers from two boys who tried it:

"When you read on that thing, all the words just come out like that. I'm serious!"

"When I got up there, well . . . when I started to read, I mean, I don't know, it was probably like a miracle. I started laughing because I couldn't help it because I was reading almost 100 percent better."[19]

Peer tutoring

Medcalf has also built on earlier work by Professor Ted Glynn, of the University of Otago, in developing a successful peer tutoring program in reading, using "pause, prompt and praise" techniques.

Here one student in an primary school simply acts as a mini-teacher for another student. Generally the mini-teacher is only a little bit more advanced—so both the tutor and her buddy benefit. The tutor very definitely is not the best reader in the class—although she may end up that way. Effectively it's one-to-one teaching without taking up the time of an adult teacher. Each "tutor" is trained in "pause, prompt and praise" techniques: to praise good work in everyday language ("Neat," or "Nice one!"); to pause for ten seconds while a reader may be having difficulty (so the tutor can think of ways to help); and to prompt with suggestions.

"Look, Listen" method for parents

- ■ Choose a very interesting book.
- ■ The print must be large. The younger the child, the bigger the print should be.
- ■ A beginner likes a picture, and not too many words, on each page.
- ■ Don't ask him to read aloud. You read to him.
- ■ Use your finger or another pointer in unison with your reading.
- ■ Read in phrases, with emphasis on meaning.
- ■ Match the speed of your reading to your child's ability to follow the text.
- ■ Both you and your child must be happy and relaxed.

Summarized from
FORBES ROBINSON'S
Look, Listen:
*Learning To Read Is Incredibly Simple**

*Distributed by J.K. Marketing, P.O. Box 366, Nelson, New Zealand.

Flaxmere Primary School teacher Rhonda Godwin sums up the results: "We've had tutors who came into the program reading about a year to a year and a half below their chronological age, and they made up to two years' gain after working on the program for about ten weeks."[20]

Over six months the average gain for tutors has been four years—and for the slower learners just over two years.[21]

The "Look, Listen" method

Another New Zealand innovation has made similar dramatic improvements in teaching reading to whole classes at once. Teacher Forbes Robinson has shown its effectiveness for years, and has proven it in practice around America, Britain and Canada. He calls it the "Look, Listen" method. Robinson is a fan of the Doman theory which proposes that youngsters can easily learn to read when they're exposed to big print.

For a classroom setting, Robinson recommends a piece of technology that predates television: the opaque projector. "Unlike the overhead projector, the opaque projector requires no transparencies. Its operation involves no preparation at all."[22] To use it to teach reading, you simply select a suitable book, preferably with attractive illustrations, slip it into position in the projector, turn on the power, and it projects the pages, in full color, either one or two at a time, on to a jumbo-sized screen: preferably 8ft. x 8ft (250 x 250 cm). The opaque projector also comes with a "magic pointer"—and the teacher can move this quickly to follow the words as they are projected on to the screen and he reads them.

Where Robinson's techniques have been researched, the results have been excellent:

At Putaruru Intermediate School in New Zealand, the "Look, Listen" method was used with 140 grade 7 and 8 students, aged 11, 12 and 13. All had "reading ages" two to six years below their chronological ages. All 140 were taken in groups of about 30 in half-hour sessions four times a week for 12 weeks. The 63 students in grade 7 were tested before and after the trial, and 40 of them made between two and three years' progress in the 12 weeks, 17 gained between one and one and a half years and five gained half a year. The school was so impressed with the results it introduced the program for adults as well.[23]

At the Language Development Center at Chelmsford Hall School, Eastbourne, England, the same method was used to teach reading to 106 children with severe reading difficulties—aged between four and 14. All

Learning is the greatest game in life and the most fun.

All children are born believing this and will continue to believe this until we convince them that learning is very hard work and unpleasant.

Some kids never really learn this lesson, and go through life believing that learning is fun and the only game worth playing.

We have a name for such people.

We call them geniuses.

GLENN DOMAN
Teach Your Baby Math*

*Published by the Better Baby Press, at The Institutes For The Achievement of Human Potential, 8801 Stenton Avenue, Philadelphia, Pennsylvania 19118, USA.

106 pupils averaged eight months' progress in six weeks.[24]

In several schools in Scotland, the Robinson method was used to help fifteen 11-to-13-year-olds diagnosed as having very low I.Q.s: between 40 and 70. They were taken for 45 to 50 minutes a day for just under six weeks, and made ten months' reading improvement.[25]

At the Fairbank Memorial Junior School in Toronto, Canada, a mid-city multi-racial school with a large proportion of youngsters learning English as a second language, after 20 minutes twice a day for only ten days, progress for children in grades 2 through 6 ranged from just under five and a half months to one year.[26]

As D.B. Routley, principal of the C.E. Webster Junior Public School in Toronto, wrote after seeing the results at his school: "During my 24 years in the field of education, I have never seen an in-service program for teachers that has produced such a positive impact on students as the program designed by Mr. Robinson."[27]

New Zealand's Reading Recovery program

All those six programs can be operated by normal classroom teachers. But the best-known New Zealand catch-up program is organized by teachers who need to be specially trained. It is known as *Reading Recovery,* first developed by Professor Marie Clay of the University of Auckland.

In New Zealand, while the official age for starting school is six, nearly every child starts at five. By six, many children with reading difficulties are identified in the *Reading Recovery* program, and helped for half an hour each day by a specially trained *Reading Recovery* teacher. *Reading Recovery* has been operating as a government-funded program through-out New Zealand since 1984. On average, youngsters catch up within 16 weeks. About 97 percent maintain and improve their ability as they proceed through school.

The program has been taken up in some parts of America, Britain and Australia.   An official British educational report on the New Zealand scheme gives it high praise—but stresses two additional points:

1. Literacy is accorded a "supremely important" place in the New Zealand education system, so "it can be no surprise that the target group of clients for *Reading Recovery* was identified and a program devised for their aid."

2. "It is already clear that the New Zealand system is well on the way

Release the native imagery of your child and use it for working material.

SYLVIA ASHTON-WARNER
Author of *Teacher**

*One of the keys to Ashton-Warner's success, as covered by
Lynley Hood in *The Biography of Sylvia Ashton-Warner,*
published by Viking, Auckland, New Zealand.

to identifying the next frontier, the third-wave children—that small core who do not appear able to accelerate at the rates of the majority of pupils for whom the scheme is the appropriate measure." [28]

Despite that international praise, many New Zealand primary schools say that combinations of other programs—as reported in this chapter— are much more effective, and certainly much more cost-effective, in teaching youngsters to read.

Personal key vocabularies

Other than Marie Clay and former Director of Education, Dr. C.E. Beeby, the New Zealand educational innovator best known in other countries is probably the late Sylvia Ashton-Warner. She first burst to prominence internationally with her book *Teacher* in 1963. It was based largely on her work teaching at primary schools in New Zealand rural areas with a mainly Maori population. And her supporters* would say it provides one of the main effective answers to that "third wave" reading problem. In the early 1950s, New Zealand introduced into its schools the *Janet and John* series of readers, a British modification of the American *Alice and Jerry* series. But even then teachers were encouraged to make up their own books based on children's own lives.

In listening to young Maori children, Ashton-Warner"came to realize that some words—different words for each child—were more meaning- ful and memorable than others." When she asked a young child to write about a "train" he wrote about a "canoe".

She then started to listen to each child and selected the key words "which were so meaningful to him that he was able to remember them when he had seen them only once". As Lynley Hood writes in *Sylvia,* her biography of Ashton-Warner: "Her pupils learned to read from their personal key vocabularies. Nearly every day, from their experiences at home or at school, Sylvia helped each child select a new key word. She wrote the word with heavy crayon on a stout piece of cardboard and gave it to the child. The word cards became as personal and precious to the

* *Those reading Sylvia Ashton-Warner's work for the first time should, in fairness, be made aware that, among her many excellent other qualities, she was also eccentric and prone to exaggeration. While she can claim credit for inventing the key vocabulary concept, many of her writings wrongly imply that she was a lone voice crying in New Zealand's educational wilderness for child-centered education. In fact, Beeby, as head of the Department of Education, was pioneering that very concept, in a rational and effective way.*

There is no reading problem. There are problem teachers and schools.

HERBERT KOHL
*Reading, How To**

*Published by Penguin, London.

children as the imagery they represented. Children who had labored for months over 'See Spot run' in the new *Janet and John* readers took one look at 'corpse', 'beer' or 'hiding' and suddenly they could read.

"The stories from which the key words were born were told in colorful Maori-English. Sylvia recorded them faithfully on to big sheets of paper and pinned them around the walls: 'I caught Uncle Monty pissing behind the tree. He got wild when I laughed at him.' 'My Dad gave my Mum a black eye.' It wasn't exactly what the Education Department had in mind when it advocated the use of children's experiences in the teaching of reading, but it certainly worked. The excitement and the sense of release created an unprecedented enthusiasm for reading."[29]

She realized that children were more interested in their own stories than hers. So she helped her students write them. She put the stories to music. And she constructed her own graphic presentations about their dreams and experiences. She regarded each child as highly creative, and encouraged them to work with clay and paint.

Above all, she summed up her philosophy in one memorable sentence: *Release the native imagery of your child and use it for working material.*

Some of the same techniques have been used by Felicity Hughes to teach English in Tanzania[30] and by Herbert Kohl to effectively teach reading to youngsters from minority cultures in California.

Beginning School Mathematics

New Zealand's success in reading recovery has been matched with some innovative approaches to teaching elementary mathematics. The *Beginning School Mathematics* program, for example, includes very brightly-colored puzzles and games. For their first two years at some schools, youngsters use these and other manipulative material to learn about the main relationships that underlie mathematics.

American writer Schulz summarizes her impression of the program in action: "As we enter the classroom, a glance at the six- and seven-year-olds tells us BSM is in full swing. Four students make geometric shapes by stretching rubber bands across pegs on a board. Children at a table draw pictures using cardboard circles, squares and triangles. One boy weighs household objects on a scale, guided by a sheet that asks, for example, if a cork is heavier than a paper clip. Six students stand in line by height and answer the teacher's questions about who is first, second

Children learn best when they are helped to discover the underlying principles for themselves.

PETER KLINE
The Everyday Genius*

*Published by Great Ocean Publishers Inc, 1823 North Lincoln Street, Arlington, VA 22207.

and third in line, and who is standing between whom."[31] Many New Zealand teachers, however, find this approach is tied far too closely with Piaget's developmental "timetable", and that much better results can be achieved by a variety of even earlier hands-on projects, including variations of the Montessori program.

Computerized catch-ups

Other intermediate schools have found great success by using the international *Technic Lego* program. Others are also using some of the excellent computer math programs that are now readily available. Among the best are those pioneered by the Computer Curriculum Corporation, based on years of research at Stanford University in California, not just for math but for a wide variety of subjects.

And in China, Clever Software Company has developed CD-ROM *Computer Tutor* programs to guarantee school examination success.

The SEED mathematics program

In the United States, the best non-computer catchup mathematics program we have seen is called SEED: Special Elementary Education for the Disadvantaged.[32]

In Dallas, Texas, Philadelphia, Pennsylvania and Oakland, California, teachers using the SEED method have been successfully teaching advanced high school mathematics to ten-year-old African-American children, from low-income families, who only a few months before were up to two years behind in math.

Three other "medical-educational" programs

This is not a book on medical problems, but no survey of effective catchup methods would be complete without reviewing three programs with strong "medical-educational" links.

Program one is the method developed by Glenn Doman and his team in Philadelphia at The Institutes for the Achievement of Human Potential to assist children with severe brain damage. Following on from the pioneering work of Professor Temple Fay, Doman's team has effectively taught many blind children to see, deaf children to hear, and handicapped children to perform at "normal" levels: by physically "repatterning" other parts of the brain to take over from damaged cells and sections. His breakthrough book, *What To Do About Your Brain-Injured Child,* is as

If you're told your child has A.D.D.S., look at his role models!

Orville Wright, one of the first two men to fly, was expelled from school because of bad behavior.

Ludwig van Beethoven was rude and ill-mannered and was subject to wild fits of rage.

Pope John XXIII was sent home with a note saying he continually came to class unprepared; he did not deliver the note.

Louis Armstrong, the great jazz singer and saxaphone player, spent time in an institution for delinquent boys.

Paul Cezanne, the painter, had a bad temper and would stamp his feet in hysterical rage whenever he felt thwarted.

William Wordsworth, the poet, was described before his eighth birthday as a "stubborn, wayward and intractable boy".

Sarah Bernhardt was expelled from school three times.

Will Rogers was incorrigible at school and ran away from home.

Arturo Toscanini was an obstinate and disobedient boy; once he made up his mind not to do something, nothing could make him change his mind.

THOMAS ARMSTRONG
The Myth of the A.D.D.S. Child*

* Published by Penguin, New York.

inspiring and challenging today as it was when first published in 1974.

Program two is the Tomatis Method, first developed 50 years ago by French physician, psychologist and educator Dr. Alfred Tomatis. The method uses filtered and unfiltered sound to "reeducate" the ability to listen and process sounds, both through the intricate mechanisms of the inner ear and through the body. The Tomatis method is used in more than 200 centers worldwide. Some of its results are outstanding, not merely to improve listing ability, but to develop superior skills in speaking, reading, writing, sports, social interaction,motor development and music.

Program three covers the natural alternatives, developed by Thomas Armstrong, to the medical treatment of the so-called Attention Deficit Disorder Syndrome—a malady that is claimed to inflict about two million American children.

A.D.D.S. is supposedly characterized by three main features: hyper-activity (fidgeting, excessive running and climbing, leaving one's class-room seat), impulsivity (blurting out answers in class, interrupting others, having problems waiting turns) and inattention (forgetfulness, disorgani-zation, losing things, careless mistakes).

In recent years psychiatrists across America have prescribed, for so-called A.D.D.S., millions of doses of Ritalin, a drug originally approved to control mild depression and senility in adults.

Now no one would deny that many children regularly display the three characteristics of being hyperactive, impulsive and inattentive.

But Dr. Armstrong, who has spent years researching different learning styles, puts clearly the viewpoint the current authors have come to share: "A.D.D.S. does not exist," he writes in *The Myth of the A.D.D.S. Child.* "These children are *not* disordered. They may have a different style of thinking, attending, and behaving, but it's the broader social and educa-tional influences that create the disorder, not the children."

Dr. Armstrong's book outlines "50 ways to improve your child's behavior and attention span without drugs, labels or coercion". Those ways range from changing eating habits to physical education programs, from martial arts classes to the use of relaxing background music, from channelling energy into creative arts to computer training.

All are the kind of sensible, common-sense activities highly recom-mended to all parents and schools, not just to help underachieving children to catch up early in their life but to avoid the dropout dilemma later.

How to solve the dropout dilemma

❏ **Adapt Japan's business methods for school.**

❏ **Use the world as your classroom, and study all subjects together as integrated projects.**

❏ **Study in cooperative groups.**

❏ **Paint the big picture first, then fill in the details.**

❏ **Learn in shorter bursts, with built-in success-steps along the way.**

❏ **Apply the lessons from SuperCamp.**

How to get "high" on education and not on drugs, gangs and crime

Is it really possible for nearly all students to succeed at high school?

Are there some guaranteed methods to get teenagers "high" on achievement instead of on drugs, gangs and crime? And ways to slash dropout rates even among those entering high school way behind others? Is it actually possible for nearly every student to *love* high school? Fortunately, our research says: Yes. And outstanding high schools are already achieving these results by using:

❏ Common sense lessons from the world's best businesses.

❏ Methods that captivate youngsters' emotions so they *want* to stay in school.

❏ Sound link-ups between university research breakthroughs, competent high school teachers and new technology.

❏ New group study techniques that are lifting examination "failures" into the ranks of high-achievers.

❏ Methods that focus on what we want for youth, not what we don't want.

❏ Short graduated courses where everyone can achieve step-by-step success—at any age.

❏ Outstanding, concentrated out-of-school SuperCamps that result in marked increases in academic results, motivation and confidence.

❏ New teaching techniques to make sure that all individual learning styles are catered to.

For working models of teenage success stories we've chosen examples from as far apart as the southeast panhandle of Alaska, the

Mt. Edgecumbe's innovative teaching methods challenge students and draw raves from business leaders.

*Reading, Writing and Continuous Improvement**

*Article in *Competitive Times* magazine, published by GOAL/QPC (Number 1, 1991).

breathtakingly beautiful national parks of New Zealand and a SuperCamp movement that has now spread from California to Singapore.

1. Using Japan's business methods to improve school

If you had to nominate any American state as a revolutionary high school leader, Alaska would not top many lists. In area it's the biggest of the 50 United States—twice the size of Texas. But it has the second lowest population: about half a million people, and only one metropolitan area, Anchorage, with a population as high as 200,000. Its native population is diverse: Caucasian, Eskimo, Eleuts and several Native American Indian tribes, many of them centered around small community towns of only 150 to 200 people, living on extremely low incomes, in a climate where the temperature in winter can reach -17 degrees Fahrenheit or -20 degrees Centigrade. Hardly a recipe for soaring educational success.

Yet one school in Alaska in recent years has earned an accolade as a world leader. It has also shown how great ideas can stem from other fields—in this case from Japan's quality revolution inspired originally by the American W. Edwards Deming.

TQM (Total Quality Management) and CIP (the Continuous Improvement Process or Kaizen) have been among the main processes used to transform Japan from a devastated, shattered and beaten society into a world economic leader within 40 years.

Now Mt. Edgecumbe High School, in Sitka, Alaska, has pioneered similar methods for education.[1] Mt. Edgecumbe is a public boarding school with 210 students and 13 teachers. Eighty-five percent of its students come from small villages. Most are Native Americans, descendents of the Tlingit, Haida and Tsimpshean tribes as well as Eskimo tribes and Aleuts. Forty percent of its students had struggled at other schools. But in recent years the school has achieved one of America's highest levels of graduates moving on to higher education.

In many ways it was transformed by the vision of two people: former Superintendent Larrae Rocheleau and former teacher David Langford. Mt. Edgecumbe was originally opened in 1947 as a school for Native Americans. But in 1984 it was converted into an "alternative" experimental school, with Rocheleau in charge. Visitors to the school have described him as a practical idealist. One of his first objectives was "to turn these students into entrepreneurs who would go back to their villages and make a difference".[2] These dreams succeeded in part, but they really

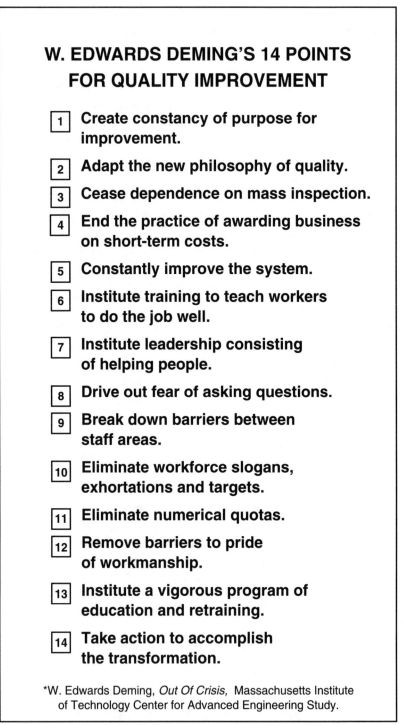

W. EDWARDS DEMING'S 14 POINTS FOR QUALITY IMPROVEMENT

1 Create constancy of purpose for improvement.

2 Adapt the new philosophy of quality.

3 Cease dependence on mass inspection.

4 End the practice of awarding business on short-term costs.

5 Constantly improve the system.

6 Institute training to teach workers to do the job well.

7 Institute leadership consisting of helping people.

8 Drive out fear of asking questions.

9 Break down barriers between staff areas.

10 Eliminate workforce slogans, exhortations and targets.

11 Eliminate numerical quotas.

12 Remove barriers to pride of workmanship.

13 Institute a vigorous program of education and retraining.

14 Take action to accomplish the transformation.

*W. Edwards Deming, *Out Of Crisis,* Massachusetts Institute of Technology Center for Advanced Engineering Study.

started to take off about four years later when teacher Langford, on a visit to Phoenix, Arizona, attended a business TQM meeting. He became convinced that the same processes that had transformed Japan could transform a school. He persuaded Rocheleau to attend a further seminar, and Mt. Edgecumbe has never been the same.

How do you summarize a school that has turned nearly every other educational system upside down and inside out? Let's try:

❏ *Teachers and students are all regarded as co-managers. They set their own targets and goals, individually and collectively. And they evaluate themselves regularly against agreed standards of excellence. There are no "incompletes" and "F" grades at Edgecumbe. Each task is not complete until it is regarded as meeting standards of excellence way above those ever achieved in any school examination.*

❏ The first computer course begins by teaching speed typing. All students do their homework on a computer, using word processors, spreadsheets and graphic programs to produce 100 percent perfect results—just as their future businesses will demand excellence in typing, spelling, accounting, financial and sales reports.

❏ Collectively the school has identified its "internal" customers (students, teachers, administrators and other staff) and its "external" customers (universities and colleges, military, industrial and service work force, homes and society in general).

❏ All activities at the school have been planned in conjunction with those "customers".

❏ Students and staff have drawn up their own "mission statement". Among many other points, it stresses that: "The school places high expectations upon students, administrators and staff. Program and curriculum are based upon a conviction that students have a great and often unrealized potential. The school prepares students to make the transition to adulthood, helping them to determine what they want to do and develop the skills and the self-confidence to accomplish their goals. Students are required to pursue rigorous academic programs that encourage them to work at their highest levels."[3]

❏ *The first week of school each year is used for building self-esteem and quality training.* Says a joint student-teacher report: "By spending the first week focusing on why students attend school, they are ready to learn and seem hungry to begin. We focus on reaching out to find out what you are truly capable of accomplishing, not just getting it done."

Mt. Edgecumbe High School's

Constancy of Purpose*

The aim of Mt. Edgecumbe High School, Sitka, Alaska, is to produce QUALITY individuals.

Our actions are based on the following beliefs:

1. Human relations are the foundation for all quality improvement.
2. All components in our organization can be improved.
3. Removing the causes of problems in the system inevitably leads to improvement.
4. The person doing the job is most knowledgeable about that job.
5. People want to be involved and do their jobs well.
6. Every person wants to feel like a valued contributor.
7. More can be accomplished by working together to improve the system than by working individually around the system.
8. A structured problem-solving process, using statistical graphic problem-solving techniques, lets you know where you are, where the variations lie, the relative importance of problems to be solved, and whether the changes made have had the desired impact.
9. Adversarial relationships are counter-productive and outmoded.
10. Every organization has undiscovered gems waiting to be developed.
11. Removing the barriers to pride of workmanship and joy of learning unlocks the true untapped potential of the organization.
12. Ongoing training, learning and experimentation is a priority for continuous improvement.

*Published by Mt. Edgecumbe High School (October 30, 1990).

❏ As part of this initiation all students and all staff take part in a Ropes course—very similar to some Outward Bound courses and some Super-Camp activities. They describe it as a great confidence builder. Says TQM specialist Myron Tribus: "It does for all students what competitive athletic contests are supposed to do for a few. But it does it better. As I see it, the school is trying to develop autonomous team players."[4]

❏ *Students decided it was inefficient to have seven short study periods a day, so the school switched to four 90-minute classes. This schedule allows time for lab work, hands-on projects, field trips, thorough discussions, varied teaching styles and in-depth study. The reorganized schedule also allows for an extra three hours of staff development and preparation time each week.*

❏ Because students are viewed as customers, the school tries to provide what they want. Students have repeatedly requested more technology, so the school has added dozens of computers, and opened the computer lab, library and science facilities at night for all pupils. As one report puts it: "Quality implementation is heavy on resources because students do the work and learning, not the teachers. The average number of hours of homework has risen to 15 per week. Studying, working together, and achievement have become a habit."[5]

❏ *CIP has prompted teachers to rethink their teaching styles. One science teacher says he has changed from being an 80 percent lecturer to a 95 percent facilitator.*

❏ Discipline problems? "Improving the entire education system, with student/customer needs first, has virtually eliminated classroom discipline problems . . . students acquire a sense of belonging and see the value in each class. Students help control and prevent discipline problems through positive peer pressure."[6]

❏ *All students set improvement goals, such as receiving all A's, avoiding conduct reports and reducing tardiness.*

❏ *All students receive 90 minutes per week of quality-improvement training and school-wide problem-solving.*

❏ All staff members have been trained in flowcharting. Flow charts of long-range projects are posted so that everyone can see how their part fits into the whole of each project.

❏ *Because one of the school's goals is to develop "Pacific rim entrepreneurs" the students have set up four pilot "companies":* Sitka

Deming's 14 points

as modified by students for education*

Deming's 14 points for Total Quality Management have been applied to many businesses. But here is how one class at Mt. Edgecumbe High School in Alaska has modified them for education:

1. Create constancy of purpose toward improvement of students and service. Aim to create the best quality students capable of improving all forms of processes and entering meaningful positions in society.

2. Adopt the new philosophy. Educational management must awaken to the challenge, must learn their responsibilities and take on leadership for change.

3. Work to abolish grading and the harmful effects of rating people.

4. Cease dependence on testing to achieve quality. Eliminate the need for inspections on a mass basis (standardized achievement test, minimum graduation exams, etc.) by providing learning experiences which create quality performance.

5. Work with the educational institutions from which students come. Improve the relationships with student sources and help to improve the quality of students coming into your system.

6. Improve constantly and forever the system of student involvement and service, to improve both quality and productivity.

7. Institute education and training on the job for students, teachers, classified staff and administrators.

8. Institute leadership. The aim of supervision should be to help people use machines, gadgets and materials to do a better job.

9. Drive out fear, so that everyone may work effectively for the school system. Create an environment which encourages people to speak freely.

10. Break down barriers between departments. People in teaching, special education, accounting, food service, administration, curriculum development and research, must work as a team. Develop strategies for increasing the cooperation among groups and individual people.

11. Eliminate slogans, exhortations and targets for teachers and students asking for perfect performance and new levels of productivity. Exhortations create adversarial relationships. The bulk of the causes of low quality and low productivity belong to the system and thus lie beyond the control of teachers and students.

12. Eliminate work standards (quotas) on teachers and students (e.g. raise test scores by 10% and lower dropouts by 15%). Substitute leadership.

13. Remove barriers that rob the students, teachers and management of their right to pride and joy of workmanship.

14. Institute a vigorous program of education and self-improvement for everyone.

15. Put everybody in the school to work to accomplish the transformation. It is everybody's job.

*Published by Mt. Edgecumbe High School (October 30, 1990).

Sound Seafoods, Alaska Premier Bait Company, Alaska's Smokehouse and Fish Co. and the Alaska Pulp Corporation—all under the umbrella of Edgecumbe Enterprises. The "parent company" started its first salmon-processing plant in 1985, run by students themselves. The goal was to give students the skills and experience needed for running an import-export business aimed at Asian markets. By the 1988-89 year, the company was already making four annual shipments of smoked salmon to Japan. Each subsidiary company now links hands-on experience with the academic curricula. So math students calculate the dollar-yen exchange rate. Pacific Rim geography is studied in social studies. Art students design promotional brochures and package labels for products. And business and computer students learn how to develop spreadsheets to analyze costs and project prices.[7]

❏ Myron Tribus provides a word picture of how the business projects link with other studies: "In the class on entrepreneurship, taught by Marty Johnson, I watched the students prepare and package smoked salmon for sale in Japan. The students had used a taste panel of local Japanese to determine the flavor and texture Japanese people liked the most. They then developed a standard procedure to produce the same taste and texture every time. To achieve the desired taste required using a certain kind of salmon, exposing it for a certain time and temperature, using a special brining solution, which they had determined experimentally yielded the proper taste, and a certain amount of time in the smoke from the right mixture of wood shavings, using slices of fish cut to a certain thickness and size. By studying the packages of smoked fish sold in Japan, they developed an attractive package which would fit in small Japanese refrigerators. They developed their own distinctive label, in Japanese of course. And they test-marketed the product in Japan."[8] That marketing includes study trips to Japan and other Pacific rim countries.

❏ *All students learn either Chinese or Japanese, and their curriculum is strong in the history, culture and languages of the Pacific rim, English, social studies, mathematics, science, marine science, computers, business, and physical education.*

❏ The school's mission statement stresses that "opportunities for leadership, public service and entrepreneurship are integrated into the program, both during and after regular school hours".

❏ Each student is assisted, guided and challenged to make choices about future academic or technical schooling and alternative methods of making a living. Enter a business class and you'll watch students pre-

The Mt. Edgecumbe High School model

❏ Teachers and students are co-managers.

❏ Excellence is regarded as the norm.

❏ First week each year is esteem-builder.

❏ Teachers are now 90 percent facilitators.

❏ Students determine and control discipline.

❏ Everyone learns speed typing.

❏ Everyone uses computers to publish work to professional standards.

❏ School operates four pilot companies to put theory into practice.

❏ All students learn Chinese or Japanese.

❏ Russian, physics, calculus and advanced quality training have been added to the curriculum, at students' requests.

❏ Classes work without supervision.

❏ Staff training is top priority.

❏ Each teacher has own computer.

❏ Teachers, students learn to develop and use multimedia such as laser discs, hypercard and presentation software.

❏ 50 percent go on to college.

paring spreadsheets to reflect what it will cost them to live in their chosen lifestyle after graduation, taking into account mortgage payments, taxes, cost of living changes and projections for such variables as the cost of transportation and schooling.

❑ Frequently whole classes work without supervision—as they will be required to do in the outside world—so the teachers are free to put extra time into study and further course preparation.

❑ Each curriculum is constantly being revised. As a result of student surveys and requests, Russian, physics, calculus and advanced quality training have been added.

❑ In the CIP media class, students teach other students. There is no administrator or teacher in the room. Twenty-five student trainers have assumed responsibility for training other students in the quality sciences.

❑ *Staff training receives top priority. Teachers are constantly encouraged to internally challenge and justify each and every learning process.* The school has developed two research and development classes, science and technology and media CIP. These continually experiment with new technologies in equipment and human relations.

❑ Each teacher has his or her own computer, with training in many applications. The school has also pioneered multiple uses for multimedia technology such as laser discs, hypercard applications and presentation software.

❑ Every student receives a "Stats for Success" handbook. It is used to record homework, weekly plans, organize their time and graph progress. The entire emphasis is on self-discipline and self-motivation.

And the success ratio? Mt. Edgecumbe's simple goal is stated boldly: to produce QUALITY individuals. Almost 50 percent of all graduates have entered college and are still there or have graduated— much higher than the national average. There have been hardly any dropouts. And the school is confident that all its students will continue to grow and learn.[9] Says *Competitive Times* magazine: "Mt. Edgecumbe's innovative teaching methods challenge students and draw raves from business leaders."[10] Adds Tribus: "I wish I could find the same thirst for learning in the rest of the country."[11]

Mt. Edgecumbe is, of course, a boarding school, but its TQM and CIP-Kaizen principles have lessons for educational systems at every level— and especially for turning previous "failures" into successes.

The old method of operating high schools is separated from the real world.

PAT NOLAN
Director of Integrated Studies Program
at Freyberg High School*

*Author interview at Freyberg High School, Palmerston North,
New Zealand (1991). Dr. Nolan is Senior Lecturer in Education
at Massey University, Palmerston North, and Director of the
university's Educational Research and Development Center.

2. Integrated studies use the world as a classroom

If Mt. Edgecumbe, Alaska, is an unlikely place to start a revolution, the lush, green, heavily-afforested national parks and soaring mountains of New Zealand seem even further removed from the traditional schoolroom. But link them with the latest computer technology, a dedicated team of university innovators and some flexible teachers from Freyberg High School in the small city of Palmerston North, and again the result is surprising.

Every innovation has its visionary driving-force. Freyberg's was Dr. Pat Nolan, senior lecturer in education at Massey University on the outskirts of Palmerston North. Massey was originally an "agricultural college" and it is closely linked with several nearby farm research institutes. So its hands-on tradition is a long one. Pat Nolan marries his love of education with a passion for exploring the New Zealand outdoors: its towering volcanic snowfields, clean sparkling rivers and forests rich with native trees and birds. He's also a computer buff, who now heads Massey's Educational Research and Development Center, a pioneer in providing data-based services to other educational institutions.

Nolan has put all his passions together in the Freyberg "integrated studies program". But it's no mere dream. Nolan sees it as the kind of alternative educational program that "might go the next step in providing for all high school students the kind of results previously enjoyed by only the top 30 to 40 percent".[12]

He says "the old method" of high school studies is separated from the real world. "We've all been through the school system. What we've experienced is a compartmentalized or segmented curriculum, where subjects are locked up in their little boxes, with tight little boundaries around them. So we learn mathematics, physics and English separately. Seldom do we see the connection between subjects. Yet it's by linking subjects together and seeing the interconnections that we come to understand the real world better. And that is basically what integration is all about: developing ways of teaching—and experiencing—knowledge in a way that establishes the interconnections in the minds of the students, and has them actually using that knowledge to create new solutions."

Similar arguments, of course, have been expressed for many years. In New Zealand alone five separate educational inquiries, from 1943 to 1987, have stressed the benefits of integrated studies.[13] But many high

The three key elements of integrated studies

 1 Interesting out-of-class project activities, combining research and exploration.

2 Student use of computer as a tool for information processing and analysis.

3 History, geography, science, math, economics, writing, computing and other studies are linked together, not taught separately.

Summarized from *Case Study of Curriculum Innovation in New Zealand: The Freyberg Integrated Studies Project,* by C.J. Patrick Nolan, then Associate Director of Educational Research and Development Center, Massey University, Palmerston North, New Zealand, and David H. McKinnon, Visiting Research Fellow, Education Department, Massey University, published by Massey University (April 23, 1991).

school principals and teachers have not always been convinced. The best primary school teachers in New Zealand have been "child-centered" facilitators for many years, but many traditional high school and university teachers have been "one-subject lecturers". Integrating several subjects together means change, and change often brings fear and stress.

But it may well be the computer that forces the "integration" changes that so many reports have urged. Most computer programs of course are very specialized. But every sensible business now integrates many of those programs to solve interconnected problems. A finance director uses computer spreadsheets to compile a company's annual report; a designer uses the same raw database to produce graphics for the same report, and uses other computer programs to produce allied artwork and camera-ready pages. Entire business plans, and quick product changes, now emerge from the bar-codes flashing through thousands of different supermarkets—charting market research trends on suppliers' data bases on the other side of a continent. Customer order-forms are instantly translated into production schedules and raw-material purchase orders.

Business revolves around integrated specialists, both self-acting and working in groups. The information revolution now integrates that specialist work. And Nolan says that the real world demands changes in traditional subject-by-subject schooling. He believes changes are demanded even more by the shortage of jobs that previously required no skills.

"In the past," he says, "people who have been relatively unsuccessful at school—relatively unskilled, relatively unknowledgeable—have been able to walk out in days of plenty and pick up a job and do well enough. Those days are now gone—but, not only that, the days of narrow vocational training have also gone."[14]

So Nolan's integrated studies program has linked Massey University educational research with field-trip study projects, IBM-sponsored computer studies and the New Zealand national high school curriculum. His pilot program started in 1986 with sixth form students at Freyberg. The first integrated studies course combined biology, computer studies, English and geography. The elements were drawn together around a central theme: preservation and management issues confronting New Zealand National Parks. That theme was the common thread that bound the subjects together in a coherent program. Out-of-class field research trips were a major part of the project. In Nolan's words: "These national park field trips confronted students not only with physical adventure and

So this is school: a week tramping and canoeing in some of the world's most beautiful scenery.*

*Integrated studies students at Freyberg High School in Palmerston North, New Zealand, frequently take a one-week journey down New Zealand's beautiful Wanganui River, combining the study of history, geography, ecology, the environment, land use and science, then integrating the project by computer analysis and writing projects.

Information obtained by author interviews with teachers, students and project directors, Freyberg High School.

challenge, but generated the experiences, data and information needed to sustain a program of integrated studies for a whole year. Computers also played a central role in supporting the theme; allowing the analysis of large and relatively complex data-sets not normally considered or done at this level. They also allowed extended studies in specific subjects and helped motivate students."

During that pilot program, students' examination results were checked against a similar group taking the standard high school courses. "We had hoped to demonstrate that integrated study students would do better than those experiencing normal secondary school teaching. And that's precisely what we've been able to accomplish." Because the pilot was with senior students—normally high achievers anyway—Nolan would have been happy to say that the pilot group had done no worse. *"But what we were able to show was that their academic performance was significantly better. In English and geography, students scored 20 to 30 marks higher* and in mathematics and science they on average scored ten to 15 marks better."*[15]

Next, a full program was continued with students starting from their first year at high school. Earlier research had shown that four different types of integrated-curriculum approaches could be used. The Freyberg team used all four: to develop student-centered inquiry, practical thinking skills, thematic studies and correlation between subjects.

The New Zealand high school curriculum also encourages students to develop positive attitudes, knowledge and skills in each subject area. So Freyberg used these as the core of their approach. And they linked that core to the four integrational themes—by out-of-class activities and computer studies.

"Over the next three years," reports Nolan, "we had out-of-class field trips, as short as one to two hours up to two to three days in junior school and seven to eight days in senior school." One class spent a week on the Wanganui River. But before it went, it split into study-groups. One researched the interconnection between the river and agriculture; another gathered information for an environmental impact report; another prepared to test the river's chemical composition and water-flow; another researched the Maori history of the area. "The whole project was curriculum-driven," says Nolan, "but most activities included adventure

---

* In most New Zealand school examinations, students are assessed out of a possible score of 100. "Marks" are therefore given as a percentage.

The real power of the computer will be as a student-controlled learning tool.

PAT NOLAN
Massey University*

* Author interview, Palmerston North, New Zealand.

and outdoor education components, learning bushcraft, camping and survival skills, as well as learning to work in groups, researching specialist subjects and then integrating them into a total report."[16]

Pat Nolan believes big issues are at stake with the integrated-studies experiment. "For years we got away with a system where unskilled people could walk into jobs, even if they'd failed school exams. That situation has changed, and I don't believe it is ever going to return. What society demands now is the kind of knowledge and skills that we've always claimed we wanted our students to have. We've wanted them to be knowledgeable in science, in mathematics, in communication skills; we've wanted them to have political and social understanding. We've wanted them to be original thinkers—in charge of their own futures, making decisions for themselves with confidence in their own ability. Now those things are imperative. We need students who can think about issues in the round, who are holistic thinkers, who can bring knowledge and ideas from many different disciplines to bear on the problem or an issue."[17]

He says society is also "looking at the day in the very near future when computers will be as commonplace as pocket calculators are today, and where they will be nearly as affordable. Not only that, teachers won't be able to teach effectively unless they're competent and confident in using computers in virtually all subjects in the curriculum. The real power of the computer will be as a student-controlled learning tool, and our Freyberg project has been in part to anticipate that day."

And the results are already in. New Zealand has a national School Certificate examination, in specific subjects, which students can take after three years of high school. When Freyberg integrated-studies students took those specific examination subjects, they scored signifi-cantly better marks than students who had not been through the pro-gram—up to 30 percent better.[18] And all the students we met told us that the whole integrated field-trip program has been fun and confidence-building.

What pleases Nolan even more is that nearly all students involved in integrated studies have made this same kind of learning gain; most of those who would previously have failed examinations have now suc-ceeded.

Since 1991 all Freyberg's first- and second-year students have handled social studies and English as integrated studies. On associated field trips,

Adults in the real world would never tolerate the built-in failure rate of schools.

DON BROWN
New Zealand educational consultant*

*Author interview, Kapiti College, Paraparaumu, New Zealand.

science, math and related subjects have been included. "We have no separate computer studies department," says new principal Russell Trethewey, "and computer work and field trips play key parts in all studies. Students revert to the subject curriculum in the third year, to sit national exams, and the results there are also well ahead of the national average."[19]

Freyberg also has shown the fastest growth in roll numbers of any school in New Zealand's North Island: almost double in four years.

3. Group study and "big picture" techniques

That same motivation spurs on educational consultant Don Brown, who has also introduced two other "success" innovations to a high school near Palmerston North: Kapiti College.

"For years, 30 percent of New Zealand's population," says Brown, "have been leaving high school without a single qualification, and for years we've had a School Certificate exam which actually and deliberately failed 50 percent of youngsters. Now if we did that out in the real world we would have to say that 30 percent of the population would never get a drivers' licence, and 50 percent of them would be continually sitting and resitting the exam to try and get one. Adults would never tolerate that, but that's the system we've had in schools."[20]

To change that, Kapiti college has introduced two separate American-inspired initiatives aimed at preventing dropout failures.

The first is called cooperative learning. "Very simply," says Brown, "that means that instead of working individually with everybody in competition with each other, you develop interdependence within teams." *The second innovation comes directly from the jigsaw, "big picture" example: see the pieces first and it's easier to put together.* So a Kapiti class not only works in cooperative groups—the teacher puts them in the complete picture before they start. They call the technique *The Advance Organizer.*

Brown again: "The advance organizer gives you the picture before you have to look at the bits, and then invites you to bring the bits together to make the picture like it was presented to you in the first place."

It is, of course, the kind of thing any competent company manager would do: spell out a year's program in advance so his staff know where they fit in the picture. And at Kapiti College these two systems are showing especially good results for those who would otherwise be

Average students have gone from 50 to 70 percent. And one-time slow-learners have gone from 37 to 63 percent.*

*Results of Cooperative Learning and "Advance Organizer" programs working together, as summarized in New Zealand television series *Where To Now?* in 1991 and reprinted in *Pacific Network* magazine, published by the Pacific Foundation, Auckland, New Zealand (February 1992).

classed as underachievers. "When we have targeted that group of young-sters," says Brown, "we can demonstrate two things: first, that the overall group mark goes up, but that the bottom third mark goes up faster than that."

In one of the schools using these two systems, "average" students have increased their grade in standardized national exams from 50 percent to 70 percent. And onetime slow learners have increased their average of 37 percent to better than 63 percent. [21]

4. Six-week courses build success step by step

Another New Zealand high school has dramatically improved stu-dents' job prospects by offering a wide range of concentrated courses that each require only six weeks' study.

Tikipunga High School is in the northern city of Whangarei, centered on an area with high unemployment. Over 78 percent of its families live on welfare benefits—the typical recipe for educational disaster.

Tikipunga has reversed this outcome by planning for step-by-step success. "Our experience has shown us," says former principal Edna Tait, "that even the most able students respond more positively to a short-term learning span, with a very clear set of goals, that are described, so they can achieve them; and knowing that at the end of that six weeks they will receive a statement which describes very precisely the achievements that they have made in a particular area of learning."[22]

Students take standard subjects like English, math, science and social studies, and every one learns basic computer skills in a series of six-week courses. Then they have a wide choice: they can take a six-week course in welding, cooking, car repairs, videotape production and woodworking or, for a career servicing the tourist industry, they can take a six-week course in bone-carving souvenirs. The school also has a great interest in art; original works by local painters line its corridors. And Tikipunga has an amazing 90 percent pass rate in national art examinations.

Edna Tait stresses that Tikipunga's assessment system is not a pass-fail system. The statements at the end of each six weeks explain exactly what each student has achieved.

And virtually anybody can take any unit—whether aged 15 or 50. "We've had one 82-year-old woman in a third form (9th grade) Maori class, and she was a joy to work with." One big benefit of the six-week modules: it's easy to redo a module if you feel you need more experience.

At this high school anyone can take a six-week study unit: from 15-year-olds to 82-year-olds.

EDNA TAIT
Former Principal, Tikipunga High School,
Whangarei, New Zealand*

*Abbreviated from author interview.

In this way, the whole school works very much along similar lines to business where, say, computer staff will regularly reattend short training sessions to master a new application, or move on to a higher level.

Says Tait: "One of the real benefits is the way every student gains confidence. Success builds on success."

And the practical results? "When we did an analysis of what had happened to our leaving students, very few were either not in some form of tertiary or other learning or in paid employment."

5. SuperCamp brings it all together

What would happen if all of these approaches were linked with the world's most effective learning and self-esteem-development techniques and where students end up loving to be at school?

That answer, too, is being given decisively—and resoundingly—in a program that started in California, has now spread to several other American states, and has been introduced in Singapore, Russia, Canada and Hong Kong. The program is called SuperCamp. And it shows that while dramatic changes may not come overnight, they can certainly happen after ten nights.

SuperCamp is an intensive training and development program, mainly for teenagers but also for older college students. Some students are sent by their parents—generally because of low grades or lack of motivation. Others want to come because their friends have loved it so much. After only ten days, there is increased motivation, self-esteem—and later quite remarkable achievements in academic results.

A major seven-year doctoral study[23] involving 6,042* students found after only ten days that 84 percent reported having increased self esteem, 81 percent more self-confidence and 68 percent increased their motivation.

The results don't stop there. American high schools grade students from A to F. *And after attending SuperCamp for only ten days, previously low-achieving students have reported an increase of 1 GPA (grade point average). F students have become D; D's have become C's; and C's have increased their ratings by half a grade point.*

So what are the SuperCamp's secrets? The program, which is based on a unique prototype developed in 1982, is a dual curriculum consisting

* Now more than 25,000 students have attended SuperCamp.

Why SuperCamp works so well

SuperCamp works because of our commitment to the total experience. At the core of our program are three important concepts:

 We provide an environment where maximum learning is possible—by building rapport between all participants and developing self-confidence.

 We teach in a variety of learning styles so that all types of learners can understand the material.

3 **We teach them the skills they need to learn any subject rather than specific course material.**

BOBBI DePORTER
President of SuperCamp*

*Author interview.

of (1) a learn-to-learn academic curriculum and (2) a personal growth and lifeskills curriculum. It uses all of the techniques we have outlined under "true learning" methods—an integrative accelerated learning model.

And it certainly is accelerated. The ten-day academic curriculum includes creative writing skills, creativity skills, speed reading, test preparation and memory-training skills in a learn-to-learn context.

The personal growth/lifeskills curriculum includes activities that develop physical skills, values, and the ability to communicate with peers and parents. Both the academics and the personal growth/lifeskills are embedded in music, play and emotion.

And the entire ten-day program, in our view, is an ideal model for the introduction to every high school's year—although SuperCamp's day runs from 7 a.m. to 10:30 p.m.

Day 1: Arrivals, introductions, team-building, security.

Day 2: Memory day—an introductory day that builds confidence, safety, trust and an attitude that learning is fun—with activities that range from morning boogie to Mind-Mapping techniques.

Day 3: Communications day, covering a wide range of learning-to-learn communications skills.

Day 4: Academic class day, including speed reading, academic strategies, creativity, writing, math, and learning styles.

Day 5: The ropes course—to give youngsters an opportunity to experience breakthroughs, stretch their self-imposed limits, work within a team to accomplish a task and to receive support.

Day 6: Academic class day.

Day 7: Relationship day—to learn to work on relationships with self, peers and parents; to increase self esteem.

Day 8: Academic class day, including group projects.

Day 9: Integration day, including personal mission statements, confidence-building exercises, goal-setting and school simulation.

Day 10: Review and graduation.

But that bald written summary does no justice to a ten-day adventure course of fun, games, participation and activity. Follow co-author Vos, as a formed SuperCamp facilitator, and you start to capture the flavor of the camp:[24]

❏ Overnight a bare college classroom had been transformed, deco-

Wings to fly

Ponder on the lives of men
What they do
Where they've been.
Stop to question
Asking why
Some men walk
Others fly.

Some are living with their lot
They live their lives and daily plot
The course which leads not up not down
But simply takes them round and round
While others hoping will not stand
For mediocrity in man
And daily striving, move ahead.

Refusing death, and all that's dead,
Again just question
Asking Why
Some men walk
Some must fly.*

Steven E. Garner

Reprinted with permission

*Typical poem used to start a goal-setting session at a
Jeannette Vos writing class at SuperCamp.

rated with live plants, neatly butcher-papered tables, pitchers of iced
lemon water, peripheral posters all over the walls, an acoustically sound
"ghetto blaster " in place, a "Welcome" sign and happy face on the neat
flip-chart—the atmosphere already orchestrated.

❏ At 10 a.m., the students arrive. No bells, only rock music—loud
and energetic, the way teenagers like it.

❏ A poem to start the day (Steven Garner's *Wings to Fly)* as an
introduction to individual goal-setting, then with direct involvement
from the start as each student is asked to identify his or her overall goals
in creative writing.

❏ Teacher dons a chef's hat, introduces "visualization" techniques—
imagining dining in a wonderful restaurant.

❏ Station WIIFM (What's In It For Me) takes the air—tackling
students' "hidden agendas": "If you could choose from the whole area of
writing, what would be something that could really help you?" Students
state the learning outcomes they'd like without realizing that they are
"buying in" to the agenda on a subliminal level. The teacher puts the
outcomes in "clusters"—a brainstorming technique developed by Gabriel
Rico in *Writing The Natural Way*. No set piece of literature here to study;
the students will learn to write from their own creative perspective.

❏ The "clustered outcomes" poster goes on the wall—to add to the
subconscious messages.

❏ Then "future pacing"—visualizing how they would like to feel in
the evening when the class is over and they've achieved their aims—with
Chariots of Fire music playing in the background.

❏ Another break; then, because many students have said how hard
they feel it is to start creative writing, "cluster" and fast-writing techniques are explored—and used through the multiple intelligences.

❏ But it soon becomes obvious that, as with most new creative
writers, students write with static words, not picture words. So the chef-
hatted teacher produces a pizza oozing with cheeses and zesty sauces—
so the "picture words" can be "tasted".

❏ By lunchtime, the creative writing session has become one of
pleasant achievement. The teacher gets feedback from students, then a
quick review and a preview of the wonderful things to come.

❏ After lunch, they're "hyperactive" but after the inevitable sugar-
intake "high" comes the early-afternoon slump. To combat it, the teacher

"Clustering" for creativity

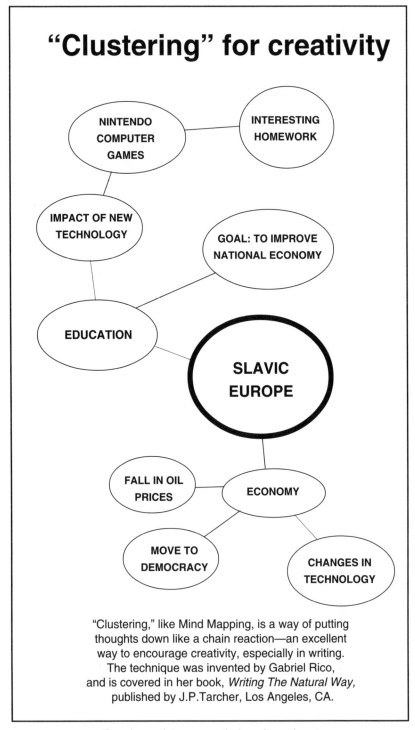

"Clustering," like Mind Mapping, is a way of putting thoughts down like a chain reaction—an excellent way to encourage creativity, especially in writing. The technique was invented by Gabriel Rico, and is covered in her book, *Writing The Natural Way*, published by J.P.Tarcher, Los Angeles, CA.

reads a lively descriptive piece called *Lady and the Chick,* from Rebecca Kaplan's book *Writers In Training.*   The students have fun as they attempt to act out some of the parts. The emotion keeps them involved in learning.

❏ More creative writing—but only after a "state change" of stretching. Then off to building on the "cluster" and "fast write" techniques—expanding on to comparison-contrast demonstrations with Koosh-ball activity. Then another break. [Breaks and state changes play an important part in the learning process. They create more "firsts" and "lasts" and thereby better retention.]

❏ Near the close of the afternoon, the teacher models a memorable childhood experience: "The forgotten immigrant"—her own version of learning English as a Second Language back in 1949.

❏ The day is beautiful, so it's outside for writing exercises, after talking about story formula and visualizing possible plots, characters and settings—all to background music.

❏ After the outdoor writing exercise, students evaluate their own work and feelings to date. Their teacher reads the evaluations to check progress and work out gaps that need to be plugged, needs that have to be met after dinner.

❏ After the meal a quiet descends. A student's father has died. So the teacher changes pace, and reads a student composition from a previous class about a girl whose grandfather has died. "Maybe just writing about our families would help," she says, using the flexibility based on student needs that should be built into all good teaching.

❏ Then the shared stories, and a run around the buildings to let off steam—typical of the "state changes" built into each session.

❏ By 8 p.m.: time for some poetry readings—and their own poetry attempts, to soft background music.

❏ 8:15 p.m.—time to share their efforts. A hush falls as the first student reads his poem. A 16-year-old boy begins to cry in front of the other 35 students. Then another, then all, while the students empathetically continue to share their writing and their feelings.

❏ By 8:45, it's obvious the sharing could go on all night, but they have to stop for a general camp get-together to debrief the day and to talk more about beliefs, values and behavior.

❏ By 10:30, they've evaluated their teachers, gone to bed—and

SuperCamp's report card

| 25%   50%   75%   100% |

68% increased motivation

73% improved grades

81% developed more confidence

84% increased self-esteem

96% retained positive attitude toward SuperCamp

98% continued to use skills

Jeannette Vos's doctoral dissertation* involved a detailed survey of 6042 SuperCamp graduates, ages 12-22.   Some of the highlights are above. In addition to this data, 98% of students with a GPA (grade point average) of 1.9 or less in high school improved their grades by an average of one grade point.

*An Accelerated/Integrative Learning Model Program Evaluation: Based on Participant Perceptions of Student Attitudinal and Achievement Changes, by Jeannette Vos-Groenendal, ERIC and Northern Arizona University, Flagsaff, Arizona (1991).

lights are out. The teacher smiles; her ratings were good that day.

A typical day at SuperCamp, if any day could be said to be typical. Each day the staff model the key principles of self-esteem and highly motivated achievement. And the results, as we've reported, are lasting.

And how do parents feel about it? An overall positive attitude towards the learning experience is expressed by 92 percent of parents and 98 percent of students.[25]

Learning Forum, parent company of The SuperCamp organization, is now working with different American schools and several entire districts to incorporate the program outlined in co-founder Bobbi DePorter's book *Quantum Learning,* and in the more recent *Quantum Teaching.*

Quantum Learning for Teachers is a professional development program for educators "to put joy back into the learning process". And the results speak for themselves:

❏ Thornton Township High School District, South Holland, Illinois, has three high schools, each with approximately 2,200 students. A big percentage of those come from low-income families, including 83 percent from African-American families. Since 1992 Learning Forum has organized multiple day trainings to put the SuperCamp principles into school settings. By 1998 detailed research[26] showed both teachers and students dramatically increasing their effectiveness.

❏ In spring 1997, incoming Thornton ninth graders were identified as performing well below grade level in math and English. They were given the opportunity to attend a 22-day Quantum Learning summer school. And after that many showed a two-year gain in math (for those who had not yet reached grade level) and a six-year gain for those who had. English grades were also up dramatically.

❏ Grossmont Union High School District in La Mesa, California, has spent more than a year tracking students being taught with the *Quantum Learning* methods. Result: 18 percent of students scoring C- or lower have now raised their grades substantially.

❏ And at California's Rancho Bernardo High School, *Quantum Learning*-trained Teacher of the Year Lori Brickley reported: "Quantum Learning's methods made things happen with the kids that I couldn't believe. Six weeks into this school year my 'at-risk' students achieved a one-point grade jump."

Add all these ingredients together and you're starting to find a recipe that will create the schools that tomorrow demands.

12 steps to a great school system

1 Plan schools as life-long year-round community resource centers.

2 Ask your customers first: your students and parents.

3 Guarantee customer success and satisfaction.

4 Cater to all intelligence traits and all learning styles.

5 Use the world's best teaching, study and learning methods.

6 Invest in your key resource: teachers as facilitators.

7 Make everyone a teacher as well as a student.

8 Plan a four-part curriculum, with personal growth, lifeskills and learning-how-to-learn linked with all content.

9 Change the assessment system.

10 Use tomorrow's technology.

11 Use your entire community as a resource.

12 Give everyone the right to choose.

The 12 steps to transform a nation's education system

Almost anything we can conceive is now possible.

And that applies equally to schools and education. So every plan to improve a school system should start with a vision of what it should be, even if that will need to be regularly updated.

Every community also has existing educational assets—land, buildings, teachers and administrators—and, like any great success story, the best educational achievements will come by starting with our assets, defining the vision, and creatively planning to link the two.

It also seems to us that any sensible vision should include these factors:

❏ Lifelong continual learning will be a key fact of life for everyone.

❏ Inside that context, everyone should be encouraged to plan his or her own curriculum for life.

❏ While there is no one right way to teach or learn, there are many techniques to enable anyone to learn faster, better, smarter. And an open-minded search for new ideas is central to tomorrow's world, and central to tomorrow's schools.

❏ Every state or country also has different school-health relationships, administrative systems, teacher training programs. And, as in any other field, progress will often depend on the vision and drive of individual leaders: principals, teachers, parents, administrators and political leaders.

Against that background, we believe these should be the 12 main steps to an excellent school system:

We talk a good fight about wanting to have excellent schools when in fact we're content to have average ones.

DAVID GARDNER*
"Nation At Risk" Commission

*Quoted in *Newsweek* (April 19, 1993), ten years after he chaired America's National Commission on Excellence in Education.

1. Schools as lifelong, year-round community resource centers

How on earth did most schools ever become 9 a.m. to 3 p.m. teaching centers for only five days a week and often for under 200 days a year? They're probably the most under-used major resource in any country.

In many parts of the world governments, like businesses, are decentralizing, and school-based management systems are on the agenda. That agenda should include transforming the traditional school into a lifelong, year-round community resource center.

In an age of instant information, every community will need an information resource center. And well-organized schools can fill that role. Even if home-based, individually-paced, interactive, electronic learning methods proliferate—as we believe they will—community resource centers will be in even more demand.

And Kimi Ora Community School in West Flaxmere, Hawkes Bay, New Zealand, is one model for creating such a center, although it has yet to achieve the high academic levels that are needed to match its excellent concept of community participation. It's in the heart of a New Zealand district devastated by the closure of a major industry. In that way it typifies many of the social problems arising from a fast-changing world.

Other suburbs may be built around industries or shopping malls. Flaxmere's rejuvenation has been centered on its school. But it's much, much more than a school. "Kimi Ora could be translated from the Maori as : 'To seek total well-being,'" says initial director Lester Finch.[1]

"The people in the community named it Kimi Ora because it matched the concept that they had of the school when it was first planned—that there should be a center, a school, which sought total well-being, and concentrated on families rather than individuals. Kimi Ora typified the approach that this community wanted this school to take, and that was an holistic approach which regarded education as a whole-of-life process and involved families."

New Zealand in recent years has turned its school administration system upside-down. A central government Department of Education has been changed into a much smaller Ministry of Education. This concentrates largely on policy advice to Government, but also providing overall curriculum guidelines. School District Education Boards have been abolished. And now schools "run themselves"—each one admin-

This resource center includes a preschool with three language choices, a primary school, adult classes, doctors, nurses, a physiotherapist, a naturopath, fitness classes, parenting-skills programs, its own minister and its own newspaper.

*Kimi Ora Community School, West Flaxmere, Hawkes Bay, New Zealand.

istered by a Board of Trustees, mainly elected by local parents, but with the school principal and teacher and student representatives.

West Flaxmere's plans for a new school came just before the new school-based management system was to be introduced nationally. And it has therefore been a model for many other existing schools.*

Kimi Ora starts with preschool, with children from as young as two. And it starts with choices. Between 60 and 70 percent of pupils are Maori, so at preschool they can, if they wish, start in a totally Maori environment—at the kohanga reo or Maori language nest. Or they can start in an all-English class or a bilingual class.

The preschool has an array of child-development equipment, geared to each age-group: a range of colorful books, puzzles and manipulative educational playthings. The infants grow up learning about hygiene—washing hands after each visit to the toilet and before every snack or meal. They learn about nutrition, washing and cutting up fruit and vegetables for lunch in the spotlessly clean kitchen.

The entire preschool makes full use of one of our most underutilized resources: grandparents. Visit any of the activities each day and you'll find grandparents leading action songs, dancing and other activities.

Parents, too, are welcome—and even young babies. And not just at the play center. The school also has a full health center. A health nurse is always on hand. Local doctors take turns to staff the medical center. There's a fulltime dental nurse.

At primary school, pupils can choose bilingual classes, in English and Maori, or they can learn solely in English. They've got a good range of computer equipment.

Other services include a public health nurse dealing with families, a physiotherapist and a naturopath. Kimi Ora also runs its own community newspaper, has its own community minister, operates its own community barter system and sports teams, has its own fitness, adult education and computer classes, and runs its own cafeteria, where parents, teachers and adult students mix every day.

Since earlier editions of this book, Kimi Ora School has been criticized by New Zealand's Education Review Authority for not meeting national academic standards. Accepting that criticism, in our view, does not nullify its place as a model for community involvement. Many other models covered in this book have changed as school principals have changed, but they have been selected because of concepts that deserve to be copied and improved.

Give your students and parents a fail-safe guarantee

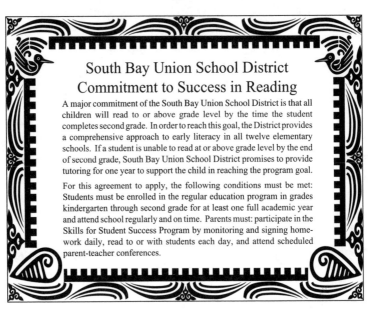

South Bay Union School District
Commitment to Success in Reading

A major commitment of the South Bay Union School District is that all children will read to or above grade level by the time the student completes second grade. In order to reach this goal, the District provides a comprehensive approach to early literacy in all twelve elementary schools. If a student is unable to read at or above grade level by the end of second grade, South Bay Union School District promises to provide tutoring for one year to support the child in reaching the program goal.

For this agreement to apply, the following conditions must be met: Students must be enrolled in the regular education program in grades kindergarten through second grade for at least one full academic year and attend school regularly and on time. Parents must: participate in the Skills for Student Success Program by monitoring and signing homework daily, read to or with students each day, and attend scheduled parent-teacher conferences.

The wording on the Commitment To Success In Reading contract issued to parents and students by the South Bay Union School District, Imperial Beach, Southern California.

The actual guarantee is on parchment with a gold embossed seal. It guarantees that all children will read at or above the national average by the time the student completes second grade. The district provides a structured one-on-one academic mentoring program to assure that the child will reach the program goal. The mentoring program HOSTS (Help One Student To Succeed) provides the proper interventions as early as possible.

For the guarantee to apply, parents must commit themselves to helping students by reading to them every day, and by monitoring and signing all homework.

2. Ask your customers

How did a poor community come up with such an all-embracing concept as Kimi Ora? Somebody thought to ask them! It was almost as simple as that. Concerned with a rising street-gang problem among Maori youth in New Zealand's capital city of Wellington, then Prime Minister Rob Muldoon visited some gang members and asked their advice. What they said was simple: Give us a chance to prove ourselves.

So when Muldoon learned of plans for a new school at Flaxmere, he invited the local school district administration to take up the challenge to survey the community.

If that's what can happen if an entire community is asked to plan a new school from the ground up—or the community up—what would happen if a school's other main customers were asked: the students? Alaska's Mt. Edgecumbe High School did just that, and the results are inspiring.

3. Guarantee customer satisfaction

Every successful business in the world is based on building and keeping satisfied customers. Nearly every good manufactured product comes with a written guarantee. But very few schools offer the same type of guarantee. Why not?

"If public schools are going to survive, we have to be held accountable for the product we turn out,"[2] says innovator Phil Grignon, former Superintendent of the South Bay Elementary School district in San Diego, California, where 84 percent of families are below the federal poverty line. So the district has been offering a "Commitment To Success In Reading" written guarantee to all its 10,500 students. That guarantee promises that all children will read at or above the national average by the time the student commmpletes second grade. If the student does not reach that level, the district "will provide intensive one-on-one tutoring" to ensure that minimum result.[3]

To take advantage of the guarantee, each parent or guardian must in turn agree to read to students at home for at least 20 minutes each day, to check and sign homework, and to attend quarterly parent-teacher workshops. The same guarantee is being given to the district's 35 percent of students who have Spanish as a first language.

The guarantee program has been one of several innovations in the South Bay district. Others include an Early Literacy Intervention program and a one-to-one tutoring program called HOSTS (Help One

School guarantees Master Students*

❑ **Every student will become a Master Learner by age 12 or 13.**

❑ **Students will be able to track and apply Continuous Improvement philosophy to their own learning.**

❑ **95% will achieve A level standing in their academic work.**

❑ **Advanced technology will be available to students at all times.**

❑ **High school graduates will possess thinking and processing skills that exceed many University graduates.**

❑ **Students will be immersed in a value-based culture.**

❑ **We will exceed all current standards set by Alberta Education.**

❑ **We will equip all students as knowledge workers with skill sets to succeed in an ever-changing world.**

* Adapted from The Master's Promise, or guarantee to parents, of Master's Academy and College, 4414 Crowchild Trail SW, Calgary, Alberta, Canada T2T 5J4. Email: tomrudmik@masters.ab.ca

Note: The Master's Academy started as an elementary school, but is adding one grade a year, up to 12th grade.

Student To Succeed). Both start before school, and have seen youngsters progressing one to three years in growth as measured by the Jerry Johns Basic Reading Inventory Test.

An even stronger guarantee comes from Master's Academy and College in Calgary, Alberta, Canada. Its promise: that students will become "Master Learners" by age 12 or 13. [4]

"Academically, that means a guarantee that 95 percent of our students will achieve A level standing in their academic work," says visionary Superintendent Tom Rudmik. He's spent years researching many models of learning, including attending one of co-author Vos's ten-day Learning Revolution workshops.

He puts his goals boldly: "The future of Master's Academy and College is driven by a powerful and compelling vision. Our mission is to develop Master Learners who will be knowledge workers of the 21st century—young people of academic excellence and noble character." [5] In the Canadian school system, 65 percent examination results are classed as average, 80 per cent outstanding, and 90 percent is very rate. Rudmik's goal is for 95 percent of students to achieve 80 percent or better. The college is strongly based on values, character development, quality, high technology and a strong emphasis on positive, bold, creative thinking. It also aims to share great learning principles with schools worldwide.

4. Cater to all intelligence traits and learning styles

In many ways, this is probably the most important single innovation that could be made to greatly reduce school dropout rates.

In our view, research by Howard Gardner, the Dunns and Barbara Prashnig shows beyond doubt that most dropouts do not learn best in schools that are geared almost exclusively to only two of the seven-or-more "intelligence traits". And most, too, are unfairly handicapped in a school environment which discourages kinesthetic learning.

The Key School in Indianapolis and New City School in St. Louis, Missouri, show what can happen when an entire school is designed to encourage every student to develop each "intelligence"—and cater to different learning styles.

A similar example comes from Cascade Elementary School in the Washington State school district of Marysville. Teacher Bruce Campbell has been a longtime fan of Gardner's theory, and has developed a class-room setup with seven learning centers: a building and moving center for

John Eliot is America's best elementary school model for integrative accelerated learning.

JEANNETTE VOS

kinesthetics, a reading center, a math and science center, a working-together center (to develop interpersonal intelligence), a personal work center (for intrapersonal intelligence), a music center and an art center.[6]

Campbell is a "thematic" teacher—and his students normally divide into seven different groups to explore each day's theme, moving from center to center for about 20 minutes at a time. His experience has also shown that the seven-center approach helps children develop all their talents.

At the start of the year, most students describe only one center as their favorite. By midyear most have three or four favorites, and by year's end every student nominates at least six centers as preferences.

Gardner's more recent suggestion of an eighth intelligence ("naturalist") gives teachers the chance to add nature-study centers—as many schools already do.

5. Use the world's best teaching techniques

No school, lifelong learning resource center or business training and retraining unit can exist without skilled teacher-facilitators. And no changes in education will be successful without a major emphasis on teacher training and continual retraining.

John Eliot Elementary School in Needham, Massachusetts, typifies what is needed. It is the most multicultural school in the district. Its students include African Americans, Haitians, Hispanics, Vietnamese and many others from Asia and elsewhere—in an area where average incomes are low.   Unlike Kimi Ora, it was an existing school when it started its big turn-round. Five years later its students had the top grades in Massachusetts.

One catalyst was principal Miriam Kronish. But another was her husband, Herbert, an architect. When he decided to go back to college to get a masters degree in education, fortunately that included an introduction to integrative accelerated learning techniques by Dr. John Grassi. "He was so enthused," recalls Miriam Kronish, "it got me involved."[7]

Grassi was obviously another catalyst. Talk to principal Kronish by phone and the enthusiasm bursts through the fiber optics: "John Grassi? He is a renaissance man, a man of the future. He is a musician, a poet, a conjuror.   He's uplifting, inspirational, a change agent.   And he's knowledgeable in all educational fields: preschool, elementary, high school and college; and in most areas: math, geography, science."

Attendance problems? We have none. Children don't want to stay away, even when they're sick. That's our problem, not non-attendance.

MIRIAM KRONISH
Principal, John Eliot Elementary School,
Needham, Massachusetts*

*Author interview by phone.

Kronish says the change in the school has been dramatic. The key to those changes? "Teacher training would be the first. Our teachers have all had regular training with John Grassi. But we're not talking about lectures. We generally organize five sessions of two hours, spread over two months. In that way, each session is a practical model that can be put into action immediately. So we do one session on ideas in math, one on social science, one on language arts—and we put them into practice straight away. We experiment."

And what is the difference? "Teacher excitement. Student excitement. The teachers immediately started to write plays, music, skits. They encouraged identification and personification from the start: the students acting out the role of all people and subjects studied. And the children, they flowered."

Enter a John Eliot classroom today and you're likely to see fourth-grade students learning grammar by performing a debate as members of a baseball team: some playing the part of nouns, verbs, adverbs and adjectives, and discussing who's most important to the team. Go back the next day and you're likely to see that same group repeating the process in other classrooms.

"Every student has become a teacher," says Kronish. "The barriers have been broken down. The whole program has changed everyone in the school."

One of the keys has been the accelerated, integrative learning techniques. And how would Kronish describe them? "First, it's integrative; it integrates music, art, poetry and drama with every other subject. And it integrates critical thinking skills across the board. I think that's a major reason we topped the MEAP* examinations: every child is involved in developing higher-level critical thinking skills. They do this from kindergarten onwards, so by fourth grade it's second nature. We've learned to use all our senses, our bodies, as part of the learning process."

A typical classroom? "Relaxing, bright, calm, fun-filled. Each class has a tape recorder, and we regularly play relaxing music, baroque music when appropriate, and music for many other purposes."

And how might the new integrated techniques apply, say, to a science class? "Well, you might see students acting out the role of molecules, or playing the part of some endangered species. It internalizes learning. And it's fun."

* Massachusetts Educational Assessment Program.

Four myths of learning

School is the best place to learn.

Intelligence is fixed.

Teaching produces learning.

We all learn the same way.

JEANNETTE VOS*

* Principles explored in The Learning Revolution international workshops.

Regular updates: www.thelearningweb.net

John Eliot School involves the whole community. How does it do it? Says Kronish in her simple, direct, enthusiastic way: "Fully. For instance, the school has recently put on a 90-minute presentation on famous black Americans. A teacher played the role of a cable television interviewer, and students played the roles of famous people. All parents were invited. And they were amazed, thrilled, astounded, proud. Not only did the students learn history, the parents did, too. The parents also help in many other ways. We're not a rich community—far from it. But parents devote talents and time, coming into school on their days off, just being a vital part of the school, because you can't have a good school without an involved community."

The future of education in America? "Wow!" says Kronish. "If we had the power—and we do—number one would probably be teacher training. It's not enough to only read of these new techniques. You have to be trained in them, in the same way an actor or a poet is trained. Then you can transfer it to others. So we need to encourage all our universities and colleges to introduce the principles of integrative accelerative learning. It's the wave of the future.

"American education also needs to pay much more attention to research and development. Use the breakthroughs that have already been achieved.

"Next, we need much more collaboration between classroom teachers and specialists—to break down the barriers. And the whole community needs to be involved: parents, businesses, everyone."

And how have teachers reacted? Miriam Kronish practices what she enthuses. The phone is instantly handed to fourth-grade teacher Rosemary Greene: "I've been a teacher for 20 years, and I genuinely feel reborn. And the students: they've become 'invested', excited, involved."[8] The results, of course, speak for themselves.* In part you'll

In the first edition of this book, co-author Vos nominated John Eliot school as the best in America, and Kronish as the best principal. Obviously others now agree. In 1995 she won both the Massachusetts state award and the national award for Outstanding Elementary Principal, the latter granted by the United States Department of Education and the National Association of Elementary School Principals. Since then she's won two additional awards: the Golden Foundation Award which honors excellence in education, and the 1996 Educator of the Year Award from the Boston University international honor society called Pi Lambda Theta. Since that first edition, John Eliot School has been visited by hundreds of teachers from round the world.

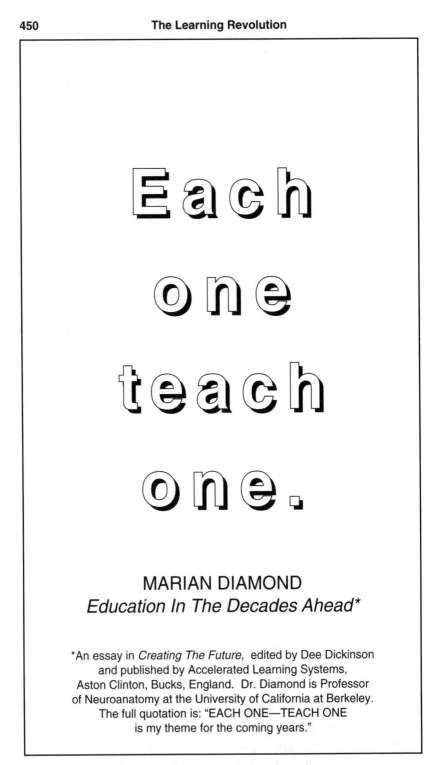

MARIAN DIAMOND
*Education In The Decades Ahead**

*An essay in *Creating The Future,* edited by Dee Dickinson
and published by Accelerated Learning Systems,
Aston Clinton, Bucks, England. Dr. Diamond is Professor
of Neuroanatomy at the University of California at Berkeley.
The full quotation is: "EACH ONE—TEACH ONE
is my theme for the coming years."

find them in the examination results: overall top in a state well known for educational innovations. But the real results you can see on the faces of the students, teachers and parents—if you haven't already caught them in the words of the principal.

6. Invest in your key resource: teachers

Here, too, the John Eliot experience is a model. America, in particular, has probably the world's most thoroughly-researched educational break-throughs, including the teaching and learning methods covered in these pages. Yet amazingly most of those methods are not being modeled at the university level—to train the teachers of tomorrow—let alone being used throughout elementary and high schools.

One teacher-training college leading the way is Cambridge College [9] in Massachusetts — in a program pioneered by Dr. John Grassi and with Dr. Mahesh Sharma and co-author Vos as foundation members—which now has 350 teachers going through each summer's course for a master's degree. Charlotte La Hecka's work at the University of Houston also provides an excellent model, and Jeannette Vos's International Academy for The Learning Revolution has now been accredited by both Cambridge College and the University of California at San Diego's Extension to offer credits in accelerated, integrative learning towards a masters degree.

7. Make everyone a teacher as well as a student

Again, John Eliot is a model: every student, every parent and every teacher is encouraged to become not only a learner but a teacher.

Many problems of staff "burnout" would be solved by the simple step of involving parents, grandparents and the community in the teaching process—and students too.

8. Plan a four-part curriculum

Computer-based programs, interactive video discs and personalized telecommunications make it increasingly possible for everyone to plan one's own continuing study program. And schools as community resource centers will provide a smorgasbord of courses and resources for a wide range of age-groups, particularly as planning one's continuing lifelong education becomes as normal and as easy as watching television.

Schools, however, will also be required to continue their present role

Model for an interlinked four-part curriculum

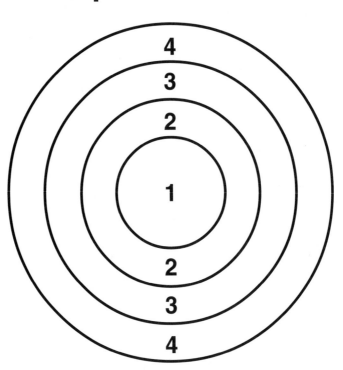

1. Personal growth curriculum, *including self-esteem and confidence-building.*

2. Lifeskills curriculum, *including creative problem-solving and self-management.*

3. Learning-to-learn and learning-to-think curriculum, *so learning can be lifelong and fun-filled.*

4. Content curriculum, *generally with integrated themes.*

Devised by Jeannette Vos, and demonstrated in her international training programs.

as core-curriculum providers. Here our own research points strongly to the need for a four-part curriculum, as important in continuing education as it is in childhood and teenage years:

1. A personal-growth curriculum, involving self-confidence, motivation, communications skills and relationship skills.

2. A lifeskills curriculum, including self-managing, creative problem-solving, career planning and replanning, economics, conflict-management and computer-based technology.

3. A learning-to-learn and learning-to-think curriculum, including the type of brain-compatible "how to" skills covered extensively in this book, so that lifelong learning can be fun-filled, fast and effective.

4. A content curriculum, with integrated themes.

Although all are interrelated, we have purposely placed content last— reversing most current school practices.

We have placed personal growth as first, for major reasons:

❏ Nearly everyone has learning blocks, but traditional schooling has succeeded in only one major way: in turning most people off, at a time when their enthusiasm for learning is vital.

❏ Emotion is the gateway to learning—and each person's emotional state is affected by communications skills, relationship skills, motivation and self-esteem: the personal-growth skills. If those aspects are not addressed, the gate will close.

❏ Real listening and speaking skills are of high importance in all aspects of life and work, yet are downplayed in many educational institutions.

❏ Self-confidence and self-esteem are vital to all learning, and education that fails to address them will fail in its other tasks.

In a world where everyone needs to be a self-manager, practical lifeskills training also needs to be included in all education, from pre-school to advanced business study. These skills include: creative problem-solving, critical thinking, leadership skills, global perspective, the confidence to play a full role in determining the future of society, and the ability to plan one's life in an era of incredible change.

Learning-how-to-learn has been a continuing theme of this book and is the bridge to all content learning. Learn how to learn and you can apply the principles to anything. Yet this most important of all specific skills is seldom taught in school.

People will exceed targets they set themselves.

GORDON DRYDEN
Out Of The Red*

* "Learning the importance of that sentence—and applying it—
has taught me more [about business] than any dozen textbooks
on management."   Book published by William Collins Ltd.,
Auckland, New Zealand.

In specific content courses, we believe the great need is for integration: to link art with science and all other subjects; to integrate all studies into more global understanding, so that Russian or French language training, or Chinese or Italian cooking, becomes linked with an understanding of others' cultures. In this way, as Mt. Edgecumbe, Freyberg and John Eliot schools have proven in practice, the world emerges as an interactive whole.

9. Change the assessment system

It would take another book, or a large part of a book, to report on worldwide moves to gain better educational assessment systems. In a summary of key principles for school reform, these to us are the main points:

❑ Too much traditional teaching and too much traditional testing have been directed to only two segments of overall intelligence.

❑ Most people who have emerged successfully through the school system have been strong in those two "intelligences". These have gone on to become the arbiters of future teaching and testing methods.

❑ Just as new learning methods should involve the whole person, so should assessment methods.

❑ The search for excellence is a justifiable goal, in personal life, school and business—and much of our present schooling is aimed at "success" rates that fall far short of excellence.

❑ Pencil-and-paper test assignments test only a very small part of anyone's ability in almost any subject, except perhaps for mental mathematics or handwriting.

❑ In a world where self-management will be required of all, continuing self-assessment is needed—another reason that confidence-building should include the confidence to continually assess one's own improvement.

❑ Excellence will often come from joint efforts with others, so peer-assessment should be encouraged. In fact, it can often be linked with self-assessment: evaluating yourself, then discussing that evaluation with the people you work with.

❑ It is one of the great truisms that we all learn from our mistakes—and a positive attitude towards mistakes and risk-taking is a positive part of growth: seeing mistakes as steps toward excellence. No examination

Recommended assessment system for the 21st century

50% self assessment.
30% peer assessment.
20% teacher or boss assessment.

JEANNETTE VOS*

* As outlined at her international training seminars.

system should penalize risk-taking or creativity, or imply that there is only one right answer to any problem, except perhaps for simple arithmetic (even then Einstein would not have produced his theories of relativity had he not challenged basic mathematics).

❑ Critical thinking is a vital skill. Free and open-minded contributions to problem-solving are essential in all aspects of life. Any assessment methods should encourage this, not pigeonhole anyone in the "only one right answer" mode.

❑ Teacher assessment is at least as important as student assessment. Every professional seminar presenter hands out evaluation forms. They're vital self-correcting feedback. And all teachers following this pattern are modeling a positive attitude toward continual growth by the free, fair and frank exchange of opinions.

❑ Competent school teachers and administrators will apply the same principles to parent-teacher relationships: sending home teacher-evaluation forms regularly as part of the school-home confidence building, part of the new customer-service concept.

❑ In fields where competence can be measured at specific levels, this generally involves performing the task in practice: typing at 65 words a minute, playing a piano, riding a bike, running or swimming at a certain speed. In all cases, the real test is competency in the task, not competency in writing about it.

❑ The Japanese have used the excellent American-developed Deming methods of total quality management to produce cars and electronic components of excellence. Mt. Edgecumbe High School has shown how to interpret those principles into school education—and into different assessment methods. All school systems would be wise to take heed.

10. Use tomorrow's technology

We've already made our views clear on one other matter: new methods of instant communication ging with them the biggest change in civilization in centur

This revolution will soor son with the tools to obtain all the information he or t is needed and in whatever form: print, photograr n screen or facsimile transmission.

River Oaks Scho ario, Canada, is typical of what will soon be happening at it is a primary school that has been

People anywhere will be able to take the best courses taught by great teachers.

BILL GATES
The Road Ahead

* Published by Viking, New York.

set up with a particular vision of how it can help its students march confidently into the instant-information age.[10] Every student in every class has the opportunity to link with the school's overall computer network. CD-ROMS are a fact of life. And the school doesn't even own a printed encyclopedia. All of its big reference library is on both interactive video discs and CD-ROMS—instantly accessible to anyone in the school, and in a variety of forms: so that pictures and facts can be combined for printouts, photos can be married with information.

Every student at the school is already a computer programmer, and his own curriculum designer.

Lester B. Pearson School, a Canadian high school, is another model for the computer age. It has 300 computers for 1,200 students. And it has one of Canada's lowest dropout rates: 4 percent compared with a national average of 30 percent.[11]

Even more spectacular results are shown by Christopher Columbus Middle School in Union City, New Jersey. In the late 1980s, the state test scores were so low and the absentee and dropout rates were so high among the children of the school district that the state was considering taking it over.[12] More than 90 percent of children came from families with English as a second language.

Bell Atlantic, the area telephone company, agreed to help by providing computers and a network linking students' homes with classrooms, teachers and school administrators. All were connected to the Internet, and teachers were trained in using the PCs. The teachers in turn set up weekend training courses for parents.

Within two years both the dropout rate and absenteeism had dropped to almost zero, and the students are scoring nearly three times higher than the average for all New Jersey inner-city schools on standardized tests.

Highly-advanced computers have the ability to serve as both tutors and libraries, providing instant information and feedback to individual students. "Virtual reality" technology already enables anyone to participate in experiences as varied as history and space travel.

This type of technology will make it possible for each student, of any age, to tailor an individual curriculum and eventually to actually experience each lesson. Interactive computer-satellite-video-television and electronic games technology provide the combined catalyst that will finally force a much-needed change in the teacher's role: from *information* to *transformation*. And every school system in the world, if it's not

The world is on the verge of a revolution, the like of which has not been seen since Gutenberg ran the first Bible off a printing press 500 years ago.

GILBERT WONG
Getting Wired*

*An article published in the New Zealand Herald, Auckland, New Zealand, July 10, 1993.

already doing so, should be matching every progressive company in keeping up with the full scope of technology and its impact on society and on education.

11. Use the entire community as a resource

Again, John Eliot, Kimi Ora, Mt. Edgecumbe, Freyberg, the Key School in Indianapolis, and many of the other models we have quoted, underscore the common sense of moving schooling away from the traditional classroom. How the world ever came to confuse classroom teaching with real learning is a mystery of its own. Probably only the dedication of enthusiastic teachers, principals and administrators has enabled this system to last so long—in spite of itself. But that tradition is rapidly coming to an end. And the lessons are clear from other industries that failed to correctly analyze their future role in a world of rapid change. After opening up much of the world last century, railway company after company collapsed, because they thought they were in the railways business, not the people-moving and transport business. Hollywood almost died through the start of television, because it wrongly thought it was in the movie-film business, not the entertainment business.

And if schools do not lead the educational changes, and make themselves the new community resource centers for lifelong learning, then the world is well served by other innovators waiting to fill the gap.

12. For everyone: the right to choose

The coming changes will be dictated, we believe, by another inevitable fact of life: the growing one-world economy and the consumer's right to choose.

The whole world now is not only one giant electronic, automobile, fast-food and financial services market; it is also a major one-world educational market. It is now possible for the works of our most brilliant educators and schools to be translated into forms that can, in turn, be made available instantly to anyone who wants them, anywhere, any time. The day of the school monopoly on education is rapidly ending.

This presents both corporations and educational organizations with the world's biggest business challenge: and possibly the most exciting marriage in history.

The Internet is a tidal wave. It will wash over the computer industry and many others, drowning those who do not learn to swim in its waves.

BILL GATES
Chairman of Microsoft*

* Quoted by Ray Hammond in *Digital Business*,
published by Hodder & Stoughton, Britain.

Big growth opportunities
for 'the learning organization'

An unusual new marriage is taking place.

The current partners are Hollywood and Silicon Valley. But the most attractive potential suitors are education and business. The challenge: to create some of the world's greatest opportunities—to merge the talents of great educators and innovative businesses.

Already the reasons are clear and the models exist in five related areas:

1. Electronic, interactive, multimedia software presents almost unlimited potential for learning and education.

2. Accelerated learning skills, in particular, provide a virtually-untapped business opportunity.

3. Successful manufacturing and retailing companies can prosper even more by selling services: by providing the training necessary for customers to use their products much more effectively.

4. Every successful company has to become a continuous learning organization, and every individual needs to continue to relearn throughout life.

5. Schools and colleges can follow university research departments in using their expertise to form strategic alliances with businesses.

Electronic multimedia opportunities

Audiotapes, videotapes, compact discs, CD-ROMs, electronic games, laser discs, and the growth of the Internet itself, provide the most striking examples of the shape of the exploding interactive learning revolution: the ability to communicate information instantly to almost anyone.

I'm not at all shy about predicting that by 2005 the Internet will be as big as the telephone system today.*

VINTON CERF
*"Father of the Internet"**

* Interview with *The Wall Street Journal,* June 17, 1996.

The examples abound, the potential is enormous:

❏ More than ten million people have improved their health and fitness at home by exercising to actress Jane Fonda's *Workout* video-tapes. Millions have followed up the early home experience by joining regular health and fitness clubs.[1]

❏ Traditionally British taxi-drivers have spent a four-year "apprenticeship" learning to navigate the winding backstreets of their capital city before getting a full license to drive one of the famous London black cabs. Now a new driver can install a *TravelPilot* electronic navigation system, enter the desired destination, and instantly be guided there by instructions on a small screen. More than a million Japanese cars are fitted with similar navigational aids. And half the 70,000 new Mercedes S-class cars sold in Germany each year come with the same type of system.[2]

❏ Forty years ago it took a six-year apprenticeship to learn typesetting on a now-defunct Linotype machine. Today journalists joining Trends International, a Pacific-rim publishing company, can become proficient typesetters and compositors *in a day.*[3]

Their company has taken the extensive Adobe Pagemaker computer software guidebook and compressed it into nine pages of simple instructions. Trends now produces 27 different high-class home-improvement "annuals" each year. Any newly-employed journalists can now select from a range of preset pages, displayed on their computer screen, and proceed immediately to produce similar pages for *Kitchen Trends* or *New Home Trends.* They are learning, in a day, the core of typography, typesetting, layout and page-composition skills that once took years.

Trainee teachers, and students in individual classrooms around the world, will have instant access to similar learning templates on the Internet, downloading everything from Mind Maps to study modules.

Journalists, of course, include typewriting skills in their basic training. But others can easily pick up typing by using the Mavis Beacon or similar quick-learn courses that come with almost any new personal computer.

❏ To learn something much more complicated, like film or videotape production, try a digital video disc with one of the greatest movies and a built-in visual essay on how the film was made.

Laser discs and DVDs offer much sharper images than standard videotape. They also offer random-access capabilities: you can preselect any movie scene and instantly jump to it, like music tracks on a compact disc.

Attend the world's greatest film seminars, led by the world's greatest producers, directors, writers.

CHRIS McGOWAN & JIM McCULLAUGH
Entertainment In The Cyber Zone

* Published by Random House, New York.

Voyager Company released the first of its annotated Criterion Collection line with *Citizen Kane* and *King Kong* in 1984, and they've followed up with such classics as *Close Encounters of The Third Kind, The Magnificent Ambersons, Alien, Raging Bull* and *The Player.*

More than 8,500 titles are now available on laser disc, including many of the world's greatest movies in annotated form. As a typical example, you can view the Kirk Douglas masterpiece *Spartacus,* with commentary by Douglas, novelist Howard Fast, producer Edward Lewis, production designer Saul Bass and film restorer Bob Harris, a video interview with actor Peter Ustinov, screenwriter Dalton Trumbo's scene-by-scene analysis, Saul Bass's storyboards and titles, deleted scenes analysis, additional music by Alex North, newsreel footage of the film's premiere, archival interviews and additional memorabilia.

What better way to study movie making than seminars by the world's greatest producers, especially if you can immediately experiment yourself with videotape, film or editing equipment?

❏ Or how about music? Great interactive CD-ROMs are becoming teachers "for a whole new generation of aspiring singers, songwriters, conductors, composers and musicians".[4]

On Dorling Kindersley's *Musical Instruments* CD-ROM, you can hear the tones and timbre of about 200 instruments, from the Australian *didgeridoos* to the Japanese *shakuhachi* flutes. You'll find around 1,500 sound samples, more than 500 high-quality photos and extensive text. And you can explore the instruments in four different ways.

Benjamin Britten's *The Young Person's Guide To The Orchestra* has long been a classic on both audiotape and videotape. The CD-ROM version offers "musical notation of every melody, lets you know which instruments are playing at all times, and includes 50 audio examples. And you get to play conductor, too."[5]

To study jazz, pop, rock, western of any other music, you can easily find an interactive CD-ROM that enables you not only to learn and appreciate, but to play along as well.

To explore the baroque, classical and romantic music recommended for enhancing learning ability, try Alan Rich's three-part *So I've Heard* series. *Bach and Before* takes you from ancient Greece and Egypt to the baroque glories of Bach and Handel, with 50 musical examples and dozens of detailed notes—which you can display on screen or not. *The Classical Ideal* guides you through Haydn, Mozart and the mainly 18th

A glimpse of the future: now

Some interactive music CD-ROMs

Explora 1: Peter Gabriel's Secret World—includes 100 minutes of video, more than 100 still images. Click on any line and you move to the video. Or call up interviews with Gabriel or the producers to discuss the interpretation of each tune. Sample tunes from each Gabriel catalogue. Watch a recording session. Check out the instruments of other countries. Hear musical excerpts from 42 albums by artists from around the world. Visit the World Music Festival: a Grammy rehearsal by Gabriel, the drummers of Barundi. And interact with the disc's interface which lets you set your own visual background to the music: an Egyptian darabuka drum with its clay body, floating above the planet—stars, ocean, sky. And if you're done with the program, sit back and browse through a beautiful full-colour booklet that's included with the CD-ROM. *A MacPlay/Interplay CD-ROM.*

Jazz: A Multimedia History—spans 1923 to 1991 with facts, figures, images and sounds, from Louis Armstrong to Miles Davis, Duke Ellington to Herbie Hancock. "An excellent interactive tour through America's greatest native artform." *An Ebook/Compton New-Media CD-ROM.*

Heart: 20 years of rock & roll—An interactive musical biography, fronted by sisters Ann and Nancy Wilson, Heart is one of rock's most durable bands, having sold more than 30 million albums. Includes clips from more than 100 songs, 20 minutes of video clips, three hours of interviews, As you play any song from any of Heart's albums, the screen can display its lyrics and history. "The Player feature will probably be imitated often by music discs in the future." *The New CD Music Show/Compton's New-Media CD-ROM.*

Time Warner's Audio Notes—such as *Johannes Brahms: a German Requiem,* with the Atlanta Symphony and Chorus, 50 side journeys into historical, musical and biographical topics, 40 examples of sound and music. *Times Warner CD-ROM.*

These notes abbreviated from Chris McGowan and Jim McCullaugh's excellent book, ENTERTAINMENT IN THE CYBER ZONE *Exploring the Interactive Universe of Multimedia* published by Random House, New York.

See other notes on Page 336.

century European classical music. And *Beethoven and Beyond* moves you through "the bold, restless, passionate Romantic era".[6]

❏ Geography? In 1985, two young Iowa trivia-game fans, Doug and Gary Carlston, turned one of their games into a computer floppy-disc hit called *Where In The World Is Carmen Sandiego?* It was a pioneer in the field to be known as "edutainment": the fusion of education and entertainment. Since 1985, the Carlstons and their Broderbund Software company have released eight titles in the series, and nearly four million Carmen Sandiego floppy disc programs have been sold.

The deluxe CD-ROM edition appeared in 1992, and today hundreds of thousands of children and their families are learning the basics of geography as they search for Carmen around the world, using 3,200 clues—including 500 in foreign languages—130 photographs, hundreds of animations, and 150 audio excerpts of traditional music.

Also in 1992, Broderbund released *Just Grandma and Me,* a CD-ROM that has since led to the *Living Books* series in partnership with Random House. The series introduces children to the interactive wonder of great stories: in English, Spanish and Japanese, all on the one disc.

Young painters can practice with Broderbund's *Kid Pix;* young musicians can have fun with Philips's *Children's Musical Theater;* and learn to read with The Learning Company's *Reader Rabbit.*

Older children and adults can plan an entire city of the future with *SimCity 2000,* learn every aspect of chess from the brilliant *Chessmaster 4000 Turbo* CD-ROM, or play a world master at bridge.

❏ The biggest commercial success of all has been in the form of video and computer games. Nintendo's *Mario* and Sega's *Sonic the Hedgehog* have become worldwide hits. By 1993 Nintendo had sold more than 100 million cartridges of its *Super Mario Bros.* By mid-1999, after a major recession in the Japanese economy, rival Sony was making 42 per cent of its total profits from its *PlayStation* video games.

❏ To make your own interactive, animated computer game, you can now invest in an inexpensive *Klick & Play* package from Britain's Europress group—developed by François Lionet and Yves Larnoureu. And for even less, try The Perian Spring's *Digital Chisel* software. It costs much less than many excellent professional programs such as Macromedia's top-rated *Director* series. (Check it out on the Internet: www.pierian.com—and see what students are designing with it.)

These highlights provide only a glimpse of the soaring potential.

The Internet features that will change your life:

It's <u>global</u>, <u>personal</u>, <u>interactive</u>, <u>low cost</u> and <u>forever growing</u>.

RAY HAMMOND
Digital Business*

*Published by Hodder and Stoughton, London, with a companion edition available free on the Internet.

Many breakthroughs have emerged only in the last five years. Significantly, nearly all have been developed in the business world, not in the world of "education". Many of the greatest successes have been produced by school dropouts or very young graduates. Since the early 1990s the merger between Hollywood, Silicon Valley, and the Microsoft base in Washington state, has blossomed. Key aspects of the new revolution will come from the further blending of talents from the movie, computer, music and electronic games industries, linking those abilities to good educational practice. But so far traditional school systems have been left far behind in the race.

Says Bill Gates: "The average primary or secondary school in the United States lags considerably behind the average American business in the availability of new information technology. Preschoolers familiar with cellular telephones, pagers and personal computers enter kindergarten where chalkboards and overhead projectors represent the state of the art."[7]

Equally important, the structure of most school systems is not designed to multiply brilliant teacher talent. Great teachers are skilled in a variety of abilities: subject knowledge, empathy, communications, warmth, interactivity, music, art, graphics and some aspects of multimedia presentations.

In school those talents will be confined to 20 to 40 students at a time, when today they could be instantly available to the world.

Seldom do teachers get the opportunity to link their most outstanding talents with the diverse skills of others. To make even a good videotape, for instance, requires a wide blend of talent: producer, director, scriptwriter, camera-sound crew, video editor, music composer, musicians, sound mixer, graphic designer and many more. What chance has "education" got to compete unless it can reorganize to blend the same kind of multifaceted talents, store the results digitally, and then "repackage" them in any interactive form required as the new multimedia platforms converge?

Accelerated learning business opportunities

Virtually every learning and teaching breakthrough highlighted in this book, for instance, represents an opportunity to take new methods of learning and turn them into commercial opportunities.

Every achiever in every field has the expertise that can now be multi-

Master it Faster

M Mind Set for success

A Acquire information

S Search out meaning

T Trigger the memory

E Exhibit what you know

R Reflect how you learned

BY COLIN ROSE
Master it Faster*

* Published by Accelerated Learning Systems Ltd.,
50 Aylesbury Road, Aston Clinton, Aylesbury,
Bucks, England HP22 5AH.

plied a million-fold through interactive multimedia and networked communications.

In theory, the marriage required is simple. As we covered in the introduction to this book, the opportunity exists to:

❏ Take the knowledge of the world's best "subject specialists", in mathematics, chemistry, English, Japanese, geography or anything else;

❏ Marry it to the expertise of the world's best accelerated-learning specialists—the people whose ideas shine throughout this book;

❏ Link that to skills of the world's best experts in interactive multimedia—the programmers, designers, editors and artists;

❏ Simplify those concepts into a basic template that every good teacher or trainer can use to create interactive learning programs;

❏ Use the world's most efficient electronic distribution systems;

❏ And along the way use the same new interactive techniques to train the parents and teachers who will be at the heart of the new child-development revolution; and the managers, trainers and staff who are rethinking and replanning their own business futures.

One to seize the opportunities is British innovator Colin Rose. His Accelerated Learning Systems group has specialized for more than a decade in Lozanov-type do-it-yourself foreign-language programs.

Now Rose has combined all the best principles he's learned from language learning into a new English-as-a-Foreign-Language course for Japanese. Students can choose their method of learning: guidebook, videotape, audio tracks or interactive interactive CD-ROM form.

Colin Rose's newest book is *Master It Faster,* designed specifically to help older students and adults learn much faster, make good decisions and think creatively. And he's linked up with Britain's Campaign for Learning to produce a guidebook on *Creating a MASTER Organization.* MASTER is a mnemonic from the words: Mindset for success, Acquire the information, Search out the meaning, Trigger the memory, Exhibit what you know, and Reflect on how you have learned.

Rose's company in 1996 also launched its new *FUNdamentals* program, designed to shows parents a range of dozens of activities that will enable their families to read, write, do basic mathematics and much more—before starting school. It includes extensive videotape, more than 1,000 activities, a detailed guidebook, and a variety of word-cards, phonic cards, reading games, math games and writing templates.

The successful companies of the next decade will be the ones that use digital tools to reinvent the way they work.

BILL GATES
Business @ The Speed Of Thought*

* Published by Viking, a division of Penguin Books.

On the other side of the world Malaysian-born chartered accountant Peter Ho, now based in Auckland, New Zealand, and former diamond-drilling expert Colin Burr, now based in Adelaide, Australia, have designed an accelerated-learning course entitled *Accounting is Ezy,* which is successfully teaching the principles of accountancy to non-accountants in two days.

Smart entrepreneurs are also applying their talents to financing the electronic revolution in schools. Bill Gates, in his latest book, *Business @ The Speed Of Thought,* highlights the example of Bruce Dixon, a Melbourne, Australia, school teacher with the core of a financing idea. Writes Gates: "Out of many discussions, conferences, and brainstorming with teaching colleagues emerged the radical idea of having all the students finance their own machine. Dixon, by then a technology consultant to schools, worked out a financial model. For a monthly fee, students lease a machine and software; the vendor provides maintenance and upgrades; and when the student graduates the family keeps the machine."

Selling services and training with your products

More and more major companies are also finding that their path to the future lies in adding new services—often high quality training—to their traditional role as manufacturers or retailers.

Probably the most dramatic example is the world's second most valuable company:* America's General Electric Co. Its market worth at the end of 1998: $360 billion. Its 1998 turnover: more than $100 billion. Profits: $9.3 billion.

For years a leader in manufacturing, GE "can no longer prosper selling manufacturing goods alone".[8] Says Chief Executive Jack Welch: "Our job is to sell more than just the box."

The Welch formula is based firmly on several key trends highlighted in chapter one of this book: from the service society to the global economy. In 1995, GE's international revenues soared to $27 billion. The most spectacular gains both inside North America and around the globe have been made in linking superb servicing to manufacturing.

* In The Fortune 500, released in April 1999, Microsoft topped GE as the company with the world's highest market value: $418 billion. Early in 1999 Microsoft reorganized itself into eight separate groups: each one to concentrate on servicing different customers.

GE has spent $80 million building a state-of-the-art training center complete with a TV studio to develop educational programming.

'JACK WELCH'S ENCORE'
*article in Business Week**

* October 28, 1996.

Nearly 80 percent of GE's profits now come from services—up from 16.4 percent in 1980. And a large slice of those profits are coming from GE Finance—by financing a wide range of services and products, and not only products produced by GE.

Visit the Milwaukee headquarters of GE Medical Systems and you get some idea of the scope of the changes. For years it sold CAT scanners, magnetic resonance imagers and other medical imaging equipment, to organizations like Columbia/HCA Healthcare Corp. with its 300-plus hospitals. Then in March, 1995, GE persuaded Columbia to let it service all the chain's imaging equipment, including that made by GE's rivals. By 1996 GE had added managing virtually all medical supplies to the deal—most of them product lines GE isn't even in.

Yet that is just the beginning. GE Medical has spent $80 million building a state-of-the-art training center, complete with a TV studio, to develop educational programming.[9] For fees ranging from $3,000 to $20,000, hospitals can tune in to live broadcasts on subjects such as proper mammography techniques. And the company regularly runs management seminars for hospital executives. Topics include strategic planning, employee evaluations and time management.

Where GE goes today, others follow tomorrow. Since winning the Malcolm Baldridge National Quality Award, Xerox has been selling its quality-enhancing skills along with its products.[10] At Otis Elevator, two-thirds of its $5 billion turnover now comes from servicing and maintenance.[11] And Dell and Gateway are two companies that have based their growth on superb customer servicing through staff training.

Developments like this are seen by corporate "reengineering" guru Michael Hammer as "the next big wave in American industry".[12] They are also forcing companies to completely rethink their own roles: just what is the purpose of business in a world of supersonic change?

The company as a learning organization

"Forget all your old tired ideas about leadership," says *Fortune International.* "The most successful corporation of the 1990s will be something called a learning organization."[13]

But it will be much more than that. And Bill O'Brien, former Chief Executive of America's Hanover Insurance, puts one of the real challenges: "Our grandfathers worked six days a week to earn what most of us now earn by Tuesday afternoon. The ferment in management will

Training results with accelerated learning methods

Bell Atlantic C & P Telephone Co.:[1]

4-week and 6-week customer rep.
training course and 12-day technical course.
42, 57 and 50 percent training time reduction.
Dropout rate reduced 300 percent.
$700,000-a-year saving in training costs.

Northeast Medical College:[1]

Forty percent of first-year medical students
failed their final exam in anatomy. The course
was redesigned with integrative learning
principles—and 100 percent passed.

Intel Corporation:[2]

Participants on one course achieved a
knowledge-gain of 507 percent compared with
14 percent by traditional methods.

1. Information supplied by Laurence D. Martel, President,
   National Academy of Integrative Learning,
   Hilton Head, South Carolina.

2. Information from The Center for Accelerated Learning,
   Lake Geneva, Wisconsin.

continue until we build organizations that are more consistent with man's higher aspirations beyond food, shelter and belonging."[14]

Tom Peters talks about an "organization-as-university."[15] And more and more companies are fitting that model.

❑ Quad/Graphics, the Wisconsin printing company with a $500 million-a-year turnover, has been specifically set up as a learning organization. All employees sign up as students. They work a four-day, 40-hour, flex-time week. On the fifth day they're encouraged to turn up in the company's classroom—without pay; and about half do. Everyone in the company is encouraged to be both a student and a teacher. You don't get promoted until you have trained your successor.[16]

❑ At Johnsonville Foods, another Wisconsin company, nearly every worker is taking a company-paid economics course at the local community college. Most work in small group projects. Each is encouraged to be a self-acting manager. Says one plant manager: "We're teachers. We help people grow. That's my main goal. Each person is his or her own manager."[17]

❑ In 1996 leading European managers for the third year running voted ABB, the Swiss-Swedish engineering group, as their most-admired company, and its president, Percy Barnevik, as Europe's most respected business leader.[18] More than any other company, it has led western Europe's advance into the former communist-bloc countries. Barnevik says the group's aim is "the massive transfer of knowledge from west to east". After the fall of the Berlin Wall, ABB quickly invested in Poland and the Czech Republic. Now it is using Czech and Polish engineers to train staff at newly-acquired businesses in the Ukraine and Russia. And its companies in smaller countries, such as Norway, Sweden, Denmark and Finland have been entrusted with supporting emerging businesses in Lithuania, Latvia and Estonia. The pattern is also being repeated in Asia.

❑ In Taipei, the China Productivity Center is playing a major part in Taiwan's drive to lift its income per person from $7,900 in 1990 to $20,000 in 2000.[19] The CPC has pioneered new methods of bringing automation and total quality management techniques to Taiwan. Its main drive now is to add the world's best accelerated learning techniques to CPC's already big range of training skills. Former president Casper Shih is in no doubt about educational priorities: "The ideal purpose of education should be to instill the ability to learn. Teach how to learn, not what to learn, and the learning opportunities are endless."[20] He sees the

Model for a learning organization*

Overall focus on the future

Including The Shape of Things to Come, the Learning Revolution, the Thinking Revolution and the Instant Communications Revolution.

Twin senior executive focus

Management: **to set and achieve short-term goals through other people;** *Leadership:* **to create and inspire a new self-generating future with even bigger goals.**

The corporate culture

Everyone an enthusiastic learner.
Everyone a teacher, mentor, coach.
Everyone a creative thinker.

Everyone a positive contributor.
Everyone a self-acting manager.
Every stakeholder involved.

Training and development

Help everyone to set and achieve personal as well as corporate goals. All training does not have to lead to specific job-related skills. It is enough to add knowledge skills and learn to learn.

Communications loop

Make it easy to create, simplify and store all vital information, and make it instantly available to everyone. Reward people for sharing ideas. Crush out the "Not Invented Here" syndrome.

Model constructed by Gordon Dryden for The Burton Group Plc., Britain, based on discussions with Chief Executive John Hoerner.

widespread use of new learning methods—including "learning with the heart as well as the head"—as the key to Taiwan's place in the 21st century.

Inventec is typical of Taiwan's new learning-based industries. One of its most recently-developed software products, *Dr. Eye*, translates English text into Chinese, and Chinese into English. Its products are selling so fast that Inventec has hired 1,600 extra software engineers to staff its operations on the Chinese mainland.

❑ In Britain, one of the country's oldest flourmills, in Yorkshire, has become a model of modern efficiency by linking together new training methods with "upside-down" management. In 1990 Rank Hovis's Selby mill was the group's worst performer, unprofitable, with terrible industrial relations—and about to be closed.

Today all its staff regard themselves as co-managers, its output is up by 85 percent per person, customer complaints are down by 66 percent, the mill is profitable, and it has won the National Training Award and the Industrial Society's special award for "unlocking people's potential".

Rank Hovis's former National Training Manager David Buffin says the key is to "involve everyone in a passionate application of simple things".[21]

❑ Also in Britain, John Hoerner, Chief Executive of The Burton Group, would agree. He heads one of Britain's major retail chains, with a turnover in excess of $3-billion, a staff of 44,000 and more than 600 outlets in six chains, including the giant Debenhams subsidiary with its 88 department stores.

In 1995 Hoerner set out on a program to change Burton's corporate culture. That year he and 400 leaders from other British companies spent a day at a planning seminar on "the new millennium", organized by Speakers International, one of the British management-development and training companies specializing in accelerated-learning methods. The presenters: Gordon Dryden, on *The Shape Of Things To Come,* and Stephen Covey, on the theme of his book, *The Seven Habits of Highly Effective People.* The other main activity: an interactive, accelerated-learning business game, *The Gold of the Desert King,* to hone decision-making skills, with all the teams in middle-east dress.

Hoerner and his Burton co-leaders decided to repeat the exercise in 1996 for all their own senior executives. Since then they've introduced programs to spread the culture throughout the company.

Eight steps to a learning organization

Step 1.   Check out the big picture of what can be. Observe the models for the future.

Step 2.   What's happening? Assess your current reality. Get the negatives out. What does not serve you? Failure equals feedback.

Step 3.   What do you want instead or in addition? Dream! Create the vision! Focus on it!

Step 4.   Check the ecology. What are your resources? Is your workplace (or life) safe for thinking? Align your behavior with intention.

Step 5.   Go for it! Clarify the outcomes, make them specific. Visualize using all of the senses. PLAN: Personal Learning Action Plan.

Step 6.   Align with others. Create the environment of interdependence. Gain support. Build team structures. "Each one teach one."

Step 7.   Evaluate, review, celebrate. Did you reach your goal? Were you successful? How successful? Regroup if necessary.

Step 8.   Recycle. Multiply your successes.

JEANNETTE VOS*

* The Learning Organization workshop,
Gallivare, Sweden, 1996.

The group's Dorothy Perkins women's wear chain, for example, has more than 500 branches. Every branch manager and all area and regional managers have been through Speakers International peak-performance training. Walk into a training session and you're likely to see petite women managers breaking through thick boards with their bare hands, learning to juggle and developing new memory-training techniques.

Says Personnel Director Kim Morton: "We want all our people to realize they can develop talents beyond what they may have thought possible." [22]

Her company is also using other training in innovation techniques and Kaizen continuous-improvement methods to increase the supply of ideas from all 6,000 staff members.

In three separate 1996 trials using accelerated learning methods, store sales in three months increased by 10 percent. In the full 1995-96 financial year, Dorothy Perkins increased its profits from $6.6-million to $25-million. The total Burton Group raised its full-year profits by 54 percent to $246-million. [23]

"We certainly can't attribute all that to training," says John Hoerner. "But the ability to use new methods to improve the skills of management and staff is undoubtedly a key factor. That involves, firstly, all senior executives combining both long-term leadership and short-term management roles. It involves a corporate culture where everyone is encouraged to be a lifelong learner, and a creative, self-acting manager. It involves training and development programs that produce specific results both for the group and for all the individuals involved in it. And it entails efficient communications so we can duplicate innovations that work." [24]

The school or college as a business venture

Author Alvin Toffler has described knowledge as "the ultimate business resource".[25] And where university-based knowledge has already teamed up with innovative business, the results have changed the world. The Stanford University-venture capital-brainpower base for Silicon Valley, M.I.T.'s Media Lab, and the bonds between the giant Japanese companies and their universities are striking examples.

Now some schools and colleges are moving in the same direction. Mt. Edgecumbe High School in Alaska is one model. Another comes from British twin entrepreneurs Peter and Paul Templeton. Their family runs two private London colleges, Lansdowne and Duff Miller, which

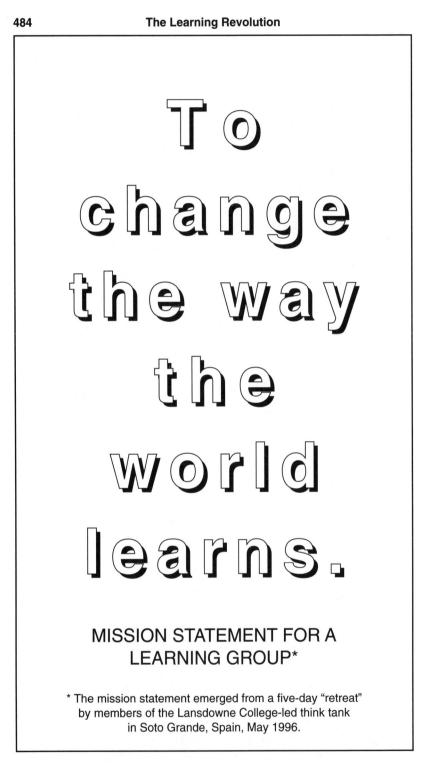

To change the way the world learns.

MISSION STATEMENT FOR A LEARNING GROUP*

* The mission statement emerged from a five-day "retreat"
by members of the Lansdowne College-led think tank
in Soto Grande, Spain, May 1996.

have both introduced accelerated learning methods.   And they have launched several "strategic alliances" from their school base.

They're now co-owners of the British franchise for Stephen Covey's Center for Principled Leadership. They're partners, too, with innovators Andrew Hughes-Hallett and Alex MacPhail in Speakers International, corporate development specialists and "big-events" organizers. A Fast Forward subsidiary produces audiotapes and study notes—produced by the chief examiners—to help high school students pass their senior exams. And the college staff and Speakers International work together to use accelerated-learning techniques for developing other programs. A Speakers International associate company, The Catalyst Group, has instant access to a database of every book currently in print, so it can instantly locate and supply books, tapes and other resources for self-improvement, management and learning.

Lansdowne College also flew nine of its teaching staff to the 1996 International Alliance for Learning Conference in Orlando, Florida. And the college involves specialist facilitators from its associate companies in seminar and workshop activity.

Every A-level Lansdowne student is offered an individual learning-style check. Courses are tailored to individual talents. And working-style checks are offered to the staffs of corporate clients.

As a typical cooperative arrangement involving the Templeton group, several hundred corporate clients turned up in Birmingham, England, at 7 o'clock one morning in 1996 for an interactive satellite presentation. Beamed out of the United States, it featured Stephen Covey, Tom Peters and Peter Senge, sharing views on the challenges of tomorrow's world and answering immediate queries from dozens of countries.

About 220,000 business people around the world took part in that interactive exchange. Paul Templeton says that typifies the potential to engage the world's best teachers to teach students of every age, anywhere on earth.[26]

In May 1996 the Templetons took 20 key members of their college and associated companies on a five-day "retreat" in Spain to see how best to be a catalyst for new learning methods. Peter Templeton outlined a template to link "all who want to make the journey into a virtual learning company".[27] And by the end of five days, the team had fleshed that out into a core of key steps around an agreed mission statement that sums it all up: "To change the way the world learns."

Our deepest fear is not that
we are inadequate.

Our deepest fear is that we are
powerful beyond measure.

It is our light, not our darkness,
that most frightens us.

We ask ourselves: Who am I to be
brilliant, gorgeous,
talented and fabulous?

Actually who are you not to be?
You are a child of God.

Your playing small doesn't serve the world.

There is nothing enlightened about
shrinking so that other people
won't feel insecure around you.

We are born to manifest the glory
of God that is within us.
It is not just in some of us; it's in everyone.

And as we let our own light shine,
we unconsciously give other
people permission to do the same.

As we are liberated from our own fear
our presence automatically liberates others.

MARIANNE WILLIAMSON
*A Return For Love**

* Published by HarperCollins, New York. (Note: This text is often
attributed to Nelson Mandela, who quoted it in his 1994 inaugural address
as the first black President of South Africa.)

How any country can lead the learning revolution: and so can you

Now it's your turn. The Learning Revolution is yours to shape.

Almost everything that idealistic dreamers ever imagined is now possible. The knowledge exists to create the world's first truly learned society. That learning revolution will flower fastest when it brings together all these elements:

❑ Introduce great infant-development and parenting programs.

❑ Lead the world in interactive communications technology.

❑ Choose from the proven best methods of learning.

❑ Mount school-business partnerships and initiatives.

❑ Make teacher retraining a top priority.

❑ Provide farsighted government leadership.

❑ Make lifelong learning a philosophy.

❑ Build on the strengths of each nation's own culture.

❑ And encourage students to be teachers as well as learners.

Already exciting models are showing that revolution in action.

The Singapore centralized leadership model

On a centralized Government level, the biggest challenge has been thrown down by the Government of Singapore.

Its masterplan we've already covered: a $US1.5 billion program to introduce the world's best educational technology to schools and society. It is using that for teaching new skills, with high emphasis on creative thinking and lifelong learning. It's also built in positive steps to ensure

One model for a 21st century school

- ❏ Design school from scratch as a self-directed inquiry and discovery center.
- ❏ Carefully select an inspiring principal.
- ❏ Principal chooses top-quality staff committed to school's philosophy.
- ❏ Use $NZ400,000 establishment grant to provide world-class IT resources.
- ❏ Plan computers, VCR and multimedia tools to support learning philosophy.
- ❏ Set up multiple-intelligence centers to cater to each learning style.
- ❏ Start de Bono *Six Thinking Hats* in infant years to build creative skills.
- ❏ Provide each teacher with a personal laptop computer and Internet link.
- ❏ Make every learner a teacher and vice versa.
- ❏ Build warm personal and multimedia home-school reporting links.
- ❏ Form business partnerships.
- ❏ Link with schools around the world, from China to America.

Tahatai Coast Primary School, New Zealand*

* Papamoa, Bay of Plenty, New Zealand. Highlights summarized from article, *What's So Special About Tahatai Coast?* by principal Mark Beach and Raewyn Baldwin-Denton, June 1997; and several author visits to the school.
Mark Beach's email address: markb@tahatai.school.nz

that all students from poorer families can benefit. Singapore's society, of course, is highly centralized: with strong government leadership and a high level of disciplined conformity. Only a handful of its public schools are independently run. And one of them, Raffles Girls School, thinks it has already achieved most of the targets set by the Government for 2002. Sit with bubbling, energetic principal Carmee Lim in her office and you catch the enthusiasm that has made Raffles the top high school in the state.

Switching on her computer, she spends half an hour showing you the Raffles web site: the color photographs of hundreds of students on Outward Bound courses; others on field trips to China and Australia; yet others producing a wide range of computer programs; the entire school on community-service projects; all students surfing the Internet. Like Miriam Kronish at John Eliot School in Massachusetts, Carmee Lim is the epitome of tomorrow's school leader: with the common sense and sparkling drive needed to turn schools into self-directed learning centers.

The decentralized New Zealand model

For a decentralized economy, some of the best models are emerging in New Zealand. All of its 2,700 schools, public and private, are now run by independent parent-elected boards of trustees. And the public policy is competition for excellence.

Go into Tahatai Coast School at Papamoa in the North Island's Bay of Plenty region, and you'll see what can happen when a new primary "school of tomorrow" is designed from scratch. When you drive up to its entrance you think you've arrived at an upmarket Californian ranch-style private condominium complex.

Go into any of the classrooms and you'll find students working in Howard Gardner-style multiple-intelligence groupings, with teachers catering to individual learning styles. In every room you'll find de Bono *Six Thinking Hats* material. And every classroom is linked to the entire world: by satellite, cable and interactive electronic networking.

Innovative principal Mark Beach and his staff have traveled extensively in the United States and Canada to pick up new ideas. He also says Tahatai Coast School has been fortunate with another big "plus": it was designed as a new-era school. And it has been able to select staff to fit the new philosophy. "For the first ten jobs," he says, "we had 200 applicants, so we've been able to select exceptional people."[1]

As a new school, Tahatai Coast received an establishment grant of

A Swedish model for the future

❏ Build a school for children from age three: "An extraordinary school for ordinary children".

❏ Make its motto: "A school valuing chickens and computers"—blending nature with the world's best technology.

❏ Build on the concept of many intelligences so education is tailor-made for each student, respecting unique talent and ability.

❏ Set up a "Knowledge Port" as an Information technology center, with three arms:

● A multimedia communications and production center.

● A multimedia publishing company, specializing in learning material.

● A training center for teachers and others who work with children, with special emphasis on new technology.

❏ Establish two other projects to promote the concept of lifelong learning:

● A "school without walls" so students can learn from a variety of experiences.

● A multimedia center to act as a family and community resource.

The Welfare Renaissance: The New Swedish Model*

* By Helen H. Wallenberg and Michael S. Bogolea, published by The Carpe Vitam Foundation, Lemshaga, 13461 Ingaro, Sweden, which operates the project.

$216,000. It spent most of this on "big budget high tech items". But for many others it has had to raise the money. And here too it is one of many schools making the most of a joint venture with Telecom, New Zealand's main telephone company. Tahatai is a Telecom site school. That means 5% of the income from specified "family and friends" long-distance calls is donated to the school. But those donations come only from homes and businesses signed up by the school. So the program both helps pay for the school's computers and personally involves its community directly in the funding and learning process.

In 1999 Tahatai became one of 23 model schools selected by New Zealand's Ministry of Education to be the on-site staff-development training centers for information technology. These centers are spread around New Zealand — a country the same area as Oregon — so collectively they can cater to the needs of principals and teachers across the island nation. This is an adaptation of the "Navigator Schools" model used with great success by the Australian state of Victoria.

The new Swedish models

Swedish innovators are seeking to blend the skills of entrepreneurs with the best elements of a decentralized welfare state.

Swedish publishers Ingemar and Gunilla Svantesson, for instance, have used *The Learning Revolution* as the "umbrella" to launch other books. Their company has brought several international specialists to Sweden for seminars, following several successful Vos tours.

Helena W. Wallenberg has gone even further, and set out a plan for "a welfare renaissance". This promotes "an alternative which changes the philosophy of welfare from welfare entitlement to welfare responsibility, from educationally dependent to educationally empowered".[2] With colleague Michael S. Bogolea and others, she has established The Carpe Vitam Foundation. It has set up a model school-of-the-future, a multimedia publishing company, a community educational center integrated into the business community, and a teacher-training center.

Their new school is The Lemshaga Barnakademi, designed as "an extraordinary school for ordinary children"—a school "valuing chickens and computers" so that it links nature with the best in technology. It has students from three to 15. From as early as three years, they are exposed to languages, mathematics and science. Many aspects of the school are based around Howard Gardner's concepts of multiple intelligence.

The art of teaching is developing into the art of teaching children to teach themselves.

HELENA H. WALLENBERG and
MICHAEL S. BOGOLEA*

* In *The Welfare Renaissance: The New Swedish Model,*
published by The Carpe Vitam Foundation,
Lemshaga, 13461 Ingaro, Sweden.

Regular updates: www.thelearningweb.net

Its next project is a "Knowledge Port: a school without walls, where we try to integrate seventh, eighth and ninth grade with high school, and actually move the children around to workplaces, study halls, language institutes, gyms etc. for a more reality-based education". The foundation is also working "on a community-based media center open to everyone. The idea is that it will be the core that connects all the schools and families in the community." Helena Wallenberg is now pressing for companies to get tax-credits for investing in "enterprise zones" that will be built around lifelong learning centers.

In the city of Lund, in the south of Sweden, are 38 relatively new preschool centers and three combined early-childhood and elementary schools operated by a group known as Pysslingen. The project is administered by private enterprise, working with local authorities, aimed at providing high-quality "educare". "The goal," says leader Monica Lundberg, "has been to combine the best from the public sector—fair distribution—with the best from private enterprise: efficiency." [3]

Monica Lundberg says the business-school model has proved so effective that many local governments—which are in charge of Swedish schooling—now turn to Pysslingen to run their government programs. Pysslingen is also setting up an integrated combined early-childhood-elementary school center for disabled children, combining accelerated learning methods with new methods for physical training.

The certification model

Sweden is also showing the way in training teachers in a combination of the best methods outlined in this book, so they can become certified "learning revolution" practitioners.

More than 25,000 Swedish teachers have so far been trained by co-author Vos. Most started off at short workshops, but many have followed-up with one-week courses.

From Gullivare schools, in Sweden's Arctic Circle, for example, 45 teachers attended Jeannette Vos's Module One certification program in 1997. Fifteen of them came to Module Two, on group dynamics, and Module Three, on curriculum design.

In 1998 they have taken two final modules on advanced techniques. And those qualifying go on to train other teachers in the same methods. Jeannette's Learning Revolution Academy is now running similar modules each year in San Diego, California, as well as Sweden.

An Apple for the student!

West High School in Columbus, Ohio, U.S.A., is the original model for the Apple Classrooms of Tomorrow project, which has been running since 1985 to test the impact of computing in a variety of teaching environments.

Each year 120 of the school's 1,200 students go to special ACOT classes where top teaching and learning methods are linked to the world's best information technology.

And the proof is in the eating.

Of the remainder of the school roll only 15 percent graduate and go on to college, while 30 percent drop out early.

Of the ACOT students, 90 percent go on to college, and the drop out rate is nil.

DAVID C. DWYER
Education & Technology*

* Published by Jossey-Bass publishers, San Francisco, and
Apple Press, to summarize the first decade of ACOT.
Dr. Dwyer, who directed ACOT's research and managed
the program for much of that decade, is one of the book's editors.

Corporate leadership models

In the corporate world, the models also abound:

❏ From Andersen Consulting's highly-impressive company university in St. Charles, Illinois, where the world's largest firm of management consultants spends more than $400 million a year on internal staff training—using the latest in multimedia, interactive case-study models.

❏ From Stan Shih's Acer Group and the $7 million it has contributed to set up The Acer Foundation.

❏ From the United Kingdom's biggest company, British Telecommunications, which is mounting a five-year, nine-figure millennium project to involve Britain's 60 million population to communicate better.

❏ And from Apple Computers, which has pioneered one of the longest partnerships between the corporate and school worlds.

Its Apple Classrooms of Tomorrow (ACOT) project has been running in America since 1985.   Some of the results have been spectacular.[4]

West High School in Columbus, Ohio, is the original ACOT model. It operates as a school within a school.   It caters each year to 120 of the school's 1,200 students.   Of the total school roll, only 15 percent of students have gone on to college. Of those attending ACOT: 90 percent.

Students at Bell High School in southwestern Los Angeles County—a high poverty area—have won more than 100 awards for producing their own videos as key components of their multimedia ACOT program.

Lincoln High School in San Jose, California, has worked in closely with a local television station and the police department to pioneer digital photography.   Its students have even collaborated with NASA scientists to produce an interactive educational CD-ROM about the effects of space on the heart.

But despite these great examples, America—the richest nation on earth—continues to provide the greatest possible contrasts: corporate leaders in informational software and hardware yet with a public school system that veers from brilliant to appalling. By contrast, companies such as Microsoft, Oracle, Hewlett-Packard and Netscape are revolutionizing the entire field of instant communications.   And several of them are revolutionizing their businesses into learning organizations.

GE Chief Executive Jack Welch is caught up in building what he calls a learning culture in a highly diversified corporation that was founded more than 100 years ago by Thomas Edison.   And as Robert Slater quotes

CEO's dream for GE: "I hope it will be the greatest learning institution in the world."

JACK WELCH
Chief Executive of GE*

* Quoted by Robert Slater in *Jack Welch and The GE Way,*
published by McGraw Hill, New York.

the company's leader in *Jack Welch and the GE Way:* "What sets GE apart is a culture that uses this wide diversity as a limitless source of learning opportunities, a storehouse of ideas whose breadth and richness is unmatched in world business. At the heart of this culture is the understanding that an organization's ability to learn, and translate that learning into action rapidly, is the ultimate competitive business advantage."

Welch is consistently voted by his peers as America's most-admired corporate manager. Before he took over the company, fully 80 percent of General Electric's earnings came from its traditional electrical and electronic manufacturing businesses. As we saw in the last chapter, now more than 80 percent comes from selling services, training and finance. Asked by Slater whether GE would look like it does today in 20 to 30 years time, Welch replied: " I doubt it. I hope it will be the greatest learning institution in the world."

The give-it-away model

We believe the Netscape concept of free software through the Internet will also be one of the main breakthroughs to revolutionize the delivery of learning programs: give it away—and sell the add-ons.

The whole culture of the Internet has been built around an open environment, where people around the world freely share knowledge. University researchers have been using it for years to swap information, so the pattern of the future is already set.

We're convinced that sometime soon most complex computer programs will be stored at central Internet web sites, and you'll be able to access them instantly through a "network computer"—call it what you like—connected to your television set, or as a combined TV-PC.

We're also convinced that one path to the future involves combining the abilities of the world's best teachers and making them available to all the world through interactive multimedia sources. Any school system not developing that concept will be left behind and surpassed by individual and corporate initiatives.

The Internet selling model

But the Internet is not only great for exchanging information; it's emerging as a potent new way to sell learning products.

By May 1997 Dell Computers were achieving $1 million in sales a day

Learning Revolution model for tomorrow's textbook/CD-ROMs

This book by itself incorporates several principles of accelerated learning.

The left-hand pages are designed to provide both an overview of all the main points and to be reproduced as posters.

The Learning Revolution CD-ROM that has been produced to accompany this book takes the concept much further.

The CD-ROM contains full-color-slide presentations of the poster pages, with these features:

❏ 16 different presentations, with recorded commentary.

❏ 300 color slides

❏ It can run on any PC or Apple Mac with a CD-ROM drive.

With it, you can:

❏ View each audiovisual presentation on your computer, or use a multimedia projector for classroom or public presentations.

❏ Select any slide and print it, in color, on an ink-jet or color laser printer.

❏ Transfer the CD-ROM to your computer hard-disc.

❏ Mix the slides with your own

if you want to make a Microsoft *PowerPoint* presentation.

❏ Mix slides with other applications, like encyclopedia clip art.

❏ Update your slides with new information off the Internet.

❏ Make the CD-ROM package available to all students, on individual PCs, through a school's own Intranet internal network.

The book/CD-ROM package is a multimedia format ideal for "the textbooks of tomorrow".

With study material in this format, teachers and university lecturers can:

❏ Make an "accelerated learning" textbook available to all students on a particular course.

❏ Have access to professional color-slide and videotape presentations for big-screen viewing.

❏ Produce key points as color posters as lasting reminders.

❏ Provide all students with access to facts and illustrations to use in their own study projects.

And all at a tiny fraction of the cost of providing separate 35mm slides or "overheads".

from the Internet, and by early 1999 that was up to $18 million a day.

"Virtual book companies" such as Amazon, in the United States, and the Internet Book Shop and Blackwells, in England, now offer millions of titles for ordering on line. We predict this model will be one of the most successful commercial applications of the learning revolution.

The business-teacher-multimedia model

The barriers between business and education are rapidly coming down, and that, too, is an essential part of the breakthrough.

Again several initiatives in innovative New Zealand show the models:

❏ Publisher Wendy Pye has become one of New Zealand's wealthiest business women. Dismissed by New Zealand News Ltd. when it was taken over by an investment company, she formed Sunshine Books. Its philosophy: teaching children to read. Its theoretical base: New Zealand's detailed reading research. Its authors: some of the world's best, starting with Joy Cowley and June Melser. Its big breakthrough, apart from Wendy Pye's entrepreneurial brilliance: setting up a television production partnership between her, Brian Cutting—a reading expert and former teachers' training college lecturer—and television network pioneer Tom Parkinson.

That led to the production of *The Magic Box* television series which now screens Monday to Friday on the United States Learning Channel to an audience of 15 million, promoting sales of the books it features. Sales to date of Sunshine Books: 85 million units.[5] Sunshine is also a leader in learning on the Internet. The company has seven-year-olds in countries and states as diverse as South Africa, Alaska, New Zealand, Singapore, Poland, Canada and America designing their own books on line.

❏ Also from Auckland, Jerome and Sophie Hartigan are turning their *Jumping Beans* physical brain-development programs for infants into a franchised network, and developing *Beanie* as a book and television cartoon character to cover the main principles of learning.

❏ Barbara Prashnig's Creative Learning Company, with its physical base in Auckland, New Zealand, is typical of the coming links between good educational research, an innovative interactive multimedia product, and the Internet. Her new Working Styles Analysis[6] is readily available on the Web. To check your own style, you can download a questionnaire, fill it in and order an inexpensive computerized printout.

❏ Another New Zealand entrepreneur, David Perry, has taken his

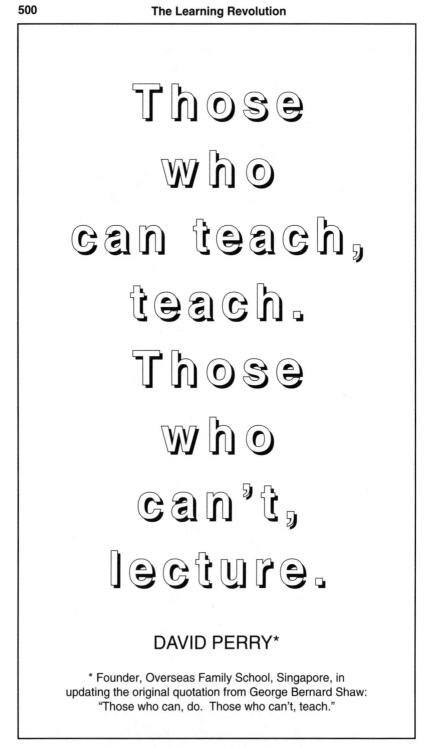

Those who can teach, teach. Those who can't, lecture.

DAVID PERRY*

* Founder, Overseas Family School, Singapore, in
updating the original quotation from George Bernard Shaw:
"Those who can, do. Those who can't, teach."

talents abroad in a different way. Called in to Singapore to rescue one international school from bankruptcy, he went back later to set up a much larger one. In the buildings of the former Singapore Teachers Training College, his Overseas Family School now has 1,700 students, and a management split that could be a model for the world.

Teachers applying for jobs are sent a copy of *The Learning Revolution* to indicate the school's overall philosophy. But David Perry stresses: "We don't try and tell good teachers how to teach. Instead, we make a very distinct split between the teaching and management functions. We spend a great deal of time selecting able teachers from around the world. Management then provides all the resources needed for those excellent teachers to do an excellent job."[7] And that means that every teacher can concentrate 100 percent on developing each child's natural ability. With students from around the world, the school looks like a mini United Nations. And it is.

The Overseas Family School has students from early childhood to high school, and a developing college-level campus operated in conjunction with California State University, the world's biggest teacher-training college.

The Foundation model

Variations of the "Foundation model" are also showing the way—often set up with grants from business following the patterns originally set by the Ford and Carnegie Foundations in the United States.

❏ In Britain, the Royal Society for the encouragement of Arts, Manufactures and Commerce has launched a four-year nationwide Campaign for Learning. Sir Christopher Ball is chairman. Its aim: "To change the culture and gradually transform the U.K. into a 'learning society'." To that Ball adds a personal vision: "For every individual to have a Personal Learning Action Plan (PLAN), every organization to become a learning organization, and for everybody to be in reach of an accessible provider of learning opportunities — whether in a school, college, university or in employment or in the home."[8]

❏ In America the Johnson Foundation—financed by Johnson Wax— has recruited John Abbott from Britain's Education 2000 Foundation to promote the search for new learning methods.

❏ From New Zealand again comes an unusual hybrid from the rapid changes in finance, banking and internationalization. For over 100 years

The new model: how to make the impossible possible. And we're doing it.

HANS HAAKONSAN
Norway's Telenor*

* Author interview, Norway.

New Zealand communities have owned "trustee" savings banks, with their profits distributed to the communities they serve. But when the Government opened up New Zealand banking to international competition in the 1980s, the trustees of the Auckland Savings Bank made a bold decision: they sold 75 percent of their bank to the Commonwealth Bank of Australia. They put the $NZ350 million proceeds into the ASB Charitable Trust, and invested them around the world. It is now by far New Zealand's biggest trust, disbursing millions of dollars a year for major educational, cultural and charitable projects.*

The international conference model

International conferences on new methods of learning and education provide another gateway to the future.

Singapore was one of 44 countries that sent delegates to Arthur Andersen's 1997 *Learning for the 21st Century* conference in Chicago. Significantly Singapore's delegates were chosen by the Ministry of Education and the National Computer Board.

The Singapore Government in mid-1997 also paid for every school principal and deputy principal in the country to attend a one-week International Conference on Thinking. The keynote presenters read like a *Who's Who* from the pioneers in creative thinking: Howard Gardner from Harvard; Robert Sternberg from Yale; Edward de Bono from England; Israel's Reuven Feuerstein; Venezuela's former Minister for the Development of Human Intelligence, Luis Machado; David Perkins from Harvard; and such thinking-skills pioneers as Paul MacCready, Robert Sylwester and Richard Paul—all brought to Singapore to stimulate the drive for creative thinking.

The "learning organization" model

Hundreds of companies are also taking advantage of new methods of learning to build their corporations into learning organizations.

❏ Norway's Telenor telecommunications company is using accelerated learning techniques to develop its 18,000 staff. It's using the Nor-

* A donation of $NZ2 million from the ASB Charitable Trust in 1990 enabled co-author Dryden and Lesley Max to form the Pacific Foundation. It paid for most of the "Where To Now?" television series and a range of New Zealand parent-education programs, including a pilot project for combining parenting education with a preschool and health center.

A cluster model for a 'learning industry'

The Learning Web

An "open university" on the World-Wide Web, co-ordinating the flow of information to and from schools, universities and lifelong learners. Possibly organized by a Learning Web Foundation or company with schools as shareholders.

Learning Network Service

Companies selling and servicing computers, intranet systems and multimedia products to schools, universities, businesses and homes.

The Web's Product Labs

Product development centers, some linked to universities, others to businesses, including venture capital companies to finance exports.

The Training Network

Separate but inter-related specialists: some coaching teachers and trainers in new learning methods, others in multimedia and computer recources.

The Publishing Network

Publishing books, CDs, CD-ROMs, laser discs, videos, TV programs and course material; plus Internet and printed Learning Web magazines.

Learning Web Shops

Retail outlets franchised internationally to instantly fill orders for learning products, courses and programs promoted through the web site.

Students produce multimedia products in school and college pilot companies

Condensed from the actual model that led to the formation of The Learning Web Ltd., publishers of this book.

wegian translation of *The Learning Revolution* and Peter Senge's *The Fifth Discipline* as models. Telenor sent two senior executive officers, Hans Haakonsan and Earnst Risan, to one of co-author Vos's ten-day workshops in San Diego for training. It also bought a copy of *The Learning Revolution* for every staff member involved in a pretest of its total program. And a year later it sent more trainers to Vos workshops.

Haakonsan says Telenor is now "focusing on values, instead of rules".[9] The *base values* are "responsibility, respect, creativity and integrity". And the *key values* are "customer satisfaction, good bottom line, good teamwork and focus on long-term development".

One of the big challenges, he says, is in building appropriate mental models. An example? "How to make the impossible possible—and we're doing it."

Accelerated-learning methods are being adopted, too, in more and more American businesses. The Center for Accelerated Learning in Lake Geneva, Wisconsin, for instance, reports results like these:

❑ Judy Authier of Cooperators Insurance says: "Our investment in accelerated learning has paid us back ten-fold." [10]

❑ Kimberly-Clark's Randy Atkins says: "Accelerated learning is the best training investment our organization has ever made." [11]

❑ On one course at Intel, participants on an AL course achieved a 507 percent knowledge gain, compared with 23 percent by "normal" training methods.[12]

❑ Of Travelers Insurance representatives studying a computer system, 67 percent learning by AL methods end up in the highest quartile of grades, compared to only 14 percent by traditional methods.[13]

The "cluster" model

One of the best model of all, for any small country or state to profit most from the learning revolution, is the "cluster" model.

This is the concept promoted extensively by the Harvard Business School and especially Professor Michael Porter who argues that industries develop best around "clusters of excellence".[14]

The outstanding example of this is California's Silicon Valley. It has radiated out from the brilliant leadership of Stanford University and especially Professor Fred Terman, Bill Hewlett, David Packard, Bob Noyce and the other engineers who originally formed Fairchild

Relearn the best from our past

As Confucius said 2,500 years ago:

- ❏ Blend the the best of the new with best from the old.
- ❏ Learn by doing.
- ❏ Use the world as classroom.
- ❏ Use music and poetry to learn and teach.
- ❏ Blend academic and physical.
- ❏ Learn how to learn, not just facts.
- ❏ Cater to different learning styles.
- ❏ Build good values and behavior.
- ❏ Provide an equal chance for all.

CHEN JINGPAN
*Confucius as a Teacher**

* Published by Foreign Language Press, Beijing, China.

Semicoductor. Spin-offs from their examples have spawned just about every company in Silicon Valley, and many more around America.

Singapore provides another example. Its government has used its multi-billion-dollar national superannuation fund to finance many high-tech industries, and has provided generous tax-breaks to attract 3,000 international companies to the city state.

The Chinese back-to-your-roots model

One of the most exciting models of all is to rediscover the great strengths of a society's own culture. That's why China is one of the most exciting countries in the world to visit today. Probably no society has a stronger "learning ethic" than China. No large developing country is racing harder to join the world of space-age communications; by 2001 China will rank next to the United States in the number of Internet connections. Yet China is striving, too, to marry the era of "networked intelligence" to its own traditions and roots.

In doing so it is rediscovering that many of today's most effective learning methods were those first taught 2,500 years ago by Confucius and his close followers, particularly Mencius. Many critics credit Confucius with a Chinese preoccupation with examinations, forgetting that he urged these in particular to select, on merit, the main advisers the country's rulers. But many of his other concepts are even more valid now than they were when he became China's most famous early teacher:

❑ Confucius urged blending new ideas with old proven concepts.

❑ He was a democrat—and wanted to bring about social reforms through education.

❑ He believed strongly in "learning by doing".

❑ Confucius used the whole world as his classroom. He did not teach in the confines of a school.

❑ He used music and poetry extensively in both learning and teaching.

❑ He believed that learning how to learn was as important as learning information.

❑ He believed that everyone had different learning abilities, and able teachers should cater to these individual abilities.

❑ And he believed strongly in the importance of values and courteous behavior, still two key characteristics of Chinese schooling.[15]

The human brain: a springboard from which we can leap into the magical world of genius.

By DILIP MAKURJEA
*Superbrain**

* Published by Oxford University Press, Singapore

In many ways he introduced much of the original Learning Revolution, and we have rediscovered it. Link many of those traditional truths with the latest brain research, and the latest in instant communications, and you have the potential for China to once again lead the world.

And perhaps that is not surprising. For more than 2,000 years the Chinese learned mathematics with the world's earliest accelerated-learning "tool", the abacus or *suanpan*. With columns of moveable beads, it can be used to add, subtract, multiply and divide, from single units up to trillions. Two of the other great "learning tools" for teaching mathematics—playing cards and dominoes—were also invented in China centuries ago. So, too, were paper and printing.

Invent your own model

But why wait for anyone else when you can create your own model?

❑ In Singapore, Indian-born former senior shipping executive Dilip Mukerjea has become so fascinated by new learning methods that he now guarantees to teach anyone to become a competent freehand artist in five days, using methods developed by Betty Edwards and illustrated in *Drawing on The Right Side of the Brain.*   He's taking up the Government's challenge for private-sector participation in its "learning revolution" by teaching students, parents and teachers the key principles of Mind Mapping, super memory, effective reading and creativity.

❑ In Australia, one of the world's most effective facilitators, Perth's Glenn Capelli, has taken much of the learning-revolution research and turned it into songs, television scripts and interactive corporate and school training programs.   His keynote topics illustrate his unique approach: On humor and health: *what we learn from apple juice;* Dealing with change: *what we learn from raindrops;* Continuous improvement: *what we learn from frogs;* Entheos—the power of enthusiasm: *what we learn from optimism;* If we're so smart, how come we're so dumb? *what we learn from whales;* The art and science of relationships: *what we learn from cereal boxes.*[16]

❑ In Auckland, New Zealand, school teacher Kristine A. McLaren has developed a complete *Integrated Reading Program* for young children, and is marketing it internationally with her accountant husband.

❑ In Dunedin, New Zealand, several key staff members at the University of Otago, have been collecting some of their country's best examples of learning through computers and the Internet. They are now

What have you done today that

no one

else in the

world

has done?

School sign in West High School,
Columbus, Ohio, U.S.A.*

* Sign posted in the Apple Classroom of Tomorrow (ACOT)
site at the school.

publishing them as series of books through Otago University Press. The latest: *Net-Working: Teaching, Learning & Professional Development with the Internet,* edited by Hong Kong-born Dr. Kwok-Wing Lai, Senior Lecturer at the university's School of Education.

❏ From Canada, Lane Clark is building an international reputation as an expert skilled in training teachers to blend the world's best learning methods with the world's best interactive, digital technology. Her staff-development model is based very much on theme-based inquiry learning, but showing how students can use digital technology to retrieve information. In a typical month, you're likely to find her running staff development courses for schools in Canada and the United States, Tahatai Coast School in New Zealand and in Western Australia running extended courses for the Center for Excellence in Education.

❏ From the New Zealand city of Christchurch come other examples of the enormous strides that can be made when students are encouraged to learn in their own way, with their own style, at their own pace.

When co-author Dryden in 1991 produced six one-hour television documentaries on new world learning breakthroughs, one of the most spectacular individual examples came from Christchurch. Michael Tan, son of Malaysian-Chinese parents, was that year studying senior high school mathematics—at the age of seven. By the end of the year he'd passed New Zealand's top secondary school examinations—while spending his spare time playing table tennis, basketball, the classical piano and working on the family's home computer. Father Choon Tan, a modest engineer, insisted that "it all comes down to love, really".[17]

When Jeannette Vos went back to Christchurch in 1994 as the guest keynote presenter and workshop facilitator for the Canterbury College of Education—the city's teacher training university—she dined with one of her workshop attendees, Chrystal Witte, the mother of 11-year-old Daniel Witte. Many teachers regarded Daniel as a discipline problem. But over dinner, a different story emerged. At age four, Daniel had built an electronic circuit board. At aged nine, he had hacked into his father's office computer. But at primary school he'd continued to get into trouble until his parents found outlets for his scientific bent. In Jeannette's view, he was gifted, but bored. Chrystal and her husband Stephen obviously agreed. And their big breakthrough came when Papanui High School agreed to enroll Daniel, aged 12, at a *fourth-year* secondary school level.

By the end of 1995, he'd passed six bursary exams and won the

Now go out and change the world.

CHARLES KRAUTHAMMER
Time magazine

* June 28, 1993, essay based on his commencement address
at McGill University, Montreal, Canada.

school's physics prize. By the start of 1996, Christchurch's main newspaper, *The Press,* could report: "Most 13-year-olds will start secondary school next week. Daniel Witte will start university. Too young to have a cheque book, hold a driver's license, or vote, Daniel has enrolled at the University of Canterbury to study electrical engineering. He sat bursary at 12, scoring an A."[18]

And by mid-1999, Christal Witte could report: "Daniel is firing on all cylinders, and continues his Electronic and Electrical Engineering degree in his fourth year. What is truly wonderful is to see and feel his enthusiasm, passion and motivation for the work he has chosen to do."[19]

Like Choon Tan, whose elder son David had earlier become New Zealand's youngest-ever Ph. D., the Wittes say their son is "not a genius, just passionate". They believe many children would do better at school if allowed to progress at their own pace. "If he had gone on in the system as he was," says Stephen Witte, "he'd probably have been diagnosed as having attention-deficit disorder syndrome or something like that."

Both Michael Tan and Daniel Witte were given their first chance to study at high-school level by Christchurch's Hagley Community College.

An excellent book, *Learning To Learn,* by Christine Ward and Jan Daley, has been based on their introduction of accelerated learning methods to Christchurch's Cashmere High School.

And the first edition of *The Learning Revolution* was launched at a South Pacific university marketing educators' conference at nearby Lincoln University.

So the catalyst can be anyone, anywhere: in business, at school, in a community or a family. It needs to be, for the evidence is overwhelming:

❑ The world is racing into an interactive era that is changing every aspect of the way we communicate, learn, live, work and play.

❑ These changes demand a complete rethink on how we learn; how we can rekindle the learning enthusiasm we embraced as small children; how we can go on learning and relearning throughout life; how we can provide the same stimulation to those coming after us; and how we can positively reshape the world.

❑ The tools are here. The time is now. The script is yours to write —or dance, or sing, or play, or act, or draw, or orchestrate.

Anyone can lead the world into the 21st century. Why not you?

Chapter reference notes ███████████

Where the same reference source is used more than once, subsequent references are abbreviated in this way:

6: 1.2 — meaning: see chapter 1, note number 2.

G.D. is Gordon Dryden, and J.V. is Jeannette Vos.

Other page references are from this edition of *The Learning Revolution.*

Introduction

1. From Robert Reich, *The Work Of Nations,* Simon & Schuster (1991).

2. Kevin Kelly, *New Rules For The New Economy,* article in *Wired* magazine (September, 1997).

3. Larry Downes and Chunka Mui, *Unleashing The Killer App,* Harvard Business School Press (1998).

4. Don Tapscott, *Growing Up Digital,* McGraw Hill (1998).

5. Introduction.4.

6. See chapters 6 and 7 for full reference notes.

7. *Fortune 500 Rich List* (1997).

8. Information supplied by The Center For Accelerated Learning, Lake Geneva, Wisconsin, U.S.A. (1996).

9. Results provided to J.V. by Leo Wood (1996).

10. John Medcalf, *TARP: The Tape Assisted Reading Program,* summarized on pages 384-385 of this book.

11. From G.D. visit to Beijing (1998).

12. *Celebrating Multiple Intelligences: Teaching for Success,* New City School, St. Louis, Missouri (1994).

13. Full details, from page 402.

14. Speech by Teo Chee Hean, Minister of Education, announcing Singapore's IT masterplan (April 28, 1997).

15. *The Straits Times,* Singapore (July 31, 1997).

16. Full details, from page 331.

17. European Union unemployment figures: *The Economist* (Sept. 28, 1996).

18. Jeremy Rifkin, *The End of Work,* Tarcher/Putnam (1995).

19. Study by Social Market Foundation, based on survey of 500,000 1995 pupils, summarized by *The Sunday Times* (August 25, 1996).

20. David Blunkett, since appointed Education and Employment Secretary, *Labor to target reading ability,* in *The Times* (May 30, 1996).

21. Introduction.10.

22. Skills-knowledge estimate by Secretary's Commission on Achieving Necessary Skills (SCANS), *What Work Requires of America's Schools,* U.S. Department of Labor (1991).

23. Introduction.18.

24. See chapter 7 for detailed research.

25. Elizabeth G. Hainstock, *The Essential Montessori,* Plume/Penguin revised 1997), provides excellent summary of Montessori history, critics and principles.

26. David Hood, in *Education In Change,* Bridget Williams Books (1993).

27. SuperCamp research by Jeannette Vos-Groenendal, *An Accelerative/Integrative Learning Model Program: Based on Participant Perceptions of Student*

Attitudinal and Achievement Changes, unpublished doctoral dissertation, ERIC and Northern Arizona University (1991).

Chapter 1: The future

1. Sources for most information are cited at the foot of page 38.

2. Bill Gates, *The Road Ahead,* Viking Penguin (1995).

3. John Naisbitt and Patricia Aburdene, *Megatrends 2000,* William Morrow (1990).

4. Total number of book-titles published in the world in 1990: 842,000, according to the Unesco Statistical Yearbook (1992).

5. See *Internet users 'likely to reach 500m by 2000',* article in *Financial Times* (May 13, 1996). Many other forecasters choose the higher number.

6. *The Learning Revolution* cover story, *Business Week* (February 28, 1994).

7. Michael A. Cusumano & Richard W. Selby, *Microsoft Secrets,* Harper-Collins (1996), give the figure of $75,000 for Microsoft's purchase of Q-DOS. Robert X. Cringely, *Accidental Empires,* Penguin (new edition, 1996), gives the figure at $50,000.

8. Bill Gates, *The Road Ahead,* Viking Penguin (1995).

9. David Sheff, *Game Over,* Coronet (1993).

10. Ray Hammond, *Digital Business* (1996).

11. *Winner take all,* article in *Time* (September 16, 1996).

12. Nicholas Negraponte, *Being Digital,* Vintage Books (1995).

13. 1.12.

14. *The Information Appliance,* annual report on information technology, *Business Week* (June 24, 1996).

15. Introduction.2.

16. 1.15.

17. Stan Shih: interview with G.D. in Taiwan (June 1996).

18. *The World Economy Survey,* supplement to *The Economist* (Sept. 28, 1996).

19. John Naisbitt predictions in this chapter, unless sourced to a book, are from a G.D. interview in Cambridge, Mass., soon after the publication of *Megatrends 2000* (1990).

20. Gordon Dryden, *How to Become an Educational Silicon Valley,* article in *New Zealand Herald* (August 26, 1998).

21. *Wired Is a Way of Life,* part of the cover story in *Newsweek* (November 9, 1998).

22. 1.20.

23. 1.20.

24. 1.21.

25. Sterling Seagrave, *Lords of the Rim,* Corgi (1996).

26. Daniel Burstein and Arne de Keijzer, *Big Dragon,* Simon & Schuster (1998). Also: Jim Rohwer, *Asia Rising,* Nicholas Brealey (1996), whose excellent book uses a World Bank forecast showing China reaching world top ranking earlier in the 21st century. Both forecasts are based on what economists call "purchasing power parity", rather than gross national product using international exchange-rate comparisons: PPP being a more accurate guide to what people can actually buy with their income.

27. Peter Drucker's forecasts are in *The New Realties,* Harper & Row (1989); John Naisbitt's in *Megatrends 2000* and *Megatrends Asia;* Kenichi Ohmae's in *The Borderless World,* Fontana (1990); and Robert Reich's in *The Work of Nations,* Simon & Schuster (1991).

28. *Europe's Most Respected Companies,* survey in *Financial Times,* (Sept. 18, 1996) updates Tom Peter's figures, including reductions in the number of ABB business centers. Barnevik has since stepped down as CEO, and is now non-executive chairman.

29. Franchising predictions from Steven S. Raab, with Gregory Matusky, in *Blueprint For Franchising a Business,* John Wiley (1987).

30. Louise E. Boone and David L. Kurtz in *Contemporary Business,* and *Contemporary Marketing,* Harcourt Brace (1996) provide franchising summaries. Also: John A. Quelch and Nathalie Laidler, *Mary Kay Cosmetics: Asian Market Entry,* in *Global Marketing Management: Cases and Readings,* Addison-Wesley (1995).

31. 1.19.

32. World tourist predictions: John Naisbitt & Patricia Aburdene, *Megatrends 2000,* Morrow (1990).

33. Japanese tourist goals, from Maarten Wevers, *Japan, its Future and New Zealand,* Victoria University Press (1988).

34. Charles Handy, *The Age of Unreason,* Hutchinson (1989).

35. 1.19.

36. *Tomorrow's Second Sex,* article in *The Economist* (September 28, 1996).

37. Tony Buzan: interview in Marlow, England, with G.D. (1990).

38 to 42. 1.18.

43. Most data on the aging of the population from Ken Dychtwald, *Age Wave,* Bantam (1990).

Chapter 2: Why not the best?

1. Richard L. Measelle and Morton Egol, *Transforming Education: Breakthrough Quality at Lower Cost,* Arthur Andersen (1996).

2. Canadian Royal Commission report, *The Love Of Learning* (1995).

3. Don Tapscott, *Growing Up Digital,* McGraw Hill (1998).

4. 2.3. But also: *The Digital Economy,* McGraw Hill (1996), and the book edited by him, *Blueprint to the Digital Economy,* McGraw Hill (1998).

5. John Naisbitt, *Megatrends Asia,* Simon & Schuster (1996).

6. Quoted in 2.3.

7. Don Tapscott, *The Digital Economy,* McGraw Hill (1996).

8. 2.3.

9. Early childhood brain development: see more detailed research, pages 227-231.

10. New Zealand hearing problems: *Child Hearing in New Zealand, Strategic Directions,* N.Z. Health Department (1991). American figures from Burton L. White, *The First Three Years,* Prentice Hall (1986).

11. Prof. Crawford: interview in London, with G.D. (1990).

12. University study showing percentage of new mothers "at risk": a 10-year research project carried out by the Psychology Department, University of Otago Medical School, Dunedin, New Zealand, and summarized in *Pacific Network,* Pacific Foundation, Auckland, New Zealand (February, 1992).

13. H.D. Hirsch, *Cultural Literacy,* Bantam, Australia (1988).

14. Elizabeth G. Hainstock, *The Essential Montessori,* Plume, New York (1996). Paula Polk Lillard, *Montessori: A Modern Approach, Schocken Books,* New York, has additional information on Professor Kilpatrick's role in curbing the Montessori movement in America.

15. John Morss, *Growing Up,* Longman Paul, New Zealand (1991). Margaret Donaldson, *Children's Minds,* Fontana/Collins, Glasgow (1978), also covers critiques of Jean Piaget.

Chapter 3: Meet your amazing brain

1. Ronald Kotulak, *Inside The Brain,* Andrews and McMeel (1996).

2. 3.1

3. 1.37.

4. Robert Ornstein and Richard F. Thompson, with illustrations by David Macauley, *The Amazing Brain,* Houghton Mifflin Company (1984).

5. Introduction.18.

6. 3.4.

7. 3.4

8. Paul D. MacLean, *The Triune Brain*

in Evolution, Plenum (1990).

9. Howard Gardner, *Frames of Mind,* Basic Books (1983).

10. Colin Rose: interview in Aston Clinton, Bucks, England, with G.D. (1990).

11. Marian Diamond, interview in Berkeley, CA, with G.D. (1990). For more scientific data, see Marian Cleeves Diamond, *Enriching Heredity,* Macmillan (1988).

12. For excellent coverage of the history of Polynesian Pacific explorations, see the Australian Broadcasting Commission's television series, *Man On The Rim,* especially episode 11, *The Last Horizon.*

13. According to the BBC television series, *The Story of English,* the English language has over 550,000 words, but the number continues to increase. The TV series has been adapted as an excellent book: Robert Crum, William Cran and Robert MacNeil, *The Story of English,* Faber and Faber/BBC Books (1986).

14. Specific Diagnostic Studies Inc. analyzes student profiles through its Learning Channel Preference Checklist. It has now collated results from 5,300 students, grades 5 through 12, in the United States, Hong Kong and Japan.

15. Wilder Penfield and Herbert Jasper, *Epilepsy and the Functional Anatomy of the Human Brain,* Little Brown (1954).

16. 3.1

17. Candace B. Pert, *Molecules of Emotion, Why You Feel The Way You Feel,* Simon & Schuster (1997).

Chapter 4: A do-it-yourself guide

1. Marilyn King, from *Dare To Imagine,* an article in *On The Beam,* published by New Horizons for Learning (Fall, 1991).

2. Colin Rose, *Accelerated Learning,* Dell (1985).

3. Terry Wyler Webb, with Douglas Webb, *Accelerated Learning With Mu-*

sic—a Trainer's Manual, Accelerated Learning Systems, Georgia (1990).

4. Georgi Lozanov, *Suggestology and Outlines of Suggestopedy,* Gordon and Breach (1978); Donald Schuster and Charles Gritton, *Suggestive Accelerative Learning and Teaching,* Gordon and Breach (1985); Lynn Dhority, *The ACT Approach: The Artful Use of Suggestion for Integrative Learning,* Gordon and Breach (1991); Richard Bandler and John Grindler, *Using Your Brain For a Change,* Real People Press (1986); Georgi Lozanov and Evalina Gateva, *The Foreign Language Teachers Suggestopedic Manual,* Gordon and Breach (1988); Tony Stockwell, *Accelerated Learning: in Theory and Practice,* EFFECT (1992).

5. Tony Buzan, *Make The Most Of Your Mind,* Linden (1984).

6. 3.11.

7. Accelerated Learning Systems, 50 Aylesbury Road, Aston Clinton, Aylesbury, Burkc, HP22 5AH, England.

8. 3.13.

9. J.A. van Ek, *The Threshold Level for Modern Language Learning in Schools,* Longman Paul (1976) for Council of Europe. The most-used 1700 words in the English language, from the Extended Ayres List, are listed by Romalda Bishop Spalding in *The Writing Road to Reading,* Quill/William Morrow (1990).

10. The 12-act play system is used by Accelerated Learning Systems, U.K.

11. 4.4.

Chapter 5: How to think for successful ideas

1. *The Adult Learner,* article in *New Horizons for Learning* magazine (spring 1993).

2. *The World Book Encyclopedia.*

3 Frank Rose, *East of Eden: The End of Innocence at Apple Computer,* Arrow Books (1989).

4. John F. Love, *McDonald's: Behind The Arches,* Bantam (1986).

5. *The Sunday Times Rich List* (1996).

6. Part of this chapter originally appeared in Gordon Dryden's *Out Of The Red,* William Collins (1978).

7. Slywotzky, Adrian J.; and Morrison, David J., *The Profit Zone,* Times Books, (1998).,

8. 5.7.

9. Ogilvy, David, *Ogilvy on Advertising,* Crown Publishers (1983).

10. Peter Ellyard, speech to New Zealand school principals (1992).

11. William J.J. Gordon is the founder of Synetics Educational Systems Inc.

12: Peter Evans and Geoff Deehan, *The Keys to Creativity,* Grafton (1988).

13. Alex Osborn, *Applied Imagination,* Charles Schribner's Sons (1953).

14. James L. Adams, *Conceptual Block-busting,* Penguin (1987).

15. Masaaki Imai, *Kaizen: The Key To Japan's Competitive Success,* Random House (1986).

16. 5.15.

17. Toshihiko Yamashita, *The Panasonic Way,* Kohansha International (1987).

18. Edward de Bono, *De Bono's Thinking Course,* BBC Books (1982).

19. Roger von Oech, *A Whack On The Side Of The Head,* Warner Books (1983).

20. 5.14.

21. 5.18.

22. Edward de Bono, *Teaching Thinking,* Penguin (1977).

Chapter 6: Right from the start

1. Professor Marian Diamond points out (letter to authors, June, 1993) that, while no one develops another cortical brain cell from the time of birth, brain cells do continue to multiply after birth: in the dentate gyrus of the hippocampal complex; granule cells in the cerebellum; and nerve cells in the olfactory epithelium.

2. Interview with G.D. (1990).

3. Dr. Ian James, interview in New York, with G.D. (1990).

4. Jane M. Healy, *Your Child's Growing Mind,* Doubleday (1987).

5. 2.12.

6. *Children in Crisis,* article in *Fortune* (August 10, 1992).

7. 6.6.

8. The Diagram Group, *The Brain: A User's Manual,* Berkley Books (1983); Richard M. Restak, *The Brain: The Last Frontier,* Warner Books (1979).

9. 3.4.

10. G.D., *Where To Now?* television series, produced by Pacific Foundation, New Zealand (1991), scripts reproduced in *Pacific Network* (February, 1992).

Chapter 7: The vital years

1. Benjamin S. Bloom, *Stability and Change in Human Characteristics,* John Wiley (1964).

2. 1.37.

3. 7.1.

4. Research on male-female brain differences summarized in *The Learning Brain,* by Eric Jensen, published by Turning Point for Teachers (1994).

5. Dr. Phil Silva, Director of the Dunedin Multidisciplinary Health and Development Research Unit, University of Otago Medical School, interview in Dunedin New Zealand, with G.D. (1991).

6. The Christchurch study is financed by the New Zealand Medical Research Council. Percentages are from Dr. David Fergusson, Program Director, in interview with G.D. (1991).

7. Research by Jack Canfield, 1982, covering 100 children each assigned to a researcher for a day; results summarized by Bobbi DePorter, *Quantum Learning,* Dell (1992).

8. Richard M. Restak, *The Infant Mind,* Doubleday (1986).

9. Ruth Rice, *The Effects of Tactile-Kinesthetic Stimulation on the Subse-*

quent Development of Premature In-fants, University of Texas (1975).

10. Prof. Lyelle L. Palmer, *Kindergarten Maxi-Stimulation: Results over Four Years,* at Westwood School, Irving, Texas (1971-75); *A Chance to Learn: Intensive Neuro-Stimulation in Transition Kindergarten,* at Shingle Creek Elementary School, Minneapolis (1989-90); and *Smooth Eye Pursuit Stimulation Readiness in Kindergarten,* at Shingle Creek Elementary School, Minneapolis (1990-91).

11. Palmer interview and correspondence with J.V. (1993).

12. Information gained during Minnesota visit by G.D. (1995).

13. Interview with J.V. (1996).

14. Notes provided by Jerome Hartigan to G.D. (1995).

15. Janet Doman interview in Philadelphia with G.D. (1990).

16. Dorothy Butler, *Babies Need Books,* Penguin (1984).

17. 3.13.

18. 4.9.

19. Peggy Kaye, *Games for Learning,* Noonday Press (1991).

20. G.D. first interviewed Glenn Doman, in Melbourne, Australia, for New Zealand radio and television in 1974; he has studied the Doman method in action in Australia, New Zealand and especially at The Institutes for the Achievement of Human Potential in Philadelphia, in 1988 (for one week), 1989 (for one week), in 1990 (during a three-day television recording session) and during the preparation of this book. Dryden has yet to meet one published critic of Doman who has actually visited The Institutes or studied his work at first hand. In fact, one highly qualified professor, and the leader of a model school, interviewed for this book, publicly criticized Doman's methods while admitting to using them extensively.

21. Glenn Doman interview in Philadelphia, PA, with G.D. (1990).

22. Dr. Noor Laily Dato' Abu Bakar and Mansor Haji Sukaimi, *The Child of Excellence,* The Nury Institute, Malaysia (1991).

23. Felicity Hughes, *Reading and Writing Before School,* Jonathan Cape (1971).

24. 3.11.

25. All details of the Missouri Parents As Teachers program obtained by G.D. during videotaping visit to St. Louis, Missouri (1990).

26. 7.25.

27. Ferguson Florissant School District data from visit to the district by G.D. (1990).

28. Phone interview with G.D. (1994).

29. Burton L.White, *The First Three Years Of Life,* Prentice Hall (1986). Note that, while this is an excellent book overall, many other child-development specialists disagree with Dr. White on the use of "baby bouncers" and "walkers". Dr. White correctly recommends that these should not be used for more than 15 minutes at a time; others say that any use of them encourages some parents to use them as "baby sitters", and prolonged use can cause developmental problems, particularly if they are used as a substitute for the important neurological stage of crawling.

30. Interview entitled *The Brains Behind The Brain,* in *Educational Leadership* (November, 1998).

31. 7.30.

32. Article, *Forward* (October 9, 1992).

33. The HIPPY program has been introduced into New Zealand by the Pacific Foundation. Details have come from Foundation Executive Director Lesley Max.

34. Amy J. L. Baker and Cyaya S. Piotrikowski, in *The Effects of Participation in HIPPY on Children's Classroom Adaptation: Teacher Ratings,* published by the National Council of Jewish Women, Center for the Child, New York.

35. 7.22.

36. Co-author Dryden was the original Chief Executive of the Pacific Foundation.

37. Interview with G.D. (1997).

38. G.D. visit to Sweden (1990).

39. Paula Polk Lillard, *Montessori: A Modern Approach,* Schocken Books, provides an excellent guide to Montessori's work.

40. Details of the Foundation Center for Phenomenological Research gained on a visit by G.D. to the Artesia II Montessori center, at French Camp, CA. (1990). Information updated from Foundation Center, email to authors (1999).

41. 7.40.

42. Maria Montessori, *The Montessori Method,* Schocken Books (1964): first published in English in 1912.

43. Pauline Pertab interview with G.D. in Auckland, New Zealand (1993).

44. Both G.D. and J.V. visited Montessori International in 1995 and produced a pilot television program on its methods.

45. G.D. videotaped the Montessori Farm School program in 1995 for *FUNdamentals.*

46. New Zealand Ministry of Education, *Education for the 21st Century,* (July, 1993).

47. California early-childhood attendance figures as at 1992.

48. Information supplied by the Academy to J.V. (1996).

Chapter 8: The secret heart of learning

1. Introduction. 22.

2. Published by R.S.A., London (1990).

3. *Children in Crisis* reports, *Fortune International* (August 10, 1992).

4. 8.3.

5. 6.10.

6. Georgi Lozanov, *Suggestology and Outlines of Suggestopedy,* Gordon and Breach (1978).

7. Joseph Romanos, *Makers of Champions: Great New Zealand Coaches,* Mills Publications, Lower Hutt, New Zealand (1987).

8. Tom Peters, *Thriving on Chaos,* Pan (1989).

9. Hewlett-Packard, from personal visit by G.D. to Silicon Valley headquarters (1981).

10. Toshihiko Yamashita,*The Panasonic Way,* Kodansha (1987).

11. 8.8.

12. Akio Morita, *Made In Japan,* Signet-Dutton (1986).

13. G.D. and J.V. visit to Andersen Consulting University, St. Charles. Ill. (1998).

14. Robert Slater, *Jack Welch and the GE Way,* McGraw-Hill (1999).

15. 3.10.

16. Northview Elementary School information, originally from *Schools in America,* PBS TV documentary, produced by MacNeil Lehrer (1990). Amended grade-average figures supplied by Dr. Yunk to authors (1993).

17. 8.16.

18. All information from personal interviews by G.D. (1991).

19. Robert C. Christopher, *The Japanese Mind,* Pan (1984).

20. Japanese experiences, unless otherwise attributed, from Jeannette Vos research visit to Japan as a Stanford University Japan Project Fellow (1991).

21. Katherine Lewis, *Cooperation and Control in Japanese Nursery Schools,* published in *Comparative Education Review* (Vol. 28, No. 1, 1984).

22. 8.19.

23. John Naisbitt, *Megatrends Asia,* Simon & Schuster (1996).

24. 8.23.

Chapter 9: True learning

1. Guggenheim School information collected by G.D. during videotaping of *Where To Now?* television program in Chicago (1990) and follow-up interview with Nancy Ellis, new Guggenheim principal, by J.V. (1993).

2. *Accounting is Ezy,* presented by Nimai & Partners, 23 Grand Central Ave., Hallet Cove, Adelaide 5158, Australia.

3. French course at Beverley Hills High School, Sydney, Australia, from Seven Network TV magazine program, Sydney (1990).

4. 240 teaching games, by Tony Stockwell, of Liechtenstein, devised for individual clients. See his summary in *Accelerated Learning in Theory and Practice,* EFFECT, Liechtenstein (1992). The book is written in the form of a Lozanov-type presentation.

5. *The Great Pacific Century Marketing Game,* devised by G.D., which is now being adapted as part of *The Ideas Revolution.*

6. Figures compiled from seminar registrations.

7. Devised by Andrew Smith, of Personal Effectiveness Consultants Ltd., P.O. Box 33385, Takapuna, Auckland, New Zealand.

8. J.V. is one of the facilitators at this program, organized by Dr. John Grassi.

9. From Glenn Capelli seminar at SALT Convention in Minneapolis, MN. (1992).

10. 9.4.

11. Interview with G.D., Washington, D.C. (1990).

12. Interview at Sodertalji High School, Sweden, with G.D. (1990).

13. Interview in San Francisco, California, with G.D. (1990).

14. In Stockwell's book, 9.4.

15. Capelli *Attitude* tape from True Learning Center, Perth, Australia.

16. 4.3.

17. 4.3 summarizes.

18. 9.13.

19. 4.3.

20. Sheila Ostrander and Lynn Schroeder, *Superlearning,* Dell (1969), reported claims that some students had learned up to 3,000 foreign words in a day. Lozanov in 8.6 records 1,000 to 1,200 words being learned per day, with a recall rate of 96.1% (see table, page 308). The present co-authors have seen no authenticated research evidence to justify higher claims than this, and have seen no evidence outside Bulgaria of figures as high as 1,000 to 1,200.

21. 4.3.

22. Book, 9.4.

23. 9.13.

24. 4.3.

25. Interview with GD (1990).

26. 9.1.

27. 9.3.

28. Written analysis of Dr. Dhority's results, provided by Dr. Palmer.

29. Conversation with J.V. (1993).

30. Interview with J.V. (1996).

31. Interview with J.V. (1996).

32. School results summary provided by Leo Wood (1996).

33. Lyall Watson, *Supernature,* Coronet. A three-hour G.D. interview with Lyall Watson on Radio i in Auckland, New Zealand, in 1973 (plus an interview with Glenn Doman in Melbourne, Australia, in 1974) provided the initial catalyst for the research by G.D. that eventually led to this book.

34. 9.20.

Chapter 10: Do it in style

1. From *Learning and Teaching Styles and Brain Behavior,* newsletter of the Association for Supervision and Curriculum Development and the Oklahoma State Department of Education, Oklahoma (1988).

2. *Survey of Research on Learning Styles,* in *Educational Leadership* (Vol. 46, No. 6, March 1989).

3, 4 and 5. 10.1.

6. Howard Gardner, *Frames Of Mind,* Basic Books (1983).

7. Lloyd Geering, *In The World Today,* Allen & Unwin and Port Nicholson Press, Wellington (1988).

8. Michael Grinder, *Righting The Educational Conveyor Belt,* Metamorphous Press (1989).

9. Rita Dunn, Jeffrey S. Beadry and Angela Klavas, *Survey of Research on Learning Styles,* in *Educational Leadership* (Vol. 46, No. 6, pages 53-58).

10. 10.9.

11. From a summary of the Dunns' research, *Learning and Teaching Styles and Brain Behavior,* published by the Association for Supervision and Curriculum Development and the Oklahoma Department of Education Newsletter (1988) .

12. Interview with GD (1999).

13. Creative Learning Company's website: www.clc.co.nz.

14. Anthony Gregorc, *An Adult's Guide to Style,* Gabriel Systems, Maynard, Mass. (1982).

15. This test, while adapted from Anthony Gregorc's, first appeared in this form in: Bobbi DePorter, with Mike Hernacki, *Quantum Learning,* Dell Publishing (1992).

16. Adapted from book in 10.15.

17. Robert Sternberg, *Beyond I.Q.,* Cambridge University Press, U.S.A. (1985).

18. Howard Gardner, *The Unschooled Mind,* Basic Books (1991).

Chapter 11: Catching up quick

1. From *Children in Crisis,* Fortune International (August 10, 1992).

2. 3.11.

3. 7.10.

4. Helen Keller, *The Story Of My Life,* Doubleday (1954); Helen E. Waite, *Valiant Companions: Helen Keller and Anne Sullivan Macy,* Macrae (1959); Norman Richards, *Helen Keller,* Children's Press

(1968).

5. Thomas Armstrong, *In Their Own Way,* J.P. Tarcher (1987).

6. Brigette Allroggen, *Munich Institute of Technology,* in *Three In One Concepts Newsletter,* Three In One Concepts, Burbank, CA. (1993).

7. Kathy Carroll, interview with J.V. (1993).

8. Gordon Stokes and Daniel Whiteside, *One Brain: Dyslexic Learning Correction and Brain Integration,* Three In One Concepts, Burbank, CA. (1984).

9. Paul and Gail Dennison, *Brain Gym,* Edu-Kinesthetics, Ventura, CA. (1988).

10. Sierra Vista Junior School results reported in *Diffusing Dyslexia,* by Lee Wasserwald, special education teacher, in *1985 Grant Results Report,* available through Three In One Concepts, Burbank, CA.

11. G.D. videotape interviews with Hartigans (1996).

12 Renee Fuller, *In Search of the I.Q. Correlation* and *Ball-Stick-Bird Series,* Ball-Stick-Bird Publications, Stony Brook, New York; and *Beyond I.Q.,* an article by Fuller summarizing her work, *In Context* magazine (winter 1988).

13. Elizabeth Schulz, *A Long Way To Go,* article in *American Teacher* magazine (February 1993).

14. Four-minute reading program, and Donna Awatere quotation, from *Pacific News,* magazine of Radio Pacific, Auckland, New Zealand (1981).

15. Interview with G.D. (1991).

16. *The New Zealand School Journal* is published by Learning Media Ltd, Wellington, New Zealand.

17. John Medcalf, quotes from interview with G.D. (1991), and some material summarized from his book, *TARP: The Tape Assisted Reading Program,* Special Education Service, Flaxmere, Hastings, New Zealand.

18. 11.17.

19. Marie Garbo, *Igniting The Literacy Revolution Through Reading Styles,*

article in *Educational Leadership,* Association for Supervision and Curriculum Development, Alexandria, VA. (October, 1990).

20. Rhonda Godwin, interview with G.D. (1991).

21. Research data gathered by John Medcalf and related to G.D. in interview (1991).

22. Forbes Robinson, *Look, Listen: Learning To Read Is Incredibly Simple,* J.K. Marketing, Nelson, New Zealand (1986).

23. 11.22, and in *The Putaruru Experiment,* a Television New Zealand documentary, TVNZ archives.

24. 11.22. Eastbourne children's reading ability tested before and after the experiment, using the Schonell Graded Word Recognition Test.

25. 11.22. Scottish results evaluated using Burt Word Reading Test.

26. 11.22. Canadian results derived from the Schonell Graded Word Recognition Test.

27. 11.22.

28. *Reading Recovery in New Zealand,* a report from the Office of Her Majesty's Chief Inspector of Schools, published by the British Government Office for Standards in Education, London (1993).

29. Lynley Hood, *Sylvia: The Biography of Sylvia Ashton-Warner,* Viking, Auckland, N.Z. (1988). Sylvia Ashton-Warner, *Teacher,* Penguin (1966).

30. 7.23.

31. 11.13.

32. SEED information, mainly collected by G.D. on visit to SEED office in Oakland, CA (1989).

Chapter 12: High school reform

1. Our thanks to The Management Edge Ltd., P.O. Box 12461, Wellington, New Zealand, and especially to Ross Peddler, Director, for assembling various reports on Mt. Edgecumbe High School.

2. Myron Tribus, *The Application of Quality Management Principles in Education at Mt. Edgecumbe High School, Sitka, Alaska, (1990),* reprinted in *An Introduction to Total Quality for Schools,* American Association of School Administrators (1991).

3. Mission Statement, supplied by the school.

4. 12.2.

5. *Opportunity and Solution Overview,* report by Mt. Edgecumbe High School (October 30, 1990), available through the school.

6. 12.5.

7. 12.2, and pilot-company organizational graphics from the school.

8. 12.2.

9. The goal to produce quality individuals, from the school's *Constancy of Purpose* statement (October 30, 1990). 46 percent of school graduates are attending post-secondary school.

10. *Reading, Writing and Continuous Improvement,* an article in *Competitive Times,* the Total Quality Management Newsletter, published by GOAL/QPC (Number 1, 1991).

11. 12.2.

12. Dr. Nolan: interview in Palmerston North with G.D. (1991).

13. C.J. Patrick Nolan and David H. McKinnon, *Case Study of Curriculum Innovation in New Zealand: The Freyberg Integrated Studies Project,* Massey University (April 23, 1991).

14 to 18. 12.12.

19. Interview with G.D. (1997).

20. Don Brown, interview with G.D. at Kapiti College, Paraparaumu, New Zealand (1991).

21. 12.20.

22. Edna Tait interview, with G.D. at Tikipunga High School, Whangarei, New Zealand (1991).

23. Introduction 15.

24. From J.V. diary notes of her first day as instructor at SuperCamp.

25. 12.23, with specific parent comments from SuperCamp files.

26. Abstract from 1998 masters dissertation by Sarah Singer-Nourie, who is one of the co-authors of *Quantum Teaching.*

Chapter 13. Planning tomorrow's schools

1. Lester Finch: interview in West Flaxmere, New Zealand, with G.D. (1991).

2 *South Bay Schools Go Extra Mile For Reading Success,* article in Los Angeles Times (June 1, 1992). Phil Grignon is no longer superintendent of the district.

3. Information from J.V. and G.D. interview with Dr. Susan Schmidt, of the South Bay School District, San Diego (1992), updated by Al Walters, South Bay Union School District Director of the local HOSTS program (May, 1999).

4. From Master's Academy and College Promise, supplied by Superintendent Tom Rudmik by email to JV (May, 1999).

5. 13.4.

6. Information on Cascade Elementary School from *A Teachers' Perspective,* by Bruce Campbell, in *Creating The Future,* edited by Dee Dickinson, Accelerated Learning Systems, England (1991).

7. Miriam Kronish: interviews from Needham, Massachusetts, by phone with G.D. and J.V. (1993). J.V. also has first-hand experience with John Eliot School's accelerated integrative learning program.

8. Rosemary Green: interview by phone from Needham, Massachusetts, with G.D. (1993).

9. J.V. is a longtime senior summer staff member at Cambridge College.

10: River Oaks School information: from Apple Computer presentation at Auckland College of Education, New Zealand (1992).

11. 1.2.

12. 1.2.

Chapter 14: Tomorrow's business world

1. Chis McGowan and Jim Mc-Cullough, *Entertainment in the Cyber Zone,* Random House (1995).

2. *Wired* magazine, British edition (September 1996).

3. From G.D.'s personal experience as publisher of *Trends.*

4 to 6. 14.1

7. 1.2.

8. *Jack Welch's Encore,* cover story in *Business Week,* international edition (October 28, 1996).

9. 14.8.

10. 14.8.

11. 14.8.

12. 14.8.

13. Peter M. Senge, *The Fifth Discipline,* Random House (1992).

14. 14.13.

15. Tom Peters, *Liberation Management,* Knopf (1992).

16. 14.15.

17. 14.15.

18. *Financial Times* supplement (September 18, 1996).

19. Casper Shih interview with G.D. in Taiwan (June, 1996) and portfolio of speech notes provided by China Productivity Center.

20. 14.19.

21. Rank Hovis information and quotations gained on GD visit to Selby, 1996.

22. *The Burton Way,* summary prepared by G.D. after discussion with John Hoerner and senior executives of The Burton Group (July, 1996).

23. Interview with G.D. (Sept. 1996).

24. 14.23.

25. Alvin Toffler, *PowerShift,* Bantam (1990).

26. Interview with G.D. (Sept. 1996).

27. Interview with G.D. (Sept. 1996).

Chapter 15: Just do it!

1. Interview with G.D. (July 1997).

2. Quotes from Helena H. Waldenberg and Michael S. Bogolea, *From Welfare to Renaissance: The New Swedish Model,* Carpe Vitam Foundation, Lemshaga, Sweden (1997).

3. Letter to J.V. (January, 1999).

4. All Apple ACOT examples quoted from *Education & Technology,* edited by Charles Fisher, David C. Dwyer and Keith Yocam, published by Apple Books and Jossey-Bass Publishers (1996).

5. Main Wendy Pye information taken from Paul Smith, *Success in New Zealand Businesss,* Hodder Moa Beckett (1996), and newspaper files.

6. Developed by Barbara Prashnig and Professor Ken Dunn, produced by Creative Learning Co., New Zealand.

7. Interview with G.D. (May 1997).

8. Christopher Ball in *For Life: a vision for learning in the 21st century,* RSA, London, UK (1996).

9. Letter to J.V. (1996).

10. Information supplied by The Center for Accelerated Learning, Lake Geneva, Wis., USA (1996).

11. 15.10

12. 15.10

13. 15.10

14. Graham T. Crocombe, Michael J. Enright and Michael E. Porter, *Upgrading New Zealand's Competitive Advantage,* Oxford University Press (1991).

15. Chen Jingpan, *Confucius as a Teacher,* Foreign Language Press, Beijing (1990).

16. Correspondence with G.D. (1996).

17. G.D. interview with Choon Tan and Michael Tan (1991).

18. Article in *The Press,* Christchurch, New Zealand (January 26, 1996).

19. Email to authors (May, 1999).

Acknowledgments and thanks ▰▰▰▰▰▰▰▰

Both authors thank:

* The pioneers in many fields on whose shoulders this work stands. These include: Maria Montessori, Glenn Doman, Georgi Lozanov, Jean Piaget, Roger Sperry, Robert Ornstein, Marian Diamond, Paul MacLean, Tony Buzan, Howard Gardner, Robert Sternberg, Burton L. White, W. Edwards Deming, Don Schuster, John Grassi, Lyelle Palmer, Peter Kline, Laurence Martel, Rita and Ken Dunn, Paul and Gail Dennison, C.E. Beeby, Daniel Whiteside, Gordon Stokes, Bobbi DePorter, Eric Jensen, Don Campbell, Charles Schmid, Richard Bandler, John Grinder, Michael Grinder, Freeman Lynn Dhority, Anthony Gregorc, John Le Tellier, Peter M. Senge, Charles Handy, Christopher Ball, Colin Rose, Tony Stockwell, Glenn Capelli, Barbara Prashnig, Bettie B. Youngs, Ivan Barzakov, Pamela Rand, Betty Shoemaker, Thomas Armstrong, Donald Treffinger, Tim Berners-Lee, Alan C. Kay, Bill Gates, Steve Jobs, and those whose names appear at the bottom of each left-hand "poster page" of this book.

* To all the other people around the world who have helped with interviews and assistance in many ways, notably:

* The Americas: *United States:* John Naisbitt, Miriam Kronish, Leo Wood, Mary Ellen Maunz, Nancy McNabb, Lisbeth Schorr, Dan Schorr, Jane Healy, Karen Pitman, Janet and Katie Doman, Dawn Price, Mary Jane Gill, Michael Alexander, Libyan Labiosa-Cassone, Philip Cassone, Joy Rowse, Sue Treffeison, Dee Dickinson, Nancy Margulies, Marilyn King, Lily Wong-Filmore, Susan Schmidt, Antonia Lopez, Lynn O'Brien, Valerie Barlous, Diane Loomans, Kim Zoller, Greg Cortepassi, Kathleen Carroll, Steven Garner, Mary Regnier, Von and Donna Stocking, Nancy Ellis, Peter and Anne Kenyon, and Mahesh Sharma. *Canada:* Paul Ruta, Tom Rudmik, Lane Clark, Doreen Agostino and Ed Gimpelj. *Brazil:* Eliana Rocha and E. Silva.

* The United Kingdom: Joanna Rose, Sheila Kitzinger, Norman Macrae, David Lewis, Michael Crawford, Vanda North, Peter, Paul, Katie and Claire Templeton, John Abbott, John Hoerner, Lesley Britton, Helen Watkins, Andrew Hughes-Hallett, Val and Margaret Edmunds, David Buffin, Philip Chambers, Jim and Pat Lennox, and the staff at Lansdowne College.

* Rest of Europe and Africa: *Sweden:* Ingemar and Gunilla Svantesson, Christopher Gudmundsson, Bam Bjorling, Stein Lindeberg, Stefan and Lola Holm, Pontus Pedersen, Ulla Eriksson. Agnetta Nilsson, Bengt-Eric Andersson, Bengt Lindquist, Barbara Martin, Bo Naesland, Agneta Borg, Barbro Martensson, Anders Larsson, Helena Wallenberg, Michael Bogolea, Bitte Johannesson, Gunilla Garde, Annike Airijoki, Tim Sefton, Ulf Lundberg, Mickey Thornblad,

Mats Oljons, Thomas Dahlqvist, Ingrid Bjorkegren- Frode and Kim Frode, Ann-Marie Odebas, Monica Lundberg, Kerstin Palmn, Onni Varg, and Mats and Irene Niklasson. *Norway:* Anne and Neil Carefoot. *Finland:* Camilla Newlander and Martin Grippenberg. *Liechtenstein:* Tony Stockwell. *Germany:* Rudolf Schulte, and Claudie Monnet. *The Netherlands:* Peter Schade and Nick van den IJssel. *South Africa:* Antony Lovell and Pita Ward.

* Asia-Pacific: *Singapore:* David Perry, Irene Chee, Bhim Mozoomdar, Dilip Mukerjea, Carmee Lim, Teo Chee Hean, Monica Yee, Teddy Ang, Tetsuo Nishizawa and Lim Tiat. *China:* Song Chaodi, Xie Jin, Xue Jianguo, Chen Jianxiang, Sun Bin, Steve Yan, Yan Jie, Jiang Xin, Denis Guo, the rest of the Clever Software team, and the executives at Shanghai Educational Television. *Australia:* Lindy Capelli, Keith McDonald, Alistair Rylatt. *Malaysia:* Terry Netto, Noor Laily Dato' Abu Bakar, Mansor Haji Sukaimi. *Taiwan:* Casper Shih, Stan Shih and John Wang.

* New Zealand: Noel Ferguson for The Learning Web's web site,Mark Beach, Kirsty Hayes, Jerome and Sophie Hartigan, Lesley Max, Pacific Foundation, ASB Charitable Trust, Joe Williams, Edna Tait, John Fleming, Pat Nolan, Phil Silva, Lester Finch, Bruce Kirk, Tony Hewett, Mike Gifford, John Medcalf, Lloyd Geering, Murray Brown, Don Brown, Bob Elliott, David Fergusson, Kay Bradford, Patrick Eisdell Moore, Pita Sharples, Pauline Pertab, Glenda Owen, Colin Follas, Ken Booth, Joy Clark, Graye Shattky, Choon Tan, Chrystal, Daniel and Stephen Witte, Colin Burr, Peter Ho and Kate Whitley.

Our thanks to those involved in the publishing venture, especially Bradley Winch Sr., Jeanne Iler, Susanna Polmares, Susan Remkus, Reg Birchfield, Ian and Diane Grant, Diane Rose: and to our translators in China, Taiwan, Sweden, Norway, Finland, Brazil and Korea.

Jeannette Vos thanks:

* My immediate family members and friends: Ed, Leisha and Summer Groenendal, Elly and John Van Barneveld, Jake and Jenny Groenendal, Rie and Jerry Kazimer, Carol Dempsey, Marilyn Gill, Pat Tanagon, Marina Smith, Don Lucas, Robert Jones, Jan McKittrick, Sandi Hendrickson, Helene and George Barfus, Donna Romanick, Carol Kennington, Ed Stracher, Theresa Mendivil, Jeff Haebig, Katharine Kertez, Donna Chester and Penny Wenger.

* My professional friends and colleagues and those who contributed on a personal level: Richard Packard, Mary Dereshewsky, Anne Nevin, Rolf Parta, Katharine Kertez, Robin Smith, Allison Lew, Jonathan Mitchell, Franziska Karlan, Elsie Begler. And to Gordon Dryden, whose partnership with this book has truly been a personal learning experience and revolution.

Gordon Dryden thanks:

* Margaret Dryden, for 41 years of love, wisdom, tolerance, support, great parenting and good fun. Sir Robert Mahuta, Tainui and MDC Investments for partnership in The Learning Web. And Jeannette Vos, for suggesting this book, for the outstanding teaching experience distilled into these pages, and for tolerance at seeing volumes of other material slashed and simplified in an editor's drive to make academic research understandable to general readers.

The Learning Revolution library

To start learning any subject (if you're a print-oriented learner) the co-authors recommend you read three or four simple introductory books on that subject by practical achievers, and then follow-up by reading more detailed material.

Suggestions follow, with the most simple introductory books, videotapes or kits marked *.

Obviously, new books are being published regularly, and you can update this list on the Web at:

www.thelearningweb.net.

Jeannette Vos also has additional regular updates, particularly covering seminars and training, at:

www.learning-revolution.com

WHERE DO I START?

*Rose, Colin, *Master It Faster,* Accelerated Learning Systems, UK (1999).

*Loomans, Diane; and Kohlberg, Karen, *The Laughing Classroom,* Kramer, Tiburon, CA (1993).

*Staff of New City School, *Multiple Intelligences: Teaching for Success, New City School,* St. Louis, Mo. (1994).

*DePorter, Bobbi; Reardon, Mark; and Singer-Nourie, Sarah, *Quantum Teaching,* Allyn & Bacon, Boston (1999).

MUSIC: INTRODUCTION

*Vos, Jeannette, *The Music Revolution,* Learning Web, Auckland, New Zealand (late 1999).

* Campbell, Don, *The Mozart Effect,* Avon Books, New York (1997).

*Barzakov, Ivan and Associates, *Essence & Impact* (includes *How to Use Music),* Novata, CA (1995).

*Andersen, Ole; Marsh, Marcy; and Harvey, Arthur, *Learn with the Classics,* LIND Institute, San Francisco (1999).

ACCELERATED LEARNING

*Rose, Colin; and Goll, Louise, *Accelerate Your Learning,* Accelerated Learning Systems, UK (1993): a kit.

*De Porter, Bobbi, *Quantum Learning,* Dell, New York (1992).

*Rose, Colin; and Nicholl, Malcolm. J., *Accelerated Learning For the 21st Century,* Accelerated Learning Systems, UK (1997).

* Frischnecht, Jacqueline; and Capelli, Glenn, *Maximizing Your Learning Potential,* Kendall/Hunt, Iowa (1995).

THE BRAIN

*Ornstein, Robert; *The Amazing Brain,* Houghton Mifflin, Boston (1984).

*Robert Kotulak, *Inside The Brain,* Andrews and McMeel, Kansas City, Mo. (1997).

*Sylwester, Robert, *A Celebration of Neurons: An Educator's Guide to the Human Brain,* ASCD, Alexandria, VA (1995).

*Diamond, Marian; and Hopson, Janet, *Magic Trees of the Mind: How to Nurture Your Child's Intelligence, Creativity, and Healthy Emotions from Birth Through Adolescence,* Plume, New York (1998).

*Herman, Ned, *The Creative Brain,* Brain Books, Lake Lure, NC (1989).

MIND MAPPING

*Mukerjea, Dilip, *Superbrain: Train Your Brain To Unleash the Genius Within By Using Memory Building, Mind Mapping, Speed Reading,* Oxford University Press, Singapore (1996).

*Mukerjea, Dilip, *Brainfinity,* Oxford University Press, Singapore (1997).

*Buzan, Tony, *The Mind Map Book— Radiant Thinking,* BBC, London (1993).

MINDSCAPES AND DRAWING

*Margulies, Nancy, *Mapping Inner Space,* Zephyr Press, Tucson, AZ. (1991).

*Margulies, Nancy, *Yes, You Can Draw!,* Accelerated Learning Systems, England (1991), with videotape.

*Betty Edwards, *Drawing On The Right Side Of The Brain,* Jeremy P. Tarcher, New York (1989).

CREATING NEW IDEAS

*Michalko, Michael, *Cracking Creativity,* Ten Speed Press, Berkeley, CA (1998).

*von Oech, Roger, *A Whack On The Side Of The Head,* Warner, New York (1990).

*Adams, James L., *Conceptual Blockbusting,* Penguin, New York (1987).

*von Oech, Roger, *Creative Whack Pack* (playing cards), U.S. Games Systems, Stamford, CT.

Michalko, Michael, *Thinkertoys,* Ten Speed Press, Berkeley, CA (1991).

Mukerjea, Dilip, *Braindancing,* The Brainware Press, Singapore (1998).

MEMORY

*Yepson, Roger B., *How to Boost Your Brain Power,* Thorsons, England (1987).

*Minninger, Joan, *Total Recall,* Thorsons, England (1989).

*Squire, Larry; and Kandel, Eric, *Memory: From Mind to Molecules,* Scientific American Library, New York (1999).

*Higbee, Kenneth L., *Your Memory: How it Works and How to Improve it,* Piatkus, London (1989).

Arp, Dave and Claudie, *60 One-Minute Memory Makers,* Thomas Nelson (1993).

Benson, Herbert, *Your Maximum Mind,* Avon, New York (1987).

Lorayne, Harry; and Lucas, Jerry, *The Memory Book,* Ballantine, New York (1975).

Buzan, Tony, *Use Your Perfect Memory,* Plume-Penguin, New York (1991).

INTELLIGENCE

*Goleman, Daniel, *Emotional Intelligence,* Bloomsbury, London (1996).

*Siler, Todd, *Think Like a Genius,* Bantam, New York (1997).

*Gardner, Howard, *Frames Of Mind,* Basic Books, New York (1983).

*Gardner, Howard, *The Unschooled Mind,* Basic Books, New York (1991).

FOR STUDENTS

*Cross, Ronald, *Peak Learning,* Jeremy P. Tarcher, New York (1991).

*Martel, Laurence, *School Success,* Learning Matters, Arlington, VA (1992).

*Sunbeck, Deborah, *Infinity Walk: Preparing Your Mind To Learn,* Jalmar Press, Torrance, CA (1996).

*Ellis, David B., *Becoming a Master Student,* College Survival, Rapid City, SD (1985).

FOR PARENTS

*Kline, Peter, *The Everyday Genius,*

Great Ocean Publishers, Arlington, VA (1988).

*Armstrong, Thomas, *In Their Own Way,* Jeremy Tarcher, LA (1987).

*Clark, Faith and Cecil, *Hassle-Free Homework,* Doubleday, NY (1989).

FOR TEACHERS

*Jensen, Eric, *SuperTeaching,* Kendall/Hunt, Dubuque, Iowa (1988).

*Caine, Renate Nummela and Geoffrey, *Unleashing the Power of Perpetual Change: The Potential of Brain-Based Teaching,* ASCD, Alexandria, VA (1997).

*Jensen, *Teaching With The Brain In Mind,* ASCD, Alexandria, VA (1998).

PARENTING FOR INFANTS

*Dryden, Gordon; and Rose, Colin, *FUNdamentals,* Accelerated Learning Systems, UK (1996): complete kit.

*Beck, Joan, *How To Raise a Brighter Child,* Fontana, London (1985).

*Marzolla, Jean; and Lloyd, Janice, *Learning Through Play,* Harper & Row (1972).

Healy, Jane, *Your Child's Growing Mind,* Doubleday, New York (1987).

Healy, Jane, *Endangered Minds,* Simon & Schuster, New York (1990).

White, Burton L., *The First Three Years of Life,* Prentice, Hall, New York (1986).

White, Burton L., *Raising a Delightful Unspoiled Child,* Simon & Schuster, New York (1994).

EARLY READING

*McLaren, Kristine A., *Integrated Reading Program,* Kmac For Kids, Auckland 1008, New Zealand (1999).

*Hughes, Felicity, *Reading And Writing Before School,* Jonathan Cape (1971).

*Young, Peter; and Tyre, Colin, *Teach Your Child To Read,* Fontana (1985).

*Doman, Glenn, *Teach Your Baby to Read,* Better Baby Press, Philadelphia (1979).

EARLY WRITING

*Martin, John Henry; and Friedberg, Andy, *Writing To Read,* Warner (1986).

*Spalding, Romalda Bishop and Walter T., *The Writing Road To Reading,* Quill/William Morrow, New York (1990).

CREATIVE WRITING

*Rico, Gabriel, *Writing The Natural Way,* J.P. Tarcher, Los Angeles, CA.

SPELLING

*Cripps, Charles; and Peters, Margaret L., *Catchwords,* Collins, London (1993).

*Hornsby, Beve; and Shear, Frula, *Alpha to Omega,* Heinemann, UK (1993).

MATHEMATICS

* *Help Your Child With Maths* (the book of the BBC TV series), BBC Books, London.

*Johnson, Virginia, *Hands-On Math,* Creative Teaching Press (1994).

* Doman, Glenn, *Teach Your Baby Math,* Better Baby Press, Philadelphia (1979).

GAMES FOR LEARNING

* Kaye, Peggy, *Games for Reading,* Pantheon Books (1994).

* Kaye, Peggy, *Games for Learning,* The Noonday Press (1991).

*Perry, Susan K, *Playing Smart (four to 14 years),* Free Spirit (1990).

GAMES FOR TEACHERS AND TRAINERS

*Thiagarajan, Sivasailam (Thiagi), *Diversity Stimulation Games* (1994); *Teamwork Games* (1994); *Cash Games* (1994); *More Cash Games* (1995); *Matrix Games* (1995); *Lecture Games* (1994); *Instructional Puzzles* (1995); *Creativity Games* (1996), all published by HRD Press.

LEARNING DIFFICULTIES

*Doman, Glenn, *What To Do About Your Brain-Injured Child,* Better Baby Press, Philadelphia (1974).

* Armstrong, Thomas, *The Myth of the A.D.D.S. Child,* Dutton, NY (1995).

*Vitale, Marbara Meister, *Unicorns Are Real: A Right-Brained Approach to Learning,* Jalmar Press, Torrance, CA (1982).

MUSIC FOR LEARNING

*Brewer, Chris Boyd; and Campbell, Don, *Rhythms of Learning,* Zephyr Press, Tucson, AZ (1990).

*Campbell, Don, *100 Ways to Improve Teaching with Your Voice and Music,* Zephyr Press, Tucson (1992).

*Merritt, Stephanie, *Mind, Music and Imagery,* Asian Publishing, Santa Rosa, CA (1996).

Barzakov, Ivan, *How to Read with Music,* Barzak Educational Institute, Novato, CA (1995).

MONTESSORI

*Elizabeth G. Hainstock, *The Essential Montessori,* Plume, New York (1997).

*Britton, Lesley, *Montessori: Play And Learn,* Vermilion (1992).

*Lillard, Paula Polk, *Montessori: A Modern Approach,* Schoken Books, New York.

Hainstock, Elizabeth G., *Teaching Montessori In The Home (the preschool years),* Plume, New York (1968).

Hainstock, Elizabeth T., *Teaching Montessori In The Home (the school years),* Plume, New York (1971).

Montessori, Maria, *The Montessori Method,* Schocken Books, New York (1964).

Montessori, Maria, *The Absorbent Mind,* Delta, New York (1989).

LOZANOV METHOD

*Lozanov, Georgi; and Gateva, Evalina, *The Foreign Language Teacher's Suggestopedia Manual,* Gordon and Breach, New York (1988).

*Lozanov, Georgi, *Suggestology and Outlines of Suggestopedy,* Gordon and Breach, New York, (1978).

*Stockwell, Tony, *Accelerated learning in Theory and Practice,* EFFECT, Liechtenstein (1992).

FOREIGN LANGUAGE TEACHING

*Dhority, Freeman Lynn; and Jensen, Eric, *Joyful Fluency: Brain-Compatible Second Language Acquisition,* The Brain Store, San Diego, CA (1998).

*Dhority, Lynn, *The ACT approach: The Artful Use of Suggestion for Integrative Learning,* Gordon & Breach, New York (1991, expanded edition).

FOREIGN LANGUAGE LEARNING

*Colin Rose, *Accelerated French,* Accelerated Learning Systems, Aston Clinton, Bucks, U.K. (full program).

* Colin Rose, *Accelerated Spanish,* Accelerated Learning Systems, Aston Clinton, Bucks, U.K. (full program).

*Colin Rose, *Accelerated Iralian,* Accelerated Learning Systems, Aston Clinton, Bucks, U.K. (full program)

*Colin Rose, *Accelerated German,* Accelerated Learning Systems, Aston Clinton, Bucks, U.K. (full program).

LEARNING & WORKING STYLES

*Prashnig, Barbara, *The Power Of Diversity,* David Bateman, Auckland, New Zealand (1998),

*Markova, Dawna, *How Your Child Is Smart,* Concari (1992).

*Carbo, Marie; Dunn, Rita and Ken, *Teaching Students to Learn Through Their Individual Learning Styles,* Allyn and Bacon, Boston (1991).

TEACHING THINKING

*De Bono, Edward, *Teaching Thinking,* Penguin, London (1977).

*De Bono, Edward, *Edward de Bono's Thinking Course,* BBC Books, London (1982).

*Frangenheim, Eric, *Reflections on Classroom Thinking Strategies,* Rodin, Loganholme, Qld, Australia (1995).

SELF ESTEEM

*Loomas, Diane with Julia, *Full Esteem Ahead,* Kramer, Tiburon, CA (1994).

*Youngs, Bettie, *The Vital 6 Ingredients of Self Esteem: How to Develop

Them In Your Students, Jalmar Press, Torrance, CA (1992). For teachers.

*Borba, Michele, *Esteem-Builders,* Jalmar Press, Torrance, CA (1989). For elementary teachers.

*McDaniel, Sandy; and Bielen, Peggy, *Project Self-Esteem,* Jalmar Press, Torrance, CA.

NEURO LINGUISTIC PROGRAMMING

*Bandler, Richard; and Grinder, John, *Using Your Brain For a Change,* Real People Press, Moab, Utah (1986).

*Grinder, Michael, *ENVoY: Your Personal Guide to Classroom Management,* Michael Grinder, Washington (1993).

*Grinder, Michael, *Righting The Educational Conveyor Belt,* Metamorphous Press, Portland (1989).

*Dilts, Robert; and Epstein, Todd A., *Dynamic Learning,* Meta, Capitola, CA (1996).

EDUCATION AND TECHNOLOGY

*Fisher, Charles; Dwyer, David C.; and Yocam, Keith (editors): *Education & Technology: Reflections on Computing in Classrooms,* Apple Press and Jossey-Bass, San Francisco (1996).

*McGowan, Chris; and McCullaugh, Jim, *Entertainment In The Cyber Zone,* Random House, New York (1995).

*Schank, Roger C.; and Cleary, Chip, *Engines For Learning,* Lawrence Erlbaum, Hillsdale, NJ (1995).

Lai, Kwok-Wing, *Net-Working—Teaching, Learning and Professional Development,* University of Otago Press, Dunedin, New Zealand (1999).

EDUCATIONAL KINESIOLOGY

*Dennison, Paul and Gail, *Brain Gym: Simple Activities For Whole Brain Learning,* Edu-Kinesthetics Inc., Ventura, California (1985).

*Stokes, Gordon; Whiteside, Daniel, *One Brain: Dyslexic Learning Correction and Brain Integration,* Three In One Concepts, Burbank CA (1987).

*Dennison, Paul E. and Gail E., *Edu-K for Kids! The Basic Manual on Educational Kinesiology for Parents and Teachers of Kids of All Ages,* Edu-Kinesthetics, Ventura, CA (1987).

Dennison, Paul E. and Gail E., *Brain Gym: Teacher's Edition,* Edu-Kinesthetics, Ventura, CA (1989).

Dennison, Gail E. and Paul E; and Teplitz, Jerry V., *Brain Gym for Business,* Edu-Kinesthetics, Ventura CA (1994).

MIND-BODY CONNECTION

*Pert, Candace, *Molecules of Emotion: Why You Feel the Way You Feel,* Simon & Schuster, New York (1997).

*Hannaford, Carla, *The Dominance Factor: How Knowing Your Dominant Eye, Ear, Brain, Hand & Foot Can Improve Your Learning,* Great Ocean Publishers, Arlington, VA (1997).

*Promislow, Sharon, *Making The Brain Body Conection,* Kinetic Publishing, West Vancouver, BC, Canada (1998).

Hannaford, Carla, *Smart Moves: Why Learning is Not All in Your Head,* Great Ocean Publishers, Arlington, VA (1995).

Hannaford, Carla; Shaner, Cherokee; Zachary, Sandry; and Grinde, Linda, *Education in Motion,* Edible Elephant Publications, Honaunau, Hawaii (1991).

Hartley, Linda, *Wisdom of the Body Moving: an introduction to body-mind centering,* North Atlantic Books, Berkeley, CA (1995).

TOMATIS METHOD

*Tomatis, Alfred, *The Ear of Language,* Stoddard, New York (1997).

*Gilmor, Timothy M.; Madaule, Paul; and Thompson, Billie (Editors); with Wilson, Tim, *About The Tomatis Method,* Listening Center Press, Toronto, Ont., Canada (1989).

TEACHING VALUES

*Eyre, Linda and Richard, *Teaching Your Children Values,* Simon & Schuster, New York (1993).

*Eyre, Linda and Richard, *Teaching

Your Children Joy, Simon & Schuster, New York (1994).

*Glenn, H. Stephen; and Nelson, Jane, *Raising Self-Reliant Childred in a Self-Indulgent World,* Prime Publishing (1989).

DIET AND LEARNING

*Morgan, Brian and Roberta, *Brain Food,* Pan, London (1987).

*Roberts, Gwilym, *Boost Your Child's Brain Power: How To Use Good Nutrition,* Thorsons, England (1988).

BUSINESS TRAINING

*Rylatt, Alistair; and Lohan, Kevin, *Creating Training Miracles,* Jolley-Bass, San Francisco, CA (1997).

*Bobbi DePorter, *Quantum Business,* Dell, New York (1997).

*Hayes, Kirsty, *A Practical Guide to Leadership Coaching,* The Learning Attitude, Wellington, New Zealand (1998).

LEARNING ORGANIZATIONS

*Senge, Peter M., *The Fifth Discipline,* Random House, Sydney (1992).

*Senge, Peter; Roberts, Charlotte; Ross, Richard B.; Smith, Bryan J.; and Kleiner, Art, *The Fifth Discipline Fieldbook,* Nicholas Brealey, London (1994).

THE FUTURE OF WORK

*Reich, Robert B., *The Work Of Nations,* Simon & Schuster, New York (1991).

*Rifkin, Jeremy, *The End of Work,* Tarcher/Putnam, New York (1995).

THE FUTURE

*Davis, Stan; and Meyer, Christopher, *Blur: The Speed of Change in the Connected Economy,* Addison-Wesley, Reading, MA (1998).

*Hamel, Gary, and Prahalad, C.K., *Competing For The Future,* Harvard Business School Press, Boston (1994).

*Handy, Charles, *Beyond Certainty,* Hutchinson, London (1995).

THE DIGITAL ECONOMY

*Kelly, Kevin, *New Rules For The New Economy,* Viking Penguin, New York (1998).

*Tapscott, Don (Editor), *Blueprint to the Digital Economy,* McGraw-Hill, New York (1998).

*Martin, Chuck, *The Digital Estate,* McGraw-Hill, New York (1996).

Gates, Bill, *Business @ The Speed of Thought,* Warner Books, New York (1999).

Tapscott, Don, *Growing Up Digital,* McGraw-Hill, New York (1998).

Negroponte, Nicholas, *Being Digital,* Vintage, New York (1996).

Downes, Larry; and Mui, Chunka, *Unleashing The Killer App.,* Harvard Business School Press, Boston, Mass (1998).

BUSINESS LEADERSHIP

*Slywotzky, Adrian J.; and Morrison, David, J, *The Profit Zone,* Times Books, New York (1997).

*Covey, Stephen, *The 7 Habits Of Highly Effective People,* Simon & Schuster, New York (1989).

*Semler, Ricardo, *Maverick!,* Arrow, London (1994).

TOTAL QUALITY MANAGEMENT

*Deming, W. Edwards, *Out Of Crisis,* M.I.T, Boston, Mass (1986).

*Imai, Masaaki, *Kaizen: The Key to Japan's Competitive Success,* Random House, New York (1986).

*Wilson, Mary, *The Deming Management Method,* Dodd Mead (1986).

BUSINESS DEVELOPMENT

*Boone, Louis E.; and Jurtz, David L., *Contemporary Business,* Dryden Press, Orlando Fl. (regularly updated).

*Boone, Louis E.; and Jurtz, David L., *Contemporary Marketing,* Dryden Press, Orlando Fl. (regularly updated).

*Rapp, Stan; and Collins, Tom, *Beyond Maxi-Marketing,* McGraw-Hill, New York (1994).

Other recommended reading and resources ▬▬▬

Adams, James L., *The Care and Feeding of Ideas,* Penguin, London (1986).

Andreas, Connie and Steve; *Heart Of The Mind: Engaging Your Inner Power to Change,* Real People Press, Moab, Utah (1989).

Bandler, Richard; and Grinder, John; *Transformations,* Real People Press, Moab, Utah (1981).

Beadle, Muriel, *A Child's Mind,* MacGibbon & Kee, London (1971).

Beeby, C.E., *The Biography of an Idea: Beeby on Education,* New Zealand Council for Educational Research, Wellington, New Zealand (1992).

Blakemore, Colin, *The Mind Machine,* BBC Books, London (1990), accompanies television series.

Bloom, Benjamin (Editor), *Developing Talent In Young People,* McGraw Hill, New York (1981).

Bloom, Benjamin, *Stability and Characteristics in Human Change,* John Wiley, New York (1964).

Brewer, Chris Boyd, *Music and Learning: Seven Ways to Use Music in the Classroom,* LifeSounds, Kalispell, MT (1993).

Butler, Dorothy, *Babies Need Books,* Penguin, London (1984).

Caine, Renate Nummela and Geoffrey, *Making Connections: Teaching and the Human Brain,* Association for Supervision and Curriculum Development, Alexandria, Virginia (1991).

Campbell, Don, *Music, Physician for Times to Come,* Quest Books, Wheaton (1991).

Campbell, Linda; Campbell, Bruce; and Dickinson, Dee, *Teaching and Learning Through Multiple Intelligences,* Allyn & Bacon, Boston, Mass (1996).

Carroll, Kathleen, *Science Songs and Stories For the Big Question,* Brain-Friendly Teaching and Learning, Washington DC (1999).

Carroll, Kathleen, *Sing a Song of Science,* Brain-Friendly Teaching and Learning, Washington DC (1995).

Cherry, Clare; Godwin, Douglas; and Staples, Jesse, *Is The Left Brain Always Right?* Fearon Teacher Aids, Belmont, California (1989).

Christopher, Robert C., *The Japanese Mind,* Pan, London (1984).

Clay, Marie, *The Patterning Of Complex Behavior,* Heinemann, Auckland (1979).

Costa, Arthur, *Supervision for Teaching Thinking,* Pacific Grove, California (1989).

Crum, Robert; Cran, William; and MacNeil, Robert, *The Story of English,* Faber & Faber/BBC Books, London (1986), with TV series of same name.

Csikszentmihalyi, Mihaly and Isabella, *Flow: The Psychology of Optimal Experience,* Harper & Row, New York (1991).

Davenport, G.C., *An Introduction to Child Development,* Collins, UK (1994).

De Bono, Edward, *Lateral Thinking,* Harper & Row, New York (1979).

Diagram Group, The, *The Brain: A User's Manual,* Berkley Books, New York (1983).

Diamond, Marian, *Enriching Heredity,* Macmillan, New York (1988).

Dickinson, Dee, *Positive Trends in Learning;* IBM Educational Systems, Atlanta, Georgia (1991).

Dilts, Robert; and McDonald, Robert, *Tools of the Spirit,* Meta Publications, Capitola, CA.

Dreikurs, Rudolph, *Happy Children,* Fontana, London (1972).

Drucker, Peter L, *The New Realities,* Harper & Row, New York (1989).

Dryden, Gordon, *Out Of The Red,* Collins, Auckland (1978).

Dunn, Rita and Ken; Treffinger Donald, *Bringing Out The Giftedness in Your Child,* John Wiley, New York (1992).

Dunn, Rita; and Griggs, Shirley A., *Learning Styles: Quiet Revolution in American Secondary Schools,* National Association of Secondary School Principals, Reston, Virginia (1988).

Dychtwald, Ken, *Age Wave,* Bantam, New York (1990).

Evans, Peter, and Deehan, Geoff, *The Keys To Creativity,* Grafton, London (1988), with BBC radio series.

Fabun, Don, *Three Roads to Awareness,* Glencoe Press, Beverly Hills, CA (1970).

Forester, Anne D.; and Reinhard, Margaret, *The Learners' Way,* Peguis, Manitoba, Canada (1990).

Fuller, Renee; Shuman, Joyce; Schmell, Judith; Lutkus, Anthony; and Noyes, Elizabeth, *Reading as Therapy in Patients with Severe IQ Deficits,* Journal of Clinical Child Psychology (1975, Spring, Volume IV, No. 1).

Gallwey, W. Timothy, *The Inner Game of Golf,* Pan, London (1979).

Gallwey, W. Timothy, *The Inner Game of Tennis,* Random House, New York (1974).

Goleman, Daniel; Kaufman, Paul; and Ray, Michael, *The Creative Spirit,* Dutton, New York (1992).

Goodlad, John, *A Place Called School,* McGraw-Hill, New York (1984).

Gorney, Roderic, *The Human Agenda,* Guild of Tutors Press, Los Angeles (1979).

Grassi, John, *Introduction to Geometry: A Curriculum Guide For Elementary Teachers,* ALPS Products, Framingham, Mass (1985).

Grassi, John, *The Accelerated Learning Process in Science,* ALPS Products, Framington, Mass (1985).

Gregorc, Anthony, *An Adult's Guide To Style,* Gabriel Systems, Maynard (1982).

Handy, Charles, *The Age oOf Unreason,* Hutchinson, London (1989).

Harvey, Neil, *Kids Who Start Ahead, Stay Ahead,* Avery, Garden City Park, NY (1994).

Herbert, Nick, *Quantum Reality,* Doubleday, New York (1987).

Hirsch, E.D. Jr, *Cultural Literacy,* Bantam/Schwartz, Moorebank, NSW, Australia (1988).

Holt, John, *How Children Fail,* Pitman, New York (1968).

Hood, David, *Our Secondary Schools Don't Work Any More,* Profile, Auckland NZ (1998).

Hood, Lynley, *Sylvia: The Biography of Sylvia Ashton-Warner,* Viking, Auckland, New Zealand (1988).

Hutchinson, Michael, *Mega Brain,* Ballantine, New York (1986).

Israel, Lana, *Brain Power For Kids,* Buzan Center, England.

Jung, Carl, *Man And His Symbols,* Doubleday, New York (1964).

Kao, John, *Jamming,* Harper Business, New York (1997).

Kantrowitz, Barbara; and Takayama, Hideko, *In Japan, First Grade Isn't Boot Camp,* Newsweek (April 17, 1989).

Kantrowitz, Barbara; and Wingert, Pat, *An "F" in World Competition,* Newsweek (February 17, 1992).

Keller, Helen, *The Story of My Life,* Doubleday, New York (1954).

Khalsa, S., *Edu-K for Everybody,* Edu-Kinesthetics Publications, Glendale, CA.

Kohl, Herbert, *Reading, How To,* Penguin, London (1973).

Kovalik, Susan, *ITI: The Model, Integrated Thematic Instruction,* Covington, Kent, Washington (1994).

Kriegel, *If It Ain't Broke . . . Break It!,* Warner Books, New York (1992).

Levering, Robert; Moskowitz, Milton; and Katz, Michael, *The 100 Best Companies To Work For In America,* Signet (1985).

Lewis, David, *You Can Teach Your Child Intelligence,* Souvenir Press, London (1981).

Lewis, Katherine, *Cooperation and Control In Japanese Nursery Schools,* Comparative Education Review, (Vol 28, No. 1, 1984).

Lindgreen, Henry, *Educational Psychology In The Classroom,* John Wiley, New York (1962).

MacLean, Paul D., *The Triune Brain in Evolution,* Plenum, New York (1990).

Macrae, Norman, *The 2024 Report,* Sidgwick & Jackson, London (1986).

Maguire, Jack, *Care and Feeding of The Brain,* Doubleday, New York (1990).

Maltz, Maxwell, *Psycho-Cybernetics,* Pocket Books, New York (1966).

Merritt, Stephanie, *Mind, Music and Imagery,* Aslan, Santa Rosa CA (1996).

Martel, Laurence, *A Working Solution For The Nation's Schools* (validation report on integrative learning at Simon Guggenheim School), Interlearn, Hilton Head Island, South Carolina (1989).

Martel, Laurence, *Testimonials and Comments from Corporate Customers,* Interlearn, South Carolina (1991).

Madaule, Paul, *When Listening Comes Alive: A Guide to Effective Learning and Communications,* Moulin, Buffalo, NY (1994).

Max, Lesley, *Children: Endangered Species?* Penguin, Auckland (1990).

Medcalf, John, *Peer Tutoring in Reading,* Flaxmere Special Education Service, Hastings, New Zealand.

Medcalf, John, T.A.R.P.: *The Tape Assisted Reading Progam,* Flaxmere Special Education Service, Hastings, New Zealand.

Morita, Akio, *Made In Japan,* Signet-Dutton, New York (1986).

Nash, Madeleine, *Fertile Minds,* Time magazine Special Report, February 3, 1997.

Naisbitt, John, *Megatrends,* Warner Books, New York (1982).

Naisbitt, John, *Megatrends Asia,* Simon & Schuster, New York (1996).

Noor, Laily Dato' Abu Bakar; and Sukaimi, Mansor Haji, *The Child of Excellence,* Nury Institute, Malaysia (1991).

Ohmae, Kenichi, *The Borderless World,* Fontana, London (1990).

Ornstein, Robert, *Multimind,* Houghton Mifflin, Boston (1986).

Ornstein, Robert, *The Nature of Human Consciousness,* Freeman, NY (1973).

Ornstein, Robert, *The Psychology of Consciousness,* Penguin, NY (1977).

Ornstein, Robert; and Sobel, David, *The Healing Brain,* Simon & Schuster, New York (1987).

Osborn, Alex, *Applied Imagination,* Charles Scribner's Sons (1953).

Packard, David, *The HP Way,* Harper-Business, New York (1996).

Parnes, Sidney, *Creativity: Unlocking Human Potential,* Dok Publications, New York (1972).

Penfield, Wilder; and Jasper, Herbert, *Epilepsy and the Functional Anatomy of the Human Brain,* Little Brown, Boston (1954).

Peters, Thomas J.; and Waterman, Robert H. Jr, *In Search of Excellence,* Harper & Row, New York (1982).

Peters, Tom; and Austin, Nancy, *A Passion for Excellence,* Collins, UK (1985).

Postman, Neil, and Weingartner, Charles, *Teaching as a Subversive Activity,* Dell, New York (1987).

Pribram, Karl, *The Neurophysiology of Remembering,* Scientific American (January 1969).

Pribram, Karl; and Goleman, Daniel, *Holographic Memory,* Psychology Today (February 1979).

Rapp, Stan; and Collins, Tom, *Maxi-Marketing,* McGraw-Hill, New York (1987).

Restak, Richard M., *The Brain: The Last Frontier,* Warner, New York (1979).

Restak, Richard M., *The Infant Mind,* Doubleday, New York (1986).

Roddick, Anita, *Body and Soul,* Ebury Press, London (1991).

Rogers, Carl, *Freedom to Learn,* Charles E. Merrill, Columbus, Ohio (1969).

Rohwer, Jim, *Asia Rising,* Butterworth-Heinemann, Singapore (1995).

Russell, Peter, *The Brain Book,* E.P. Dutton, New York (1979).

Schuster, Donald H.; and Gritton, Charles E., *Suggestive Accelerated Learning Techniques,* Gordon and Breach, New York (1986).

Sheff, David, *Game Over: Nintendo's Battle To Dominate an Industry,* Hodder & Stoughton, UK (1993).

Sheridan, Mary, *Spontaneous Play In Early Childhood,* Routledge, UK (1993).

Shih, Stan, *Me-Too Is Not My Style,* Acer, Taiwan (1996).

Sperry, Roger, *The Great Commissure,* Scientific American (January 1964).

Smith, Paul, *Success In New Zealand Business,* Hodder Moa Beckett, Auckland, N.Z. (1996).

Sternberg, Robert, *Beyond I.Q.,* Cambridge University Press, New York (1985).

Suzuki, Shinichi, *Nurtured By Love,* Exposition Press, New York (1975).

Svantesson, Ingemar, *Mind Mapping and Memory,* Swan, Auckland (1989).

Thornburg, David, *Multiple Intelligence Inventory,* Thornburg Center for Creative Development.

Toffler, Alvin, *PowerShift,* Bantam, New York (1990).

Townsend, Robert, *Further Up The Organization,* Michael Joseph, UK (1984).

Treacy, Michael; and Wiersema, Fred, *Discipline of Market Leaders,* Addison-Wesley, Reading, MA (1995).

Vance, Mike; and Deacon, Diane, *Think Out Of The Box,* Advantage Quest, Kuala Lumpur, Malaysia (1995).

Vos-Groenendal, Jeannette, *An Accelerated/Integrative Learning Model Program Evaluation: Based on Participant Perceptions of Student Attitudinal and Achievement Changes,* unpublished dissertation, ERIC and Northern Arizona University, Flagstaff, Arizona (1991). [UMI Dissertation Services Number: 9223732; DAI: 5304A; at www.uni.com]

Waite, Helen E., *Valiant Companions: Helen Keller and Anne Sullivan Macy,* Macrae (1959).

Wallace, Rosella R., *Active Learning: Rappin' and Rhymin',* Upbeat Publishing, Anchor Point, Alaska (1990).

Ward, Christine, and Daley, Jan, *Learning to Learn,* published by the authors, Christchrch 2, New Zealand (1993).

Watson, Lyall, *Supernature,* Coronet, London (1973).

Wenger, Win, *Discovering the Obvious,* Project Renaissance, Gaithersburg, MD (1999).

Wenger, Win; and Poe, Richard, *The Einstein Factor: A Proven New Method for Increasing Your Intelligence,* Prima Publishing, Rocklin, CA (1996).

Wenger, Win, *Beyond Teaching and Learning,* Project Renaissance, Singapore (1992).

Wujec, Tom, *Pumping Ions: Games and Exercises To Flex Your Mind,* Doubleday, Toronto (1990).

Index